European Integration and Disintegration

Europe has changed radically since 1989 and continues to change at great speed. This book deals with the principal problems and challenges confronting Europe in the aftermath of the Cold War and the collapse of European communism.

Whilst endeavouring to strike a balance between East, West, North and South, the volume is more concerned with the changing political, economic and cultural morphology of Europe, and of the relations within it, than with the formal institutional arrangements of the European Community and its successor, the European Union. There are already numerous books on the institutional development of the EC/EU, but relatively few with a wider compass, and we question the utility of narrowly mechanistic institutional interpretations of European integration.

The book emphasizes that the study of European integration should be taken in the round, avoiding a narrow and self-centred concern with the development of the 'lesser Europe' of the EC/EU. It suggests that integration should be seen neither as an inexorable predetermined process nor as an automatic consequence of high levels of economic interdependence, but rather as something that proceeds in fits and starts and sometimes suffers reverses.

Robert Bideleux is Director of the Centre of Russian and East European Studies and Lecturer in Politics. **Richard Taylor** is Professor of Politics. Both are at the University of Wales, Swansea.

European Integration and Disintegration

East and West

Edited by
Robert Bideleux and Richard Taylor

London and New York

First published 1996
by Routledge
11 New Fetter Lane, London EC4P 4EE

Simultaneously published in the USA and Canada
by Routledge
29 West 35th Street, New York NY 10001

Routledge is an International Thomson Publishing company

© 1996 Robert Bideleux and Richard Taylor,
selection and editorial material; individual chapters, the contributors

Typeset in Times by
BC Typesetting, Bristol

Printed and bound in Great Britain by
TJ Press (Padstow) Ltd, Padstow, Cornwall

British Library Cataloguing in Publication Data
A catalogue record for this book is available from the British Library

Library of Congress Cataloguing in Publication Data
A catalogue record for this book has been requested

ISBN 0–415–13740–3 (hbk)
ISBN 0–415–13741–1 (pbk)

Contents

Tables

Notes on contributors

Robert Bideleux is Director of the Centre of Russian and East European Studies and Lecturer in Politics at the University of Wales, Swansea, where he teaches on the politics of European integration. The author of *Communism and Development* (1985) and a contributor to several other books, he is currently completing two books on Eastern Europe.

Richard Taylor is Professor of Politics at the University of Wales, Swansea, where he teaches courses on Russian and Soviet cultural politics. His most recent books include *The Film Factory: Russian and Soviet Cinema in Documents, 1896–1939* and *Inside the Film Factory: New Approaches to Russian and Soviet Cinema* (both co-edited with Ian Christie and published in paperback in 1994). He is also General Editor for the British Film Institute of the four-volume *Eisenstein: Selected Works*, of which the two latest volumes were published in 1995/6.

Jonathan Bradbury is Lecturer in British Politics at the University of Wales, Swansea, where he teaches courses on British politics and European integration.

François Duchêne was born of Swiss-French parents and worked as a journalist on the *Manchester Guardian* before becoming Press Officer to the ECSC High Authority, 1952–6. He worked on *The Economist* from 1956 to 1958 and again from 1963 to 1967. He was personal assistant to Jean Monnet, 1958–63; Director of the International Institute for Strategic Studies, 1969–74; and Director of the European Research Centre, University of Sussex, 1974–82. His books include: *New Limits on European Agriculture* (1983); (with Geoffrey Shephard) *Managing Industrial Change· in Western Europe* (1987); and *Jean Monnet: the First Statesman of Interdependence* (1994).

Bruce Haddock is Senior Lecturer in Politics at the University of Wales, Swansea. He has written widely on the philosophy of history, political theory, history of ideas and modern Italian history. His principal publications include *An Introduction to Historical Thought* (1980) and *Vico's Political Thought* (1986). He is currently completing a study of Italian federalism.

Philip Lawrence is Lecturer in International Relations at the University of Wales, Swansea, where he teaches on security and international relations. He has published two books, *Preparing for Armageddon* (1988) and *Democracy and the Liberal State* (1989), and various journal articles on European security, strategy and the theory of the state. He is currently working on a monograph on the cultural roots of strategic ideology.

Frances Millard is Reader in East European Politics in the School of Social and Historical Studies at the University of Portsmouth. Her most recent book is *The Anatomy of the New Poland* (1994) and she is the author of numerous articles dealing with Polish politics and social policy.

Nikolaj Petersen is Professor of International Politics and Organization at the University of Aarhus and, since 1983, deputy chairman of the Danish Institute of International Affairs; a member of the Danish Commission for Security and Disarmament Affairs from 1981 to 1995 and its co-chairman in 1995–6. His most recent publications include: *Tysklands enhed – Europas sikkerhed* [Germany's Unity – Europe's Security] (1991); *Det nye EF. Traktaten om den Europæiske Union* [The New EC. The Treaty on European Union] (1992); *Fra Maastricht til Edinburgh. Folkeafstemningen om det nye EF* [From Maastricht to Edinburgh. The Referendum on the New EC] (1993); *The European Community in World Politics* (1993); and *Danish Foreign Policy 1967–94* (forthcoming).

Clive Ponting is Lecturer in Politics at the University of Wales, Swansea. He has published five books on British politics: *Whitehall: Tragedy and Farce* (1986); *Whitehall: Changing the Old Guard* and *Breach of Promise: Labour in Power 1964–70* (both 1989); *Secrecy in Britain* and *1940: Myth and Reality* (both 1990). His *A Green History of the World* (1991) has been translated into eight languages. His most recent works are his highly controversial, revisionist biography of Churchill (1994) and *Armageddon: World War II* (1995).

Gareth Pritchard was Lecturer in Politics at the University of Wales, Swansea. His principal interest is in Eastern Europe in the period immediately after the Second World War. He is currently completing a doctoral thesis on German workers in the Soviet zone of occupation at Swansea, for which he has undertaken extensive research in the archives of the former GDR.

Preface

This book deals with integration and disintegration in Europe as a whole and on various levels: national, supranational and subnational. Whilst endeavouring to strike a balance between East, West, North and South, the volume is more concerned with the changing political, economic and cultural morphology of Europe, and of relations within it, than with the formal institutional arrangements of the European Community and its successor, the European Union. There are already numerous books on the institutional development of the EC/EU, but relatively few with a wider compass and, in any event, we question the utility and validity of narrowly mechanistic and institutional interpretations of European integration. In this volume, accordingly, Europe is viewed as an interactive, pluralistic states-system within which processes of integration and disintegration are primarily driven by domestic (often national) interests and policy concerns – for example, the requirements of post-war (including post-cold-war) recovery, economic growth and national and/or regional security. While some of the contributors see integration more as a means of realizing specific policy objectives than as an end in itself, others (including the editors) regard it as a highly desirable goal in its own right. However, we have not attempted to impose a uniform 'party line'.

The turbulence and the accelerated pace of change in Europe since 1989 have increased the need and widened the scope for European integration, making it a much more exciting process, while also rendering it more difficult to achieve in practice and to encapsulate in neat theoretical formulations. In one way or another this book touches on most of the major developments, but it has proved impossible to cover everything of importance within the confines of a single volume. Moreover, in view of the kaleidoscopic nature of the changes still unfolding, we have tried to write about current developments in the past tense whenever possible, in the hope that this choice of tense will not jar on readers a few years from now.

European Integration and Disintegration: East and West was conceived as an integrated whole, rather than as a collection of miscellaneous essays, and it has benefited from continuing discussions and exchanges of views between most of the contributors as well as from a fruitful three-day gathering at an early stage in its gestation. We therefore consider that, like Europe, this volume is more than the sum of its parts.

Three strongly held beliefs helped to set this project in motion. First, the editors believed that the principles, practice and study of European integration should be taken in the round, avoiding a narrow and self-centred concern with the development of the *Kleineuropa* [Little Europe] of the EC/EU. Furthermore, we felt that integration should be seen as neither an inexorable predetermined process, nor an automatic consequence of high levels of economic interdependence, but rather as something that proceeds in fits and starts and sometimes suffers reverses, as demonstrated by the dramatic disintegration of the Soviet bloc in 1989–91 and the serious setbacks suffered by the EC itself in 1992–3. Finally, we also believed that EU relations with Eastern Europe should be handled not as part of the 'external relations' of the EU but as part of the internal relations of Europe as a whole and that the study, and university teaching, of European integration now requires a considerable input from specialists in Eastern as well as Western Europe. There have already been moves in that direction, but there is still a long way to go. This was our point of departure. Hailing from a background in Russian and East European studies, yet having developed an academic and political interest in and commitment to European integration, the editors have long shared a common sense of dissatisfaction and occasional irritation with the parochial mentalities of Little Englanders, xenophobes and enthusiasts for a narrowly *West* European EC/EU dominated by a Franco-German 'axis'.

The creation of the EC transformed power relationships within Europe. It greatly enhanced the EC's bargaining strength vis-à-vis non-members, not least through its ability to exclude them from its large 'common market'. It empowered its members to determine the nature and extent of their relations with non-members, some of whom could be granted entry or specific privileges and exemptions, while others could be denied such access and/or favours. The creation of the EC thus placed inter-state relations on a new footing, to the great detriment of Europe's 'outsiders'.

As the only cock in the yard, the EC was, and the EU remains, in a position to lord it over would-be members. However, the temptation to do this should, we believe, be resisted from within as well as from without. Such muscle-flexing is ultimately detrimental and demeaning to all concerned. There remains another equally interesting Europe outside the EU, much of it impatient to be allowed into this inner sanctum. We are only too aware of the objections to further 'widening' of the EU, some of which reflect genuine concern for the well-being of would-be members as well as existing ones, whilst others stem from baser instincts. But we believe that, just as the self-declared candidates for EU membership would have to make huge and often traumatic economic, legal and even cultural adjustments in order to make themselves more obviously eligible for EU membership, so the EU will have to demonstrate a reciprocal willingness to reform and to tax itself sufficiently to be able to accommodate them. The candidates have already been induced to embark on massive and painful adjustments, partly in order to enhance their eventual chances of EU membership, but further widening will not be successful unless it becomes a more genuinely two-way convergence, a meeting of minds rather than simply a one-sided Westernization of the East. Europe's 'founding fathers' never intended the EC to remain an exclusively West European club. The burdens of adjustment ought not to fall exclusively on the impoverished candidates for membership who for fifty years have been denied their fair share of the 'peace dividend' of 1945.

Robert Bideleux and Richard Taylor
Swansea, April 1995

1 Introduction

European integration and disintegration

Robert Bideleux

Schemes for European integration are almost as old as the idea of Europe as a distinct political and cultural entity and much older than the conception of a Europe of nation-states. The birth of the idea of Europe went hand in hand with the emergence of the first schemes for European integration. Indeed, the conception of Europe as a distinct entity, i.e. as something more than a mere 'geographical expression', presupposed or implied a potential basis for European cohesion and integration. On the other hand, Europe has long been subject to relatively high degrees of political, economic and cultural division and fragmentation. Europe, after all, pioneered the ideas of nationalism, nation-states and national self-determination that still threaten to fragment Eastern Europe and states such as Belgium, Spain and possibly even Italy (or Britain) into ever-smaller political units. Europe has also been profoundly divided between North and South, between East and West, and between the Protestant, Roman Catholic and Eastern Orthodox worlds. Historically, Europe has been characterized more by division and conflict than by unity and harmony.

Europeans have long disagreed as to which states and peoples should properly be included in Europe. Britons have often equated Europe with 'the Continent'. Britain's accession to the EC in 1973 was usually described as 'going into Europe'. Poles and Spaniards, similarly, speak of 'the return to Europe' in relation to membership of the European Union. There have also been long debates as to how far countries such as Russia, Turkey, Albania, Georgia, Armenia, Israel or Morocco should be included in Europe, politically, militarily, culturally or economically. They are certainly very different in some ways from Western and Central Europe, which have frequently been urged to unite against 'the Russian menace' (whether Tsarist or Soviet) and against Islamic foes (whether they be the Arabs, the Ottoman Turks, OPEC or Saddam Hussein). Many Russians as well as West Europeans still question whether Russia, which straddles the Eurasian landmass, is more European than Asiatic: this theme is taken up by Richard Taylor in Chapter 13.

The factor that must always be borne in mind in any consideration of Europe is that definitions of Europe and the configurations of European states are fluids rather than solids. They are constantly changing. In all probability, the Europe that we think we see now has no more permanence or solidity than the economic and cultural parameters and state configurations of Europe's past. This suggests that it can be reshaped by conscious design. Thus people who profess an undying allegiance to a particular nation or nation-state, which they regard as a constant or eternal feature of the political and cultural landscape, are suffering from a sad and potentially dangerous delusion. The idea of the nation and of a European order based upon sovereign nation-states is of relatively recent origin and is likely to be as ephemeral or short-lived as all previous European state configurations. It is on the eternal fluidity of European states systems, rather than on any deterministic belief in a teleological progression towards a preordained 'federal goal', that federalists should rest their hopes for a federal Europe in the twenty-first century. Since national allegiances are 'all in the mind', they are not fixed or 'set in concrete' for all time, but are subject to change, as identity and allegiance always have been. It is no accident that the seemingly solid and unassailable bipolar European order established in 1945–9, at the height of the Cold War, has already disintegrated since 1989 and that there is a debate over whether it has been replaced by multipolarity (as many Europeans fondly imagine), or (as many Arabs and Latin Americans would see it) by a unipolar 'New World Order' characterized by increased US hegemony. The nature of the new European order is one of the themes taken up by Philip Lawrence later in Chapter 4.

The apparent groundswell of support for regional integration in Europe since 1945 has in a sense been misleading, since it is clear that European integration has always meant different things to different people. For Europe's bankers and aristocrats, it may have represented a nostalgic desire to return to the Europe of cosmopolitan capital cities, relatively free trade and unrestricted travel (i.e. no passports and border controls) that existed before the First World War. For 'European-minded' socialists and technocrats, European integration represented an opportunity to plan, to regulate and to build on a scale that would transcend European national boundaries and allegiances. But for free-traders, it meant precisely the opposite: a reduction in regulation, planning and state intervention and a freeing of markets for goods, capital, labour and services. For many Roman Catholics, European integration was to be a means of uniting Christian Europe against the 'threat' of communism and the Soviet 'menace' and of binding Western Europe more closely to the USA and NATO. This was a latter-day version of medieval attempts to unite Christendom against the 'threat' of Islam and the Turkish 'menace'. Over the centuries, indeed, the vast majority of schemes for European integration and confederation have been predicated on a presumed need to unite against a common external foe and a perceived 'threat' to Christian and/or European values and civilization. This, above all else, has been what has persuaded their proponents and supporters to consider a 'pooling of sovereignty', especially in such sensitive areas as defence and, in the cases of the European Coal and Steel Community (ECSC) (1951) and the European Atomic Energy Community (Euratom) (1957), 'the production of the means of waging war'. The major schemes for West European integration after 1945 were in part 'new editions' of the nineteenth-century calls for Europe to unite against 'the Russian menace', metamorphosed into 'the Soviet threat'. Now that this perceived external threat has seemingly been laid to rest by the disintegration of first the Soviet bloc and then the Soviet Union and possibly the Russian Federation, 'wider' European integration and even a pan-European confederation have become more feasible, on paper at least. Yet the will or the motivation to integrate and to confederate has palpably diminished, as much of the previously existing fear (and hence discipline and cohesion) has been dissipated by the removal of the perceived external 'threat'; and the fragile integrative achievements of post-war Western Europe threaten to unravel in the face of the destabilizing effects of the new European disorder.

For General de Gaulle and for many 'European-minded' socialists, however, European integration was a means of giving Western Europe a more independent position in the world, as a 'third force', equidistant between the two superpowers and capable of resisting American as well as Soviet hegemonism, at a time when many West Europeans felt overshadowed by the two superpowers or dominated by a superpower condominium. They saw a confederal union of states as a means of reasserting West European autonomy and freedom of manoeuvre, i.e., Western Europe as an independent actor on the world stage. For some, the primary goal was to form an exclusive regional bloc, embracing only West European states (even excluding Britain, so long as de Gaulle was in power). For many 'Atlanticists', however, European integration was only part of the wider process of reducing and removing barriers to trade, an ongoing crusade initiated by the General Agreement on Tariffs and Trade (GATT) in 1947. By the end of the 1950s this had fully reintegrated Western Europe into the international economy, reversing the autarkic tendencies of the interwar years and of the Nazi 'New Order'. Thus, for each current in the European movement, 'Europe' has represented a different vision, a different set of goals, ideals, mechanisms and instrumentalities. For all that, these disparate ideas about Europe and European integration have continued to generate strong passions and commitment and a sense (or possibly an illusion) of inexorable movement towards 'ever closer union'.

In the 'new' post-Cold-War Europe of the early 1990s, however, disintegration was much more in evidence than integration. Comecon, the Soviet Union, Yugoslavia and Czechoslovakia disintegrated with astonishing suddenness and sometimes tragic consequences. Political disintegration among Europe's former communist states went hand in hand with economic and social disintegration, once the brief initial euphoria and sense of 'liberation' from communist dictatorship subsided. Western Europe, meanwhile, was afflicted by severe economic recession, rising social discontent, widespread disillusionment with old established political parties and politicians and a consequent 'crisis of governance'. The crisis of the 1945–89 European order coincided with (and exacerbated) a crisis of the state as an institution in the West:

> It is no longer the function of the state to protect its citizens against a well-defined single threat: the prospect of Soviet tanks rolling over Europe. The uncertainties of the present situation are multiple, diffuse. In this sense the state, too, is an orphan of the [former] Soviet Union. Deprived of its regal Hobbesian security mission, it seems incapable of finding solutions to the economic crisis and powerless to confront unemployment and monetary turmoil. The globalization of financial markets has deprived the state of its ability to control financial flows.[1]

The complacent 'triumphalism' of the assembled EC Commissioners and heads of government at Maastricht was stopped in its tracks by the initial Danish rejection of the Maastricht Treaty in June 1992 (discussed by Nikolaj Petersen in Chapter 6) and by the near rejection of the Treaty by the French electorate in September 1992. Moreover, the initial euphoria of German unification turned sour in the wake of the subsequent economic and social collapse of post-communist East Germany, the consequent escalation of the costs of unification, the ensuing rise in German (and therefore West European) real interest rates and the accompanying rise of the extreme Right – not only in Germany, but also in other West European states afflicted by lethal combinations of economic recession, 'crisis of governance' and widespread fear of large-scale immigration from the disintegrating East and economically depressed, conflict-ridden North Africa, especially Algeria. In 1993 Europe witnessed the near collapse of one of the main pillars of West European integration, the European Exchange Rate Mechanism, which threatened to derail the West European programmes for Economic and Monetary Union and for a Single European Market. Even more seriously, perhaps, the British and Danish 'opt-outs' from the Maastricht Treaty threatened to undermine one of the fundamental tenets of the EC, the principle that, once rules were adopted, they had to be applied equally to each of the member states. (Otherwise, the latter would be encouraged to 'pick and choose' which EC policies and laws they would implement and enforce and the whole process of West European integration could steadily unravel or lose cohesion and discipline.)

Superficially it seems paradoxical that, on the one hand, the EU has achieved more impressive and far-reaching economic, political and even cultural integration than any other major union of states or supranational regional bloc and yet, on the other hand, the continent of Europe is still deeply afflicted by forces of disintegration. In reality, however, European societies and polities have long been characterized by continuous tension between the forces of integration (promoting greater harmony, co-operation, 'drawing together', cohesion, prosperity, complementarity, interdependence and division of labour) and the forces of disintegration (fostering inter-state and internal friction and warfare, beggar-my-neighbour protectionism and inter-ethnic or sectarian strife), both at national and supranational levels. Until the 1940s, the main focus was on national integration, and one would encounter some quite deterministic views of the process of national integration. For example, according to the most influential analyst of the process by which the Austro-Hungarian Empire dissolved into nation-states:

> The whole history of the nineteenth century is a demonstration of a sociological law, according to which among masses of the same nationality, living under different sovereignties, there develops, with the rise of economic and cultural life, an irresistible current tending toward the unification of the whole national body into one single political and economic organization.[2]

Since the 1940s, however, the focus has of course shifted to supra-national European integration. The forces fostering cohesion and integra-tion, including Europe's shared values, elements of a common European culture and civilisation, the variegated (albeit fractured) European market and the consequent interdependencies and complementarities between European economies, have given rise to various conceptions and theoriz-ations of European integration, most notably: European federalism; neo-functionalism; theories of interdependent development; and the 'trans-actional' theory of regional integration elaborated by Karl Deutsch.[3] Since the late 1970s, however, these theories have been widely rejected and/or discredited on the grounds that they are unduly teleological or deterministic. They postulate ineluctable movement towards a predeter-mined outcome; an irresistible, technologically determined progression towards ever-increasing contact, communication, economic interdepen-dence and division of labour between European states and regions, both at supranational and at subnational levels, accompanied by a steady proliferation of international regulatory tasks or 'functions' that can best be handled by supranational agencies. 'Integration' is itself a very loaded, normative, teleological term. Nevertheless, these theoretical approaches and the tendencies they claim to discern have both reinforced and drawn strength from European federalist theses that the European nation-states system, along with the underlying ideas of 'the nation' and 'national self-determination' as the appropriate basis of the European political order, were obsolescent or outmoded and a threat to European peace and prosperity. European federalists argued that there was an increasing need for a supranational federation with directly elected federal institutions and agencies, in order to secure European peace and prosperity. During the 1950s and 1960s, this deterministic, teleological integrationism appeared to highlight and even provide the 'dynamic', the 'logic' and the dominant motives behind the processes of integration among the states which came together to form the European Coal and Steel Community (ECSC) and the European Economic Community (EEC) and, to a lesser degree, among the states which formed the European Free Trade Association (EFTA) and those that formed (or were forced together into) the Council of Mutual Economic Assistance (CMEA, commonly known as Comecon). These were the theories of integration that dominated the textbooks of West European politics and EC economics in the 1960s and early 1970s. As Milward argued in *The European Rescue of the Nation-State*:

> In their implication that governance by the nation-state was a thing of the past and governance by the supranation the image of the future, such theories did set the assumptions and the tone of political discourse about European integration and provide it with the erroneous assumptions on which so much of it now relies.[4]

Milward is one of the foremost critics of these West European teleological integrationist paradigms. He argues that they are 'far too general to serve as explanations of the specific phenomenon which distinguishes the EC, the voluntary surrender by the nation-state of specific areas of national sovereignty to the Community's own political structures'[5] and that:

> there is nothing in the observation of the general trend towards greater interdependence associated with the process of modern economic development to explain why the reaction of the state to it should be to make this surrender, unless it is assumed that interdependence does lead in a linear continuum to the supersession of the nation-state and that the 1950s were the historical moment when the continuum had arrived at that point.[6]

However, the nineteenth and twentieth centuries witnessed numerous customs unions which did not survive and the view that 'the process of economic development leads through interdependence progressively to integration is . . . too simple a conclusion'.[7] The supposedly inexorable growth of international economic interdependence can be halted or even thrown into reverse 'by an act of national political will'.[8] The biggest and most extreme examples were, of course, provided by the ambitious autarkic policies pursued by Nazi Germany [*Großraumwirtschaft*] and by the USSR under Stalin, which managed to minimize their 'dependence' on external resources and markets and to insulate their economies and societies from external economic pressures and foreign ideas. Europe's smaller fascist states moved in a similar direction, albeit on a more limited scale, as did the neo-Stalinist states established in Eastern Europe after the Second World War. More generally, protectionism, the expanding roles of the state in 'national' economic development and the growth of 'political' interference in international flows of trade, labour and capital all helped to set limits or erect barriers to the growth of international economic interdependence and specialization in twentieth-century Europe. Indeed, 'Some measurements of the extent of interdependence suggest that it was in fact greater between 1890 and 1914 than in the 1950s',[9] when the major European breakthroughs to increased international economic and political integration took place. 'Interdependence is not, therefore, a phenomenon which has progressively and inexorably developed in twentieth-century western Europe.'[10] Likewise, although physical contacts between European peoples steadily increased from the 1940s to the 1970s, most of the increase was in the form of tourism. The biggest increases in tourism were to Franco's Spain and, to lesser degrees, to Greece, Italy, Portugal, Yugoslavia and Turkey; yet, with the exception of Italy, these countries were not in the forefront of moves towards closer international integration in that period. Similarly, while problems that require supranational 'functional' regulation by international agencies have proliferated since 1945, it is by no means clear that problems and tasks of this sort have required forms of international organization different from 'the successful regulation of international postal or railway traffic in the mid-nineteenth century' or that there was any direct linkage between 'attempts at functional regulation of problems of this kind and the actual history of European integration since 1945'.[11]

Furthermore, contrary to the frequent claims that there was a widespread and unified (West) European movement towards a more federal, supranational polity in (Western) Europe in the wake of World War II, in reaction to the experience of fascism and the failure or inability of Europe's nation-states system to cope with the 1930s Depression and the rise of fascism, Milward argues that the advocates of a supranational federal polity for (Western) Europe were 'of little importance or influence in the political life of their own countries' and that they 'had practically no influence on the negotiations' leading to the formation of the ECSC in 1950–2, because 'the idea of a peacefully united Europe' was less potent and pervasive than 'the idea of resurrecting the conquered nations'.[12] Thus, the chief architects of the ECSC, Jean Monnet and Robert Schuman, were also prominent among the architects of French *national* reconstruction. Moreover, studies of French post-war diplomacy indicate that 'integration was an attempt to restore France as a major national force by creating an integrated area in Western Europe which France would dominate politically and economically'; likewise, West Germany embraced 'European integration precisely in order to establish itself as the future German nation-state'.[13]

In this respect, however, Milward has greatly overstated his case. For the six founder members of the ECSC and the EEC, 'European idealism' and 'national self-interest' happily coincided. There was little conflict between the two. Nevertheless, Milward has seriously underestimated the strength of the underlying commitment to the construction of a federal Europe, especially on the part of the West German government. On 11 January 1952 Heinrich von Brentano, who was soon to become West Germany's Foreign Minister (1955–61), declared:

> We are not signing the Schuman Plan because it improves our economic and political position, but because we regard the basic idea of close co-operation between all European states as a good one. At the same time we welcome it in the economic and political interests of Germany.[14]

Furthermore, in a speech in Königstein on 22 July 1956, Brentano expounded his federal vision and the principle of 'subsidiarity':

> Europe will not be a unitary State of unorganized individuals of different languages, but a close community of national States. However, a national State as the basis for such a community of States will not be the end of the development. . . . Europe and its individual member States will live together according to the principle of subsidiary function; that is to say, a task will be undertaken by the next highest level only when the lower level cannot carry it out with its own resources.[15]

Thus the notion of 'subsidiarity' was already present at the inception of the EEC and, contrary to the assumptions of some of the European leaders assembled at Maastricht in December 1991, the concept *presupposed* a federal structure for Europe. The British Tory Eurosceptic notion of 'subsidiarity' as a bulwark *against* federalism is therefore nonsensical. In a speech in Rome on 23 January 1960 Brentano elaborated on this theme:

> I am firmly convinced that the solution to the terrible problems which face us today can best be found in a free, democratic and irrevocable unification of the European peoples. . . . Parallel with this dawning of a European task, the political ideas of the German people also began to turn to federalism. Federalism was understood as a hierarchic structure of communities, each of which was expected to perform those tasks which naturally fell to its lot, and to surrender those tasks beyond its resources to the next higher stage in the hierarchy.[16]

In his memoirs, Konrad Adenauer, who served as Chancellor of West Germany from 1949 to 1963, similarly stated:

> We had to get away from thinking in terms of national states. The last war, the development of weapons technology, and, indeed, of all technology, had created new conditions in the world. There were now two world powers: the United States and Soviet Russia. There was the

British Commonwealth whose power was on the decline. The countries of Western Europe to which we belonged were impoverished by wars and weakened politically. They were no longer in a position to save European culture if each country acted by itself. The peoples of Western Europe had to unite politically, economically and culturally. It was the only policy that could enable them to protect the peace, to rebuild Europe, and to make it again a real factor in world politics, in cultural and in economic matters.

The creation of the Council of Europe, the founding of the European Community for Coal and Steel, and the establishment of a European Defence Community were to serve the pacification of Europe. The supranational organizations in particular were to bring the contracting powers so close together through renunciation of sovereignty that wars inside Europe would become impossible. With much care and circumspection a political constitution for Europe was already being worked out.[17]

However, while Milward's rather one-sided emphasis on national self-interest as the driving force behind West European integration is mistaken, it is equally apparent that at least some of the 'founding fathers' of the ECSC and the EEC saw no fundamental antithesis or contradiction between supranational integration and national self-interest. The former was partly an enlightened means of realizing the latter, but it was also more than that. The whole would be greater than the sum of its parts. Thus Milward is on safer ground when he argues that the formation of the EC facilitated 'the reassertion of the nation-state' as the basic building block of the post-war political order in Western Europe because, without the EC, 'the nation-state could not have offered to its citizens the same measure of security and prosperity which it has provided and which has justified its survival'.[18] Thus the EC was created, not in opposition to the nation-state, but as part of the post-war rehabilitation of six West European nation-states, following the collapses they had suffered at various points between 1940 and 1945. 'The development of the EC . . . was . . . a part of that post-war rescue of the European nation-state, because the new political consensus on which this rescue was built required the process of integration, the surrender of limited areas of national sovereignty to the supranation.'[19] Therefore, the formation of the EC could be described as a kind of insurance policy taken out by six restored and enhanced national states, allowing them to maximize *national* income, *national* welfare and *national* security, while minimizing the potential risks and costs of any return to the beggar-my-neighbour protectionism and autarky and destructive conflict of the sort that had almost destroyed them during the 1930s and Second World War.

The extreme example of a nation-state that has relied on the exigencies of EC membership to provide a degree of national purpose, cohesion and discipline which it seems incapable of providing for itself has been Italy. Since the late 1960s, EC membership has been central to the Italian political consensus, as the one policy on which all the major political parties can agree (the Communist Party was the last to fall into line). The requirements of EC membership have underpinned and provided the driving-force behind the principal programmes of reform and 'moderniz-ation', especially the liberalization and 'opening up' of the Italian economy to foreign capital, technology, ideas and competition and reforms to bring Italian society closer to North-West European standards in education, social provisions, public health and legal and business practices (although the 1990s revelations of the continuing scale and pervasiveness of cor-ruption and malpractice suggest that these reforms never went far enough, or that they were honoured more in the breach than in the observance). During the 1980s and early 1990s, moreover, Italy's participation in the Exchange Rate Mechanism and its strong commitment to eventual partici-pation in Economic and Monetary Union provided the principal sources of enhanced monetary and budgetary discipline, which drastically reduced Italy's hitherto chronic 15–20 per cent per annum inflation rate to around 4 per cent per annum and strengthened the lira (excessively so, it could be argued). The new monetary and budgetary disciplines also elicited heroic efforts to tighten up tax collection and reduce social security fraud, albeit at considerable social cost to the poor, and significant personal and poli-tical cost to Italy's inveterate tax dodgers and their 'patrons'. Indeed, common membership of the EC could in the end prove to be the only poli-tical and economic framework within which the prosperous semi-corrupt North can continue (or consent) to co-habit with the impoverished and thoroughly corrupt South. (These themes are taken up by Bruce Haddock in Chapter 7.) In a similar vein, it is widely believed that only EC member-ship can provide a framework within which Flanders can continue to co-habit with Wallonia in a single Belgian state, especially since the death of King Baudouin in July 1993 removed a potent focus of common allegiance, and the August 1993 Federal Constitution spawned separate mutually antagonistic regional governments and parliaments in Flanders and Wallonia. These two would-be nation-states also seemed fated to share Brussels as the bilingual capital of both Belgium and the European Union. Likewise, as argued in Chapter 8, post-Franco Spain has come to depend on EC membership to hold together an increasingly fissiparous kingdom.

Conversely, it can be argued, countries such as Britain, Sweden and Switzerland did not feel any need to become founder members of the EC during the 1950s because their economies and institutions had not collapsed (and had to some extent emerged with enhanced strength and legitimacy) during the 1940s, precisely because they had passed the supreme test: they had safeguarded the sovereignty and security of their states and citizens in a time of war, through military victory in the case of

Britain and through armed neutrality in the cases of Sweden and Switzerland. During the war Portugal sided with the Allies, despite the fascist leanings of the Salazar regime during the 1930s, and both sides grudgingly accepted Spanish and Irish neutrality. The anomalous cases are Norway and Denmark, both of which were occupied by Nazi Germany and yet decided that their safest 'insurance policy' was membership of NATO rather than the EC, towards which their electorates have remained ambivalent ever since – witness the initial Danish rejection of the Maastricht Treaty on European Union in June 1992 and the strength of Norwegian popular opposition to EC membership in 1972 and in 1992–4. But the fact that other West European states have never really felt the same post-war anxieties or the same need for mutual economic and political assurances as the six founder members of the EC partly explains why those six have remained much more committed to 'ever closer union' (including Economic and Monetary Union) than the outer ring of 'half-hearted Europeans'.

With regard to the motives of the Six, Milward's crucial arguments are that the EC 'was not the supersession of the nation-state by another form of governance . . . but was the creation of the European nation-states for their own purposes' and that 'there has surely never been a period when national government in Europe has exercised more effective power and more extensive control over its citizens than that since the Second World War'.[20] This was part of the strength of the impetus behind the creation of the EC. Therefore, in Milward's analysis, both the champions of a more federal EC and the die-hard opponents of 'deeper' integration within the EC have fundamentally misunderstood the complementary and mutually supportive (rather than antithetical) relationship between the EC and its member states. 'To supersede the nation-state would be to destroy the Community. To put a finite limit to the process of integration would be to weaken the nation-state, to limit its scope and to curb its power.'[21] Yet the assumed antithesis or polarity between the EC and the nation-state is still deeply entrenched in current academic thinking on European integration. Thus a major recent textbook by Loukas Tsoukalis asserts that, 'As integration approaches the very heart of economic sovereignty, the resistance of the European nation-state is bound to grow.'[22] However, if the EC and the West European nation-states need (and, indeed, complement) each other, as Milward and some of the founding fathers have argued, there is no *a priori* reason why such antagonism should grow. Indeed, it has not always been assumed that there is an antithesis between a supranational European union or confederation and a Europe of nation-states. According to Forsyth, confederal union has been 'one of the . . . classic forms of relationship that states adopt to guarantee or underwrite their continued existence as states'.[23] And some of the leading nineteenth-century advocates of a 'united' federal Europe, including the French radical Henri de Saint-Simon, the Italian nationalist Giuseppe Mazzini and the writer Victor Hugo, tried to side-step or reconcile the potential conflicts or contradictions between a Europe of nation-states and a European federation by postulating a 'brotherhood' or 'fraternity' of European nations. They assumed that the natural relationship between democratic nations was a 'fraternal' harmonious one, that dynastic, proprietorial and mercantile rivalries were the primary sources of inter-state conflicts and that, if all nations were democratized and cleansed by shifting power from selfish and self-seeking rulers and vested interests to the people, the nations would live together in harmony and the root cause of inter-state conflict would be eliminated.[24] According to Saint-Simon, the 'balance of power' system was 'the falsest combination possible, since peace was its aim yet it has produced nothing but war'.[25] And in 1849 Mazzini declared that the states of Europe 'become more and more intimately associated through the medium of democracy. . . . They will gradually unite in a common faith and a common pact in all that concerns their international life. The future of Europe will be one, avoiding both the anarchy of absolute independence and the centralization of conquest.'[26] Even Winston Churchill, in his famous speech on the need for a 'United States of Europe', spoke of familial relations between the European nations: 'The first step in the re-creation of the European family must be a partnership between France and Germany.'[27] But perhaps they all forgot that brothers, like families, sometimes quarrel. . . .

However, while Milward's work has provided a powerful antidote to the deterministic teleological integrationism of the 1950s and 1960s, it also propounds a relatively monocausal and mechanistic interpretation of the process of West European integration since 1950. Milward presents West European integration as the result of a specific conjunctural convergence and package of economic policies needed to sustain and perpetuate the remarkable upsurge of economic growth initiated by 'national' post-war economic reconstruction and the European Recovery Programme, rather than as a dynamic process which has in fact continued through many ups and downs and widely differing economic conjunctures and policy mixes. Milward's interpretation of West European integration also rests upon a somewhat questionable view of the state as a national actor maximizing economic self-interest. He has not explained very convincingly how the calculus of 'national' economic self-interest is reflected in (or translated into) the political behaviour of voters or parties or governments, although he has acknowledged the problem:

> the national interests which have underlain the process of integration are made up of positions taken by interest groups which are themselves compromises in consensus-building at a micro level before they become part of the greater compromise represented by a national policy.

For example, 'Not only was the French state apparatus divided on what the national interest in respect of the Common Market treaty was, the sectional interest groups who sought to affect its decisions were also divided.'[28] It is difficult to see how such fractured and divided 'national interests' could have asserted themselves as driving forces behind the integration process.

Milward's characterization of the emergence of the European Communities as 'an integral part of the reassertion of the nation-state as an organisational concept'[29] is also difficult to reconcile with observations that the rhetoric which propelled and proclaimed West European integration was anything but nationalistic. On the contrary, it pronounced the need for limitations, surrenders and 'pooling' of national sovereignty. Moreover, he has confused the issue by equating the *nation-state* (meaning a country and/or political community) with the state as an agency, and by using the terms interchangeably. Thus he has misleadingly quoted the increased power of the state over its citizens since 1945 as evidence of 'the reassertion of the nation-state'.[30] Yet it is perfectly possible to imagine a federal European 'superstate' which could exercise unlimited power over its citizens, and – at the other extreme – a Western Europe composed of ultra-liberal (i.e. completely *laissez-faire*) sovereign nation-states. The reassertion of 'nation-states' is far from synonymous with increased 'state power' over individuals. In addition, there are difficulties in reconciling Milward's emphasis on the interests of nation-states with his equally strong emphasis on the primacy of economic interests, as the nation-state is not a narrowly (or even primarily) economic concept.

Finally, Milward's reinterpretation of West European integration has largely omitted the roles played by some other significant players in the process (especially the USA and the multinational companies) and by the security concerns of the founder members of the EC, by their desires to unite and to strengthen themselves against the Soviet (alias communist) 'threat' and to constrain or forestall the potential renewal of German military and political hegemony in Europe in the wake of the much-needed revival of the West German economy. As François Duchêne has remarked:

> The key was . . . the security needs of the continental neighbours of the new postwar Germany and especially of France, the only state placed to launch a new policy. Germany was still the potential hegemonic power in Europe outside the USSR and might have reached a bilateral accommodation with it. The risks of a third bid for such domination had to be removed. This could not be assured by insurance policies, which had failed between the wars, but only by a basic political process designed to supersede the old national rivalries. This demanded that everyone be equal before new rules, and that 'European' bodies should have the power to take decisions without national bias. Supranationality followed, not only to reach effective decisions, but to guarantee the levels of trust to implement them. This was agreed first for the ECSC

then the Common Market, both expressing the same policy of absorbing Germany into a new European civil system via unity.[31]

Milward has argued that some of the security concerns of the Six were ill founded. But what counted was not the validity of these concerns so much as the fact that they existed in the minds of voters and governments at the time. As a biographer of Jean Monnet, for whom he worked as an assistant during the 1950s, Duchêne is in an unrivalled position to recall and comment upon the motives and world-view(s) of the founding fathers of the ECSC and the EEC. In Duchêne's opinion, the overriding motive for both France and Germany was the need to maintain the process of Franco-German reconciliation in a framework strong enough to make it irreversible. In this sense the EEC really was the progeny of the ECSC. Both were eventually political (not economic) instruments to cement Franco-German reconciliation and to rehabilitate Germany in ways that would be non-threatening to its neighbours, especially France. Thus the origins of the ECSC and the EEC lay, not just in the two World Wars, but in the Franco-Prussian War of 1870–1. Yet the European Communities were formed by the Six (not two) states because France, having been defeated by Germany in three successive wars, felt the need to bring in others to counterbalance and dilute German power and potential dominance.

While the deterministic, teleological, integrationist theories of the 1950s and 1960s have been strongly challenged and to a large extent discarded, however, 'No historian has tried to construct . . . any alternative theoretical explanation.'[32] Equally, while there has been an abundance of (widely challenged) theories of European integration, there have been few (if any) theories of European disintegration which could help to explain the setbacks of the early 1990s, such as the initial Danish rejection of the Maastricht Treaty in 1992, the near collapse of the ERM in 1993 and the resurgence of the ultra-nationalist far Right, as well as the more cataclysmic disintegrations which took place in the East, especially in the former Soviet and Yugoslav federations. In principle, however, theories of disintegration can be just as teleological and deterministic as theories of integration. Indeed, whereas Western analyses of the USSR used to emphasize the apparent solidity and impregnability of the Soviet 'monolith' from the 1930s to 1985, the sudden disintegration of the Soviet Union between 1989 and 1991 led to a new emphasis on its inherent fragility, artificiality and lack of legitimacy, implying that the Soviet experiment had been doomed from the start. Similarly, the final dissolutions of the Tsarist, Habsburg and Ottoman Empires in the wake of the First World War have often been presented as the culminations of inexorable processes of disintegration, moving irresistibly towards their 'inevitable' denouements. There have been numerous deterministic, doom-laden accounts of the protracted decline and disintegration of the Tsarist and Habsburg Empires, disregarding the evidence and counter-claims that, until 1916, even their most restive national minorities were only demanding limited autonomy within multinational imperial federations (rather than independent statehood) and that, since these multinational empires had been undergoing economic booms and were in no sense 'bursting at the seams' before 1914, they could probably have endured for several more decades if their collapse had not been prematurely induced by military defeats in the First World War.

Instead of attempting to counterpose any deterministic theory or theories of *disintegration* to equally deterministic theories of European or national or imperial *integration*, however, it is more fruitful to explore the theme that Europe has long been characterized by continuous tension between forces of integration and disintegration, at national, subnational and supranational levels. Since the Middle Ages, Europe has had much more fragmented and pluralistic states systems than almost any other continent (the obvious exception being Africa, where settled states systems were late to develop). While other continents have usually been dominated by large empires and/or strong hegemonic powers until quite recently, peninsular Europe has long consisted of large numbers of small and medium-sized states. Only Eastern Europe has been ruled for long periods by imperial powers displaying at least some of the characteristics and staying power of Asiatic empires. The Habsburgs, Napoleon and Hitler achieved temporary hegemonic 'superpower' dominance of Western and Central Europe, but their ascendancies were mercifully short-lived. The endemic political fragmentation of Europe has been a source of both weakness and strength, disunity and cohesion, conflict and co-operation, beggar-my-neighbour protectionism and healthy economic and political pluralism and competition. It has also given rise to the circumstance that West European integration has occurred, not between a hegemonic power and its client states (as is the case, for example, between the former USSR and its 'allies', or as could be the case between the USA and its North American neighbours), but between essentially more equal small and medium-sized states. For short periods, there have been fearfully destructive wars between European states and, in the twentieth century, these have drawn other continents besides Europe into two unprecedented World Wars. Yet, over much longer periods, there have been mostly creative or productive tensions and complementarities between European states. These have been at the root of Europe's successes as well as its failings and shortcomings.

In his magisterial study of *The European Miracle*, E. L. Jones attributes mediaeval and modern Europe's distinctive political fragmentation, cultural pluralism and economic diversity, and the correspondingly large scope for interregional trade, specialization and capital accumulation, primarily to its 'special features of site, location and resource endowment'.[33] Large spatial variations in climate, geology, soils and vegetation have given Europe an unusually diverse (if not especially rich) natural resource base and, since not everything is found or produced in the same places, this has given rise to large interregional complementarities and exceptionally extensive opportunities for interregional trade. Moreover, intra-European transport costs have been much lower than those of other (mostly much larger) continents, because 'Europe was a peninsula of peninsulas with an exceptionally long, indented coastline relative to its area' and an abundance of navigable rivers.[34] These conditions were conducive to multilateral long-distance trade in mundane bulk commodities such as grain, timber, dried fish, salt, wine, wool and, in modern times, iron ore and coal. European governments found it more rewarding to tax such commodities than to appropriate them (and to encourage trade rather than to plunder or monopolize it), in contrast to governments and rulers in continents where trade mainly consisted of low-bulk/ high-value commodities such as gold, silver, herbs, spices, silk, tea and, most recently, oil. The comparatively high profile and wide distribution of trade (and of tax revenues derived from it) gave European governments and rulers strong incentives to establish and uphold law and order. Moreover, the wide dispersal of river basins and level areas of fertile (often alluvial) soil, many of which became mediaeval centres of political and economic power, fostered a plurality of European states. Advances in both military and civilian technologies, which gradually increased the optimum size of states, facilitated territorial amalgamation and conquest. This reduced the total number of separate political units from one thousand in 1300 to five hundred in 1500 and twenty-five by 1900. Nevertheless, 'Amalgamation went so far but no further: never to a single empire. Amalgamation costs were high. Major natural barriers protect several parcels of territory the size of modern nation-states', particularly in Western Europe.[35] The European 'miracle' is that, through shifting and balancing alliances and the emergence of a system of international law, a pluralistic European states system and balance of power endured for so long, against all the odds and against so many challenges for the mastery of Europe. 'States systems are fragile and precarious. Any conflict between members is likely to draw in others and threaten the survival and stability of the whole.'[36] This pluralistic states system has given Europe important advantages over continents dominated by great imperial powers. In the long run, imperial polities tend to breed debilitating court intrigue, sycophancy, vice, corruption, conspicuous consumption, even more conspicuous construction and stultifying cultural uniformity. In the pluralistic European states system, by contrast, 'wrong-headed and incontrovertible decisions' could not be imposed on Europe as a whole by a central authority.[37] Even more importantly, Europeans 'escaped the grasp of a single political-religious order. . . . Limited diversity, for all the waste of intra-Christian conflicts, gave Europeans some freedom of thought.'[38] Above all, while all-powerful empires have minimal incentives to adopt new methods of organization, production and warfare, European states have always been surrounded by actual or potential competitors. 'The states system was an insurance against economic and technological stagnation.' Competition for military, dynastic, commercial and industrial advantage has provided constant spurs to adaptation and innovation, while religious and later political refugees and economic migrants have repeatedly (and often unwittingly) transferred skills and know-how from state to state.[39] 'All in all, the competitiveness and 'genetic variety' of the states system helped to generalize best practices. . . . This was done by voluntary and involuntary movement of capital and labour.'[40] The emergence of elements of a common European culture, facilitated by increased contact, mixing and cross-fertilization and by the generalization of 'best practice' under the spur of inter-state rivalry and commercial competition, fostered 'unity in diversity' and 'gave Europe some of the best of both worlds'.[41] By the eighteenth century 'in important respects Europe had become a unified market area for . . . capital and labour and increasingly for goods'.[42] 'The states system did not thwart the flow of capital and labour to the constituent states offering the highest marginal returns.' Attempts to curtail these flows were (and still are) largely ineffectual.[43]

The member states of the EU would be foolish to throw away these vital age-old strengths and advantages of the European states system by forming a single European superstate. What Milward does not emphasize sufficiently is that the continuing dynamism and vitality of the EU requires a plurality of competing member states just as much as Europe's nation-states need an EU for their economic prosperity and survival. A pluralistic states system does not, however, have to be based on the idea of the nation-state. Other permutations are conceivable. There are still parts of Eastern Europe, the former Soviet Union and even parts of Western Europe (Belgium, Spain, the British Isles) where, taken to its logical conclusion, the attempt to construct (or reconstruct) polities on the basis of the idea of the nation-state is or would be a recipe for economic disaster and human tragedy, for Balkanization. Indeed, a slightly worrying aspect of *The European Rescue of the Nation-State* is the implicit apotheosis of the nation-state, on whose altar twentieth-century Europe has already sacrificed so much.

Furthermore, in his summary analysis of the processes of state building and 'national integration' in mediaeval and modern Europe, E. L. Jones suggestively observes that cycles of integration and disintegration appear to have been 'subject to an almost rhythmic alternation'. In his view:

> the state may have been able to extend and consolidate its position when there was population growth and economic expansion but made little headway during phases of contraction. Successful periods seem to have been between the eleventh and thirteenth centuries; again during the

late fifteenth and sixteenth centuries; and once more after the middle of the eighteenth century. Setbacks . . . and threats of dissolution were more evident following the Black Death and during the 'General Crisis' of the seventeenth century. . . . When there was economic and population growth there were more buyers and sellers and therefore increasing numbers of transactions. . . . Kings shared in the prosperity and they could get on with building their states without excessive resistance from the lesser lords. During the periods of contraction there were fewer pickings. There was more discord between and within states.[44]

Similarly, in the West European economy since the mid-nineteenth century (if not earlier), international integration appears to have advanced most vigorously during the major periods of boom, such as the 1850s–60s, the 1950s–60s and the late 1980s; and it has suffered its most dramatic reverses during periods of economic depression, such as the mid-1870s–80s, the 1930s, the mid to late 1970s and the early 1990s. Instead of an inexorable process of ever-increasing international interdependence and integration, one should perhaps postulate an pattern of ebb and flow.

Nevertheless, European integration since 1945 (and probably earlier) has not been merely (or even mainly) a matter of economics, let alone the national economic interests of nation-states. As already intimated, schemes for both national and supranational integration have often been motivated by security concerns and fear of a common external foe. Such fears and concerns were, in large part, what motivated the US-sponsored European Recovery Programme (1948–51), the abortive European Defence Community and the formation of the ECSC and the EEC; they were partly what prompted Franco-German reconciliation and made the ECSC and the EEC acceptable to Germany and France; these same factors largely explain American support for these initiatives and the willingness of the State Department to overrule the objections of economic departments who were fearful of erecting obstacles to a liberal multilateral trading system; and they largely explain why European 'neutrals' such as Sweden, Switzerland, Austria and Finland virtually excluded themselves from the ECSC and the EEC. The end of the Cold War has unravelled the post-1945 Cold War framework within which those developments took place. France has lost the privileged political and military positions in Western Europe conferred by the Cold War East–West division of Germany and Europe and by the initial omission of Britain from the ECSC and the EEC. A united Germany is no longer so willing to accept and defer to French political leadership in return for West German economic dominance of the European Union; Germany now wants a political status and role commensurate with its economic strength. In 1994 Austria, Sweden and Finland finally decided to join the EU, with effect from January 1995, the end of the Cold War having reduced the significance of 'neutrality', although the political and economic challenges and implications of full membership also exacerbated the Swedish and Finnish political and economic crises, which full membership was intended to resolve. (Indeed, many Swedes remain reluctant to abandon a tradition of neutrality which, like that of the Swiss and unlike that of the Austrians and the Finns, dated back to their experiences in the Napoleonic wars and was not imposed on them by the USSR and the exigencies of the Cold War.) However, since Sweden, Finland and Austria had already been brought into the Single European Market by the inauguration of the European Economic Area in January 1994, for them full membership of the EU implied only a small step towards further economic integration, even though it was a large step politically. It was also expected to lead to increased pressure for further enlargement of the EU to include Poland, Hungary, the Czech Republic and the Baltic states.

The end of the Cold War and communist rule also intensified East European desires to 'come in from the cold' politically, economically and militarily. In an ideal world, East European states would be admitted to the EU and NATO on a rapid time-table, just as soon as they have established stable liberal market economies and parliamentary democracies. Unfortunately, the EU was felt to be not yet sufficiently strong and integrated to be able withstand the additional stresses and burdens that any major 'Eastern Enlargement' would impose on its institutions, decision-making, social and regional funds, 'sensitive industries' and Common Agricultural Policy, not to mention the fears that unrestricted rights of migration from the East and North Africa might fuel further rises in West European unemployment and of the neo-fascist and anti-immigrant Right. Nor could the EU afford to disregard the likely effects of its *Ostpolitik* on Russia and the Ukraine, which did not want to be wholly excluded from any new 'European architecture'. Likewise, it was unlikely that Eastern European states would gain full membership of NATO as long as there continued to be high risks of conflict in the East, not least within those Eastern European states that are unwilling to uphold and observe human (including 'minority') rights and fundamental freedoms. In many respects the East–West division of Europe predated the Cold War and would probably long outlive it. These issues are taken up in Chapters 12–14.

In addition, the collapse of the Soviet bloc, the end of the Cold War and the permanent or temporary demise of socialism and communism as alternatives to either liberal or social democratic capitalism has had a major impact on party systems and ruling coalitions in Europe, above all in Italy, where these tectonic shifts helped to unravel a highly corrupt party system and a system of coalition government which was based on keeping the Communist Party out of office. Similar, albeit less marked, political realignments occurred in other European states (particularly those with significant communist parties and/or anti-communist Christian Democratic parties), while communist and socialist parties continued their retreats from socialist programmes and doctrines. This overlapped with the more widespread disaffection with long-established political parties, the rise or re-emergence of strong regional, environmental, anti-party, anti-corruption and neo-fascist movements, the breakdown of the post-war consensus and the 'crisis of governance' which was occurring in Eastern as well as Western Europe. Most governments no longer even pretended to be able to guarantee either full employment or economic prosperity and preferred to claim that such matters were essentially governed by global market forces outside their control.

The chapters in this volume clearly demonstrate that Europe is in a period of fundamental realignment and régime change, as it was in the years 1945–57. The régimes and alignments that emerged between 1945 and 1957 became stable and even appeared to have solidity and permanence. But one vast structure, the Soviet bloc, has clearly disintegrated and new patterns of reintegration in the East (and between East and West) have barely begun. The considerable integration achieved by the EU has frayed at the edges, especially on its frontiers with Scandinavia and Eastern Europe; and it has lost its sense of direction, as it did in the late 1970s and early 1980s. The deregulatory, deflationary, free-marketeering régime and policy convergence around which the EU set out to build the Single European Market, the Maastricht Treaty, the European Economic Area and the programme for Economic and Monetary Union was not strong enough to sustain either economic growth or monetary stability or full employment or deeper integration during the early 1990s, thus forcing both the EU and its member states to rethink their programmes, priorities and presumptions at a time when they would have preferred not to have had to do so! Hence the appearance of European disarray and disorientation during the early 1990s. Among other things, this volume aims not only to explain how these situations came about, but also to present the choices and challenges that Europe currently faces and to suggest the directions in which the various parts of Europe are likely to move in the later 1990s.

FURTHER READING

F. Duchêne, *Jean Monnet: the First Statesman of Interdependence*, New York: W. W. Norton, 1994.
A. Milward, *The European Rescue of the Nation-State*, London: Routledge, 1992.
A. Milward *et al.*, *The Frontier of National Sovereignty*, London: Routledge, 1993.
O. Nørgaard, T. Pedersen and N. Petersen (eds), *The European Community and World Politics*, London: Pinter, 1993.
J. Story (ed.), *The New Europe*, Oxford: Blackwell, 1993.

NOTES

1 K. Kaiser, C. Merlini and D. Moisi, 'Hurry to Put European Union Back on the Rails', *International Herald Tribune*, 28 October 1992, p. 6.

2 O. Jászi, *The Dissolution of the Habsburg Monarchy*, Chicago: Chicago University Press, 1929, p. 403.
3 M. Hodges (ed.), *European Integration*, Harmondsworth: Penguin, 1972, pp. 9–28, remains one of the best introductions to these theories.
4 A. Milward, *The European Rescue of the Nation-State*, London: Routledge, 1992, p. 12.
5 Ibid., p. 7.
6 Ibid., p. 7.
7 Ibid., p. 8.
8 Ibid., p. 8.
9 Ibid., p. 9.
10 Ibid., p. 10.
11 Ibid., p. 14.
12 Ibid., p. 16.
13 Ibid., p. 17.
14 Speech to the *Bundestag*, reprinted in: H. von Brentano, *Germany and Europe*, London: André Deutsch, 1964, p. 53.
15 Ibid., p. 109.
16 Ibid., pp. 165–7.
17 K. Adenauer, *Memoirs, 1945–53*, London: Weidenfeld & Nicolson, 1966, p. 437.
18 Milward (n. 4 above), p. 3.
19 Ibid., p. 4.
20 Ibid., p. 18.
21 Ibid., p. 3.
22 L. Tsoukalis, *The New Economy of Europe*, Oxford: Oxford University Press, p. 3.
23 M. Forsyth, *Unions of States*, Leicester: Leicester University Press, 1981, p. 204.
24 F. Hinsley, *Power and the Pursuit of Peace*, Cambridge: Cambridge University Press, 1962, pp. 102–6.
25 Cited in: Hinsley, p. 102.
26 Hinsley, p. 113.
27 Churchill's attitude towards Europe is examined by Clive Ponting in Chapter 3.
28 A. Milward *et al.*, *The Frontier of National Sovereignty*, London: Routledge, 1993, p. 190.
29 Milward (n. 4 above), p. 3.
30 Ibid., p. 18.
31 Letter from François Duchêne to the author, 2 February 1994.
32 Milward (n. 4 above), p. 18.
33 E. L. Jones, *The European Miracle: Environment, Economics and Geopolitics in the History of Europe and Asia*, Cambridge: Cambridge University Press, 1981, p. 226.
34 Ibid., p. 90.
35 Ibid., p. 106.
36 Ibid., p. 108.
37 Ibid., p. 109.
38 Ibid., p. 112.
39 Ibid., p. 119.
40 Ibid., p. 123.
41 Ibid., pp. 110–11.
42 Ibid., p. 113.
43 Ibid., p. 117.
44 Ibid., pp. 128–9.

2 French motives for European integration

François Duchêne

The paradox of the European Union from the first day to this has been that, while its aims – notably of Franco-German reconciliation – have been political, its successful vehicles, such as the Common Market, have been economic, and its direct political achievements at best marginal. Since a French initiative set the policy going, assessing its French roots is an important part of understanding the Union now.

After the war the need for Europeans to unite was a cliché. Under the German wartime occupation, the idea came from both sides: from the Resistance and from Hitler's propaganda for a New Order. After the war unity was widely accepted as the only recipe for peace after all the failures and blood-letting of the previous generation. To avoid the fate of the city states of ancient Greece and Renaissance Italy, Europe's former great powers, which had come down so abruptly in the world, had to draw urgently on new sources of vitality in the face of the New Romes of East and West. Unity was one of the great themes of renewal in continental Europe in the immediate post-war years.

This should not be discounted as passing rhetoric of little relevance in the long run. It motivated the active minorities who launched the European Communities and kept the unifying impulse alive even at times, such as after the rejection of the European Army, when it seemed terminally impaired. The leaders of the so-called 'Third Force' political parties, mainly socialist and Catholic, who ran the French Fourth Republic until the return to power of de Gaulle in 1958, were – or became for the most part – stoutly committed to integration.[1] Robert Rothschild, the chief of staff of Paul-Henri Spaak in the negotiations on the Treaties of Rome, and later Belgium's ambassador to France and then Britain, has said of those years among decision-makers in the six founding member states of the European Community that to declare one was not 'European' was an 'abomination'.[2] A strident nationalist such as Michel Debré was regarded as slightly touched. Such convictions were a significant ingredient in, and precondition for, the launching of the European Community. They operate even now in the power of attraction which a club of states engaged in a political process under the rule of law exerts on outsiders used in the past to the insecurity and rigours of the balance of power.

Yet, had European convictions sufficed, one would have expected them to produce results soon after the war when the ideological magnetism of European unity was at its purest. A slight hiatus might have been allowed for the first aid of reconstruction. But once the Marshall Plan brought in the Americans with their strong desire to see the Western Europeans overcome their divisions, governments should (on this assumption) have displayed a practical will to turn European rhetoric into acts. That is conspicuously what they failed to do. The period from the Marshall to Schuman Plans, from June 1947 to May 1950, is a cemetery for aborted European schemes. The Council of Europe, the Franco-Italian customs union and Finebel all laboured mightily to miscarry, notably because governments were not ready to give up their individual vetoes in the interests of effective joint decision-making.[3] On the eve of the Schuman Plan, early in 1950, the Americans were so resigned to the impossibility of European unity that attention began to shift to woolly concepts of Atlantic political co-operation.[4] One of the many schemes promoted in April 1950 was a French one for an Atlantic High Council for Peace, advanced by none other than Georges Bidault, the head of the very government that was to propose the Schuman Plan three weeks later.

The issue that, more or less at the last moment, blew away the fog on the landscape was the reappearance of Germany on the political scene. It was the calendar of German revival that concentrated neighbours' minds and fixed the European breakthrough in May 1950 and not before.[5]

In theory, Hitler's ruin in 1945 offered an opportunity to reshape Germany, which France had not enjoyed even in 1919. De Gaulle responded in the spirit of the novelist François Mauriac's grim Cold War joke that France loved Germany so well she preferred to have more than one of them. This did not quite extend to Henry Morgenthau's notion of turning Germany into a pastoral zone. Still, de Gaulle and his successors in Paris did seek to form several regional states and to internationalize the Ruhr, whose heavy industries were still regarded (oddly, in the age of superpowers and atomic weapons) as the sinews of militarism. But France was alone in wanting this, and the years to 1950 brought an increasingly desperate retreat from her preferred position.

The initial desire to have several German mini-states fell foul of the desire of both superpowers, for different reasons, to maintain Germany, the fulcrum of the balance of power, as a single entity. Then, from 1946–7, as the Cold War gradually crystallized, each superpower confirmed its grip over its own Germany. This simple partition put paid to hopes of regional mini-states. Then the Marshall Plan, designed to make Western Europe prosperous and self-reliant, demanded the revival of West Germany at its economic heart. At the first London Conference in May–June 1948 the Americans, backed by the British, made it clear that, whether the French liked it or not, the 'Anglo-Saxons' would move to a joint administration of their two occupation zones, a Bi-Zone, generally assumed to be the first step towards a new German state. The French were horrified. The parliamentarians in the National Assembly narrowly endorsed a decision that they could not prevent, but made a scapegoat of Georges Bidault, the Foreign Minister since September 1944, who lost his hitherto inviolable job. By this time – indeed since the Marshall Plan a year earlier – the French had fallen back on trying to establish international controls over the Ruhr.[6] By 1949 this too looked more and more of a forlorn hope, for the German Federal Republic was set up in May and Konrad Adenauer became its first Chancellor in September. By May of 1950 it was clear to Bidault's successor as Foreign Minister, Robert Schuman, that – again whether the French liked it or not – the Americans and British were about to lift production controls over the Ruhr and an increasingly sovereign German Federal Republic.

France's pre-Schuman Plan policy of trying to control Germany from the outside failed for three reasons. The first was that France was too weak to impose it, just as she had proved too weak to contain Germany between the wars. The second was that France's post-war hopes of the USA containing Germany, and so relieving France of the trouble, also implied that France had no real ability to control events. The USA was now building up West Germany as a front-line bastion of the West, not repressing her, and France at most could only slow the process. Third, the past ensured that any attempt at French control was bound to re-awaken the habitual hostility between French and Germans. This became evident early in 1950 over French measures to annex the Saar 'economically' and use this coal and steel region as a partial makeweight in the unequal industrial balance between the two countries. A policy with better prospects than Balkanizing Germany, relying on America to repress her or pinching strips of territory, had to be devised.

Schuman, in launching his famous Plan in May 1950 (or rather in giving Jean Monnet the political cover to launch the Plan), now broke with all French approaches to Germany since Richelieu by proposing a partnership with the Federal Republic. The French coal and steel industries would be placed in a common pool with those of Germany and any other participating states. All of them, including the Germans, would be equal before the laws of this international régime. It would be run by a joint High Authority and other institutions enjoying real powers to take decisions. The Schuman declaration of 9 May 1950 stated that this was a first step to the ultimate goal of a federal Europe.[7]

It has been argued that, despite these declared intentions, the Schuman Plan was really an extension by other means of traditional French policies of control over Germany. Sir Oliver Harvey, the British Ambassador in Paris, observed that:

the Schuman Plan seems to be an attempt to substitute for repressive institutions such as the High Commission or the Ruhr Authority, whose effectiveness is thought to be diminishing, a new organisation which would have some chance of being permanently accepted by the Germans because they would have within it equal status with the French . . . it seems to [the latter] the only chance of preventing exclusive German control of the Ruhr, which to their minds still represents the greatest potential danger to French security.[8]

During the negotiations on the Schuman Plan, Ruhr industrialists, while paying lip-service to European integration, attacked it as 'a protective screen for inefficient French steel' and made no bones about their preference for a revival of the pre-war steel cartel.[9] The theme has been revived in the 1980s by the economic historian, Alan Milward. His study, *The Reconstruction of Western Europe, 1945–1951*,[10] argues that the Schuman Plan was primarily designed to save the Monnet investment plan's ambitions to make France competitive with Germany in steel and manufacturing.

Monnet himself, on 3 May 1950, in a key memorandum for Schuman, stated that, if the Germans were allowed to prevent French steelmasters from buying Ruhr coke and coking coal on the same terms as their German competitors, French industry might sink back into the second-class status and protectionism of the 1930s: 'our industrialists consider that dearer steel handicaps the whole of our manufacturing'.[11] It was therefore a matter of economic survival for France to establish a joint control of the prices 'of these basic commodities in Western Europe'. There are reasons for discounting the validity of such arguments and even the depth of Monnet's belief in them. As one of his closest associates at the time, Jacques Van Helmont, has remarked, it gave him, in dealing with sceptics not least in the French Parliament, 'one of those unanswerable arguments he liked to have, of a totally concrete kind'.[12] But, if the French Parliament had to be persuaded in those terms, then, whatever Monnet's private views might be, that shaped the action.

Nevertheless, if the Schuman Plan was an extension of traditional French policy by other means, it was a very odd version of it. For the means transformed the traditional policy itself. It was obvious there would have to be 'equality' in any scheme if there were to be a permanent settlement with Germany.[13] The Germans, from Adenauer down, would take nothing less. That was hard enough for many French to swallow five years after the war. Further, if the new system was to be effective, it had to be able to take decisions when the partners fell short of unanimity. National vetoes had to be limited. In theory, as the subject of a thousand speeches, this was nothing new. It was widely accepted that no collective would work if each member state could pick and choose decisions as it pleased and block the rest. The League of Nations, the Council of

Europe, even the United Nations, were object lessons. The Schuman Plan was not to repeat such mistakes. The difficulty was in the corollary: if Germany was not to be allowed to go her own way and France, Germany and their partners were all to be equal before the rules, France must lose the freedom to do as she liked along with everyone else.

For France's neighbours, this was precisely what made the Schuman Plan serious. J. van den Brink, the Dutch Minister for Economic Affairs in 1950, has recalled that 'Holland was normally rather suspicious of any proposal from France. We always thought there was some ulterior motive. . . . But, when I heard that the French were ready to bring their own coal and steel industry in . . . this had body, flesh and blood.'[14] But equality and the loss of a free hand were exactly what most French politicians and diplomats could scarcely bear to concede. Officialdom was viscerally incapable of giving up a great power's pride in unilateral behaviour. Even strong 'Europeans' were schizophrenic. René Pleven, the Minister for Defence in Bidault's government, approving European controls on German coal, amazed Monnet's deputy, Etienne Hirsch, by wondering aloud whether they need apply to French iron ore (in any case, a much less strategic asset).[15]

The Schuman Plan implied other audacities by the lights of the time and place. A partnership with Germany was in the medium run (at the latest) quite incompatible with an 'economically' French Saar. The Saar was ethnically as German as Hesse or Hanover and the Germans (particularly in the light of their claims on the Russians for reunification) would never concede such a denial of the right to self-determination. Schuman and Monnet did all they could to marginalize the Saar in the Schuman Plan negotiations. But they were sailing close to the rocks as regards opinion in Paris. Another strong 'European' in the Bidault government, the Minister of Justice, René Mayer, told Adenauer nearly three years later that he regretted the Saar had not been settled in the Schuman treaty. He meant that France's economic annexation should have been recognized.[16]

Just as shocking was the Schuman Plan's effect in jettisoning the *entente cordiale* with London, which had been France's prime insurance against Germany in two world wars. The insistence of Monnet (rather than Schuman) that the new system demanded a commitment to supranational government necessarily excluded Britain, since she would not countenance such a pledge.[17] Joining an unproven Germany without Britain was breathtaking five years after the war. Britain stood head and shoulders above her European neighbours in war and peace and was much the biggest economy in the region. In reality, though, raising anchor from the *entente cordiale* was much less risky than it seemed, much less risky than the *entente cordiale* itself had been. The Schuman Plan, superficially a shift from Britain to Germany, was in fact a transfer of French insurance from Britain to America. America was the ardent champion of European integration because she wanted harmony between France and West Germany to solidify Western Europe in the Cold War balance with the Soviet Union. America was far more of a counterweight to Germany than Britain could ever be. By her mere presence in Europe she created a safety zone. But this was not self-evident to everyone at the time. Would the USA remain in Europe and, if she did, would she back France or Germany?

It was, therefore, no accident that the Schuman treaty conference was taken out of the hands of the Quai d'Orsay. All the other delegations – from Germany, Italy and the Benelux countries – were headed in the orthodox way by diplomats (even if Walter Hallstein, hitherto a lawyer and university vice-chancellor, was as yet only one in embryo). The French were led by Monnet, a political entrepreneur and, for all his power at the time, an outsider. This anomaly cannot have been due to the Quai d'Orsay's incapacity to conceive the strategy. A note of 13 December 1948, which follows the reasoning of the Schuman Plan itself, proves otherwise.[18] But in April 1950 Schuman was unable to obtain any proposals from his Foreign Ministry to help him cope with his problem.[19] This was not surprising. The dominant officials in the Foreign Ministry were almost all representatives of the Gaullist or *entente cordiale* schools of thought, both of which came close to regarding a Community with Germany as suicide or a betrayal of France's prerogatives, and in either case to give off a whiff of treason. René Massigli, the French Ambassador in London and de Gaulle's former Commissioner for Foreign Affairs in the Committee for National Liberation in Algiers, told Sir William Strang, the Permanent Under-Secretary at the British Foreign Office on 27 June 1950 that 'the French Ministry of Foreign Affairs were solidly hostile to the Schuman Plan in its present form'.[20] He may have been exaggerating, but another ambassador remarked of Schuman: 'to think that nobody has attacked that man for having fought in German uniform' (which, as a Lorrainer when his part of Lorraine was German, he had done in the First World War).[21] The diplomats who were shortly to turn fiercely against the European Army project, could not propose a Schuman Plan, even though they did not actively oppose it. Monnet wanted to run the talks. Schuman knew he would produce results. That an interloper handled the watershed conference for French foreign policy this century shows how far the new departure flouted tradition.

In fact, the Schuman Plan initiated not so much a reversal of alliances as an embryonic revolution in foreign policy. In the Schuman Plan, the member countries renounced one of the central tenets of centuries of the balance of power: the right of the nation-state, embodied in the formal veto, to refuse to co-operate and, in the last resort, to withdraw from any contract as freely as it was entered into. By implication, under supranational bodies, set up to conceive and apply common policies, they also agreed to cease to treat one another as foreigners and instead to deal as partners in a quasi-domestic system. Decision-making acquired some of the spirit of joint responsibility taken for granted in the domestic practices of democracies, but not internationally. Of course, the new commitment was limited. The Schuman Plan was fragmentary. The bonds cementing the new relations were fragile. Nevertheless, a new principle was introduced, potentially as exclusive as the one it replaced. A first step was taken on a road that led diametrically away from the classical practices of the diplomats. No wonder most of them were unenthusiastic.

The Schuman Plan, in short, mobilized a coalition of forces – ideological, economic and political – for a new security policy towards a new Germany. This would have led to little if the Schuman Plan had remained an anomaly in the context. It would not have survived. In fact, the main features of the Schuman Plan, the focus on Germany, the political goals, the economic medium, and the divisions in French opinion over the whole strategy, have been in evidence in various ways and to a greater or lesser degree ever since. This was never clearer than in the critical period from 1953 to 1957 when the ill-fated European Army project was brought down in flames and the Common Market rose unexpectedly from the ashes.

The European Army project (or European Defence Community, EDC) was prompted by the American reaction to the outbreak of the Korean War only one week after the Schuman Plan negotiations had begun in June 1950. The American view was that the United States could only protect the West Europeans and bring troops into the region if the West Europeans helped themselves, which meant *inter alia* that West Germany must be armed. To the French, the idea that Germany should be rearmed five years after the war was deeply alarming. The EDC was the response of the French 'Europeanists' – Monnet, Schuman and now Pleven (the new Prime Minister) – trying to hitch unwelcome rearmament to the new hope of a united Europe. There would be no revival of a German Defence Ministry and General Staff because German troops would be incorporated in a European Army, with a European Defence Minister and General Staff. However, as events were to prove, the balance of French political opinion was such that in the end, by 1953–4, the motive became more to prevent any German rearmament at all than to form an EDC, which was hard to imagine without a European Government.[22] In the end, the EDC Treaty drew even fiercer fire from some of the political right (notably the Gaullists) than German rearmament itself. For these critics, preserving the 'millennial' French Army from a European merger took precedence over all else. Leading diplomats, though civil servants, fiercely aided, abetted and incited the opposition to the European Army Treaty.[23] The conclusion of what Raymond Aron called the greatest ideological and political conflict in France since the Dreyfus case was a narrow victory for the opponents of the European Army in Parliament in 1954.[24] By this time, opposition to the Treaty had spilt over in many (not all) influential quarters in France into opposition to supranational European union itself.

As Miriam Camps has written, 'anyone who had then predicted that the Six would soon be actively engaged in the creation of two new

Communities might reasonably have been dismissed as a light-headed visionary'.[25] Why such expectations were confounded is again a basic question. After France's rejection of the European Army Treaty in August 1954, powerful forces in all its Community partners leaned towards freeing trade with Britain and the other European states in the wider, looser setting of the OEEC. Freer trade did not have to mean a common market with relatively strong institutions. It also did not have to be pursued with France, perhaps the most convinced and articulate protectionist country in the region. The Germans, who were – at least in theory – most eager to cut tariffs, like Erhard and part of industry, regarded France as the last country with which to pursue a privileged trade relationship. When the Common Market was effectively (but not for the first time) injected into the political process by the Dutch Foreign Minister, Jan Beyen, in 1955, the French establishment was so opposed to free trade that the new French Government, divided between pro- and anti-Europeans and wanting (but very cautiously) to 'relaunch Europe', stressed integration in civil nuclear power – the European Atomic Energy Community (Euratom) – instead. Given all this and the French veto on the EDC, plenty of leaders in Germany and Benelux were ready to go ahead and build co-operative (but not supranational) networks with Britain and, if necessary, without France, and let her catch up later.

There was no overwhelming case on economic grounds for the six founding states – and no one else – launching the five Communities proposed in the 1950s. The Six made less sense, for instance in Euratom, than a functional group including Britain with the then biggest nuclear programme in Western Europe, Norway with heavy water, and Sweden or Switzerland with their special engineering. The (literally) Euro-sceptic French Prime Minister in 1955, Edgar Faure, would have preferred nuclear energy co-operation in the OEEC to a community of the Six.[26] As regards the Common Market, the great boom of the mid-1950s undoubtedly made things easier. A small but influential minority of senior French officials and politicians were becoming convinced that freer trade was necessary in the French interest. In the end, it became possible to find a balance between Germany's interest in French and Italian markets for manufactured exports and French, Dutch and Italian interest in German markets for food. But the French committed themselves to negotiate the Common Market only in September 1956, whereas the Germans had specifically re-embraced the Community approach well before, in July 1955.

In fact, the great boom cut both ways. The growth of exports to Germany from its neighbours between 1951 and 1958, the years relevant for defining attitudes to a still hypothetical Common Market, is very revealing. There was no clear pattern distinguishing neighbours who joined the Common Market from those who did not. Austria was far ahead of any other country. Italy, Switzerland and France came in the next group. Britain, Denmark, the Netherlands, Belgium and Norway followed in that order.[27] From such a jumble, it is hard to draw any lesson about the economic pressures to join the Common Market. The 'miracle' of the 1950s, boosting trade and growth for almost everyone, was so overwhelming that it was materially as easy for some countries to say 'no' to joining the Community as for others to say 'yes'. Except in agriculture, there was little or no commercial price to pay for staying out.[28]

Yet France's Community partners chose to attempt a common market with her; and, after much hesitation, in the winter of 1956–7, France acquiesced. Adenauer was clear, against his own free-traders, that reconciliation with France came first. In Belgium, Spaak wanted European union for somewhat similar reasons.[29] The figure in France most responsible for pushing through the Treaties of Rome, the socialist boss who became Prime Minister for a relatively long time in 1956–7, Guy Mollet – like another influential figure, the conservative, Antoine Pinay – feared that the new German Army and Ruhr industrialists might once again provide a seedbed for predatory nationalism.[30] In a new form, this was the old fear behind the Schuman Plan. Interestingly, it was shared by the German socialists, who were only won over to the 'European' camp after the failure of the EDC and through Euratom, partly for these reasons. The men who settled the issue in favour of the Community of Six had political concerns uppermost in mind. It was no accident that all five Communities of the 1950s, the three born alive and the two that miscarried, were based on the six states ready to enter into supranational commitments.[31]

France's sense of vulnerability was not unique. For West Germany, a post-war pariah, the Community provided an accommodating context for revival and an insurance against the risk of any decline in the United States' security guarantee. For the Benelux trio, initially very wary of supranationality, it increasingly represented protection against both conflict, and a domineering alliance, between France and Germany. It gave small countries a say in the formation of policies almost wholly lacking in the old balance of power. For all member states, large and small, it meant extra insurance in face of both superpowers and (on another plane) of the rapid globalization of the world economy. This was a formidable list of security reasons for states to feel committed to the Community. They made, and make, it a highly political edifice even without a political union.

Interestingly enough, the reasons for the groupings that emerged were political not just on one but on both sides of the supranational fence. The Six were willing to commit themselves because of the importance to them of Franco-German reconciliation. The other states were not, either because of a great-power mentality, in the case of Britain, or of various forms of neutrality with most of the others, and also in Britain and Scandinavia a certain insularity and disdain for the continentals, a sense of superior virtue to them. In short, economic factors were the enabling base of the Common Market as of the Schuman Plan, but security concerns focused the political outcomes.

The political shaping power of the European framework can be seen in the case of the Saar. In 1950 this offered every sign of becoming a classic territorial dispute of the kind that produced so many *casus belli* in the past and that even without war could generate endless bad blood. A settlement of the Saar question by France and Germany was a precondition of any true negotiation of the Treaties of Rome. It took the whole of the first half of 1956 to return the Saar to Germany on economic terms acceptable to France. The annexation of the Saar had been designed to reduce the potential disparity between French and German steel productions when they were still roughly equal. By the time the territory was handed back, steel production in Germany and the Saar together was twice that of France.[32] Yet the very next step was the Common Market. Obviously, in the perspective of a partnership, the old yardstick of the balance of industrial power, at least in the old guise, had become irrelevant.

Then why have the achievements of the European Community and now Union been so much more economic than political? At least two features tend to make economic integration easier. The first is the crude but relevant proposition that governments find it hard enough to integrate businessmen; it is even closer to the bone to integrate themselves. The most political aspect of economic integration, monetary union, still, despite thirty years of effort, eludes the authors of the Single Market.[33] Second, economic integration has run before the wind of international forces, such as the freeing of trade in the great post-war boom, the emergence of the so-called multinational corporations and now the rush to a global economy. These have all gathered momentum over recent decades, making the Single Market only a particular (if striking) expression of a wider phenomenon. In contrast, political integration (in money, law and order, foreign policy and defence) has tended increasingly to cut across the grain of the revival of the nation-state buoyed up by economic recovery and the return of the traditional self-confidence which was at a low ebb after the war. In the long run, the internationalization of the economy tends to undermine the nation-state, but in the short run it has defused the post-war sense of acute crisis without which great political changes are hard to generate.

Certainly, the French division of opinion over European integration – to the point of schizophrenia in individual politicians – has been very much to the fore from first to last. This was dramatized before the Common Market was even in place by the return to power of de Gaulle in June 1958. He made the Common Market possible in many ways, but was determined to excise its federal elements, which he did in the Community's so-called 'empty chair' crisis of 1965–6. It was another twenty years before François Mitterrand, a socialist President rooted in the Fourth Republic, made it possible for the Community to put an end to semi-paralysis by a return to qualified majority voting in the Council of Ministers. Throughout these twenty years, the French attitude to the Community was closer to those of de Gaulle in the 1960s or the British at all times than it was to that of the founding fathers. Even under Mitterrand, the French desire to run an independent foreign and security policy soaked in 'grandeur' and the dislike of handing over to the European Parliament the kinds of powers needed to close the European Union's 'democratic deficit' have resembled British attitudes more than German support for federalism. It is an irony and a success that Germany should be the champion of a policy originally designed to contain or convert her.

For most of the post-war period, France and Britain have been identical in their need to posture as great powers exercising the great power's privilege of unilateral decision-making. If Britain today can aspire to be an effective obstacle to further European Union of a federal kind, this is largely because the ambiguity of the Gaullist inheritance in Paris casts doubt on a clear Franco-German alignment of the kind that was decisive in 1950 and 1956. Yet, for all the parallels, one major contrast sets France and Britain apart. For the French, Germany has been and is the decisive influence in the shaping of foreign policy. For Britain, Germany has been relatively marginal and largely left to the Americans to handle. Britain has gone into the European Union because she cannot afford to stay out, not because she feels she must subordinate other policy priorities to the German imperative. The British emphasis wherever possible on NATO and free trade in the approach to European Union shows that Germany is still treated as an actor in an environment defined by the USA. It can even be argued that this policy, by bringing in the New World to weigh on the balance of the Old, is a functional equivalent in dealing with a would-be united Europe of the old balance-of-power policy towards threatening hegemonists when Europe was divided. France, however, as she has shown by her stubborn and costly attachment to monetary union, cannot stand aside in this ambivalent way. France treats Germany as a problem too important to be left to anyone else. The German issue has made few inroads on the psychology of the British establishment, but it has profoundly shaped that of France.

FURTHER READING

F. Duchêne, *Jean Monnet: the First Statesman of Interdependence*, New York: W. W. Norton, 1994.

P. Gerbet, *La Construction de l'Europe*, Paris: Imprimerie Nationale, 1983.

J. Gillingham, *Coal, Steel and the Rebirth of Europe, 1945–1955*, Cambridge: Cambridge University Press, 1991.

A. Milward, *The European Rescue of the Nation-State*, London and New York: Methuen, 1992.

R. Poidevin (ed.), *Histoire des débuts de la construction européenne, mars 1948 à mai 1950*, Brussels: Bruylant; Milan: Giuffrè; Paris: L.G.D.J.; Baden-Baden: Nomos, 1986.

K. Schwabe (ed.), *Die Anfänge des Schuman-Plans* [The Beginnings of the Schuman Plan], Brussels: Bruylant; Milan: Giuffrè; Paris: L.G.D.J.; Baden-Baden: Nomos, 1988.

E. Serra (ed.), *Il Rilancio dell'Europea e i tratatti di Roma* [The Relaunching of Europe and the Treaties of Rome], Brussels: Bruylant; Milan: Giuffrè; Paris: L.G.D.J.; Baden-Baden: Nomos, 1989.

J. van Helmont, *Options européennes, 1945–1985*, Brussels: Commission des Communautés Européennes, 1986.

NOTES

FRUS   Foreign Relations of the United States
USNA   US National Archives
FJME   Fondation Jean Monnet pour l'Europe
FNA   French National Archives

1 At first, the French socialists were reluctant to embark on the Communities without Britain. As British reluctance became clear, notably over the European Defence Community (EDC) treaty, their attitude changed. After the rejection of the EDC treaty in 1954, their leader, Guy Mollet came round to Jean Monnet's view that the 'British respect facts' and that the six founding states should go ahead, leaving the door open for the UK to join later.

2 Baron Robert Rothschild, interviews with author, 6 March 1986.

3 The OEEC was more successful, notably in establishing an important European Payments Union; but it too ran out of steam in the early 1950s.

4 US State Department, Foreign Relations of the United States (hereafter FRUS), 1950, vol. III, pp. 64, 75, 91–2, 617–18 and 896–8; also US National Archives (hereafter USNA), RG 59, 840.50R, 7th meeting, Strategic Defense Policy Planning Staff, 24 January 1950.

5 In September 1949, at one of the periodic meetings of the Foreign Ministers of the Allied Occupying Powers in West Germany, the US, the UK and France (Dean Acheson, Ernest Bevin and Robert Schuman), Acheson put a gun to Schuman's head, asking him to outline a common policy for West Germany at the next Foreign Ministers' meeting with the implication that, if Schuman did not, the US would have to define a policy with or without the French. The next Foreign Ministers' meeting was finally fixed for 11–12 May 1950. The Schuman Plan came in the nick of time; FRUS, 1949, vol. III, pp. 610 and 623; B. Clappier, 'Bernard Clappier Témoigne' [Bernard Clappier Bears Witness], in: H. Rieben (ed.), *L'Europe: une longue marche* [Europe: A Long March], Lausanne: Fondation Jean Monnet pour l'Europe (hereafter FJME), 1985, p. 22.

6 Clayton–Monnet series of meetings, FRUS, 1947, vol. II, 30 July 1947 ff., pp. 1011–37; A. S. Milward, *The Reconstruction of Western Europe, 1945–1951*, London: Routledge, 1984, pp. 74–5 and 141 ff.

7 See, for example: H. Rieben (ed.), *Des Guerres européennes à l'Union de l'Europe* [From European Wars to European Union], Lausanne: FJME, 1987, pp. 292–6.

8 R. Bullen and M. E. Pelly (eds), *Documents on British Policy Overseas. Series II, vol. I: Schuman Plan*, London: HMSO, 1986; Harvey-Younger, 16 June 1950, pp. 183–5; and Franks-Makins, 14 July 1950, p. 259.

9 French National Archives (hereafter FNA), 81 AJ (Schuman Plan), # 138, Part 1/IV A. François Poncet, 31 October 1950; # 139 Part 3/I Bureau-Monnet, 7 April 1951; USNA, RG 59, # 4946, 850.33, Bohlen-SS tg 2093, 18 October 1950. Germans sometimes talked of the Coal and Steel Community as 'the policy of Richelieu' (to control Germany) if France gave up political union: Winrich Behr-Max Kohnstamm, M. Kohnstamm, diary entry 23 November 1954, interviews with author, 18 January 1986.

10 Milward (n. 6 above), pp. 369–71, 380, 396.

11 FJME, Lausanne, R. Schuman papers, 4-1-2 Monnet-Schuman, 3 May 1950, reprinted in *Le Monde*, 9 May 1970. René Pleven, the Minister of Defence in the Bidault Government told his British counterpart, Emmanuel Shinwell that 'in a very short time . . . Germany would undersell France in coal by 25% and in steel by 15%'; Bullen and Pelly (n. 8 above), p. 38. In the light of such categorical statements, it is ironic to find Monnet complaining over five months later to the Prime Minister, the Foreign Minister and the Minister for Industry that it was impossible to winkle the costs of production of the steel industry out of the steel division of the Ministry of Industry; FNA, 81 AJ 135 M1/b, Monnet-Louvel, 24 November 1950.

12 Jacques Van Helmont, interviews with author, 28 April 1988.

13 E. Hirsch, *Ainsi va la vie* [Such is Life], Lausanne: FJME, 1988, pp. 102–3.

14 J. van den Brink, interview with author, 17 May 1989.

15 Bullen and Pelly (n. 8 above), Harvey-Younger, 16 June 1950, p. 183; Hirsch (n. 13 above), pp. 107–8.

16 FNA, 373 AP (Private Archives), René Mayer papers, # 17, 12 May 1953; Virginia Historical Archives, Richmond VA, David Bruce diary, 24 March 1953.

17 USNA, RG 59, 850.33, 26 May 1950.

18 French Foreign Ministry Archives, Z-Europe, Allemagne, 40, Z-18-1, pp. 210–13.

19 J. Monnet, *Mémoires*, Paris: Fayard, 1976, p. 346; R. Mischlich, *Une Mission secrète à Bonn*, Lausanne: FJME, 1986, p. 51; J. Sauvagnargues, interviews with the author, 22 April 1988, pp. 21–2.

20 Bullen and Pelly (n. 8 above), p. 224, n. 2.

21 Mischlich (n. 19 above), p. 38; J. Guyot, interview with author, 21 April 1988.

22 Which is why in the summer of 1952 proposals for a European Political Community (EPC) came to the fore. But, tied to the European Army project, and difficult to embody in a practical way without a wholesale transfer of political sovereignty (which Belgium and France at least had no intention of making), the EPC died with it.

23 According to Pierre Mendès-France (*La République moderne. Propositions*, Paris: Gallimard, 1962, p. 38), Alexandre Parodi, the Secretary-General (or civil service head) of the Quai d'Orsay, and René Massigli led the fierce opposition in it to the EDC Treaty.

24 After an impassioned debate, the Chamber of Deputies voted on 30 August 1954 by 319 to 264 to pass on to the next item of business, and so in effect to bury the Treaty. When the vote was announced, the majority rose to their feet, some to sing the Marseillaise, others the Internationale. The decisive factor was the split in equał parts of the hundred socialist votes. If the socialists had voted *en bloc* in favour, the result would have been reversed. They did vote *en bloc* for the Treaty of Paris (Coal and Steel Community) in December 1951 and the two Treaties of Rome (Common Market and Euratom) in July 1957. The reference to the Dreyfus case is in R. Aron and D. Lerner (eds), *La Querelle de la C. E. D.* [The Quarrel over the EDC], Paris: Colin, 1956, p. 9.

25 M. Camps, *Britain and the European Community 1955–1963*, Oxford: Oxford University Press and Princeton, NJ: Princeton University Press, 1964, p. 20.
26 Belgian Ministry of Foreign Affairs Archives, van der Meulen papers, 5216, 17.771/4, Guillaume-Larock, 19 April 1955.
27 A. S. Milward, *The European Rescue of the Nation-State*, London: Routledge, 1992, p. 136, Table 4.3. The order was as inextricably mixed for exports to Western Europe as a whole (excluding Germany): the Netherlands came first, followed, in that order, by Austria, Switzerland, Italy, Denmark, the UK, Sweden and Norway, with France, Belgium and Portugal bringing up the rear.
28 Access for agricultural exports to the German market, by far the fastest growing, was an argument very much in favour of a common market for the food exporters, the Netherlands, France and Italy. But the Germans were not at all keen to open their highly protected farm sector to competition. It took six years of table-thumping by de Gaulle after the Common Market was established to obtain a Common Agricultural Policy in the EEC.
29 Rothschild, interviews with the author, 13 and 20 February 1986.
30 M. Kohnstamm, diary entry 7 November 1956, interviews with the author, 3–8 July 1986; *Der Spiegel*, 9 October 1954, pp. 36–9; Van Helmont, interviews with the author, 14 May 1986.
31 The European Coal and Steel Community, the European Economic Community (Common Market), the European Atomic Energy Community (Euratom) survived; the European Defence Community was stillborn and the European Political Community partly negotiated and never initialled.
32 OEEC, *Industrial Statistics 1900–1959*, Paris: OEEC, 1960, p. 93, Table 54.
33 Public proposals for monetary union go back at least as early as November 1959, when the Action Committee for a United States of Europe, chaired by Jean Monnet, recommended the establishment of a European Reserve Fund along lines he prepared in 1957 with a group including the distinguished Belgian Yale economist, Robert Triffin.

3 Churchill and Europe

A revision

Clive Ponting

During the process of ratifying the Maastricht Treaty differences of view within the Conservative Party over European policy were severe and openly expressed. During the run-up to the 1996 Inter-Governmental Conferences these differences are likely to re-emerge. However, nearly all Conservatives would agree that, for better or for worse, it is their party rather than the Liberals that can lay claim to be the originator of the European idea. This assertion is based less on the Macmillan Government's belated bid to enter the EEC in the early 1960s than on the widely held belief that Sir Winston Churchill was one of the earliest advocates of the European idea. It is argued that, when in opposition between 1945 and 1951, he worked determinedly to further the cause of European unity and to place Britain at the centre of that movement. Many Conservatives and other commentators would go further and assert that one of Churchill's many claims to greatness was his post-war vision of a united Europe – a vision which, it is believed, he set out in his Zurich speech of September 1946. I shall argue that such views are a serious misunderstanding of Churchill's position, and in particular of his views about Britain's role in Europe.

In considering Churchill's views on any subject, but in particular on Britain's role in the world, it is always necessary to remember that he was educated in the 1880s and formed his views at a time when the British Empire was still expanding to its maximum extent. Churchill was an imperialist who believed that Britain was one of the great world powers and therefore on a different level from other European countries. Before he entered Parliament in 1900 he stated that one of his political aims in life was to preserve and, if possible, expand the British Empire. In Churchill's view of the world – which was widely shared by his generation – threats to Britain's security could come from Europe (for example, Germany in the early twentieth century), whereas Britain had wider interests which meant that it could never be a purely European power. Britain's imperial interests were regarded as forming the basis of its claim to be a world power and were therefore of pre-eminent importance.

After the First World War Churchill's political attitudes were increasingly shaped by the multitude of threats he saw as undermining the world he had known in his first forty years – in particular, revolution at home and abroad and increasing challenges to British rule from within the Empire, especially in Egypt and India. From the mid-1920s he adopted the position of an isolationist – seeking to detach Britain from European quarrels. As Chancellor of the Exchequer in the 1924–9 Baldwin Government he opposed Austen Chamberlain's negotiation of the Locarno Treaty on the grounds that it could involve British intervention in Europe. His views remained unchanged in the early 1930s. On 23 November 1932 he told the House of Commons that Britain should undertake no commitments in Europe that the United States would not support.[1] Since the United States was not even a member of the League of Nations and took little interest in Europe's political problems, Churchill obviously intended that Britain should do likewise. In this way, he believed, Britain would be able to concentrate its resources and efforts on the Empire.

Hitler's appointment as Chancellor in Germany on 30 January 1933 made no difference to this stance. A month later, speaking to his constituents, he reassured them that 'there is no likelihood of a war in which Britain would be involved' and he praised the foreign policy of the government because 'they have very rightly refused to extend our obligations in Europe or elsewhere'.[2] In the middle of April 1933 he told the House of Commons that 'we have no right to meddle too closely in Europe'.[3] He opposed any close association with France (which he had long thought should come to an agreement with Germany) and argued that Britain should be neutral in any future European war. On 14 March 1933 he told MPs: 'I hope and trust that the French will look after their own safety, and that we shall be permitted to live our life in our island without being again drawn into the perils of the continent of Europe' and reminded the House that 'we have to be strong enough to defend our neutrality'.[4] Again on 12 August 1933 he told his constituents that Britain should be 'strong enough if war should come in Europe to maintain our effective neutrality'.[5] Churchill's attitude remained unchanged for some years. As late as July 1935 in an open letter he criticized Labour Party foreign policy because it would endanger peace in Europe by Britain 'meddling too much in foreign quarrels which it is beyond our power to heal'.[6]

Although Churchill for long opposed Britain's involvement in Europe, in the 1930s he came under the influence of Count Coudenhove-Kalergi and his Pan-European Union and was an advocate of his ideas. But on one essential fact Churchill was certain – European union might be possible for the continental states but it could not involve Britain. As early as February 1930 he wrote in the *Saturday Evening Post* that, 'We see nothing but good and hope in a richer, freer, more contented European commonality. But we have our own dream and our own task. We are with Europe, but not of it. We are linked but not compromised. We are interested and associated but not absorbed.'[7] Those were to remain Churchill's views, and the basis for his European policy, for the rest of his life.

The collapse of the old Europe in the summer of 1940 led Churchill, like many others, to think about the future of the continent after the defeat of Germany. The scheme that he devised was not only far-reaching but also eccentric. The boundaries of Europe were to be re-drawn – not only those of the defeated states but also those of the neutrals and, even more remarkably, of the victors themselves. Churchill told his Cabinet colleagues that there were only five great European nations that should remain as independent states – England [sic], France, Italy, Spain and Prussia.[8] The other European states would be grouped into four confederations. The Northern bloc would consist of the Scandinavian countries and the Netherlands and would have The Hague as its capital. Mitteleuropa would consist of Czechoslovakia and Poland. The Danubian Confederation consisting of Bavaria, Württemberg, Austria and Hungary would have Vienna for its capital. The Balkan Confederation would be under the leadership of Turkey and would have what Churchill still quaintly called Constantinople for its capital. The five independent powers and the four confederations would form a Council of Europe which was to control an internationalized air force with individual countries only allowed to maintain a militia. For Churchill the key to this arrangement was always the Danubian Confederation, the dismemberment of Germany and the restoration of the Habsburgs. (He devoted considerable effort during the war to secure the latter objective.) In December 1942 he wrote: 'The separation of the Austrians and the Southern Germans from the Prussians is essential to the harmonious reconstitution of Europe.'[9]

Churchill never addressed the very obvious objections to this grandiose scheme. He did not consider the potential for national and ethnic conflict that the confederations would contain. In particular it was difficult to imagine that the Christian Balkan nations, so recently independent, would agree to be dominated by their old enemy – Muslim Turkey. Neither did Churchill spend time considering how such a scheme might be implemented. Would these states, some of them with long and historic traditions of independence, agree to give up that independence? Would the states involved form these confederations as a matter of free choice or were they to be coerced? If the latter, who would apply coercion and what methods would be involved? The Foreign Office was well aware of these objections and treated Churchill's views with disdain and avoided taking any action to implement them.

Nevertheless Churchill stuck to his views and his Prime Ministerial files contain extensive correspondence with Coudenhove-Kalergi and various draft schemes from him on the subject of European Union. In November 1942 Churchill again lectured the Cabinet on the future of Europe.[10] His views were once more eccentric and perhaps a little naive about likely post-war power politics. He argued that the only way to run Europe was for both Britain and the Soviet Union to keep out of European affairs and for a Grand Council of Prussia, Italy, Spain and a Scandinavian Confederation to be formed: France was notably missing from this arrangement. Despite the opposition of his colleagues, Churchill put these views to President Roosevelt in early 1943 and again during a visit to Washington in May of that year.[11] He suggested that the future world organization should eliminate the influence of the small powers by only allowing the major victors and the European confederations to join. Under the world organization there would also be a series of regional councils, including one for Europe. At a lunch at the White House he expounded on these ideas more fully. They were close to the ideas he expressed in 1940 but were less firm in some respects, reflecting Churchill's habit of constructing grandiose schemes without giving much attention to practicalities. Within Europe there would be the Danubian Confederation (including Bavaria) and Prussia would be independent. 'France would be made strong even though she did not deserve it. The Scandinavian countries would be a single bloc. He had no ideas about handling Switzerland or the Low Countries.' He went on: 'there ought to be three regional organizations and one supreme. He visioned [sic] the USA, British Empire and Russia really running the show.'[12] The three regional organizations would cover Europe, America and the Pacific, while Africa and Asia would remain European colonies. Remarkably, Britain, in order to emphasize its world role, was to be the only state with membership in all three regional organizations. Churchill's musings were rejected by Roosevelt at the Quebec conference in August 1943 and by the Soviet Union at the Moscow meeting of foreign ministers that autumn.[13]

Although Churchill continued to dabble in the idea of a Habsburg restoration, he took little interest in post-war planning after the rejection of his pet ideas. On one point however he was clear and consistent with his pre-war views. Britain should seek to remain detached from European affairs. He told the Cabinet in November 1944: 'No immediate threat of war lay ahead of us . . . and we should be careful of assuming commitments consequent on the formation of a Western bloc that might impose a very heavy military burden upon us.'[14] Two days before giving the Cabinet these views he had told Eden, the Foreign Secretary, in even more blunt language that he was opposed to a Western bloc. He thought it might take ten years to build such a bloc and he was scathing about the likely membership: 'The Belgians are extremely weak and their behaviour before the war was shocking. The Dutch are entirely selfish and fought only when they were attacked and then for a few hours. Denmark is helpless and defenceless and Norway practically so.'[15] His views of France, and especially de Gaulle, were equally sour.

In the immediate post-war period Churchill reversed his judgement about a Western bloc because of what he saw as the Soviet threat.

However he did not change his deeply held views about Britain's role in Europe and the world. The first clear statement of his post-war views can be found in the 'Iron Curtain' speech given at Fulton, Missouri, in March 1946.[16] This was not simply a call for an Anglo-American alliance against a world-wide communist threat that was already dividing Europe and threatening subversion in Western Europe. The speech had, for Churchill, a much more important message about Britain's role in the post-war world. Although he did not articulate such views in public, he realized that Britain's position had weakened in relation to the United States during the Second World War both militarily and economically. Nevertheless he was convinced that Britain could, and should, remain a worldwide imperial power. He therefore used the threat of communism to argue for a fifty-year alliance between the United States and Britain to enable them to rule the world. The United States would provide the bulk of the military power and the British Empire would provide the worldwide chain of bases for the deployment of alliance forces. The vital point for Churchill was that in these circumstances the United States would have a vested interest in continuing to prop up the weakened British Empire.

Given this global perspective Europe was bound to play a subordinate role in Churchill's post-war perspective. His vision for Europe was set out in his speech in Zurich six months after the Fulton speech.[17] Remarkably, Martin Gilbert's exhaustive official biography does not quote from the speech. The reason for this omission may be that the speech contains the opposite view to that normally ascribed to Churchill. The Zurich speech accepted the division of Europe into East and West and called for a Union of Western Europe, built around a partnership between Germany and France, as a bulwark against communism. However, Churchill's speech was not forward-looking but drew rather on his long-held views about Britain and Europe. This new 'United States of Europe' (in reality Western Europe) would, he argued, be part of a regional structure within the new United Nations Organization. He went on:

> There is already a natural grouping in the Western hemisphere. We British have our own Commonwealth of Nations. And why should there not be a European group? . . . We must build a kind of United States of Europe. . . . The first step in the recreation of the European family must be a partnership between France and Germany . . . under and within the world concept [the United Nations – CP] we must re-create the European family in a regional structure. . . . In all this urgent work France and Germany must take the lead together. Great Britain, the British Commonwealth of Nations, mighty America, and, I trust, Soviet Russia – must be the friends and sponsors of the new Europe.

Two important points need to be made about the Zurich speech. First, at no point did Churchill suggest that Britain should be a member of any

United States of Europe. This was perfectly consistent with the proposed post-war framework he had outlined on many occasions during the war. Britain would, in the words of his newspaper article first published in 1930, be 'with Europe, but not of it . . . linked but not compromised . . . interested and associated but not absorbed'.[18] Second, the development of a 'Western bloc', which he had opposed during the war, would now have a vital impact on Britain's strategic role. To the extent that Western Europe became stronger and more united in the face of increased Soviet power, it would reduce the need for any British intervention on the continent. This again was consistent with Churchill's views in the 1920s and 1930s that Britain should, if possible, stand aside from Europe. Such a disengagement from Europe would enable Britain to concentrate on its imperial role and its relationship with the United States. Britain would, once again, be a global power with a peripheral interest in ensuring a stable and prosperous Europe. Britain's world role and relationship with the United States was always crucial for Churchill. At the Albert Hall rally in April 1947, grandly entitled 'Let Europe Arise', he specifically made it clear that 'we shall allow no wedge to be driven between Great Britain and the United States of America'.[19] Six months later at the Conservative Party conference he stated that Britain should be the 'vital link' between the United States, the Commonwealth and Europe – again making it clear that Britain was not simply a European power like the other lesser members of what might become the 'United States of Europe'.[20]

In the aftermath of the Zurich speech Churchill, with his great post-war prestige, was seen as one of the advocates of a European Union. Although he was prepared to use the rhetoric of European unity, partly in order to embarrass the Labour Government, which was developing cold feet about progress in this direction, he showed no enthusiasm for developing a blueprint for a united Europe. At the May 1948 Hague conference on European Union (a peculiar mixture of politicians – many out of office – and unelected people) he proposed a 'European Assembly' to, as he grandly put it, 'enable the voice of a United Europe to be heard'.[21] What Churchill did not spell out was how such a European Assembly would be linked to the governments of Europe and what powers it would have apart from debate and propaganda. In private two years later he told one of the strongest pro-European Conservatives, Harold Macmillan, that the Council of Europe could 'never at this stage in affairs deal with problems which belong to executive governments'.[22]

In practice Churchill was opposed to the development of European institutions that had supranational overtones – a view that was essentially identical to that of the Labour Government. In November 1949 he accepted the government's view that Britain could not join any European economic system if the Commonwealth was excluded.[23] However he then went on to take the unrealistic position that the Commonwealth could be part of a European trading bloc.[24] Later he tried to maintain his European credentials by arguing that Britain should take part in the talks on the Schuman plan to create a European Coal and Steel Community. However, the caveat he entered – that Britain should oppose the supranational elements in the plan – would have destroyed the basis for the talks.[25]

Churchill played an equally ambiguous role in the other key issue of the early 1950s – the creation of a European Defence Community and a European Army. In August 1950, after the outbreak of the Korean war, which he thought presaged a Soviet attack on the West, he advocated a European Army under a unified command.[26] He once again failed to set out the crucial details about how such an army would be created, how it would be commanded and, most important of all, at what level it would be fully integrated. This latter point was crucial in meeting French concerns over German rearmament. In addition he gave no more than an ambiguous commitment that Britain would play 'a worthy and honourable part'.[27] In private Churchill was quite clear both that the European Army should not be integrated below divisional level, which did not meet French requirements, and that the British commitment should be very limited.[28] He therefore later opposed the so-called Pleven plan for an integrated European Army.

On his return to power in the autumn of 1951, Churchill and his colleagues were forced to take decisions about their policy towards Europe. Their decisions were consistent with Churchill's long-held views rather than the rhetoric he had adopted in the late 1940s. On 22 November 1951 the Cabinet agreed that, in effect, their policy would be the same as that of their Labour predecessors.[29] Britain would be enthusiastic about discussing European unity but would oppose any concrete steps in that direction. The supranational elements of the Coal and Steel Community would be rejected, Britain would not join the European Defence Community, and would only be associated with it. In the last resort the Cabinet – and Churchill in particular – viewed this movement towards Western European unity as something for the states on the continent: Britain, for its own reasons, would help in that process but it was not part of Europe.

On 29 November 1951 Churchill circulated a paper to his colleagues grandly entitled 'United Europe'.[30] He recalled his Zurich speech of 1946 but made clear in private what he had never made explicit in public: 'I have never thought that Britain . . . should become an integral part of a European Federation.' A week later in the House of Commons Churchill announced that 'we do not propose to merge in the European Army'.[31] In private Churchill believed that a European Army would not fight and that Britain should anyway stand aside. As he told his doctor Lord Moran: 'I love France and Belgium, but we cannot be reduced to that level.'[32] In the middle of December 1951 Eden sent Churchill a minute arguing that Britain could not merge its defences with the continent – only inter-governmental co-operation as in NATO was possible. Similarly,

Britain was willing to support efforts towards a European federation but would not join such a grouping. Churchill replied 'I feel we are in general agreement.'[33]

This policy was carried out over the next few months. Britain stood aside from the debates about the European Defence Community and only intervened over two years later after the French rejection of the EDC in order to secure agreement on the European defence identity it had always favoured. Similarly, Britain remained aloof from the establishment of the European Coal and Steel Community in August 1952 and only sent an observer to its headquarters in Luxembourg. Indeed Britain tried to sabotage moves towards any supranational institutions by suggesting the so-called 'Eden Plan' in March 1952.[34] This proposed to put both the Coal and Steel Community and the Defence Community, if it was established, under the weak co-operative structure of the Council of Europe. These moves designed to enfeeble the new institutions were rejected by the other Western European states. In private Churchill also went back on his 1949 view that Britain could join a European economic grouping if the Commonwealth was also included.[35] On 15 May 1952 he told the Cabinet that he 'would certainly deprecate any project for economic association between Europe and the sterling Commonwealth'.[36]

British policy for the rest of the Churchill administration (and long after) remained one of maintaining a healthy distance from moves towards European integration on the basis that Britain as a world power simply could not merge its interests with lesser European powers. Churchill would have fully endorsed Eden's speech, made at Columbia University during their visit to the United States in January 1952, which argued that Britain could not join a European federation because Britain had world-wide interests and without them 'we should be no more than some millions of people living on an island off the coast of Europe, in which nobody wants to take any particular interest'.[37]

In his memoirs Harold Macmillan, a great admirer of Churchill, tried to paint a portrait of him as an early advocate of the policy he himself finally adopted in the early 1960s – entry into the EEC. He wrote that Churchill believed that 'Britain could play a full role in Europe without loss or disloyalty to the traditions of her Empire and Commonwealth'.[38] He argued that Churchill had a clear programme when in opposition between 1945 and 1951 but that, once in power, 'I realised that he had now abandoned or postponed any effort to realise his European conception.'[39] Such views, repeated on many occasions since, bear no relation to the reality of Churchill's position, which was consistently maintained over a number of decades.

Churchill was an English imperialist who believed in Britain's world role. Europe was simply one area of interest in which Britain had to be involved. The more stable and prosperous Europe was, the less claim it would have on British resources and the more effort Britain could devote to its own world role. Although Churchill was an advocate of European union, he never believed that Britain should take part in that movement: that process was reserved for the lesser European nations. Churchill stuck by this position with an unusual consistency – in the 1930s, during the Second World War, when he was in opposition and after his return to power. Occasionally his rhetoric seemed to imply some greater degree of commitment to the cause of European unity, but in practice this made no difference to his views about the correct policy for Britain.

Throughout his political career Churchill showed no desire to be a forward thinker who wanted to chart out new territory. Instead he wanted to hold back the course of history and preserve for as long as possible the world he had known in his childhood. Unfortunately it was his fate that his political career coincided with Britain's rapid decline as a world power – a development which became particularly acute during the Second World War. As a response Churchill looked for ways to preserve Britain's position. One possibility was to reduce the need for Britain to take a major interest in the affairs of Europe. European Union, by producing a stable and prosperous Western Europe, would significantly assist this process. Britain would then be able to use its diminishing resources, in conjunction with the United States, on a worldwide basis, thereby preserving both its influence and empire. Churchill's hopes for the future, in particular his aim of fifty years of Anglo-American hegemony, were to prove vain. To claim him as the original 'pro-European' Conservative is a serious misunderstanding of his views. Even to claim him as a 'Thatcherite' on Europe would misrepresent his position. He believed in an imperial Britain as a world power. On that basis Britain could never be part of a European federation.

FURTHER READING

M. Gilbert, *Churchill, Volume 8: Never Despair 1945–65*, London: Heinemann, 1988.
C. Ponting, *Churchill*, London: Sinclair-Stevenson, 1994.
J. Young, 'Churchill's "No" to Europe: The Rejection of European Union by Churchill's Post-War Government 1951–52', *Historical Journal*, 1985, vol. 28, pp. 923–37.
J. Young (ed.), *The Foreign Policy of Churchill's Peacetime Administration 1951–55*, Leicester: Leicester University Press, 1988.

NOTES

Public Record Office abbreviations:
CAB   Cabinet Records
PREM   Prime Ministerial Papers

1 *Hansard*, 23 November 1932.
2 *The Times*, 25 February 1933.

3 *Hansard*, 13 April 1933.
4 Ibid., 14 March 1933.
5 *The Times*, 13 August 1933.
6 Ibid., 21 July 1933.
7 *Saturday Evening Post*, 15 February 1930; see also: *News of the World*, 29 May 1938.
8 J. Colville, *The Fringes of Power*, London: Collins, 1985, pp. 312–13; entry dated 13 December 1940.
9 PREM 4/33/3, 13 December 1942.
10 CAB 65/36 WM 146 (42), 15 November 1942, and PREM 4/100/7, 18 October 1942.
11 PREM 4/30/11, 12 April 1943.
12 M. Blum, *The Diary of Henry Wallace*, New York: Random House, 1976, p. 202; entry dated 22 May 1943.
13 *Foreign Relations of the United States: The Conferences at Washington and Quebec 1943*, Washington, DC: US State Department, 1970, p. 743.
14 CAB 65/48, WM 157 (44), 27 November 1944.
15 CAB 121/1614, 25 November 1944.
16 *The Times*, 6 March 1946.
17 Ibid., 20 September 1946.
18 *Saturday Evening Post*, 15 February 1930.
19 *The Times*, 19 April 1947.
20 Ibid., 5 October 1947.
21 Ibid., 15 May 1948.
22 H. Macmillan, *Tides of Fortune, 1945–1955*, London: Macmillan, 1969, pp. 218–19.
23 *Hansard*, 28 November 1949.
24 Ibid.
25 *The Times*, 24 July 1951.
26 Ibid., 12 August 1950.
27 Ibid.
28 Lord Moran, *Churchill: The Struggle for Survival, 1940–1965*, London: Constable, 1966, p. 312.
29 CAB 128/23, CC (51) 88, 22 November 1951.
30 CAB 129/48, CC (51) 32, 29 November 1951.
31 *Hansard*, 6 December 1951.
32 10 January 1952. Lord Moran, *Churchill: The Struggle for Survival, 1940–1965*, p. 362.
33 CAB 128/25, CC (52) 53, 15 May 1952.
34 PREM 11/153, 15 December 1951.
35 CAB 128/25, CC (52) 53, 15 May 1952.
36 Macmillan (n. 22 above), p. 156.
37 *The Times*, 12 January 1952.
38 Macmillan, p. 506.
39 Ibid.

4 European security

A new era of crisis?[1]

Philip Lawrence

Key assumptions concerning European security have gone through an accelerating process of change since the end of the Cold War. Initial considerations were focused on grasping the new realities in Europe. Cold warriors were reluctant to relinquish their former assumptions concerning East–West conflict. However, in the early 1990s a new consensus emerged on the security issue in Europe. It was recognized that the former problem of controlling a confrontation between heavily armed blocs had been replaced by a situation that was more fluid and less tangible.

The scope of the new European security debate was extremely broad, with the consequence that questions of strategy and defence could not be separated from larger issues of history, politics and theory. The benefit of this was that security thinking encompassed a rich tapestry of conceptual frameworks and argumentation. The cost was that discussion of security matters lost shape and direction. There is now an urgent need for a reformulation of the nature of the security question. The more optimistic visions of Europe's new future were clearly ill-founded. The critique of Cold War thinking failed to see the dangers in the post-Cold War environment. Moreover, idealistic assumptions concerning a new security architecture for Europe greatly exaggerated the power and scope of the dominant institutions. By 1995 optimism had been replaced by a sense of failure and a growing realization that a series of mistakes had been made in the security arena, particularly in former Yugoslavia. It will be argued that new idealism is dead and that the European Union's goal of an effective common foreign and security policy will remain unattainable for the foreseeable future.

The European security problematic corresponds to the following distinct areas of intellectual concern. First, the concept of security itself; second, the new theoretical debate that the recent changes in global politics have stimulated; third, the question of European institutions and political development; fourth, the character of current armed conflicts in Europe; fifth, the nature of predictions about the immediate future and, finally, policy recommendations.

THE CONCEPT OF SECURITY

Post-1945 discussion of security matters focused almost exclusively on defence and strategy. The fundamental concerns by the late 1940s were in formulating plans and providing resources to combat a Soviet threat that was taken for granted. The perceived threat was countered by the permanent coupling of US power resources to Western Europe through the institutional mechanism of the North Atlantic Treaty Organization (NATO). At the same time this furnished a second dimension of containment by constraining the post-war development of Germany: notwithstanding formal protestation to the contrary, the division of Germany was commonly viewed as essential to European peace and stability. As the first Secretary General of NATO, Lord Ismay remarked, the purpose of NATO was 'to keep the Russians out, the Americans in, and the Germans down'.[2]

On the basis of these geo-strategic arrangements, 'security' was reduced to strategic analysis. The name of the game was, on the one hand, quantification of force levels and characteristics and, on the other, the development of sophisticated models of deterrence and defence. Thus the security analyst was *ipso facto* a defence expert who dealt with a narrow and clearly defined subject matter. The 'meaning' of security was supposedly self-evident.

By the 1980s this narrow conception of security was increasingly subject to challenge. The onset of the new Cold War and the adoption of more aggressive postures by NATO and the US during the Reagan era provoked a serious reaction against the whole edifice of Western security. In the first instance this stemmed from debates within the domain of strategic discourse. Critics argued that the new policies were destabilizing and confrontational. The deployment of new weapon systems such as Cruise, Trident and Pershing II intensified anxiety in Europe (especially in the two Germanies) and made the nuclear threat more palpable. The idea that one could be better defended and yet less secure gained common currency, as did the 'doomsday scenario' of a nuclear winter. This led to renewed stress on the mutuality of security and emphasized the need for co-operation and communication. Moreover, from 1985 onward, the new foreign policy of Mikhail Gorbachev – the 'charm offensive' of Eduard Shevardnadze, the 'new thinking' and the talk of a 'common European home' – confounded much of the traditional Western security rhetoric.

Besides attacking strategic doctrine, the 1980s discourse also broadened the notion of security. Realism had bequeathed a view of security where states posed other states a dilemma that was critical for their survival. The state's essential mission was to preserve a way of life encapsulated within a fortification, both real and metaphorical. Against this, debate in the 1980s began to stress a common way of life in Europe and a common civic culture. Moreover, the established means of realizing the Cold War vision were delegitimated. Europe was too small and too crowded for there to be serious contemplation of nuclear war. Gorbachev's notion of a common European home implied a degree of mutuality and interdependence which undercut the Cold Warriors' vision of Europe. Particularly in Germany, Poland, Hungary, Czechoslovakia and the Baltic Republics, the new holistic notion of security became increasingly attractive. In the case of Germany emotional fatigue from being at the centre of East–West confrontation had set in and German public opinion – especially the burgeoning Green movement and the lutheran Churches in East as well as West Germany – increasingly challenged the NATO view of security. For Eastern Europe the holistic vision of security and other aspects of Gorbachev's new thinking promised liberation from Soviet domination. The implications of glasnost and perestroika were well understood in Eastern Europe, even (or especially) in those states that tried to resist them. There was a gradual realization that the Brezhnev doctrine was dead.

The broadening of the notion of security away from a realist state-centric model also brought in new issues. The new vision encompassed environmental questions, social and economic issues and human rights. Pollution in Europe, acid rain and the fallout from the 1986 Chernobyl disaster provided dramatic affirmation of interdependence, while also demonstrating that security concerned much more than military threats. In a literal vein it was realized that the real security of individuals depended on a variety of complex factors which the traditional security debate had never encompassed.

The new perception of security in Europe in the 1980s also raised the very question of Europe's identity. In taking for granted a divided Europe, the Western debate envisaged a *Kleineuropa* [little Europe]. The plan was to preserve 'fortress Western Europe' through policies of exclusion. The new parameters not only raised the prospect of a wider Europe, but became linked to notions of 'liberation'. For the social, environmental and ecclesiastical movements and campaigns that were promoting the new thinking, part of the promise was of the emancipation of Europe from both superpowers and the elevation of the Eastern European states to Western European standards of political, civil and environmental practice. These moves were to a large extent by-products of the 1975 Helsinki Conference, growing international attention to 'human rights' and the birth of Charter 77 in Czechoslovakia in 1977.

The changed concept of security that emerged in the 1980s became widely accepted. As Booth and Wheeler note, 'It has become increasingly apparent that "security" cannot sensibly be conceived narrowly, and that dealing with "security in Europe" in the 1990s and beyond depends on more than strategic problem solving.'[3] However, the context in which this wider concept was to be applied in the 1990s was radically different from that of the late 1980s. The new holistic notion of security grew up in an atmosphere of idealism and optimism. The events of 1989 in Eastern Europe and 1991 in the USSR were greeted with virtual euphoria. The

Cold War had ended, the Soviet Empire had collapsed, the threat of nuclear war had been lifted and Eastern Europe had been emancipated. But by the mid-1990s the feeling was very different. The spectre of chaos haunted the former USSR, numerous civil wars had broken out and three European states had disintegrated: Yugoslavia, Czechoslovakia and the USSR. Moreover, rampant nationalism had surfaced in South-Eastern Europe. In the words of Václav Havel, 'We realized that the poetry was over and prose was beginning.'[4]

A new vision of security, which attached itself to utopian assumptions about Europe's future and identity, was now confronted by some very ugly spectacles in Europe. In essence the military threat posed by bloc systems and nation-states had given way to the problem of sub-state nationalism and the use of violence to carve out new national political structures. Moreover, Russia's initial response to its loss of empire was to show that it still had military muscle and the will to use it. Russian sabre-rattling against the Baltic states and the Ukraine, military interventions in Moldova, Georgia and Central Asia and the meaningless slaughter in Chechnya reflected the fact that President Yeltsin and others were seeking credibility through very traditional conceptions of the uses of state power. The law and order issue, as Sergei Stankevich called it, was about defining the essence of the Russian Federation by testing contending ideas of legitimate political means. What the violence showed was that old habits died hard and that democracy still sat uneasily within Russian political culture.[5] As we shall see, a bizarre feature of Western policy towards post-Soviet Russia was a single-minded concentration on economic reforms – an obsession with macroeconomic stabilization and the transition to the market with scant regard for political outcomes.

Where the proponents of the new concept of security erred was in believing that the extension of the scope of the concept of security meant that the traditional concerns could be ignored. Realism, as events in Bosnia have shown, cannot be refuted by ignoring the obvious facts of human conflict and war. The issue here is which mode of explanation best accounts for the forms of conflict that we are now witnessing. What was extraordinary about the idealist reaction to the Cold War was that it should ignore nationalism and the likely consequences of the break-up of the Soviet empire and the Yugoslav federation. Also pan-European models presupposed a degree of homogeneity in Europe which does not exist. The future identity of Central, South and Eastern Europe remains to be seen. The Cold War imposed bifurcation; the post-Cold War era permits fragmentation.

THEORETICAL DEBATES

The collapse of the USSR and the relative decline of American power unleashed a debate in international relations journals concerning the re-emergence of a multipolar global system. In the European context a neo-realist theory of the post-war reconstruction process, which high-lighted the role of bipolarity, now indicates a likely return to great power rivalry and fundamental changes in the EU and in trans-Atlantic relations, calling into question the continuation of interdependence, integration and security co-operation.

The trigger for this debate was John Mearsheimer's article, 'Back to the Future: Instability in Europe after the Cold War' published in 1990.[6] Using the structuralist realist assumptions of Kenneth Waltz, Mearsheimer argued that the end of the Cold War and the decline of bipolarity would lead to a less stable and more conflictual Europe. In particular the factor of relative gains in power and wealth would resurface as an issue for Western European states. As Mearsheimer put it, 'Without a common Soviet threat and without the American nightwatchman, Western European states will begin viewing each other with greater fear and sus-picion. . . . Consequently, they will worry about the imbalances in gains as well as the loss of autonomy that results from co-operation.'[7] This view posits the Cold War as the key organizing fact of post-war Europe and its source of stability. To put it simply, the capacity of European powers to make trouble had been taken away. As Waltz noted, 'For the first time in modern history, the determinants of war and peace lay outside the arena of European states.'[8]

The structuralist view of multipolarity also indicates a particular theory of EU integration, namely a model based on the self-interest of individual states. In the first place, as we have seen, co-operation and integration can take place because European states have been passive as regards their own security. But, in addition, the integration which has been achieved is not seen through the lens of interdependence but from a state-centric per-spective. As Moravcsik writes, 'The Community has from its inception been based on a set of interstate bargains between the leading member states – initially bilateral agreements between France and West Germany, later triangular agreements, including the UK.'[9]

With respect to security issues the realist view suggests that further EU integration will falter, that NATO will wither away and that Europe will return to being an arena of nation-states. For some this is a welcome prospect, portending a neo-Gaullist vision of a Europe stretching from the Atlantic to the Urals, free from superpower domination. For others it is an alarming scenario. Either way, however, security questions will become more complex and will demand successful readjustment to balance-of-power diplomacy. In this situation some neo-realists put their main hope in the continuation of nuclear deterrence and even advocate some degree of nuclear proliferation, particularly to European states that are stable. Paradoxically, though, their best hope would be a return to the Cold War, but this possibility rests exclusively in Russian hands.

The rude intrusion of neo-realism into the post-Cold War euphoria provided a useful antidote to unbridled utopianism. However, the image conjured up of the future is not an attractive one. Realist scholars have retained a high degree of scepticism about the fear of nuclear confrontation, but the fact is that nuclear deterrence cannot be guaranteed. Thus it is important to ask whether we want a return to the tense confrontational atmosphere of the nuclear stand-off of the early 1980s. Moreover, a new Cold War would bring an unacceptable loss of freedom and democracy. Contrary to the hyper-determinism of the realist view, a degree of autonomy is undoubtedly available to planners and policy-makers. If the wrong decisions were taken, or if politicians were continually to play the nationalist card in domestic politics, then the EU would probably be demolished. Moreover, the wrong policy orientation towards Eastern Europe could have disastrous consequences. But the point is that we are considering historical processes that are still in the making. The institutions that will mould Europe's future are still being developed. Realism, in the Mearsheimer/Waltz mode, treats history in a very remote, abstract fashion. Realism has little to say on institutions, as its view of politics is one of the articulation of elemental forces such as power. However, norms, rules, procedures, expectations and sanctions do genuinely mediate the exercise of power. The trick is to create the right institutions and to have the courage to use them. During the first half of the 1990s elements of fragmentation predominated, but these resulted from specific policy failures and confusion over the changing role of established institutions. They were not structurally determined and, hence, were also not necessarily enduring.

INSTITUTIONS

There are now a large number of institutions with responsibility for European security. As Adam Roberts has remarked, 'The proliferation of European bodies with responsibility in the security field is notorious.'[10] Indeed there probably are too many, sowing real confusion over the proper division of institutional roles and responsibilities, and the proper relationships between them. Support for the differing organizations is not simply a question of evaluations of technical competence and functions. The proponents of the varying institutions have divergent views of the nature of Europe and the nature of security. Thus the different organizations carry within them different visions of what Europe should be and how it can achieve security.

The pre-eminent security organization in Europe is still NATO, which has vast resources, an integrated command structure, and is widely perceived to have been successful. Those who advocate that NATO should continue as the primary security organ in Europe hold to an Atlanticist vision of Europe and insist on linking the US to the implementation of European security policy. This view is generally supported in Europe by Conservative and Christian Democratic parties and has held sway in the UK, Holland, Portugal and the USA. Its proponents cite the following justifications for continued reliance on NATO: (i) it links the US to Europe; (ii) it provides cost-effective defence co-operation; (iii) it is a proven alliance of democratic nations; (iv) it can shape and direct the growth of German military power; (v) it offers the best protection against a recidivist Russia.[11]

Before considering criticisms of this formulation, it should be pointed out that the Atlanticist view presupposes a continuing US commitment to Western Europe. However, various factors have called into question the future scale of the US presence in NATO. In particular, the calculus of US interests, America's changing self-image and its domestic agenda will impact heavily on the question of future entanglement in Europe. The Clinton administration was from the outset committed to restoring the primacy of the domestic political agenda. Moreover, in relation to foreign policy, Williams, Hammond and Brenner posit an identity crisis:

> the demise of the Soviet Union has also removed the dominant impulse underlying US security policy for over 40 years and deprived Washington of its intellectual and conceptual moorings, provoking what is, in effect, a major identity crisis for the United States.[12]

Indeed, the domestic challenges facing the US are serious and perhaps all-absorbing. After the triumphalism of the 1980s US policy analysts began to question whether the $2,000 bn spent on confronting a moribund adversary was well spent. The growing US preoccupations with health care, education, urban decay, declining productivity and waste and corruption have cast a cloud over the notion of victory in the Cold War. European Atlanticists must consider the real prospect of US 'disengagement' from Europe.

Notwithstanding this possibility, critiques of NATO have centred on the following factors. NATO is seen as a creature of the Cold War: its critics contend that it cannot address the new reality of Europe and that it preserves an anachronistic American hegemony. It is also pointed out that it is not supposed to engage in 'out of area' operations, although it did begin to do so under the auspices of the United Nations (UN) in the former Yugoslavia in 1993. These criticisms drew on long-standing European suspicions of US motives in Europe, particularly in France, Spain, Greece and other Mediterranean states. However, new critiques of NATO have also gained credence. NATO has recognized the need for closer ties with Eastern Europe, but the Partnership for Peace programme does not satisfy the aspirations of either Poland or the Baltic Republics. Moreover, as NATO draws closer to Eastern Europe, it seems unable to allay the fears of Russia. NATO has in fact been unable to accommodate

Russian demands for security guarantees and for a pan-European security framework. In addition NATO has largely failed to intervene effectively in the former Yugoslavia and has been paralysed by policy disagreements between Europe and the US. In this context, NATO threats and ultimata against Bosnian Serb forces sounded increasingly hollow and Serbian military and political circles became increasingly contemptuous of NATO pronouncements. Moreover, NATO and the UN have failed to see eye to eye on Bosnia. Indeed, NATO has 'been largely ineffective and irrelevant' in the former Yugoslavia and 'has been saved from a real legitimacy crisis only by the inability of other European institutions to do any better'.[13]

Thus from a number of angles there are large question marks over the viability and future of NATO. The organization is likely to persist if Atlanticists hold sway in Europe or if the prospect of inter-state conflict re-emerges. However, the greatest imponderables relate to US intentions. President Bush set a ceiling of 150,000 personnel committed to NATO in Europe. However, there are now demands for a limit of 75,000 and growing Congressional calls for defence cuts in the European theatre.

From its inception there have been those who wanted the EU to extend its supranational competences to defence and security matters. In a world of regional power blocs, it was believed that Europe would only regain its former world status if it acted in concert as a single political unit.[14] In the early 1950s two plans emerged to integrate the security efforts of European states. In August 1950, at the fifth session of the Consultative Assembly of the Council of Europe, Winston Churchill proposed a unified European Army.[15] However, the plan of René Pleven for a European Defence Community (EDC) was the more significant.[16] Conceived on the lines of the European Coal and Steel Community (ECSC) and as its military counterpart, the EDC was to have an Assembly, a common budget, a Council of Ministers and a European Defence Ministry. The plan did the rounds of European parliaments for four years until the French National Assembly voted not to ratify it in August 1954.

Following the stillbirth of the EDC, hopes for a separate security identity for Europe rested on the Western European Union (WEU), which added West Germany and Italy to the signatories of the 1948 Brussels Treaty.[17] However, the WEU failed to develop as a military alliance with common forces and its own integrated command structure. From the outset the relationship of the WEU to both NATO and the EEC was unclear. The Maastricht Treaty on European Union elevated the EU to the status of the European pillar of NATO and the WEU to the security arm of the EU, even though its membership is different. The WEU remains a very ambiguous compromise between Europeanism and Atlanticism.

Today proponents of a stronger WEU envisage a so-called Western European Defence Community (WEDC). On the other hand, Atlanticists see the WEU as a bridge between NATO and the EU. They argue for the

'Europe of facts' and not the 'Europe of words', as Douglas Hurd put it.[18] Nevertheless, the WEDC concept has gained strong support in France, Spain and Italy and certainly contains the germs of a possible future European defence capability in the context of declining US interest in NATO.

The creation of a WEDC would complement the views of those who want to see a further deepening of the EU. In June 1990 the European Council proposed 'the transformation of the Community from an entity based on economic integration into a union of a political nature, including a common foreign and security policy'.[19] The Maastricht Treaty is somewhat more tentative and speaks of 'the eventual framing of a common defence policy which might in time lead to a common defence'.[20] A WEDC would dovetail with these ideas, which presuppose a federalized European Union with a common foreign, security and defence policy. As Hyde-Price points out, however, it would have to be capable of significant 'power projection and co-ordinated military action'.[21]

Dilemmas for supporters of a WEDC include the question of a German finger on the nuclear trigger and British and French desires to maintain 'sovereign' national control over nuclear weapons. In the context of NATO and the Cold War it was obvious how Germany could be deprived of jurisdiction over nuclear weapons. But in a strong European military alliance that excluded the US, German control of nuclear weapons would be inevitable. Suffice it to say that some Europeans find this an alarming prospect and that old habits and modes of thought will have to change before it becomes possible. Opposition is strong in Holland and the UK, while Germans themselves have been split over the idea of a WEDC. It should also be remembered that Ireland is neutral and Denmark increasingly pacifist. Thus many obstacles to a WEDC exist and Europe's response to the Bosnian crisis indicates that co-ordination of foreign and defence policy is still elusive. Critics like Mark Almond see division and conflict as still very much alive in the EU: 'The European Community remains bedevilled by nationalist rivalries despite all the talk of common policies and a new united identity.'[22] On Europe's performance on the Bosnian issue Almond is scathing: 'counsels of despair encourage the West to wash its hands of the Balkan problem and let the ancient fire burn itself out'.[23]

Those who have advanced the more radical and all-encompassing notion of security that I discussed above have placed their hopes chiefly on the Conference on Security and Co-operation in Europe (CSCE) – since November 1994 the *Organization* for Security and Co-operation in Europe (OSCE) – which enshrines a pan-European vision of collective security. The CSCE began in the context of East–West détente in 1973 and led to the Helsinki Final Act which was signed in 1975. The unique feature of the CSCE was that it linked security to the issue of human rights and from the outset promoted a broad concept of peace and stability. From 1973 until 1988 there was considerable scepticism towards the CSCE in conservative circles. However, the CSCE proved itself a highly flexible tool of multilateral diplomacy and strongly encouraged the emergence of human rights movements within the USSR and Eastern Europe. In 1989 it was clear that the CSCE had gained considerable popularity in Eastern Europe and that the emancipatory movements had drawn inspiration from it. Particularly important was the fact that it bound together groups in the East and the West who wanted to overcome the divisions of the Cold War. Its human rights advocacy was exemplary. As Victor Ghebali observes, 'Human rights, a long-standing taboo in East–West relations, became within the CSCE a legitimate subject of dialogue and, gradually, of cooperation.'[24]

Although the CSCE was usually dismissed as a mere 'talking shop' in NATO circles, its valuable work in overseeing the Conventional Forces in Europe (CFE) Treaty enhanced its credibility. Robert Jackson notes, 'This role for the CSCE in monitoring the CFE gave a new Pan-European vision to military security and contributed to a growing commitment to reassurance.'[25] In the last two years the CSCE/OSCE has developed a permanent institutional structure with different agencies located in Prague, Vienna and Warsaw. Moreover, after the CSCE summit in Paris in November 1991 even the sceptics accepted that it has a role to play in the new Europe. Its new operation includes a summit every two years, biannual meetings of foreign ministers and meetings of senior officials before ministerial meetings. The minimalist view of the OSCE accords it key roles in confidence building, crisis management and arms control.[26] However, pan-Europeanists conceive of the OSCE as a European version of the UN. Thus here the support is for a pan-European security system with an OSCE Security Council able to impose a range of sanctions – including military intervention – against transgressors. However, the OSCE's current organizational structure inhibits this form of development. The member states have chosen to operate according to the principle of unanimity, and thus decisive action can always be vetoed, as it was by the USSR in 1990, Yugoslavia in 1991, and Russia in 1994. At the OSCE summit in Budapest in 1994 the OSCE's deliberations were utterly fruitless and the Russian delegation was allowed to promote propaganda gains for Serbia. With regard to Bosnia the OSCE has fared no better than other European institutions. Thus, just as it seems sensible to be cautious about a likely WEDC, it is right to be highly sceptical about the more grandiose visions of pan-European security. If EU member states cannot agree on how to defend themselves, it seems unlikely that they will be able to project deterrence and defence beyond a *Kleineuropa*. The old CSCE kept alive an image of co-operation in Europe denied by the Cold War, but the ending of the Cold War has confronted it with the real limits of pan-European consensus.

CURRENT CONFLICTS

There now seems a consensus in security circles that the big set-piece military threat posed by a major war in Europe is gone. In addition there is a widely held perception that security is no longer a question of dealing with a distinct enemy. Europe now lacks a clear strategic anthropology: the threats are now more dispersed and more amorphous. In one respect this is an immense relief; the eschatological nightmare of World War III has been cancelled. However, that threat did give clarity of vision and purpose. Also the neo-realist belief that the threat created cohesion looks even more valid in retrospect than it did at the time. Indeed, as Williams *et al.* argue, 'Preserving an alliance without an enemy and a strategy without a threat will not be easy.'[27]

The security threats of the present era centre around the problem of nationalism. But, as Griffiths argues: 'In the past 40 years, the European security debate has not paid much attention to nationalism.'[28] In consequence security analysts have not had very sophisticated models of inter-ethnic conflict to hand. Partly for this reason, the level of analysis of the role of nationalism in new conflicts in Europe has been crude and simplistic. In some accounts, particularly those given by politicians, it is as though superpower domination was holding the lid on a cauldron of seething tribal animosity. When the lid was removed the violence and the conflict spilled out. In fact current problems require a more careful analysis. It is important to realize that Yugoslavia, for example, was not under superpower domination and also that former communist élites were quite likely to manipulate and inflate national rivalries. The idea that communism was heroically holding back the tide of nationalism is nonsense. The issue is that the demise of communism has changed the political framework through which nationalism is being articulated.

Conflicts in the former USSR, tensions in the Baltic states and Eastern Europe and the catastrophe in the former Yugoslavia are examples of the problems of sub-state nationalism. They denote situations in which ethnically defined communities are not conterminous with the territorial and legal boundaries of states and where struggles to secede from states are taking place. In addition these struggles are linked to attempts to protect or unite with fellow ethnic nationals in other states. Thus the conflicts have often involved efforts to redraw political boundaries on ethnic criteria. The scope for this process was enormous. In the former USSR there were 104 nationalities of which 89 had no republic. In addition 64 million people lived in states where they were an ethnic minority, and of twenty-three inter-republican borders only three were not contested.[29] Within this mélange there was the added spice of 30,000 nuclear warheads and a large number of probably not very secure nuclear power stations. The image is clearly unsettling. As one commentator remarked, Russia is 'a Third World country with a nuclear arsenal and men floating in space'.[30] But of course there will not be conflict between all the different nationalities. What need investigation are the political and economic conditions under which inter-ethnic conflicts erupt.

In examining this issue it is useful to distinguish ethnic nationalism from civic nationalism. The former articulates political identity on the basis of the ethnic community (ethnie), the latter according to membership of a territorial state. Civic nationalism connotes a more abstract form of political identity that corresponds to a liberal notion of the state. The 'nation' defines itself through identification with the laws, procedures, rules and institutions that constitute the state. In this context proximate reinforcers of identity such as family, church, city, region or class do not compete with allegiance to the state. Civic nationalism can thus withstand cross-cutting agents of identity formation. On the other hand ethnic nationalism serves to articulate the boundaries of the state around an ethnic community which will draw on myths of common ancestry, language, shared culture, links to territory, memories, histories, names and key events.[31] But what needs to be remembered is that this is a political and sociological process. An ethnic community can rarely be defined in an obvious biological way. As Smith notes, 'Ethnicity is not about blood or genes as such, but about myths and beliefs in common origins.'[32]

According to Snyder, an instructive way to comprehend nationalism is to reflect on the purposes of human groups. He suggests that humans form groups to pursue collective goals in terms of their economic and physical security. In the modern context the most effective collective actor in these respects was the state. Nationality became a form of political identity conducive to the territorially extensive state. Political legitimacy depended on the national form because the state was larger than regional and parochial identities. Moreover the state's military operations demanded an extended focus for authority and support. As Snyder notes, 'States also had strong incentives to foster nationalism, which became a potent weapon facilitating the mobilisation of military power.'[33]

Snyder goes on to argue that states come under pressure from separatist national movements when they are perceived to fail to provide key goals in the economic and security realms. Alternatively, if states are threatened by exogenous factors, different conflict groups will manoeuvre to arrange outcomes which they find desirable. In both cases conflict is highly likely and thus nationalism heightens in order to more clearly define in-group/out-group boundaries and to increase solidarity. The key point is that the heightening of the sense of nationalism is not some psychological disorder or pathological condition; it is related to discernible economic and political processes. Nor is it a re-run of some eternal inter-tribal hatred. As Snyder notes, 'nationalism and ethnic conflict are not primarily rooted in ancient culturally engrained animosities'.[34]

Snyder's theory of nationalism is a useful antidote to the casual ideas that have been bandied about recently, although he may overstate the

degree to which nationalism is a material, strategic-utilitarian phenomenon. Traditions, histories and folklorization are parts of the process.
While in Western states periods of crisis have intensified cleavages on
class lines, in Eastern and Southern Europe cleavage has often operated
along the lines of the ethnic community.

In order to grasp this point it is necessary to look at the different paths
of political development taken in Western and South-Eastern Europe.
In Western Europe nationalism emerged when successful and large states
had been created. Nationalism lived in the present and conformed to
current experience. In Western Europe large-scale migration had ceased
and the Catholic Church helped impose cultural homogeneity. In the East
borders were still fluid, large migrations were common and there was a
fundamental conflict between the Catholic and Byzantine religions. Moreover, large numbers of ethnic communities were subject to imperial rule
of a brutal kind. In consequence (Western-style) nationalism confronted a
situation in Eastern Europe that was not conducive to the drawing of
state boundaries around a national community. According to Griffiths
this changed nationalism in Eastern Europe into something more mythic,
idealistic and historical.[35] Nationalism became associated with a messianic
mission: it had to keep alive aspirations that were denied by current
realities.

The contemporary security anxieties of Europe grew out of the situation
described above. Strongly held conceptions of national identity defined in
ethnic terms have diverged from existing state boundaries or have
challenged certain federalist forms. In each particular case the level of
military threat to Europe as a whole is low: but the ethnic mosaic of
South-Eastern Europe could knit together conflicts in a large number
of states. In addition, the cumulative effect of these conflicts could produce high levels of disorder which could in turn trigger large economic
migrations.

The context in which the worst case scenario has been realized is, of
course, the former Yugoslav Federation. A small war in Slovenia was
followed by a larger one in Croatia and a devastating one in Bosnia.
Despite some success in its early stages, EC/EU diplomacy and crisis
management in the former Yugoslavia have ultimately failed. Successive
discredited peace plans would merely have ratified Serbian gains, and
exacerbated tensions between Muslims and Croats. The UN has been
reduced to providing rations and medicine for a people who were suffering
genocide. But the Balkan tragedy has not been an irremediable act of
collective insanity: this view merely legitimizes Western failures. The truth
is that there were levers of policy that could have made a difference:
there was a political process that called for judicious analysis and careful
intervention.

In Bosnia a wilful disregard of historical facts has facilitated a crude and
false understanding of the war. The accepted axiom that the conflict

erupted because ancient hatreds could not be restrained is misleading. It is also a misconception that the conflict is a civil war. Crude nationalism has played a role in the violence, but this was imported into Bosnia from outside. It is ironic that diplomats and commentators trained in the tenets of realism failed to see that Bosnia was the victim of an external security threat. As Malcolm has observed, 'What has always endangered Bosnia was not any genuinely internal tensions, but the ambitions of larger powers and neighbouring states.'[36] Furthermore, contrary to popular belief, Serbs and Croats do not have a long history of mutual animosity. The two have fought each other mainly in the twentieth century. In the 1980s 29 per cent of Serbs in Croatia had Croatian spouses.[37] The problem in the former Yugoslavia has been political, not anthropological. In Bosnia the three main ethnic groups were highly integrated, which is why the process of prizing them apart has been so painful. The cleavages that have existed have resulted from both class and ethnicity. Christian peasants resented their Muslim landlords. In the current conflict the Serbs have also tapped into a rural antagonism towards the Muslim middle classes. In a strategy reminiscent of the atrocities of Pol Pot, the Muslim professional classes have been singled out for extermination.

Serbs endeavoured to dominate both the interwar Kingdom of Yugo-slavia and the post-1945 Yugoslav Federation. In the 1930s Croatian resistance took the form of the Ustashe, a violent, quasi-fascist terrorist movement. During World War II the Nazis installed an Ustashe régime in Croatia which murdered some 500,000 Serbs, while 200,000 Croats perished. All told Yugoslavia lost 1,700,000 dead, or nearly ten per cent of the total population. The post-war Yugoslav Federation established by Tito's partisans was supposed to give equal rights to each of the con-stituent republics, but in reality it was dominated by Serbs, especially in the police, the army and the political élites.[38] The new state was 'burdened from the very outset by the previous negative experience of centralism, unitarism, force and assimilation, outright national discrimination and colonial oppression'.[39]

Despite the problems that Bebler cites, Yugoslavia gained a reputation in the early 1970s as an ideal fusion of liberal and socialist state forms. Superficially the country seemed to be performing better than the other communist states in Eastern Europe. However, in the 1980s Yugoslavia did not escape the debt and stagnation that characterized European communist systems. Moreover, other events accelerated the state towards crisis. In 1974 a new confederal constitution was agreed to smooth the transition to a post-Tito federation. However, the cumbersome mechanism of rotating leadership paralysed the centre and pushed power to regional and republican party leaders. Thus, after the death of Tito in 1980, there was a leadership vacuum. After 1986 the economy began to disintegrate and in 1987, when Slobodan Milošević came to power in Serbia, the diver-gent political élites in the Federation began to advance disparate solutions to Yugoslavia's economic and political problems. Cohen has argued that this was the key to the break-up; élite strategies were mutually incompatible.[40] By 1987 accelerating inflation and rapid depreciation of the dinar were strengthening Slovene and Croatian demands for sweeping economic liberalization, but these were blocked by Serbia. This exacerbated the growing anti-Serbian sentiments among non-Serbs, but also enhanced Serbian support for Milošević's nationalism and his manipulation of the Kosovo issue, culminating in the abolition of the autonomy of that region. But the central point is that the growing nationalism was a response to negative experiences of communist rule. This coalesced in the late 1980s with growing demands for democratization and a fully fledged market economy. But these were blocked because 'the nationally and culturally divided Yugoslav élites were incapable, and some unwilling, to effect a speedy and orderly transition from an authoritarian order to a competitive democratic system'.[41]

It is conceivable that the centrifugal forces in Yugoslavia in the late 1980s would have broken up the state, come what may. Until 1990, however, Slovenia and Croatia were prepared to accept a loose confederation of sovereign republics. According to Bebler, timely Western support for the confederal option could have resolved the crisis: 'The West (USA and EEC) made then a cardinal mistake in not supporting the confederal option while the option still had a chance.'[42]

With this option gone, Yugoslavia descended into war and the West failed to protect the victims of genocide. In the initial conflict in the summer of 1991 the Serb-dominated Yugoslav National Army (JNA) moved to occupy Serb-inhabited territory in Slovenia and Croatia. Slovenia was soon abandoned but Milošević's nationalistic political strategy necessitated the acquisition of territory in Croatia. The territorial gains that were made in Croatia then required that the JNA acquire territory in Bosnia to link the Krajina pocket with Serbia.[43]

It was at this juncture in March 1992, before Bosnia had gained independence, that Serb militias began to terrorize Muslim villages in North-East Bosnia. According to Almond, JNA conscripts were not effective in this role which is why para-military terror groups entered Bosnia in the spring of 1992. Thus it was Arkan's Tigers, the White Eagles and Chetniks who spread violence and mayhem into Bosnia: 'Outsiders were needed who would kill anonymous victims without compunction and thereby polarise society and force people to take sides.'[44] These actions represented, not war, but criminal violence committed by Serb units against the people of Bosnia. The flood of refugees from North-East Bosnia resulted from an invasion by para-militaries and the JNA which took 60 per cent of Bosnia within six weeks. As Malcolm notes, 'this was predominantly an invasion of Bosnia planned and directed from Serbian soil'.[45]

To begin with there was little Western interest in the Bosnian conflict. But in the summer of 1992 journalists began to report on the concentration camps in Bosnia and the mass rapes of Muslim women. The international community galvanized itself to find a solution. But immediately the false assertion that this was a civil war and that everyone was equally to blame became the anchor of the West's response. The leader of the Bosnian Serb forces, General Mladić, inherited a force of 80,000 men from the JNA. The Bosnian defence forces began their belated resistance with 3,500. The arms embargo, which the UN had imposed on Yugoslavia, made little difference to the Serbs, who had inherited the arms industry of the former Yugoslav Federation, but was catastrophic for the Bosnians, who were hopelessly outgunned. By failing to see the political project behind the war, and by concentrating on halting the fighting through the arms embargo, the West actually contributed indirectly to the destruction of Bosnia.

It has been widely argued that the civil war environment prevented any useful form of military intervention. However, the fragmentation of the conflict into discrete pockets occurred gradually and was not a legitimate excuse for non-intervention. In Bosnia the Serb militia and the army could have been deterred had the West not sent out the wrong signals. Moreover, had the Bosnian defence forces been properly armed, they could probably have rolled back Serbian gains. In many respects the deployment of 8,000 lightly armed UN forces made matters worse as they became hostages to Serb reprisals. Most tragic of all was the decision taken in 1993 to protect Bosnians in 'safe havens'. The UN forces were quite simply not equipped for this task. The truth is that everything that the international community has tried to do to help the Bosnians has depended on the co-operation of the perpetrators of the worst violence. We should have no illusions: Serbia and the Bosnian Serbs have made a mockery of the rationale and effectiveness of Western security institutions.

The most serious political mistakes occurred at the outset. In 1990 Western governments believed that Serbia was divided, with a pro-peace constituency led by Federal Prime Minister Marković, but support for Marković merely strengthened the hand of the nationalists and the military. Then the German recognition of Croatia raised Croatian hopes of military support and legitimized Serbian propaganda over the vulnerability of the Serb minority in Croatia. At this point media pundits were constantly reminding us that the Serbs were fearful of a re-run of Ustashe atrocities. Furthermore, within the EU, anti-German sentiment resurrected the image of 'plucky' little Serbia. The West has been divided over Bosnia and has contributed a peace plan which is a national humiliation for the group that has behaved with the most courage and integrity. Thus Yugoslavia has not represented a cauldron of uncontrollable emotion:

it has been a massive political failure compounded by Western sins of omission.

FUTURES AND POLICY

Yugoslavia represents a nationalist tragedy in the here and now; Russia and its relationship with the former Soviet republics is one for tomorrow. In the former Yugoslavia national enmities have been interpreted through the model of ancient hatreds. In Russia it has been more common to see the notion of the 'Weimar analogy'.[46] As Galina Starovoitova – a former Yeltsin adviser on nationalities – has argued, 'We cannot exclude the possibility of [a fascist period] in Russia. We can see too many parallels between Russia's current situation and that of Germany after Versailles.'[47]

The suggestion is that Russia has been humiliated, that powerful groups feel cheated and that central material objectives cannot be achieved by the Russian state in its current form. Here, as before, however, we must discount the idea of an immutable nationalism that must run its course. The form that Russian nationalism will now take depends on the economic crisis and the viability of the Russian state.[48] What is odd is that Western policy may serve to recreate the very security threat that Western security policy previously sought to eliminate. In particular the application of economic shock therapy would appear to play into the hands of proto-fascist organizations such as the Russian National Unity group. Moreover, prolonged and acute economic pain will militate against moves towards democracy and the continuance of a liberal, pro-Western foreign policy.

According to Neil Macfarlane, Russia's unequivocal Western orientation under Yeltsin was already drawing to a close in 1993. Bearing in mind the historical ambivalence in Russia to Western values and institutions, Macfarlane identified new tendencies in Russian policy. These involved a move away from the pro-Western orientation that Yeltsin had promoted vigorously in 1991 and 1992 and which was closely associated with Andrei Kozyrev, the Foreign Minister, and Yegor Gaidar.[49] This position sought membership of the G-7 group of leading industrial nations, the World Bank, the International Monetary Fund (IMF), the General Agreement on Tariffs and Trade (GATT), NATO and the EU. In the security field its proponents advocated joining Western security structures and they supported START-2 (the second Strategic Arms Reduction Treaty) and the CSCE. However, this orientation provoked a reaction that ran the full spectrum from moderate nationalism to fascism. In nationalist, neo-fascist and neo-Stalinist circles, the Gorbachev–Yeltsin pro-Western policy is seen as a disaster: collaboration with the West is thought to have brought national humiliation and a chronic reduction in Russian power. The credibility of this view will increase if economic expectations continue to be frustrated.

Bearing this in mind, we can see that Yeltsin's foreign-policy orientation has gone through three distinct phases during the first half of the 1990s. First, the continuation of Gorbachev's pro-Western 'new thinking'. Second, as the Western embrace failed to materialize, a move towards the centre and a more cautious approach to the West. Finally, after the army stormed the Russian Parliament in October 1993, Yeltsin and Kozyrev seemingly moved closer to the military and sought to appease nationalists on the far right. Thus Zhirinovsky does not have to be in power to shape the pattern of Russian politics. The existence of the far right and their potential appeal to the military and military-industrial complex has, by itself, moved Yeltsin and Kozyrev towards a position that is increasingly ambivalent towards the West, NATO, the UN and the EU. This has also meant an independent line on Yugoslavia and intervention in Moldova and Georgia as well as Chechnya. What this suggests is that Western policies that excluded Russia from multilateral institutions and that applied economic 'shock therapy' have had highly negative results.[50] In the past Russia's relations with Europe have been conflictual and destabilizing. Thus the lesson is clear: Western policies that undermine the credibility of liberal reforms should be abandoned. As Macfarlane observes, 'international economic institutions have been instrumental in influencing Russian policy makers to adopt policies . . . that have seriously damaged the political standing of liberal reforms, while contributing greatly to social instability'.[51]

The didactic approach of the IMF, which sought to school Moscow in market economics, has clearly backfired. In 1993 Yeltsin's determination to convert arms industries to civilian use gave way to a new drive to export Russian arms to China, Iran, India and Malaysia.[52] Thus increasingly the West should relax about the format of economic institutions and concentrate on political outcomes. If NATO can only guarantee security in Eastern Europe by antagonizing Russia it is not surprising that Yeltsin should respond by constructing his own security arrangements in Russia's 'near abroad'. Indeed, it is important to note that border security is moving up the political agenda in Russia and the episode in Chechnya is redolent of a racism in Russia that the far right is articulating towards Turkey, China and Iran. The continued exclusion of Russia from multilateral institutions will increase these stresses and strains and is premised on the wrong policies.

CONCLUSION

The discussion has moved a long way from strict questions of military security. But, given the analysis above, it is possible to predict a nightmare future for Europe. In the West integration and co-operation decline under the pressure of conservative nationalist mobilization of anti-EU protest. The fissures grow under the strain of declining US influence and competing visions of Atlantic relations. In South-Eastern Europe economic failure compounds nationalist rivalry and further 'civil wars' develop. In the Russian Federation economic failure exacerbates nationalism and inter-republican conflict. Thus the neo-realist vision comes true. However, this prospect is far from inevitable. In the case of Russia concentration needs to focus on the political process and Western assistance should be freed from IMF constraints. In the case of Eastern Europe and the Balkans a correct grasp of nationalism is essential if policies for stabilization are to be pursued. The process of European political and economic integration has to embrace Eastern Europe, as should security networks. In the security sphere clarification is needed with regard to the respective roles of the EU, NATO, WEU, OSCE and the Council of Europe. If Europe is serious about human rights, the protection of minorities and international law, some military agent of intervention is necessary. If it is not, then we must be honest about our limitations and the pretence of old European dignity must be abandoned.

FURTHER READING

D. Buchan, *Europe: The Strange Superpower*, Aldershot: Dartmouth, 1993.
A. Hyde-Price, *European Security beyond the Cold War: Four Scenarios for the Year 2100*, London: Sage, 1991.
H. Maill, *Shaping the New Europe*, London: Pinter, 1993.
N. Malcolm, *Bosnia: A Short History*, London: Papermac, 1994.
S. White *et al.*, *Russia's Future*, Oxford: Polity, 1993.

NOTES

1 An earlier version of this chapter was published under the title 'European Security: from Euphoria to Confusion' in: *European Security*, vol. 3 (1994), no. 2, pp. 217–35.
2 Quoted in: A. Hyde-Price, 'Future Security Systems for Europe', in: C. McInnes (ed.), *Strategy and Security in the New Europe*, London: Routledge, 1992, p. 42.
3 K. Booth and N. Wheeler, 'Contending Philosophies about Security in Europe', in: McInnes, p. 3.
4 Quoted in: S. I. Griffiths, 'Nationalism in Central and Southern Europe', in: McInnes, p. 59.
5 See Chapter 13.
6 J. Mearsheimer, '"Back to the Future": Instability in Europe after the Cold War', *International Security*, vol. 15 (1990), no. 1, pp. 5–56.
7 Ibid., p. 47.
8 Quoted in: I. A. Caporaso, 'Has Europe Changed? Neorealism, Institutions and Domestic Politics in the New Europe', in: R. Jackson (ed.), *Europe in Transition: Management of Security after the Cold War*, London: Adamantine, 1992, p. 23.
9 Quoted in: ibid., p. 22.
10 A. Roberts, 'The United Nations and International Security', *Survival*, vol. 35 (1993), no. 3, pp. 3–30; quotation from p. 8.
11 Hyde-Price (n. 2 above).

12 P. Williams, P. Hammond and M. Brenner, 'The US and Western Europe after the Cold War', *International Affairs*, vol. 69 (1993), no. 1, p. 1.
13 Ibid., p. 11.
14 W. Nicoll and T. Salmon, *Understanding the European Communities*, London: Philip Allan, 1991, p. 106.
15 See Chapter 3.
16 See Chapter 2.
17 The original signatories to the Brussels Treaty had been France, Britain, Belgium, the Netherlands and Luxembourg.
18 Quoted in: Hyde-Price (n. 2 above), p. 45.
19 R. Jackson, 'The Changing Conditions of European Security in the Post-Cold War Era', in: Jackson (ed.) (n. 8 above), p. 11.
20 Ibid., p. 12.
21 Hyde-Price (n. 2 above), p. 45.
22 M. Almond, *Europe's Backyard War*, London: Mandarin, 1994, p. xvii.
23 Ibid., p. xiv.
24 V. Ghebali, 'The CSCE in the Era of Post-Communism: The Jewel that Has Lost Its Gleam', *Paradigms*, vol. 6 (1992), no. 2, p. 5.
25 Jackson (n. 19 above), p. 9.
26 Ibid., p. 11.
27 Williams *et al.* (n. 12 above), p. 12.
28 Griffiths (n. 4 above), p. 61.
29 Booth and Wheeler (n. 3 above), p. 22.
30 Quoted in: Jackson (n. 19 above), p. 4.
31 A. Smith, 'The Ethnic Sources of Nationalism', *Survival*, vol. 35 (1993), no. 1, p. 50.
32 Ibid., p. 51.
33 J. Snyder, 'Nationalism and the Crisis of the Post-Soviet State', *Survival*, vol. 35 (1993), no. 1, p. 20.
34 Ibid., p. 26.
35 Griffiths (n. 4 above), p. 64.
36 N. Malcolm, *Bosnia: A Short History*, London: Macmillan, 1994, p. 234.
37 Snyder (n. 33 above), p. 5.
38 A. Bebler, 'Yugoslavia's Variety of Communist Federalisms and Her Demise', *Journal of Communist and Post-Communist Studies*, vol. 26 (1993), no. 1, p. 72.
39 Ibid.
40 L. J. Cohen, *Broken Bonds: The Disintegration of Yugoslavia*, Boulder, CO, Westview Press, 1993.
41 Bebler (n. 38 above), p. 85.
42 Ibid., p. 82.
43 Almond (n. 22 above), p. 264.
44 Ibid.
45 Malcolm (n. 36 above), p. 238.
46 Snyder (n. 33 above), p. 5.
47 Quoted in ibid., p. 7.
48 See also Chapters 13 and 14.
49 See also Chapter 13.
50 See Chapter 13.
51 S. N. Macfarlane, 'Russia, the West and European Security', *Survival*, vol. 35 (1993), no. 3, p. 22.
52 Ibid., p. 14.

5 The UK in Europe

An awkward or accommodating partner?

Jonathan Bradbury

Since the mid-1980s the transfer of state powers to an EC/EU level and reforms affecting the distribution of power in EC/EU policy-making have challenged the sovereignty of member states. This chapter is concerned with the response to these developments by the United Kingdom, conventionally seen as the most awkward of the member states and a force for disintegration in the EC/EU. Such a view neglects an appreciation of the importance of accommodationism within the UK approach to EC/EU developments. This chapter is concerned to remedy this.

Existing perspectives generally suggest that UK European policy has evolved within a realist conception of what is in the national interest, rather than according to any European ideal.[1] Interests have been defined in two principal ways. First, EC/EU membership was deemed important for expanding trade opportunities in Europe, and providing an arena in which the UK economy would be made more competitive. At the time of Britain's accession in 1973 membership was seen as essential for the reversal of relative economic decline. Second, membership has been deemed important for the maintenance of great-power status after the retreat from Empire.[2] As Young argued, in an increasingly interdependent world states needed to forge relationships through which they could control the forces of interdependence so as to insulate themselves from political change and shape the world to fit their interests.[3] By the 1960s it was clear that the Commonwealth was unlikely to provide a satisfactory basis for fulfilling these needs. Meanwhile, the EC had enjoyed early success and was viewed benevolently by the US, suggesting also that the US 'special relationship' would decline in importance as the US bypassed the UK in developing relations with the EC. EC membership came to be seen as essential both as a means of shoring up the Anglo-American 'special relationship' and as a new vehicle through which the UK might exercise international influence. The conventional argument has been that the national interest was translated into the pursuit of a particular ideal for the EC/EU. UK governments have encouraged the EC/EU to develop as a large free-trade area, but sought to limit EC/EU competences and revenues in attempts to ensure that sovereignty, the bedrock of claims to world-power status, is not diminished and that the UK governmental system as a whole is not affected. UK governments have also sought to use the EC/EU as a vehicle for pursuing the UK's global aims of free trade and international security.[4]

Because of this particular conception of state interests and approach to the EC's development, the UK has been judged an 'awkward partner' with respect to continental ambitions for various forms of deeper integration within the EC/EU, and the prioritization of EC/EU developments over wider international relationships. In this perspective, awkwardness has been a consistent feature of UK European policy. It was evident in the reluctant manner in which application for membership was made by the Macmillan and Wilson governments in the 1960s and in the emphasis placed by both on the continued importance of the special relationship with the USA, factors which led to two vetoes from President de Gaulle. The approach of the 1974–9 Labour governments, which involved a controversial renegotiation of the UK's terms of entry and a referendum on continued membership in 1975, threatened UK membership once it had been achieved. Young argued that Heath's premiership in the early 1970s was an example of a willingness to forge a European future for the UK and to be more *communautaire*.[5] Nevertheless, George has argued that, even when there have been attempts at new policy departures, the historical legacy of the UK's international dependencies and the constraints of domestic political factors have pushed British governments back towards their customary recalcitrance. High among such factors have been the UK's patterns of trade and investment, doubts about the economic advantages of membership and concerns about sovereignty.[6]

It has also been argued that British awkwardness has intensified during the last decade. It has become clear that moves in the EC/EU towards 'an ever closer union' have the potential seriously to subvert the UK's sovereignty and ability to act autonomously.[7] Consequently, even though both the Thatcher and Major governments at various times may have struck a *communautaire* tone, in substantive matters they have posed alternative agendas and declined to make commitments to participation in deeper integration. In the early 1980s Mrs Thatcher sought and attained a rebate mechanism for UK net budget contributions. She supported the creation of a Single European Market (SEM) in the 1986 Single European Act (SEA). On both issues she claimed to have set the agenda and won. However, when deeper integration was threatened, she grew hostile and steadfastly refused to support either social integration or Economic and Monetary Union (EMU) leading to a single currency. Under Major the UK opted out of key developments provided for in the 1992 Maastricht Treaty with respect to social integration and EMU.[8] Assessments of the result of this approach have varied with the time of writing: Young concluded in 1992 that 'the country lies on the periphery of the continent in more than a geographical sense'; whereas George argued in early 1994, after the momentum for further integration had been eroded by popular reaction to the Maastricht Treaty, that 'developments in the EC/EU itself suggested that the British position would not need to alter too much to be central to the debate on the future'.[9]

Finally, the conventional wisdom has been that UK policy has become increasingly awkward because of the increasing significance of divisions in the Conservative Party over European policy since the late 1980s.[10] Wallace claimed that Major negotiated the opt-outs in the Maastricht Treaty because of the influence exerted upon European policy by back-bench anti-EC/EU feeling. This reflected his more general 'preoccupation with party management rather than long-term objectives'. Moreover, by the beginning of 1994, with the Conservatives reduced to a small majority since the 1992 general election, giving a greater leverage to backbench anti-EU feeling, preparation for the 1996 Inter-Governmental Conference (IGC) to review the Maastricht Treaty was even more blighted by British foreign policy being 'directed from number 12 Downing Street (the Whip's office) rather than number 10'.[11]

In these terms the UK approach has been marked out as a disintegrative force with respect to ambitions for deeper EC/EU integration since the mid-1980s. Such analyses naturally play down the integrative dimensions of UK policy. Whilst it would be impossible to argue that the UK has been a positive force for deeper integration, the 'accommodationist' element in UK policy has been too little emphasized. The accommodationist approach is implicit in the slogan 'TINA' (there is no alternative), with which government policy promoted EC membership in the 1960s and 1970s, and is a key assumption in the Eurosceptic critique of government policy in the 1980s and 1990s.[12] In conventional analysis, however, the importance of the TINA argument has clearly been understood in a limited way, thus allowing a greater focus on UK awkwardness. I shall be concerned, therefore, to re-appraise the force of the TINA argument and its implications for UK policy since the mid-1980s with respect particularly to the main developments of the EC/EU – the original commitments of the founding treaties of the EC, the SEA and the Maastricht Treaty.

Defining the importance of an accommodationist approach is of primary interest but we do not wish to throw out the baby with the bath water. We shall examine the importance of accommodationism in context. Hence, we shall look at UK policy in terms of accommodation to developments in the EC/EU constrained by certain special UK political factors, distinguishing between those that are inherent features of the UK approach and those that have the potential to make UK policy awkward only in certain ways or at certain times. This nevertheless departs from an analytical framework that examines policy in terms of a general inclination towards awkwardness or disintegration. Section 1 conceptualizes the importance of accommodationism in UK European policy and suggests its primary influence on policy in the 1960s and 1970s despite constraints. Section 2 argues that Thatcherism posed the greatest challenge to accommodation-ism, but was nevertheless fought off. Section 3 argues that the accommoda-tionist approach remains highly influential in the European policy of the Major governments. Section 4 argues that the impact of Europeanization would tend to suggest the continued importance of accommodationism in UK approaches to future developments in the EU.

1 UK RELATIVE DECLINE AND EC MEMBERSHIP

In the 1960s and 1970s government ministers were prone to suggest that there was no alternative to EC membership if the UK wished to reverse its relative economic decline and bolster its global-power status. We need to understand how deeply this was felt in order to comprehend the determination of the governing elite to accommodate the UK to EC/EU developments. Initially, this requires looking, first, at the general commit-ment to reverse relative decline and maintain global-power status and, second, at the specific commitment to EC membership.

The commitment to the reversal of relative economic decline and the bolstering of great-power status is often underestimated. Two bases of commitment are well understood. First, these aims represented the rational desires of economic and foreign policy-makers to maximize economic pros-perity and external power. Second, the reversal of relative economic decline responded to a domestic political agenda, where business demanded sup-portive policies and the electorate was concerned about levels of personal welfare. A third basis of commitment, however, is generally ignored. The reversal of relative economic decline and the bolstering of great-power status were both essential to state legitimacy itself,[13] and, in particular, to the legitimacy of two key features of the UK state: first, that it is a state based territorially upon the Union of England with Scotland, Wales and Northern Ireland; and second, that its claim to exclusive jurisdiction within its boundaries has been derived from the concept of parliamentary sovereignty. It was in the context of imperial power that British identity and the shared perception of economic benefit that bound the Union together were formulated.[14] Similarly, it was in the context of respect for and pride in the state's imperial power that social deference and acquies-cence in a hierarchical structure of power, which underpinned continued respect for parliamentary sovereignty in the face of democratic ideas of popular sovereignty, were derived.[15] Relative economic and political decline, therefore, potentially threatened the stability of the Union as well as continued respect for Parliamentary sovereignty. Evidence of this was already available by the early 1960s with the growth of Scottish and Welsh nationalist movements and the emergence of anti-establishment atti-tudes amidst the beginnings of a more permissive and assertive society.[16] During the 1960s the momentum for reform of UK political institutions increased further, adding greater weight to the need to find ways of arresting relative decline. These concerns over state legitimacy made the aim of reversing economic and political decline fundamentally important, rather than merely voluntary, policy objectives.

Commitment to EC membership has also been underestimated, for it is understood in such a way as to make it vulnerable to attack. Policy-makers may well have believed that EC membership was the crucial means to make substantive economic and diplomatic gains but it has always been controversial. Indeed successive sets of government proposals laying out the case for membership since 1973 were usually careful to make it without specific predictions about economic growth rates or political successes. More importantly, however, policy-makers believed that, even if substantive gains were not made, EC membership offered a basis for maintaining the appearance of economic and political power, an important resource in sustaining domestic state legitimacy.[17] After Suez, Britain's marginalization in superpower relations and the emergence of problems in the Commonwealth, EC membership offered new promise in this respect. The EC's standing as a major regional bloc meant that, simply by her membership and her position as one of the four key powers in the Council of Ministers, the UK had her standing as a major power in the international system recognized, reassuring a domestic audience of continued state prestige. These perceptions ensured that EC membership became central to the general project to sustain the legitimacy of an existing configuration of the state against the threats posed by relative economic and political decline. The notion that there was no alternative to EC membership was not simply a public appeal in terms of the aim of maintaining UK world economic and political power, but a private confession in terms of government's own aim of maintaining a particular configuration of the UK state.

Understanding Britain's commitment to EC membership in these terms has implications for how we understand UK behaviour within the EC. British governments may have pursued substantive goals, sought to shape the EC/EU to UK ideals, and pursued through the EC certain global aims, which established for the UK a reputation for awkwardness. However, the priority accorded to maintaining the appearance of power suggests that awkwardness has its limits. It is not necessarily rational for states to enter into conflict consistently over the substance of policies, if to do so risks defeat and indicates a clear loss of power, or if such policies could be presented in a complementary light irrespective of their substance. In particular, it is not rational to fight substantive policy battles in the EC/EU where there is a risk of omission from a core project of integration that would undermine both external and domestic perceptions of UK power in the EC/EU and, thus, in the rest of the world. On this basis accommodation to core developments in the EC/EU becomes a necessity in order to fulfil the original aims of membership.

This reconceptualization of the aims of EC membership and how they might be attained suggests that the standard disposition of those in government was one of accommodation to major EC/EU developments. There remain, of course, key substantive constraints to its operation. One is inherent and continuous: the economic and great-power objectives that underpinned the need to join the EC also reflected strong attachment to state sovereignty.[18] While needing to participate in the core developments of the EC/EU in order to sustain state legitimacy, the pretence that the UK, in its membership of the EC/EU, is merely sharing sovereignty and not giving it all up must also remain credible with the electorate or risk political destabilization at home. Hence, the very act of joining the EC, as well as subsequent accommodation to EC/EU developments, has had to co-exist with acts which continue to maintain the credibility of state sovereignty. This has always been a potentially contradictory and deeply problematic exercise for UK governments in the context of EC/EU developments which have clearly compromised the credibility of sovereignty.

Other constraints have had a varied impact over time. Foremost among these has been the influence of the Eurosceptics in both the Conservative and Labour Parties, who have found the appeal of formal state sovereignty so great that they either have never been reconciled to membership of the EC/EU or more commonly are concerned to fight within it against further losses of sovereignty and to divert it from supranational integration towards intergovernmental co-operation.[19] Eurosceptics continue to equate national power with independence rather than with interdependence and its management and to be more confident of securing political objectives, such as the reversal of relative economic decline and the maintenance of great-power status, without EC membership than with it. Their presence within the parties has varied over time but has always potentially represented an important pressure upon governments to summon up the spirit of past conflicts with Europe when going to Brussels, especially when they have managed to penetrate the Cabinet.

These constraints have ensured that the UK approach to EC/EU developments has always been deeply problematic, but in the period up to 1979 an approach which was ultimately accommodating nevertheless became entrenched as a strong influence on government policy.[20] The constraints clearly had their effect. For example, the need to emphasize the credibility of state sovereignty and to appease Eurosceptics ensured that the EC applications in the 1960s were made with an air of reluctance. The strength of Eurosceptic opinion in the Conservative Party ensured high-profile domestic conflicts over EC accession, and in the Labour Party led to the need to renegotiate the terms of entry and have them sanctioned by referendum in 1975, as well as constraining Labour policies on Europe between 1976 and 1979 on such issues as direct elections to the European Parliament. Nevertheless, the central facts remain that the leaderships of both main parties applied for membership and continued to make it a priority even after de Gaulle's vetoes. Similarly, British governments in 1973–9, while hampered by such constraints, did little to damage EC integration or the UK's standing within the EC. The Heath Government made a show of defending the national political tradition whilst negotiating terms of entry that meekly complied with the Treaty of Rome. The Wilson Government's renegotiation in 1974–5, whilst trumpeted as a great triumph for UK interests in order to underpin the credibility of effective UK power in the EC and head off Eurosceptic critics, posed only a very limited challenge to the initial terms of entry. Wilson concentrated renegotiation on the specifics, such as concessions over Commonwealth trade, avoiding any conflict over the fundamental principles of the EC founding treaties. Even then on some issues Wilson quietly backed down. The Callaghan Government, while indulging in Eurosceptic rhetoric for domestic party conferences, actually forged quite a rapport with West Germany on EC matters and, despite not joining the exchange rate mechanism (ERM) of the European Monetary System (EMS) in 1979 for economic reasons, did join the EMS itself. Nevertheless, it should be remembered that until the 1980s the capacity of UK membership of the EC to be Janus faced – to be presented as not undermining sovereignty whilst also submitting to all its rules – was comparatively easy because in the main the EC remained a limited economic organization, and the economic crisis engendered by the 1973/74 oil shock had halted further plans for further integration. The 1980s were to provide a much more fundamental challenge to the UK approach to EC membership.

2   THATCHERISM AND EUROPEAN INTEGRATION

The general outlook of the Thatcher governments of 1979–90 threatened to make the UK a genuinely awkward partner and a force for disintegration in the EC. It is important to note, however, that this did not represent an intensification of an existing trend but a new challenge at the heart of government to a hitherto prevailing disposition to be accommodating to EC developments. Views which had previously languished on the back-benches now moved on to the front benches. We need to understand the novelty of this challenge, its influence over European policy and how it was defeated.

To appreciate the novel implications of Thatcherism it is important to understand the development of European policy in terms of the broader state projects to arrest and reverse UK relative decline in order to maintain state legitimacy. These 'modernization' projects of the 1960s and 1970s involved varying designs of managed capitalism based upon neo-Keynesian macroeconomic policies aimed at maintaining full employment, a universal welfare state, corporatism and the mixed economy. They each had a role for EC membership in helping to galvanize the economy by enhancing competitiveness, technological innovation and rationalization. None of these projects, however, was pursued with much conviction or for very long, representing as they did half-hearted attempts at a developmental state without a coherent political philosophy to underpin it.[21] It was, in fact, in this wider context that membership of the EC *per se* served as a key prop for maintaining the appearance of UK power, both economically and politically, during a period of real relative decline.

The Thatcher administrations from 1979 pursued a different course. Their programme for renewal rested first on a neo-liberal design for the economy based upon the control of inflation, a reduction in the size of the state and of welfare provision and the promotion of a market economy backed by an enterprise culture. Second, they aimed to reassert the authority of the state in overseeing renewal by excluding certain interest groups from government and championing the traditional procedures of government by Cabinet accountable to Parliament, and by pursuing state interests vigorously on the world stage, in particular making a great show of standing firm with the USA against Soviet communism. Thatcherism was a radical counter-revolution against post-war prescriptions for a managed economy and a permissive state in order to recreate 'a free economy and a strong state'.[22] At its core Thatcherism relied upon the activation of national potential without assistance from outside and envisaged only a limited role for EC membership. On these grounds Mrs Thatcher has been called an agnostic on European integration.[23] She merely hoped to eradicate the ways in which EC membership impeded the general project of Thatcherism and to take advantage of ways in which it complemented it. By treating the EC as something outside the UK she sought also to use it as an arena in which the UK could appear to demonstrate its renewed national vigour. This implied a profound hostility to any deepening of integration in the EC that could erode national autonomy.

Thatcherism was a radical departure in the effort to modernize the UK and to reverse its relative decline. Of all the modernization projects since the 1960s it allocated the least significant role to EC membership. It is appropriate, therefore, to suggest that after 1979 there was the potential for a novel tension between the original purposes of the UK's EC membership and the comparative indifference towards membership within Thatcherism. It was fortuitous that in this period European integration unexpectedly leapt forwards. Consequently, Thatcherism came to pose a test of just how committed the political class was to accommodating itself to EC developments in order to sustain EC membership as a key prop to the reversal of decline and the maintenance of state legitimacy. In practice, an accommodating approach to new EC developments remained influential until 1986 but thereafter Thatcherism provoked a crisis in European policy.

Thatcherism and the EC, 1979–86

During this period the Thatcher governments claimed that European integration had started to reflect UK interests and ideals, suggesting that there could be an ideal marriage between EC membership and the imperatives of Thatcherism. Superficially, there was much to support this thesis. First, in 1984 at the Fontainebleau summit, after a four-year struggle, the Thatcher Government achieved an ongoing EC budget mechanism that guaranteed a 66 per cent rebate on UK VAT contributions set against budget receipts. The fiscal burden of membership was reduced, a feat that complemented the domestic priority of reducing the fiscal burden of the state.[24] Second, the completion of the SEM, provided for in the 1986 SEA, appealed to the Thatcherite desire to extend the market economy and promote an enterprise culture.[25] Both developments allowed the presentation of the UK as an influential member of the EC and could be claimed as victories for the resolute approach of Thatcherism towards Europe.

Closer analysis would suggest however that, whilst the Thatcher Government's domestic rhetoric may have portrayed the EC as moving in the UK's direction, from 1983 onwards it was in practice on the back foot responding to a continental agenda. The push to relaunch the EC came in 1983 from President Mitterrand and the Franco-German axis, and with it came an indifference to UK participation. Mitterrand suggested that, if the UK government was so hostile to the EC, as indicated by the budgetary crisis in which the Thatcher Government was implicitly questioning the legitimacy of the EC having its own resources, then it need not join in new initiatives. The UK could move into the slow lane of a 'two-speed Europe'. It was this threat, rather than a realization of any specific rebate objective, that concentrated the Thatcher mind on a resolution of the budgetary question at Fontainebleau in 1984 with a deal arguably less generous than earlier offers. Geoffrey Howe, then Foreign Secretary, also came forward with strong pro-European rhetoric to signal the UK's determination to participate in any new developments.[26]

The new phase of integration crystallized in the SEA. This included the SEM but in addition provided for the introduction of qualified majority voting in the Council of Ministers and new powers for the European Parliament, which the Thatcher Government viewed with disfavour as erosions of sovereignty. The SEA also provided a basis for the completion of the SEM not simply by widespread deregulation, as the Thatcher administration had hoped, but also through the harmonization at a European level of indirect taxation, movement of labour, professional standards, state aid and public procurement. It also articulated the aim of European union, paving the way for the use of the SEA to justify further deepening of integration.[27] Such re-regulation at the EC level and the potential for further integration were anathema to the Thatcher administration, but the customary priority of accommodating the UK to EC membership prevailed. Thatcher comforted herself with the belief that there was little to worry about in the short term.

A cohabitation between accommodation to new EC developments and specifically Thatcherite objectives in relation to EC membership was achieved in this period, but this was not because the EC moved consciously in a UK direction. Rather, the policy of the Thatcher governments was ultimately determined by fear of being left in the slow lane of a two-speed Europe, for it would marginalize the UK within the EC and thus potentially marginalize the UK in trans-Atlantic relations. Decline would become obvious. The continued hold of concerns about the fragility of the UK's position and the need for the support of EC membership meant that acquiescence in the continental agenda for the creation of the SEA, warts and all, was still deemed essential. It was fortuitous then that the government was also able to satisfy the objectives of Thatcherism by exploiting the latter years of Eurosclerosis to get a favourable resolution of the budgetary question and a presentation of the SEA in triumphal terms by emphasizing the SEM.

Thatcherism and the EC, 1986–90

In the late 1980s the implications of the limited UK influence over the agenda for the deepening of European integration became clear. Three developments occurred which together posed considerable dilemmas for UK policy and pushed the third Thatcher Government into crisis. First, there were significant pressures to move towards EMU, including a single currency, and some form of political union. Both of these projects threatened to circumscribe the capacity for state assertion demanded by Thatcherism as well as the credibility of national sovereignty. Second, membership of the ERM came to be seen as an essential prerequisite for participation in EMU. The UK had hung back from joining the ERM without incurring significant problems in its relations within the EC. Now the ERM became of prime political importance. Yet, in imposing the requirement upon the UK Government to maintain a fixed exchange rate within defined bands of movement, ERM membership threatened governmental freedom of action over economic policy as well as posing uncomfortable questions for the broader credibility of effective sovereignty. Finally, in 1988 the EC launched a social dimension to the SEM, symbolized by the Social Charter. This threatened the Thatcherite desire to deregulate the labour market to allow it to work more effectively and reduce individual expectations of state welfare.[28]

The response of the third Thatcher Government was determined primarily by Thatcher herself. This arose from two sources of strength. First, in 1987 she had won her third successive general election and was closely identified as a powerful electoral asset. With a large parliamentary majority she apparently had little need to bridge party divisions in defining European policy. Second, by the late 1980s Mrs Thatcher had a strong hold over the Cabinet, particularly in issues of high politics. Hers was seen as the paradigm case of prime ministerial government, even presidential government.[29] In making her response, Thatcher was strongly influenced by the celebratory mood of Conservatives following the 1987 election. Inflation had been controlled, productivity improved and unemployment was coming down. Living standards for the majority had risen in real terms over the decade and there was a growing belief that the Thatcher experiment was turning the UK economy around. Of course, by the end of the decade it was clear that the economic situation had been too strongly built upon a consumer boom, fuelled by direct tax cuts, financial deregulation and asset inflation. By 1989 her government faced problems of both product inflation and recession, and expectations of the UK economy were reversed.[30] But at a crucial juncture in the development of European integration Mrs Thatcher was strong in office and confident in the UK's own capacity to bring about the reversal of relative decline without an undue reliance on the external support mechanism of the EC. Consequently her responses were defined more clearly by the imperatives of Thatcherism than by any perception of the need to accommodate the UK to new EC developments.

Mrs Thatcher outlined her opposition to new EC developments in a speech in Bruges on 20 September 1988.[31] Her opposition to deeper integration was not entirely divisive within the government and her opposition to the Social Charter was consistent with the strong neo-liberal consensus on social welfare. Moreover the social dimension was not seen as a core project of integration so that opposition to it would not make the UK an outcast. However, her general policy profoundly worried key members of her Cabinet, led by Sir Geoffrey Howe and Nigel Lawson, the Chancellor of the Exchequer. They were more pessimistic than was she about the UK's ability to maintain great-power status without the support of EC membership. Indeed Thatcher's speeches were drawing attention to the erosion of UK sovereignty and threatened to expose the realities of relative decline. Her apparent belief that fighting an open battle over sovereignty with Europe – one that would either be lost or result in the UK's marginalization in European affairs – appeared naive, and dangerous to the aim of maintaining the authority of the UK state. In particular, Howe and Lawson were worried by Thatcher's outspoken opposition to EMU and ERM membership. They recognized that EMU was a core project of integration. For the UK to exclude itself from EMU would be to move to the slow lane of a two-speed Europe. They were anxious, therefore, that the UK should support EMU in principle. Ideally, they would then also be able to influence EMU to proceed along lines that made it more compatible with maintaining the credibility of UK sovereignty. The coded concept by which they promoted this renewed desire to assert an accommodating approach to EC developments was that of shared sovereignty. Referring to EMU, they highlighted the reciprocal gains for the EC and the UK state in terms of enhanced authority from further deepening. As a corollary to this Lawson promoted UK membership of the ERM.[32] Lawson had his own domestic macroeconomic policy reasons for supporting this move: to use ERM membership as the cornerstone of his anti-inflationary strategy now that monetarist doctrine had fallen into disrepute.[33] However, the force with which Lawson promoted ERM membership within Cabinet from 1988 onwards also derived from his belief that membership was essential to influencing the debate about EMU from the inside.[34]

Thatcher, in speaking as she did against Howe and Lawson, also departed from a line of policy that maintained Conservative Party unity over Europe. The accommodating approach was capable of embracing a wide section of the Party from *communautaire* Gaullists to mild Euro-sceptics. It entailed a willingness to participate in further integration but one that was not unconditional. However, Thatcher's efforts to lead the Party to a Eurosceptic position represented a clear choice against further participation, which was only capable of pleasing the Eurosceptic wing of the Party. This threatened to alienate completely the more 'Euro-enthusiast' and 'Euro-realist' sections of the Party. Thatcher opened the Party to the possibility of a split and electoral oblivion. As Baker and others have shown, on the two occasions in which the Conservative Party has previously split – in the 1840s and the early 1900s – the argument was over the external political economy to be pursued, and the result of failing to resolve or manage a division of opinion was disunity and electoral disaster. There was no reason to believe that European integration should not follow the Corn Laws and tariff reform as a trigger of self-destruction, and Thatcher's high-handed choice of the EC policy to be pursued threatened such an outcome.[35]

On these bases a split arose within Thatcher's third government.[36] Lawson and Howe felt Thatcher's challenge to British participation in EMU and to the maintenance of Party unity over Europe was sufficiently dangerous to warrant a struggle to overturn her policy. They sought to push her to accept UK membership of the ERM. Before the Madrid Summit of June 1989 they both threatened resignation unless she committed herself at the summit to ERM membership. This ambush achieved a commitment to entry if certain conditions were met, including a reduction of the UK inflation rate to the EC average. This advance was swiftly followed by Mrs Thatcher's revenge. In summer 1989 she reshuffled her Cabinet, effectively breaking the Howe–Lawson axis by demoting Howe to the position of Leader of the House of Commons. John Major, less experienced and thought to be a loyal Thatcherite, was brought in as Foreign Secretary. She then recalled Alan Walters as her economic policy adviser and allowed him to criticize the economic policy being pursued by Lawson, and publicly to oppose ERM membership. Lawson responded by resigning in October 1989. Major was moved to the Treasury and Douglas Hurd became the new Foreign Secretary. The battle over European policy did not, however, go away. Major and Hurd effectively re-forged the Lawson–Howe axis and pressured Thatcher to accept ERM membership. Moreover by early 1990 Thatcher was in a much weaker position. Beset by economic problems, the crisis of the community charge legislation and criticism of her as an electoral liability, she was increasingly vulnerable to attack. In spring 1990 Major presented ERM membership as the cornerstone of a policy that could deliver low inflation again by the next election and help pave the way for a fourth victory. Duly seduced, Thatcher gave a public commitment to the principle of entry. It was then largely a tactical decision as to when entry would be made, and it finally came in October 1990. During 1990 Major and the Treasury also worked to get the UK back on the inside in debates about EMU. Major made broad declarations cautiously supporting EMU, and in June 1990 offered a proposal based upon one originally devised under Lawson as to how EMU could be achieved with a hard ECU to the satisfaction of the interests of the UK and of other member states. This involved the simultaneous introduction of the hard ECU and the retention of existing currencies, leading to a competition over practical usage. This offered the prospect of EMU with the possibility of the ECU eventually becoming the common currency, thus pleasing integrationists, but also with the possibility of the continuation of the pound sterling as a symbol of the continued importance of state sovereignty.[37]

Thatcher was not, however, to be silenced. At the Rome Summit in October 1990 she openly opposed the abolition of the pound sterling in favour of a single currency as recommended by the Delors Committee on EMU. Moreover, she returned to the House of Commons and, during a stormy exchange over European policy, declared that the ECU would never become the common currency of the EC. This entirely contradicted Major's carefully crafted EMU policy, which was also the official Cabinet position. For Howe, Thatcher had gone too far in her rejection of attempts to find ways to participate in the new phase of integration. He resigned from the Cabinet and in his resignation speech criticized Thatcher for bypassing Cabinet responsibility and pursuing her own European policy to the detriment of UK interests. This gave Michael Heseltine, the former Cabinet Minister who had left office in 1985 complaining about the way in which Thatcher ran her government, the principled basis on which to challenge her for the leadership of the Conservative Party. A combination of concerns over European policy, the community charge, the recession and personal loathing then combined to leave her without sufficient Conservative Parliamentary support to continue as leader and she duly resigned.[38] The late Thatcher years had constituted the only period in which UK European policy threatened to break from accommodationism, preferring to obstruct new EC developments and adopt a position of total isolation if necessary. Other members of the Conservative Party governing élite ultimately deemed this sufficiently serious to warrant the deposition of their most successful post-war leader.

3 THE MAJOR PREMIERSHIP AND EUROPEAN UNION

The 1990 leadership election led to the installation of John Major as Party leader and Prime Minister. Thatcher and her supporters presented Major as her heir, yet this was only true in the sense that he was deeply committed to continuing the Thatcherite neo-liberal revolution to create the free economy.[39] As Chancellor, Major had positioned himself against the Eurosceptic view of EMU, seeking to influence its form by giving it qualified support. As Prime Minister, he sought to develop modern conservativism on the basis of a more general cohabitation between the Thatcherite neo-liberal project and the necessity of accommodating the UK to EC initiatives, assisted and guided within the upper echelons of the Cabinet by the broadly pro-European Douglas Hurd, Michael Heseltine, President of the Board of Trade since 1992, and Kenneth Clarke, Chancellor since 1993.[40]

Major's European policy should not be judged too harshly, for he had a very difficult hand to play. It required finding ways of agreeing on forms of integration that appeased other member states' general desires for progress, and to which the UK could accommodate itself, whilst maintaining a credible pretence of sovereignty. This trick was harder to perform, the more fundamental the issues of integration became. He faced considerable domestic political constraints: he was required to reassert cabinet government, to remedy the excesses of prime ministerial government under Thatcher, and to pursue a more consensual approach in the Party because of the small Parliamentary majority following the 1992 election. Moreover, he faced a section of the Parliamentary Party who were committed anti-Europeans or Eurosceptics, some of whom were relatively elderly, no longer constrained by career considerations and the resulting power of the Party whip.[41] Their power in the context of a small Parliamentary majority put a particular premium on the need to assuage Party concerns over the loss of national sovereignty and made it necessary to appoint some prominent Eurosceptics to the Cabinet. In the circumstances the Major premiership up to 1995 played a poor hand plausibly well, attaining most of the aims of his European policy, despite the severe constraints: a high-wire act that few in the Conservative Party or press have appreciated. In the process European policy has, in fact, remained considerably more accommodating towards integration, and much more coherent than critics would suggest.

Most significantly, Major's policy aims were achieved in the negotiations on EMU and political union leading up to the Maastricht Treaty signed in

1992.[42] Major emerged pleased that the second and third pillars of the EU, concerned with the common foreign and security policy and judicial and home affairs co-operation, were to be on an inter-governmental basis. This actually conformed with the UK ideal of close co-operation on the basis of a Europe of sovereign nations. Major also ensured that the UK emerged from Maastricht with an approach to EMU that faced both ways. First, he ensured UK participation in the principal development towards EMU. He signed up to the first and second stages of EMU, which bring it about in all but name. This has ensured the UK remaining 'at the heart of Europe' with all that that entails. Meanwhile, Major won an opt-out on the third stage of EMU – the move to a single currency – stating that this would have to be a decision to be left to a later Parliament. This meant that, while in all essentials the UK accommodated itself to the core project of EMU and thus remained at the centre of EU politics, time was bought on settling the issue of the future of the pound sterling and a single currency. The negotiation of the opt-out was presented as evidence of the credibility of UK autonomy, and the possibility of saving sterling was meant to appease the Eurosceptics. Major also negotiated an opt-out from the Social Agreement of the Treaty. This did not unduly concern Euro-enthusiasts or realists as the Social Agreement was a side-show in the development of integration, and non-participation would not centrally damage UK standing in the EU. At the same time, however, it was a further demonstration of the credibility of sovereignty and a means of appeasing further Eurosceptic opinion in the Party. Finally, the inclusion in the Treaty of the concept of subsidiarity appeared to provide a further counterbalance to the supranationalist drift of EMU, in that it provided a principled basis for the redistribution of competences between different levels of government and for the reversal of the perceived over-centralization of EU policy-making. Major's claim that the Maastricht Treaty was 'game, set and match' for the UK has often been interpreted cynically as being more like 'game, set and match' for a government struggling to manage Conservative Party divisions over Europe. Undoubtedly this was so, but it should also be recognized that at a deeper level Major led a successful effort to accommodate the UK to core projects in deepening integration whilst maintaining the credibility of sovereignty. In this way the Major premiership continued to pursue the original aims of membership in ever more difficult circumstances.

In many ways, however, the problems of Major's European policy were only just beginning. The bill to ratify the Maastricht Treaty achieved its second reading in the House of Commons in 1992 without great controversy as most Eurosceptics concluded that Major had made the best of a bad job. However, the 'no' to Maastricht in the Danish referendum in June[43] galvanized Conservative Eurosceptics into the belief that the whole Treaty could be overturned. Eighty-four Conservative MPs signed a 'fresh start' early-day motion, which achieved the postponement of the rest of the progress of the ratification bill, and in September the Conservative Fresh Start Group was formed to fight the bill's ratification. The parliamentary siege of Maastricht that ensued pushed Major's resolve to the limits. The ratification bill was finally passed in summer 1993 but not before the Party divisions over Europe had been fully exposed, leaving a permanently embittered band of Eurosceptics. Major's popularity and credibility as Prime Minister had also been undermined by the public displays of weakness and wheeler-dealing and by high-profile criticism from leading former Thatcherite ministers and traditional organs of Conservative support, such as *The Times*.[44]

The combination of these legacies has meant that the Major premiership's European policies have been subject to continued political controversy. The end of UK membership of the ERM in September 1992, because of speculative pressures on the pound, was greeted with glee by Major's opponents within his Party and the pressure against UK entry into the ERM has been maintained ever since.[45] Issues that otherwise might not have been politically significant have led to deeply troublesome challenges to Major's authority and policies – including the government's policy in March 1994 on the adjustment of Qualified Majority Voting arrangements on the Council of Ministers as a result of the 1995 EU enlargement; the bill to confirm the UK's budgetary contributions in November 1994; and UK responses to developments in the EU fisheries policy in January 1995.[46] Increasingly the fight-back of the Eurosceptics within the Conservative Party has been focused on influencing the government's approach to the 1996 IGC to review the Maastricht Treaty. Their primary aim is to unravel integration as far as possible or to gain a governmental commitment to a referendum on the outcome of the IGC, the result of which may force the government to withdraw from further integration. Eurosceptics, both on the backbenches and within the Cabinet, have campaigned either openly or in coded terms against the UK ever joining a single currency. In late 1994 eight Eurosceptic MPs had the Party whip withdrawn from them for voting against the government, and a ninth left the whip voluntarily. The whipless nine subsequently drew up an alternative Conservative manifesto on European policy, which essentially advocated the reversal of all supranationalist dimensions of the EU.[47] Increasingly they behaved as if they spoke for a majority in the Conservative Party in favour of a more Eurosceptic stance in the 1996 IGC.

In response, the Major premiership appeared to move with this feeling towards a more Thatcherite pro-sovereignty approach to policy formation for the 1996 IGC. In September 1994 Mr Major made a speech in Leiden which restated the UK preference for a Europe of sovereign nations, its tone of caution about further integration flatly contradicting the calls by the German CDU/CSU for a concerted push towards EMU and political union before the end of the century.[48] In early 1995 Mr Major struck a Eurosceptic tone in speeches and interviews and allowed leading Cabinet

Eurosceptics, Michael Portillo and Jonathan Aitken, to discuss openly their misgivings about a single currency. There was concern among pro-Europeans within the Party, prompting Lord Howe to undertake a media campaign to restate the virtues of UK participation in new EU developments and Michael Heseltine and Kenneth Clarke to reaffirm their support for the UK joining a single currency if and when it materializes.[49]

However, if we examine the substance of policy, the Major Government has not budged from its position over EMU as agreed in the Maastricht Treaty. The UK has complied with stages one and two of EMU. Since the more general collapse of the ERM in 1993 and the introduction of looser bands of alignment the Major Government has informally collaborated in exchange-rate stabilization. UK economic policy has continued to be concerned to meet the Treaty's convergence criteria for joining a single currency and the UK is likely to be eligible to join a single currency if it materializes. Despite Eurosceptic demands for clear opposition, Cabinet policy remains open-minded on whether the UK should join a single currency if it happens later than 1997. Moreover, the threat of backbench rebellions over European policy, for example on the budget issue in late 1994, has been met uncompromisingly by threats of government resignation and a general election. In the game of poker that this has involved few MPs have actually dared to call Major's bluff and, despite a small Parliamentary majority and an effective Labour Party in opposition, Parliamentary votes have been won. In this context Major's Eurosceptic tone in early 1995 is more properly seen as mood music to encourage Eurosceptics, particularly the whipless nine, back towards Party unity, and the leeway given to Portillo and Aitken as a necessary safety valve to prevent Eurosceptic disaffection within the Cabinet from leading to damaging senior ministerial resignations.

An examination of the substance of policy also suggests that the Major premiership will seek to accommodate the UK to the third stage of EMU if it takes place later in the decade. In the Council of Finance Ministers Kenneth Clarke has played a full role in discussions in EMU, merely calling for a delay in introducing the single currency to 1999 rather than 1997.[50] Major crucially has signalled his belief that the UK can join a single currency whilst retaining the credibility of sovereignty by stating his agreement with Kenneth Clarke that EMU is possible without political union.[51] Entry into a single currency will satisfy the aim of participating in the core project of integration, thus keeping the UK at the heart of the EU, an aim crucial to maintaining international prestige. However, the gradual sacrifice of the opt-out on stage three of EMU will require balancing deals to bolster simultaneously the credibility of national sovereignty and, in return for this extra step on EMU, it appears likely that the Major Government will seek a number of objectives at the 1996 IGC. Major will set a high premium on maintaining the inter-governmental basis for the second and third pillars of the EU and the Social Agreement opt-out. In addition, he will seek the minimum in institutional reform which would dilute the national veto on the Council of Ministers further, or increase the powers of the European Parliament. Rather the Leiden speech indicated Major's preference for bringing national parliaments back into the EU decision-making process. He is also likely to seek a repatriation of some powers through the application of the concept of subsidiarity.[52] Such an agenda for the IGC taken in isolation may be taken as evidence of an awkward and disintegrative approach. However, Major's European policy taken as a whole offers a plausible formula for accommodating the UK to the deepening of integration whilst also seeking to maintain the credibility of sovereignty. Of course, the more that Major can achieve in bolstering the credibility of state sovereignty the more chance he has of retaining Party unity as well but, as of early 1995, the Major Government was still resisting a Eurosceptic agenda that would make European policy genuinely and comprehensively more hostile to integration.

4 EUROPEANIZATION AND UK EUROPEAN POLICY

Recent research has suggested that the effects of EC/EU membership on the political system have been much greater than originally envisaged.[53] This Europeanization has changed the UK political context for the making of European policy. On balance Europeanization has reinforced the accommodationist approach in UK European policy, which maintains UK participation in core projects of integration whilst seeking to sustain the credibility of sovereignty. There are even some indications of more positive attitudes towards deeper integration. Nevertheless, we should not exaggerate these trends and we should note that Europeanization also exacerbates domestic constraints on the practice of European policy.

Most of the evidence suggests that many of the main actors and institutions that can influence government are broadly supportive of UK participation in EU developments. In the broad foreign policy élite – embracing newspaper editors, academics, senior figures in the armed services and so on, as well as those working inside government – UK membership of the EU is assumed to be a cornerstone of foreign policy. This assumption has been reinforced by the end of the Cold War and the resulting gradual withdrawal of the US from Europe, leaving EU states to take much bigger roles in European security.[54] Business is also broadly pro-EU. With over 50 per cent of trade now conducted with EU member states, and inward investment from the Far East thought to be attracted by the UK's place within the EU, business believes that the UK economy cannot afford to be denied the full economic advantages of participation. Both the Confederation of British Industries (CBI) and the City of London provide qualified support for EMU and believe that the UK should participate in a single currency if it materializes. At the same time the CBI also supports the UK opt-out from the Social Agreement of the Maastricht Treaty in the belief that this insures against the imposition of higher social costs.[55] This provides strong support for key dimensions of the policy that the Major premiership is pursuing.

The labour movement has also come round to support for EC/EU membership. In the 1970s large sections of both the Labour Party and the trade union movement saw the EC as a rich man's club, and in the 1983 general election the Labour Party campaigned on a policy of withdrawing from the EC as part of a general strategy of rebuilding the UK economy on socialist principles behind a protectionist wall. However, under Neil Kinnock and later under John Smith and Tony Blair, the Labour Party has adopted a social democratic outlook and re-established its support for EC/EU membership – so much so that in the 1990s Labour has increasingly come to be seen as the more pro-European of the two major parties. Blair has signalled Labour's preparedness to reverse both the UK opt-outs in the Maastricht Treaty and to join a single currency if it is established. Labour officially shares many of Major's views on political union, although Blair has suggested that Labour would countenance an increase in the use of qualified majority voting in the Council of Ministers if the UK and other big member states were to get more votes. The trade union movement similarly has converted to general support for UK membership since the unveiling of a social dimension to the SEM in 1988.[56]

Even the attitudes of some on the socialist left of the labour movement have moved in favour of European union, indeed seeking full political union to accompany EMU. This change arises from a belief that the state is no longer a large enough unit to regulate multinational capitalism. The EU appears as a more appropriate arena for pursuing socialist aims and to ensure that this may be done it is deemed vital to concentrate powers in the European Parliament at the expense of the member states. Consequently, some members of the Labour left have become as enthusiastic about European integration as the Liberal Democratic Party. Attitudes to EC/EU developments have also exhibited particularly marked changes in Wales and Scotland. In the 1970s the EC was widely seen there as a prop to the ailing UK state. But since the late 1980s structural funds assistance has been welcomed by all and the emphasis within the EU on developing a 'Europe of the Regions' has been welcomed by devolutionists in particular. Even the Scottish National Party favours an independent Scotland in Europe, although within a vision of a Europe of nations, while Plaid Cymru's articulation of Welsh nationalism is increasingly sympathetic to the development of Welsh autonomy within a federal EU.[57]

A lower-profile but equally significant development has seen a wide range of pressure groups, which make up the 'new institutions' of government, respond to the growth in policy made at EU level by opening offices in Brussels or hiring lobbyists and consultants to obtain information and influence. Most see this as a purely functional response to changing circumstances, but some pressure groups, particularly those working on issues thought to have been neglected at the domestic level, such as environmental policy and women's and minority rights, are keen to bypass the UK government by taking their message directly to EU Commission officials and to press for increases in EU power. Elected local authorities now routinely monitor EU legislation and participate in the implementation of EU structural funds policies. Consequently, a number of authorities have also joined the 'Brussels village'. For many the EU is an opportunity of escaping what they see as the stifling central controls of the UK government. Consequently, they often seek to relate to central government on an equal footing in triadic relationships with EU institutions.[58]

Such trends are striking but, nevertheless, should be viewed with some caution.[59] With respect to the Civil Service there is such a wealth of variation in approaches to EU policies across Whitehall that beyond a broad recognition of the value of EU membership generalizations about official views are unwise. Business similarly does not always sing from the same hymn-sheet. While the CBI in supporting EMU and the single currency takes a long-term view of what is in the best interests of capital, in the short term businessmen have been quite happy to take advantage of the effective devaluation of the pound sterling that resulted from its exit from the ERM in 1992 to increase exports. The Labour Party too has its Euro-sceptics, led by former Cabinet ministers, Peter Shore and Tony Benn, while a number of leading trade unions, for example the Transport and General Workers Union, remain strongly attached to state autonomy in economic policy as a means of seeking full employment. Indeed it remains unclear whether the conversion of the rest of the labour movement to Europe should be seen as a principled and deeply rooted step or simply as an act of opportunism by its leadership to reap maximum advantage from the Conservative Party's divisions on the EU – a stance that could fairly swiftly be reversed in different circumstances.

The notion that pro-European sentiment is a reaction against the domestic impact of modern conservatism can be taken further with respect to views on the periphery, in pressure groups and local government. For example, in Scotland and Wales devolution failed to attract sufficient support in the referendum held in 1979, indicating that despite relative economic decline sentiment in favour of home rule was still relatively weak. Since 1979 it is true that the EU has provided a more encouraging context for devolutionist sentiment. It is also true however that, in seeking to govern Britain in an assimilationist manner, giving all parts an equal dose of the Thatcherite medicine, Thatcherism departed from a previous consensus in which government showed a respect for the political demands of the different parts of the Union. Pro-devolutionism and greater pro-Europeanism may merely be symptomatic of a reaction against Thatcherism. If we note that the Labour Party is the largest party in Scotland and polled over 50 per cent of the vote in Wales in the 1992 election it is plausible to believe that such sentiments could be deflated merely by the election of a Labour government. The flight of some pressure groups and local authorities to Brussels is also symptomatic of the impact of Thatcherism in seeking to assert a strong state, which has had implications for both civil liberties and local democracy. Again the election of a Labour government committed to constitutional reform, including a bill of rights and entrenched rights for local government, may have a considerable impact in restoring loyalties to the UK state.

Then there is public opinion. It is important to recognize change. The electorate, long considered the least pro-European-integration in the EC, actually became increasingly reconciled to EC/EU membership from the early 1980s. Indeed the gap between the UK and EC/EU public opinion poll averages on such issues as support for continued membership and perception of benefit has narrowed. Even the reaction to the Maastricht Treaty only saw UK public opinion ratings on the EC/EU slip back to mid-1980s levels rather than to the much lower popularity levels of the late 1970s. However, we should also recognize that with respect to perception of a European identity the UK electorate is well below the EU average, and there is a very indifferent attitude towards the European elections. Mass awareness of how the EU works or what it does is low, and there is a receptiveness to the jingoistic features ridiculing the EU presented in the tabloid press. Consequently, the conclusion after the 1975 referendum that 'support for membership was wide but it did not run deep' probably remains the case.[60] Europeanization as a means of fostering new attitudes to EU membership clearly has a long way to go.

Europeanization has also bolstered the case against EC/EU membership. For it has become increasingly hard to defend the credibility of effective sovereignty. The EU has a much larger set of competences as a result of the SEA and the Maastricht Treaty. Parliamentary scrutiny of EU legislation suffers time and resource restraints. Ministerial veto in the Council of Ministers has been surrendered on a large number of issues of EU legislation. Parliament is deterred from passing legislation which contradicts European law for fear of undermining the rule of law in the EU and the means of redress through the European Court of Justice. The rule of construction which in theory defends Parliamentary sovereignty against the supremacy of European law is seen to be of little practical use. Consequently, Eurosceptics in the Parliamentary Conservative Party are opposed to any further accommodation to EU initiatives that erode sovereignty; rather they wish it to be reversed. They feel that they can tap into public opinion, draw out Labour Eurosceptic support and exploit weaknesses in the support for the EU in the UK. They also have potential financial backers. In late 1994 the fiercely Eurosceptic businessman, James

Goldsmith, offered to bankroll pro-referendum candidates at a general election. Clearly, whilst Eurosceptics ideally wish to stay in the Conservative Party and to emerge victorious in determining its government's policies, if this does not work out, they can turn to forging a new 'nationalist Conservative' grouping outside the Conservative Party.

The key battle in UK European policy in the late 1990s will be over a single currency. The Major premiership is prepared to accommodate it if it occurs, a position also taken by the Labour Party. A change of government would not, therefore, change the main thrust of government policy. On balance there is a wider array of forces supporting such an approach than opposing it. Indeed there is also some support for further transformation of UK politics as a result of EU membership and increased EU powers. But we need to be cautious about levels of support in the broader political system for UK participation in deeper integration and to note the continued presence of potentially powerful political forces that could push UK policy to a genuinely more disintegrative position.

CONCLUSION

The main argument of this chapter has been that the broad message of existing perspectives on UK government responses to EC/EU developments in the last decade is flawed because it neglects their accommodationist content in favour of a central focus on awkwardness. An accommodating disposition is to be found in élite perceptions of the fundamental importance of EC/EU membership to state legitimacy and the value to this end of using membership to help keep up the appearance of state power. There has always been a pressure on the governing élite to ensure that membership did not irrevocably undermine the credibility of sovereignty, and broader arguments within the political parties and beyond against membership and/or accommodationism at all. This has meant that UK European policy has advanced conditionally as far as continental pro-integrationists are concerned, but its underlying commitment to UK participation in core projects of integration is ultimately more significant. This accommodationism was apparent in the 1960s battle to get the UK into the EC, and in the policies of the 1970s to keep the UK in the EC, and it has continued to be influential in the 1980s and 1990s, despite the challenges mounted by Thatcherism to cast UK policy in more genuinely awkward and disintegrative light. The strings attached to UK membership have not prevented the EC/EU from developing broadly along the paths that most member states have wished to go.

The Heath and Wilson governments persuaded the British public that the UK was joining what was in essence an economic organization, which could help to reverse relative economic decline and bolster great-power status. In relation to these promised benefits, EC/EU developments since the mid-1980s have been difficult to reconcile with maintaining the credibility of UK sovereignty and the unity of the governing Conservative Party. In these circumstances the UK may have been forgiven for rethinking foreign policy. This path has, however, been forgone by post-Thatcher Conservative governments which have sought to find tolerable ways of managing the discipline of European integration. The politics of European policy since 1990 have left the Major premiership open to a variety of criticisms but these insufficiently appreciated the magnitude of the difficulties involved and the coherence of the policy that has resulted. Important components of the political system have now moved in favour of a European future for the UK, indeed offering alternative scenarios for UK European policy. But there remain domestic constraints that render the problems of forming a coherent EU policy as great as ever, and the achievements in so doing worthy of considerably more appreciation than hitherto.

At Maastricht the Major Government was able to accommodate the UK to the development of the EU in ways tolerable to its domestic constituency without preventing other member states from pushing integration along the path they broadly wished it to take. UK policy since Maastricht has left the way open to the continuation of this approach. The question remains, however, whether the constraints it imposes are too tight to allow a consensus to be reached with other member states at the 1996 IGC and beyond. For we should be clear that Major's European policy seeks to make a virtue of multi-track and multi-speed integration. This allows different policy areas to spawn different forms of integration, for example the CFSP being on an inter-governmental basis rather than subject to the role of the Commission or the European Parliament as in other policies. It also permits different rates of integration in different policy areas, enabling states to opt out altogether if they wish. Major's policy also seeks to promote the idea of a 'quasi-federal bargain' where, in return for such major steps as EMU, other policy competences, currently at the EU level, are returned to the states. Other states' aspirations for the development of the EU as a coherent and effective body, both internally and externally, may, by contrast, place a high premium on attaining a common institutional framework for all policies and common rules across all policy areas. The Commission and the Parliament would resist any repatriation of their powers, especially if this occurred in advance of the completion of EMU. In view of this, multi-track integration and a quasi-federal bargain are highly problematic. On the other hand the new Europe that has emerged out of the end of the Cold War provides no clear prescriptions for political development. The chaos of ethnic and nationalist rivalries in Eastern Europe and the assertion of localism, regionalism and state identities against the forces of internationalization suggest the need for flexibility in developing European union, particularly as the EU expands to take in new members. UK European policy, combining accommodation and the imperatives of domestic political considerations, may yet continue to dovetail with the requirements of broader European union.

FURTHER READING

S. Bulmer, S. George and A. Scott (eds), *United Kingdom and EC Membership Evaluated*, London: Pinter, 1992.

S. George, *An Awkward Partner. Britain in the European Community*, 2nd edn, Oxford: Oxford University Press, 1994.

S. George (ed.), *Britain and the European Community. The Politics of Semi-Detachment*, Oxford: Clarendon, 1992.

J. Young, *Britain and European Unity, 1945–1992*, London: Macmillan, 1993.

NOTES

1 D. Sanders, *Losing an Empire, Finding a Role: British Foreign Policy since 1945*, London: Macmillan, 1990, pp. 258–72.

2 See, for example: Sanders (n. 1 above), ch. 5; and D. Reynolds, *Britannia Overruled. British Policy and World Power in the Twentieth Century*, London: Longman, 1991, especially chs 7–10.

3 J. Young, *Britain and European Unity, 1945–1992*, London: Macmillan, 1993, p. 167.

4 P. Sharp, 'The Place of the EC in the Foreign Policy of British Governments, 1961–71', *Millennium*, vol. 11 (1982), pp. 155–71; S. George, *Britain and European Integration since 1945*, Oxford: Blackwell, 1991, especially ch. 2. George attempts to argue that such aims constitute an alternative British global idealism. Drawing from Sanders' discussion (see n. 1 above), such aims may be interpreted as too closely related to national self-interest to justify George's claim.

5 Young (n. 3 above), pp. 107–19.

6 S. George, *An Awkward Partner, Britain in the European Community*, Oxford: Oxford University Press, 1990.

7 M. Clarke, *British External Policy Making in the 1990s*, London: Macmillan, 1992, pp. 30–43, 64–8.

8 S. George, *An Awkward Partner, Britain in the European Community*, 2nd edn, Oxford: Oxford University Press, 1994, chs 6–8:

9 Young (n. 3 above), p. 183; George, *An Awkward Partner*, 2nd edn, p. 260.

10 N. Ashford, 'The Political Parties' in: S. George (ed.), *Britain and the European Community. The Politics of Semi-Detachment*, Oxford: Clarendon, 1992, pp. 119–48; D. Baker, A. Gamble and S. Ludlam, 'Mapping Conservative Fault Lines: the Problem of Typology', in: P. Dunleavy and J. Stanyer (eds), *Contemporary Political Studies 1994*, London: Political Studies Association, pp. 278–98.

11 W. Wallace, 'Foreign Policy' in: D. Kavanagh and A. Seldon, *The Major Effect*, London: Macmillan, 1994, pp. 283–300.

12 J. Bulpitt, 'Conservative Leaders and the Euro-ratchet: Five Doses of Scepticism', *Political Quarterly*, vol. 63 (1992), pp. 258–75.

13 For a general discussion of methodology, see: S. Smith and M. Smith, 'The Analytical Background: Approaches to the Study of British Foreign Policy', in: M. Smith, S. Smith and B. White (eds), *British Foreign Policy: Tradition, Change and Transformation*, London: Unwin Hyman, 1988, pp. 3–23. For a discussion of the élite methodology that the essay implicitly draws upon, see:

P. Evans, D. Rueschemeyer and T. Skocpol, *Bringing the State Back in*, Cambridge: Cambridge University Press, 1985; and J. Bulpitt, *Territory and Power in the United Kingdom*, Manchester: Manchester University Press, 1983.

14 L. Colley, *Britons: Forging the Nation 1707–1837*, London: Pimlico, 1992, introduction.

15 H. Perkin, *The Origins of Modern English Society*, London: Routledge & Kegan Paul, 1969.

16 S. Beer, *Britain against Itself*, London: Faber, 1982.

17 See: M. Hollis and S. Smith, *Explaining and Understanding in International Relations*, Oxford: Clarendon, 1991, chs 6 and 8.

18 See, for example: S. Bulmer, 'Britain and European Integration: of Sovereignty, Slow Adaptation, and Semi-detachment', in George (ed.) (n. 10 above), pp. 1–29.

19 N. Ashford, 'The Political Parties', in George (ed.) (n. 10 above), pp. 119–48.

20 The analysis in this paragraph re-interprets the evidence offered in George (n. 6 above), chs 1–4, and Young (n. 3 above), chs 3–6.

21 See: D. Marquand, *The Unprincipled Society*, London: Fontana, 1988.

22 A. Gamble, *The Free Economy and the Strong State*, London: Macmillan, 1988. See also: D. Kavanagh, *Thatcherism and British Politics. The End of Consensus?* Oxford: Oxford University Press, 1990.

23 H. Young, *One of Us*, London: Macmillan, 1990, pp. 184–5.

24 See: G. Denton, 'Restructuring the EC Budget: Implications of the Fontainebleau Agreement', *Journal of Common Market Studies*, vol. 23 (1984), pp. 117–40.

25 George (n. 6 above), chs 5–6.

26 See: Young (n. 23 above), pp. 144–9.

27 D. Judge, 'Incomplete Sovereignty: the British House of Commons and the Completion of the Internal Market in the European Communities', *Parliamentary Affairs*, vol. 41 (1988), pp. 441–55; C. Crouch and D. Marquand, *The Politics of 1992: Beyond the Single European Market*, Oxford: Basil Blackwell, 1990; George (n. 6 above), ch. 6.

28 See: P. Taylor, 'The New Dynamics of EC Integration in the 1980s', in: J. Lodge (ed.), *The European Community and the Challenge of the Future*, London: Pinter, 1989.

29 See, for example: M. Foley, *The Rise of the British Presidency*, Manchester: Manchester University Press, 1993.

30 S. Wilks, 'Economic Policy', in: P. Dunleavy, A. Gamble, I. Holliday and G. Peele (eds), *Developments in British Politics 4*, London: Macmillan, 1993, pp. 221–45.

31 M. Thatcher, *Britain and Europe*, London: Conservative Political Centre, 1988.

32 See: N. Lawson, *The View from Number 11. Memoirs of a Tory Radical*, London: Corgi, 1993, chs 39–40, 52–3, 71–7.

33 Differing views of the domestic political economy of Lawson's policy to enter the ERM may be found in: A. Scott, 'Britain and the EMS: an Assessment of the Treasury and Civil Service Committee Report', *Journal of Common Market Studies*, vol. 24 (1986), pp. 187–201; and H. Thompson, 'Why is UK Economic Policy-making Non-Strategic? The Case of ERM Membership', in: P. Dunleavy and J. Stanyer (eds), *Contemporary Political Studies 1994*, vol. 2, pp. 855–65.

34 For confirmation of Lawson's approach see the Commons report of his resignation speech, *Independent*, 1 November 1989.

35 Ashford (n. 10 above); D. Baker, A. Gamble and S. Ludlam, '1846 . . . 1906 . . . 1996? Conservative Splits and European Integration', *Political Quarterly*, vol. 64 (1993), pp. 420–34.
36 The analysis provided in this paragraph is derived from Young (n. 23 above), pp. 156–60.
37 See: W. Keegan and N. Wapshott, 'The Pound in Europe', *Observer*, 7 October 1990; Lawson (n. 32 above), ch. 80.
38 Foley (n. 29 above), pp. 179–82.
39 D. Kavanagh, 'A Major Agenda?', in: D. Kavanagh and A. Seldon, *The Major Effect*, London: Macmillan, 1994, pp. 3–17.
40 For an indication of their views, see: D. Hurd, *Our Future in Europe*, London: Conservative Political Centre, 1993; M. Heseltine, *The Challenge of Europe: Can Britain Win?*, London: Weidenfeld & Nicolson, 1989.
41 See: Foley (n. 29 above), chs 7–8; A. Seldon, 'The Conservative Party', and P. Riddell, 'Major and Parliament', in: Kavanagh and Seldon, pp. 29–45 and 46–63.
42 For a comprehensive discussion of the contents and implications of the Treaty on European Union, see: A. Duff, J. Pinder and R. Pryce (eds), *Maastricht and Beyond. Building the European Union*, London: Routledge, 1994.
43 See Chapter 6.
44 D. Baker, A. Gamble and S. Ludlam, 'The Parliamentary Siege of Maastricht', *Parliamentary Affairs*, vol. 47 (1994), pp. 37–60.
45 For a discussion of how the UK pound sterling came to leave the ERM, see *The Economist*, 9 January 1993, pp. 28–9.
46 *Guardian*, 31 March 1994; *Guardian*, 29 November 1994; *Independent*, 19 January 1995.
47 C. Brown, *Independent*, 20 January 1995.
48 J. Major, 'Europe: A Future that Works'; and CDU/CSU, 'Reflections on European Policy', both in *European Access*, 1994, no. 5, pp. 6–15.
49 A. Bevins, *Observer*, 22 January 1995; P. Webster, *The Times*, 10 February 1995.
50 See, for example: J. Palmer, *Guardian*, 17 January 1995.
51 M. White, *Guardian*, 2 March 1995.
52 This analysis is derived from Major (n. 48 above); A. Bevins (n. 49 above); and White (n. 51 above).
53 See, for general surveys: George (ed.) (n. 10 above); and S. Bulmer, S. George and A. Scott (eds), *The United Kingdom and EC Membership Evaluated*, London: Pinter, 1992.
54 D. Sanders and G. Edwards, 'Consensus and Diversity in Elite Opinion: the Views of the British Foreign Policy Elite in the Early 1990s', *Political Studies*, vol. 42 (1994), pp. 413–40.
55 W. Grant, *Business and Politics in Britain*, 2nd edn, London: Macmillan, 1993, pp. 166–92.
56 See: S. Tindale, 'Learning to Love the Market: Labour and the European Community', *Political Quarterly*, vol. 63 (1992), pp. 276–300; and B. Rosamund, 'National Labour Organisations and European Integration: British Trade Unions and "1992"', *Political Studies*, vol. 41 (1993), pp. 420–34.
57 M. Keating and B. Jones, 'Scotland and Wales: Peripheral Assertion and European Integration', *Parliamentary Affairs*, vol. 44 (1991), pp. 311–24.
58 See: S. Mazey and J. Richardson, 'British Pressure Groups in the European Community: the Challenge of Brussels', *Parliamentary Affairs*, vol. 45 (1992), pp. 92–107; and: M. Goldsmith, 'The Europeanisation of Local Government', *Urban Studies*, vol. 30 (1993), pp. 683–99.

59 Most work referred to provides a complex picture of approaches towards the EC/EU in the UK political system. See, for example: Stephen George's 'Conclusion' to *Britain and the European Community* (n. 10 above), pp. 202–7.

60 See: N. Nugent, 'British Public Opinion and the European Community', in: George, ibid., pp. 172–201; D. Butler and U. Kitzinger, *The 1975 Referendum*, London: Macmillan, 1976.

6 In the strategic triangle

Denmark and the European Union

Nikolaj Petersen

INTRODUCTION

Since 1985 Danish policy towards the European Community (EC) has begun to undergo significant change. A 'foot-dragging' posture, especially prevalent in the field of institutional reform, has gradually been replaced by a more active and supportive policy, culminating in May 1992 when the government and Parliament (*Folketing*) approved the Maastricht Treaty. Defeat in the subsequent referendum in June 1992 forced the politicians to retreat somewhat from the Treaty, however, and as a result Denmark acquired a special status within the European Union at the EC's Edinburgh Summit in December 1992. This solution was then approved in a second referendum in May 1993. Danish European policy rebounded from the extreme position of 1992, but the pendulum did not quite swing back to the pre-1985 position. However, the forthcoming Inter-Governmental Conference (IGC) in 1996 may once again tear open the divide between the politicians, the public and the European Union that was revealed in 1992–3.

The controversies over the Maastricht Treaty are a perfect illustration of what may be termed the 'strategic triangle' in Danish EC/EU politics. This triangle has three corners: the politicians, public opinion, and the EU and its member states. A sustainable Danish EC/EU policy requires not only that the politicians agree among themselves (always a dubious proposition) and with their EU partners; they also need the support of the public. But, as the Danish public is inherently Eurosceptic, political life in the strategic triangle is difficult and often frustrating.

THE MAKING OF DANISH EU POLICY

As domestic factors have a major impact on Denmark's European policy, it is natural to take a brief look at how this policy is formulated. First, Parliament and the political parties play more central roles than in any other member state. Denmark is normally governed by minority governments and, even though the effect of this is mitigated by the tendency to form broad foreign-policy coalitions,[1] the government cannot count on automatic support in the Folketing. This was especially the case with the non-socialist Schlüter government (1982–93), whose foreign and security policy was often defeated by a so-called alternative majority in the Folketing.[2]

In addition, the Folketing has exerted its power in EC matters by creating (in 1960) a powerful Market Relations Committee (*Markedsudvalget*) and gradually increasing its powers. Both in 1973 (following Denmark's membership of the EC), in 1986 (after the SEA), and in 1993 (after the Maastricht Treaty) the influence of the Folketing and the Market Relations Committee increased as a consequence of inter-party agreements.[3]

Public opinion has a significant impact on EC/EU policies because of a strong political convention to the effect that major changes in Denmark's formal relationship with the Community should be decided by referendum. The background to this is the 1953 Constitution, according to which sovereignty rights can only be delegated to international bodies by a five-sixths majority of all members of the Folketing (that is at least 150 votes for), or – failing that – by a simple majority in the Folketing followed by approval by a simple majority in a popular referendum. As a result referenda were held both in 1972 on membership and in 1986 on the ratification of the Single European Act. The twin referenda of June 1992 and May 1993 served to confirm further the convention that the people are the final arbiter of Denmark's EC/EU policy. Thus, before the last referendum seven political parties agreed that Denmark's relationship to four main aspects of the Maastricht Treaty (citizenship, Economic and Monetary Union, defence policy and justice and home affairs) should be finally decided by referendum and should only be changed by a new referendum at some time in the future.

This makes public opinion an all-important variable in Danish EC politics. Even though the issue of EC membership *per se* went off the political agenda in the late 1980s, the public remains deeply Eurosceptical, and the contents of EC/EU policy are heatedly contested as is demonstrated by the No vote in 1992. Overall, the Danish public is significantly less supportive of European integration than in most other member states except the UK. The majority of Danes instinctively prefer intergovernmental co-operation to supranational integration, and only about one fifth of the public can be characterized as convinced supporters of deeper integration.[4]

DENMARK AND THE EUROPEAN COMMUNITY 1972–90

Denmark joined the Community in January 1973 together with Britain and Ireland and following a referendum in which 63 per cent of the electorate voted Yes and 37 per cent No. The chief motivation for the Yes vote then was economic, especially the expected benefits to Danish agriculture from the Common Agricultural Policy (CAP), while the chief reason for the No vote was political, namely the fear of reduced national sovereignty and self-determination.[5] This attitudinal pattern has not changed much since then: support for the Community and the Maastricht Treaty is still mainly motivated by fears of economic loss, even though positive political arguments have also entered the debate, while opposition focuses on political threats to sovereignty and autonomy.

In the government's official motivation for joining the Community in 1973 economic arguments were pre-eminent as well and, in fact, during most of the following period Danish politicians saw the Community as principally an economic arrangement. This view was especially prevalent among the Social Democrats, many of whom remained sceptical about the Community's political goals. Danish governments, therefore, regularly rejected plans for an expansion of the Community into the political domain as suggested, for example, in the Tindemans Report (1975), the Genscher-Colombo initiative of the early 1980s or the Spinelli Plan of 1984. The Dooge Report of 1985 was sprinkled with Danish footnotes and reservations and at the Milan Summit in June 1985 Denmark opposed holding the inter-governmental conference that negotiated the Single European Act (SEA). Despite its 'foot-dragging' attitude towards constitutional reform, Denmark did, however, play a full part in economic co-operation and joined both EPC (European Political Co-operation) and the EMS (European Monetary System). And Denmark also acquired the reputation of being the 'nice guy' with respect to implementing and respecting EC policies at the national level.

The Single European Act (SEA) created political drama in Copenhagen. The Schlüter government of 1982–8, consisting of four non-socialist parties, supported the SEA, but was defeated in the Folketing by a majority coalition of opponents, most notably the Social Democrats, the Radicals (both normally pro-EC parties) and the anti-EC People's Socialist Party. Rather than accepting defeat and a difficult situation vis-à-vis the EC, the Schlüter Cabinet reacted by calling a non-binding referendum, which was held on 27 February 1986. The voters responded by approving the SEA by 56 per cent to 44 – mostly because the government succeeded in making it a question of Denmark's continued membership of the Community.[6]

After this sobering defeat the opposition parties started to modify their policies towards the Community. The Internal Market was welcomed in almost all political circles in Denmark, and the Social Democrats slowly warmed towards a general expansion of the EC's powers, for example in environmental and labour market questions (the social dimension).[7] After the European upheaval of 1989 the *Einbindung* of Germany became an important additional motivation.

Initially, the twin ideas of an economic and monetary union (EMU) and a political union caused serious domestic problems. While the government had few objections to the EMU, the Social Democrats had considerable initial reservations, not to speak of the left-wing parties, who fought the idea vehemently. To the Social Democrats the emphasis in the original EMU plan was too much on anti-inflation to the detriment of objectives like employment, environmental concerns and a more equal division of societal values. The party also objected to the idea of automatic progress through the projected three phases of the EMU.

By April 1990, after a joint French–German initiative, political union came to dominate discussions. As presented by Chancellor Kohl and President Mitterrand, political union was meant to deal with the democratization of the Community, its increased effectiveness, its broadening to new areas of competence and its inclusion of all aspects of foreign and security policy. Some of these items had already started to be discussed in Denmark: for example, the need for greater openness in the EC and a strengthening of policies concerning the environment, the social dimension, consumer protection, and so on, through more effective decision-making procedures. On the other hand the initiative raised traditionally sensitive questions for Denmark, such as an enhanced role for the European Parliament, the inclusion of security policy proper in EPC, as well as the very term 'political union'.

The initiative therefore gave rise to some disagreement in the Social Democratic Party. In the end a positive line prevailed, though motivated not least by the perceived need to find a European framework for the new Germany. By the summer of 1990 the Social Democrats had proposed an inter-party agreement on Denmark's position at the coming Inter-Governmental Conferences, and in October 1990 agreement was reached between the government parties (Conservatives, Liberals and Radicals) and the Social Democrats on a so-called government memorandum.[8] The paper, which bore unmistakable Social Democratic fingerprints, was also accepted by the Centre Democrats and the Christian People's Party. On the other hand, the People's Socialists who had gradually relaxed their opposition in principle to the Community, remained opposed to a deepening of the EC and to the notion of a European union. At the opposite end of the political spectrum the right-wing, populist Progress Party now strengthened its anti-Brussels critique and increasingly distanced itself from the official EC policy.

The government memorandum was the most pro-European statement of Danish goals so far; generally speaking it moved Danish EC policy from a relatively passive and defensive stance to an active and offensive one. It advocated a substantial widening of the EC's agenda with new areas of co-operation and proposed stronger decision-making procedures in environmental and social questions, including the use of majority decisions. It further demanded a greater degree of openness in the Community and stricter control of the Commission, the principal proposal being the creation of a Community ombudsman. The memorandum also accepted a certain strengthening of the European Parliament by expanding the co-operation procedure to new issue-areas, but did not foresee any new decision-making procedures, for the Parliament. Denmark's traditional opposition to changes in 'the natural balance' between the EC's institutions was reiterated, and the 'Luxembourg veto' was to be maintained.

The memorandum also addressed foreign and security policy. A gradual expansion of the Community's diplomatic and political tasks was welcomed, but on the continued basis of the consensus rule and expressly excluding defence policy co-operation, including 'joint military forces'. On the other hand, there was a certain readiness for practical co-ordination of EC and EPC matters, and the inclusion of the Commission in EPC, though without the right of initiative.

Finally, the memorandum referred to the proposed EMU, which was characterized as a natural offshoot of the Internal Market. Price stability should not be the only goal of the EMU; full employment and sustainable economic growth should be among its objectives as well. The memorandum did not take any firm stand on the EMU's third phase and the common currency, except for advocating a short second phase followed by a swift transition to the third phase.

DENMARK AND THE TREATY ON THE EUROPEAN UNION

During the Inter-Governmental Conferences of 1991 the Danish memorandum functioned as a delimitation of the government's room for manoeuvre.[9] It was also the background for the catalogue of draft texts for political union which were presented by the Danish government in March 1991.[10] These concentrated on giving the environment a prominent place in the overall objectives of the Union, allowing state subsidies for cultural purposes, and introducing minimum (not maximum!) levels for indirect and company taxation; furthermore, there were detailed proposals concerning the social dimension, environmental protection, consumer protection and the institution of an ombudsman. The government also proposed a short and rather conservative text concerning foreign and security policy, which referred military co-operation to the existing alliances.

During the IGC negotiations four main obstacles emerged as viewed from the Danish perspective. One was the draft formulation on the Treaty on European Union as 'a new stage in a process leading gradually to a Union with a federal goal'.[11] Foreign Minister Ellemann-Jensen (Liberal) considered this formula innocuous, but it was utterly unacceptable to the Social Democrats and a majority in the Folketing, which on 5 December 1991, just before the Maastricht Summit, enjoined the government not to accept any reference to the federal goal.

Other problems concerned foreign and security policy. It proved impossible to keep the whole range of foreign and security policy out of the treaty or to exclude the possibility of qualified majority voting. Again, the

Social Democrats firmly objected to the inclusion of defence policy in the treaty, and they were also strongly critical of associating the WEU with the Union, 'because this is the cold war model'. Already in 1990 the party had definitely rejected Danish membership of the WEU so that, when they finally acquiesced in the inclusion of a defence dimension in the Treaty, it was on the specific ground that it was tied to the WEU (which Denmark would not take part in) and that Sweden and other Nordic countries would very likely be members of the Community before the next round of defence discussions scheduled for 1996.

The third major problem concerned EMU. During 1991 the Social Democratic position on the third phase and the common currency hardened once again, leading to a demand that Denmark should not commit itself to participation in the third phase until the end of the second phase, and that the issue should be determined then by a referendum.

At the Maastricht Summit some of these problems were solved: the 'federal goal' disappeared, because it was also unacceptable to Britain; a chapter on consumer protection was reinstated in the treaty text after having been removed earlier; and Denmark got a special protocol on EMU, which noted the possibility of a Danish referendum on the third phase, and which allowed Denmark not to commit itself to it until after the conclusion of the second phase.

In important respects the Maastricht Treaty reflected Danish demands and priorities. Its formulations concerning an EC ombudsman were more or less literally copied from the Danish draft; the texts on environmental protection, the social dimension and consumer protection, while not ideal, came close to what had been demanded by the Danish government; Danish state support for the arts could continue; and Denmark got special clauses concerning EMU and also the sale of summer houses.[12]

Denmark had, however, also compromised, for example over the powers of the Parliament and the possibility of majority voting on foreign and defence policy. The inclusion of a defence dimension (Article J.4) was another such concession, even though its practical implications for Denmark would be limited as long as Denmark stayed out of the WEU.

On balance, the six pro-EC parties judged the Maastricht Treaty to be an acceptable framework for Denmark's position in Europe, and voted unanimously for it at the final parliamentary reading on 12 May, which confirmed the Treaty by 130 votes to 25. This was the first time the Social Democrats and the Radicals had managed to present an unbroken party line in a decisive EC vote; both in 1972 and 1986 there had been dissenting votes. Parliamentary opposition was now confined to the Socialist People's Party on the left and the Progress Party on the right. This vote was the culmination of the rapprochement between the Danish political establishment and 'Europe' which had started in the mid-1980s: that is, an acceptable compromise had been found between two of the corners of the strategic triangle. Now only the third corner, public opinion, remained to be included.

THE DEBACLE: 2 JUNE 1992 AND ITS AFTERMATH

Even though the six parties had voted together for the Maastricht Treaty in the Folketing, they split apart in the subsequent referendum campaign. The Liberals were openly pro-European and pro-integrationist, the Conservatives pursued a more cautious national line and kept aloof from federalist phraseology, while the Social Democrats tried to keep their distance from the governing parties by advocating a so-called 'honest yes' to the Treaty. Its campaign, however, was overshadowed by a serious leadership crisis in which the party chairman, Svend Auken, was ousted in April 1992 by a challenger, Poul Nyrup Rasmussen. As a result, the Social Democratic party machine and its activists conducted only a lacklustre campaign in favour of the Treaty.

The result of the referendum of 2 June 1992 – 50.7 per cent No and 49.3 per cent Yes – indicated that the political establishment had seriously underestimated the public's scepticism towards the European Union and overrated the degree of opinion shift as a result of the changing situation in Europe. While the politicians had reacted by a more offensive attitude to European integration, the public seemed to prefer a continuation of the old defensive attitude. The result was a serious, unexpected setback for the policy line followed since 1986. This was a special problem for the Social Democratic Party, a majority of whose voters defected from the party line.

The referendum, of course, put all the pro-EC forces in an extremely difficult political position. The Maastricht compromise between the Danish political establishment and the Community had failed to win the support of the third corner in Denmark's strategic triangle, which meant that the government was unable to deliver the ratification it had promised when signing the treaty. The task of the government and the other pro-unionist forces was therefore to find a new settlement with Denmark's EC partners which could be presented to the people with some certainty of success in another referendum, that is to find a new and more stable balance between public opinion and the European mainstream. Considering the distance between these, this threatened to be a truly Herculean task.[13]

The dilemma had three logical solutions, each of which suffered from serious drawbacks, however: a settlement that might unite the political establishment and public opinion would probably have difficulty finding favour with the other EC member states; a solution that would unite once more the Danish political establishment and its EC partners (as the Maastricht Treaty had done) was likely to be unsatisfactory to the majority of public opinion. And, finally, a compromise between the EC and public opinion, for example, on giving Denmark an associate status in the

Union, would very likely be considered unacceptable by the political establishment. The problem was compounded by the fact that the EC foreign ministers immediately after the referendum – and with the full support of the Danish Government – declared that there could be no renegotiation of the Maastricht Treaty.

After the referendum the anti-unionist parties and grassroots organizations demanded that the people's verdict should be unreservedly respected and that the government should therefore inform the other EC members of Denmark's inability to ratify the Treaty. This conclusion, however, was unacceptable to the pro-unionist parties who feared that this would imperil the entire integration process and lead to Denmark's isolation in Europe.

The government's initial strategy was to sit tight, hoping for certain changes and reforms towards democracy and openness in the Union, which could then be presented to the public in another referendum as a kind of 'Maastricht with roses' solution. This avenue was decisively rejected by the Social Democrats, however, who demanded substantial changes in Denmark's relationship with the Union. Without formally opening the Treaty Denmark should be granted certain exemptions from it, which would make it more palatable to the public than Maastricht. What was demanded was a 'Maastricht without thorns'.

Consequently, political interest came to focus on the reasons for the rejection of the Maastricht Treaty as mirrored by public opinion polls and academic surveys. These were fairly unanimous in singling out the unionist aspects of the Treaty as the problematic ones. In one survey respondents were asked their opinion of ten aspects of the Treaty, only four of which were accepted by a majority or plurality of the respondents. These were the breakdown of trade barriers (61 per cent for), the Internal Market (59 per cent), Economic and Monetary Union (45 per cent) and 'cohesion' (42 per cent). On the other hand, majorities or pluralities rejected a common foreign policy (46 per cent against), a common defence policy (50 per cent), the social dimension (44 per cent), a United States of Europe (59 per cent) and a common European citizenship (73 per cent). When asked an open question about the reason for their vote, 44 per cent of the opponents mentioned 'loss of sovereignty/national freedom of action' and 16 per cent opposition to a common foreign and security policy, while 10 per cent were generally against the Union as such.[14]

That is, people voted against the Treaty for fear of specific aspects of the European Union, especially the loss of sovereignty and national freedom of action that the Union was seen to imply. There was widespread support for the Community as a successful economic arrangement, even among the anti-unionists. But a majority of the Danish population was opposed to the Community being transformed into a union with common policies, especially in the high politics area of foreign and defence policy. They were also opposed to transferring further competences to the Community, except in narrowly defined issue-areas, such as environmental politics.

Polls also indicate that those who voted Yes were not very convinced of the political arguments for the Union. In fact, it can be estimated that fewer than 20 per cent of all Danes support a federal Europe.

Other clues as to the possible contents of a special arrangement for Denmark came from the stated views of the anti-unionist parties and organizations. In May 1992, that is before the referendum, the Socialist People's Party had published its demands for renegotiation in the case of a No vote, the most important ones being that Denmark should keep out of the EMU and defence policy co-operation and not take part in majority voting in foreign and defence policy, in union citizenship and in supra-national co-operation in the field of justice and home affairs; nor should Denmark be committed to the unionist goals of the Treaty. The same neuralgic points had been singled out in a joint declaration by the anti-unionist organizations prior to the referendum.[15]

In September the Social Democratic Party congress adopted a resolution, which mirrored some of the opponents' demands, concentrating on a rejection of participation in the defence dimension, including the WEU, and in the EMU's third phase, non-commitment towards EU citizenship and rejection of supranational co-operation in asylum and police matters. Later in the month the Radical Party adopted similar demands at their annual convention.

The way out of the impasse was a paper known as the 'National Compromise', a concept coined by the new leader of the People's Socialists, Holger K. Nielsen, who in October 1992 invited the Social Democrats and Radicals to talks on a joint initiative to solve the crisis. In a matter of a few days agreement was reached on a paper which was subsequently presented to the Conservative–Liberal Government on a take-or-leave-it basis. The paper was also accepted by the Centre Democrats and the Christian People's Party.

Basically the memorandum, which was finally agreed on 30 October 1992 as Denmark's official position in the anticipated negotiations with the other EC member states, was a compromise between the anti-unionist People's Socialists and the lukewarm Social Democratic and Radical pro-unionists. The government, and especially the Liberal Party of Foreign Minister Uffe Ellemann-Jensen, disliked the memorandum, but chose to support it as the lesser evil – the greater evil being national dissension and conflict on an issue of overriding national importance.[16]

The document, entitled *Denmark in Europe*, was subsequently presented by Uffe Ellemann-Jensen to the individual EC governments, while the new leader of the Social Democratic Party, Poul Nyrup Rasmussen, canvassed Socialist and Social Democratic parties across the Community. Fundamentally the paper was meant as a formula which would enable Denmark to sign the Maastricht Treaty and so become part of the European Union. The People's Socialists' demand for renegotiation of the Treaty was quietly dropped, as was their original demand that Denmark's 'solution' could become a model for new members of the Community, if they so wished. It was also stated in the paper that Denmark would not object to the other members' expanding their co-operation in the fields where Denmark received exemptions. These were mainly concessions on the part of the People's Socialists.

The core of the document consisted of a number of demands: Denmark should be allowed to keep out of the defence dimension and the common currency and to remain uncommitted with respect to Union citizenship and supranational co-operation in justice and home affairs; on these questions Denmark should not be bound by the Treaty's unionist goals, either. Furthermore, an agreement should be legally binding and unlimited in time.

Apart from these fundamental points, other less ultimatum-like demands were voiced, as well, such as greater openness in the EC, a clearer definition of the subsidiarity principle, less bureaucracy, and a strengthening of the EC's efforts with respect to the environment, the social dimension, the Internal Market and unemployment. Finally, the National Compromise demanded that negotiations with applicant countries should be speeded up and that their special conditions (history, culture and traditions) should be taken into account.

THE EDINBURGH AGREEMENT AND AFTER

Somewhat surprisingly in view of the negative European response to the referendum in June and to the National Compromise of October 1992, the European Council at its meeting in Edinburgh on 11–12 December 1992 largely accepted the Danish demands. The road to agreement was shorter, and the willingness of the Eleven to accommodate the Danes greater, than had been expected. The British Presidency played an important role by finding the legal key to agreement and by threatening not to ratify the Treaty until after a solution to the Danish problem had been found. Second, the Danish negotiators, Prime Minister Poul Schlüter and Foreign Minister Uffe Ellemann-Jensen, were skilful and hard-nosed in arguing a case which they themselves did not support wholeheartedly. Third, although the EC governments were severely critical, there was considerable sympathy for Denmark among their publics who were concerned about the many aspects of the Union that had caused Danish voters to say No. Finally, the Community was plagued by a host of other problems and therefore interested in disposing of the Danish one.

By and large, the Edinburgh Agreement[17] was therefore a vindication of the Danish negotiating position. On subsidiarity the European Council agreed on a number of principles which were not very explicit and operative, but which were at least compatible with the Danish notion of 'nearness'.[18] The Council also agreed to the principle of a more open Community, even though the practical outcome was quite modest: improved access for the press to Council meetings, some open debates in the Council, publication of formal votes in the Council, and so on. The Council also agreed that talks with Austria, Sweden and Finland should commence in early 1993, with accession being predicated on full acceptance of the Treaty and of the *acquis communautaire*, but with the possibility of transitional arrangements. This was highly satisfactory for the Danish Government.

The solutions to the specific Danish demands were included in a special annex to the Edinburgh communiqué. The Heads of State and Government (*not* the European Council as such) agreed on the specific points raised by Denmark, but also noted Denmark's intention not to hamper closer co-operation in the Union in these areas. On Union citizenship the decision emphasized clarification, rather than modification of the Maastricht Treaty. A Danish declaration, which the other members took note of, spelled out the difference between member state citizenship and Union citizenship, and stated that citizens of the EC either had or would receive the right to vote and to stand as candidates in local and EP elections in Denmark.

The text on Economic and Monetary Union recognized that Denmark wanted to stay outside its third phase, but would participate fully in the second phase and in the Exchange Rate Mechanism. On defence the decision acknowledged that Denmark was not obliged to become a member of the WEU and that Denmark would not participate in 'the elaboration and implementation of decisions and actions of the Union which have defence implications'. As a consequence, Denmark would renounce its right to exercise the Presidency in such cases. Finally, the decision noted that Denmark would participate fully in the Union in matters relating to justice and home affairs.

The decision finally noted that it would take effect on the date the Maastricht Treaty came into effect, its duration being governed by Articles Q and N.2. (Whether this meant 1996 (N.2) or 'indefinitely' (Q) was not quite clear.) It was also noted that Denmark might at any time return to co-operation under the Union Treaty in the exempted areas.

In a separate declaration the European Council emphasized that nothing in the Treaty prevented any member state from maintaining or introducing more stringent protection measures (if they were compatible with the Treaty, that is) concerning working conditions, social policy, consumer protection and the environment nor from pursuing its own policy with respect to the distribution of income or the improvement of social standards.

In a Final Declaration the Council struck a sort of compromise concerning the disputed *finalités* of the Union. On the one hand, it was said that, in the four specified areas and as far as Denmark was concerned, the Treaty goals should be interpreted on the basis of the Edinburgh documents. On the other hand, it was claimed that these documents were compatible with the Treaty and did not question its goals.

An overall evaluation of the Edinburgh Agreement must conclude that Danish demands were to a large extent accommodated. Denmark achieved important exemptions, not included in the original Maastricht deal, concerning EMU and defence. That is, a new deal had been struck between the political establishment and the EC which presumably was somewhat closer to the public-opinion corner of the strategic triangle. The agreement was therefore positively received by the seven parties to the National Compromise, including the Socialist People's Party whose General Council confirmed it by 33 votes to 4. Only the Progress Party maintained its opposition, arguing that the agreement did not differ significantly from the Maastricht Treaty, that is that Edinburgh was nothing but 'Maastricht with roses'.

In the circumstances, the opposition campaign before the referendum of 18 May 1993 was led by the Progress Party and, especially, the so-called June Movement, an anti-unionist grassroots organization set up in 1992. The opponents argued along several lines: Edinburgh was only a dressed-up Maastricht Treaty; a Yes would irretrievably place Denmark on the slippery slope towards full European Union; a renewed rejection would not lead to Denmark's forced withdrawal from the Community, but rather to the final demise of the Maastricht Treaty itself. (The latter argument was based on British intimations to the effect that it would be impossible for Her Majesty's Government to introduce the Treaty in the House of Commons in the face of another Danish rejection.)

The proponents also followed several lines of argument. In their view Edinburgh did differ qualitatively from the platform presented in June 1992 and, far from being democratically suspect, the Agreement signified that the politicians had in fact listened to the people and taken their views seriously. The supporters also termed it wishful thinking to suggest that another No would not have serious consequences for Denmark, which, after having had its demands met in Edinburgh, could not expect further understanding from the other EC members. A rejection of Edinburgh would therefore endanger Denmark's whole position in the Community and put her membership at stake.

In the circumstances, the result of the referendum of 18 May 1993 was perhaps a foregone conclusion. However, the victory of the Yes side, 56.8 per cent against 43.2 per cent, was not too convincing, considering the fact that seven out of eight political parties in the Folketing stood behind it. Less than a fifth of the People's Socialists followed the new party line, and Social Democratic voters were about evenly split. In Copenhagen, the nation's capital, there was a majority against (55.4 per cent), while 59.9 per cent voted for in the western part (Jutland).[19]

The vote was no breakthrough for pro-integrationist views among the public. Immediately before the referendum only 8 per cent supported the idea of a United States of Europe with a common European government, while as many as 73 per cent thought that individual member countries should retain their full independence as well as their veto power in the Community.[20] Thus, while opposition to EC membership no longer plays a role in Danish politics among either the political élite or the public, there remains a widespread public reluctance to surrender more formal sovereignty to the Community.

DENMARK AND THE EUROPEAN UNION SINCE 1993

While it is evident that Denmark received important concessions at the Edinburgh Summit, their implications for her future participation in the Union remain unclear. Since 1 November 1993 Denmark has been a member of the European Union and has participated fully in its work except in the areas covered by the Edinburgh exemptions. However, as most of these concern future options, they do not count for very much in the day-to-day workings of the Union: by mid-1995 the Edinburgh exemptions had not had any direct impact on Denmark's role in the Union. Whether Denmark will continue to participate as a 'full-blown A member', as former Prime Minister Poul Schlüter argued after the Edinburgh Summit,[21] is however debatable.

In the defence field the trend towards closer co-ordination and co-operation between NATO and the WEU, which was confirmed by the NATO Summit in Brussels on 10–11 January 1994, questions the rationale of the Danish WEU exemption and raises the prospect of a certain marginalization within NATO. In the same way, renewed talk in the summer of 1994 of an EMU phase three puts a certain strain on the Danish position.

As already mentioned, the Edinburgh Agreement allows Denmark to give up her exemptions at any time and to revert to full participation in the European Union. This is not likely to happen in the foreseeable future, though. Before the 1993 referendum the seven political parties of the National Compromise pledged themselves officially not to revoke any of the Edinburgh exemptions unless approved in a referendum. Public opinion being what it is, this agreement in practice precludes changes in Denmark's formal position in the Union under present circumstances, that is at least until after the 1996 IGC. Suggestions by the Liberals and the Conservatives in 1994 that Denmark waive its reservations on membership of the WEU and on participation in the third phase of EMU have been firmly rejected by the present government of Social Democrats, Radicals and Centre Democrats.

The implications of Edinburgh depend, of course, on the direction and tempo of future European integration. In the summer of 1994 government and opposition started to brace themselves for the 1996 IGC, which is likely to strain Denmark's relationship with the EU and also relations between government and opposition. The 1996 version of Denmark's strategic triangle may be just as difficult to handle as its 1992 predecessor.

The problem is not only that the Edinburgh exemptions may come under pressure, but more generally that the public remains deeply sceptical of further integration, while the political establishment fears both integration and abandonment. Thus, in 1994 Foreign Minister Niels Helveg Petersen (Radical) reacted strongly to German suggestions of a two-tier European Union, in which Denmark would necessarily be placed in the second tier. Denmark should, he insisted, remain part of the European core notwithstanding the Edinburgh exemptions.

The public opinion/European Union dilemma is most pronounced for the Social Democratic Party, because its rank and file are mostly anti-unionist. While Liberals and Conservatives in opposition may demand a removal of the Edinburgh reservations, the government has to tread more cautiously, both because of its own voters, and because the People's Socialists – if they were estranged from the EU decision-making process – might create problems in a new referendum. The government is therefore caught between its awareness that a public debate on Denmark's future relationship with the Union is indispensable if public opinion is to be moved before the next referendum (presumably in the aftermath of the 1996 IGC) and its reluctance to open such a delicate debate before it is absolutely necessary.

CONCLUSIONS

Denmark and the European Community, 1985–95

In the period under discussion in this chapter Denmark approached the European mainstream in a continuous move until 1992 and then retreated somewhat as a result of the referendum. These movements were characterized by different mixes of Danish concessions and demands as well as policy 'bastions' erected and abandoned.

The main concession was to the general dynamics of European integration that emerged in the mid-1980s and culminated in the signing of the Maastricht Treaty in early 1992. In the early 1990s there was a general acknowledgement in Danish political circles that the European Community had become far and away most important of the four traditional pillars of Danish foreign policy, the others being: Nordic co-operation, NATO and the United Nations.

This re-orientation was unproblematic for the non-socialist government from 1982 to 1993, but implied a greater degree of policy change on the part of the Social Democratic Party, which had been the main author of the previous, 'foot-dragging' EC policy. To an even greater extent, the re-orientation of Danish EC policy implied policy revisions on the part of the People's Socialists, as they moved from opposition to acceptance of EC membership and, finally, to a rather qualified acceptance of the European Union as well.

In concrete terms Danish concessions involved the erosion of some of the traditional 'bastions' of Denmark's EC policy. Opposition to institutional change became less absolute, the Luxembourg veto lost political significance, and Denmark abandoned its opposition to majority decisions entirely. As the 1992 referendum showed, policy makers had made too many concessions during the Maastricht process for the taste of a majority of the population. Subsequently, some concessions had to be retracted, mainly in the form of national escape clauses, which did not affect the European Union as such.

An important aspect of Danish EC policy in this period was the increasing role of the demands made of the EC system. Prior to 1985 Danish governments had certainly made demands of the system in concrete matters, but from 1985 onwards Denmark also started to make specific demands on the Community's constitutional development. These demands made a certain impact, such as in the environmental sphere or with respect to the new institution of the ombudsman. After the 1992 referendum Denmark made further demands on the EC, at least some of which were conceded in Edinburgh.

Finally, while some of the older 'bastions' were left to erode, new ones were erected, especially after 1992. After being conceded in the Edinburgh Agreements, these 'bastions' were subsequently strengthened so that they can only be abandoned by Denmark after a new referendum.

In the end Denmark has managed to adapt to the European integration process since 1985. But it has been a tough process, both externally and internally, and the main problem has not been solved, namely the discrepancy between the Danish public and the European mainstream, which makes the politics of the strategic triangle so difficult. Public opinion has certainly moved a long way since 1985 when Denmark's very membership in the EC was still at issue. But the European mainstream has moved even faster and repeatedly strained the public's relationship with the EU. Unless some radical change in public opinion occurs or the European process stagnates, Denmark's EU policy is likely to continue to be characterized by troubled manoeuvrings in the strategic triangle.

Theoretical perspectives

Denmark's strategic triangle is to a certain extent a specific national phenomenon. But there are indications that similar triangles may come to complicate the EU policies of other member states. The secular trend towards democratization will increasingly involve the publics in Union politics, especially as it acquires more and more the characteristics of domestic politics. The reactions to the Danish referendum in other countries, such as Germany and France, showed that the European public is more critical of the Union than expected and less dormant than before. Furthermore, the EU's new member states (Austria, Finland and Sweden) have entered on the basis of referenda and will presumably feel obliged to refer future changes in the Union's constitutional arrangements to public approval.

The increasing involvement of the European publics raises important problems for the Union, which may respond in two ways: by a slowing-down in its constitutional development (it is hardly cost-effective to change the constitution twice every decade) or by a dramatic constitutional revision that gives those European publics a central role in the Union, that is, some kind of federalist solution. Courses in between these two extremes involve the risk of activating national strategic triangles and, even though the Union may live with one or a few active strategic triangles, it can hardly function if the Danish model is universalized.

The problems of the strategic triangle also have important implications for the study of European integration. First, the strategic triangle draws attention to the European Union's democratic deficit and to the need to develop conceptual models for its solution: this might include a closer look at various federalist models. Second, it points to increased attention to the so-called domestic politics approach to European integration.[22] But studies of the internal dynamics of national policy making are not enough, however important they are for our understanding of the major bargains in the EU system. What is needed is an approach that takes in all corners of the strategic triangle and focuses on the interplay between the national and the communitarian as well as the national and sub-national levels. Robert D. Putnam's notion of two-level foreign policy games may be a helpful one, as it envisages national leaders playing two games simultaneously – one with other governments, and another with their domestic environments.[23] In order to succeed, policy makers must not only be able to strike a deal with their external counterparts: they also have to have the backing of their domestic environments. This perspective has recently been applied with some interesting results to EU bargaining by Andrew Moravcik who also includes institutional aspects in the analysis.[24]

A somewhat similar notion lies behind adaptation theory, which posits foreign policy as a balancing on the part of policy makers of demands and changes emanating from their internal and external environments and which focuses on various overall strategies to cope with this balancing act. This perspective, which was originally developed by James N. Rosenau,[25] has recently been discussed in relation to the making of national policies towards the European Union and may prove another fruitful way of conceptualizing the politics of the strategic triangle.[26]

FURTHER READING

C. Due-Nielsen and N. Petersen (eds), *Adaptation and Activism: Danish Foreign Policy 1967–93*, Copenhagen: Danish Institute of International Affairs, 1995.

J. H. Haahr, *Looking to Europe. The EC Policies of the British Labour Party and the Danish Social Democrats*, Aarhus: Aarhus University Press, 1993.

M. Kelstrup (ed.), *European Integration and Denmark's Participation*, Copenhagen: Copenhagen Political Studies Press, 1992.

L. Lyck (ed.), *Denmark and EC Membership Evaluated*, London: Pinter, 1992.

P. Svensson, 'The Danish Yes to Maastricht and Edinburgh. The Referendum of May 1993', *Scandinavian Political Studies*, vol. 17 (1994), pp. 69–82.

T. Tiilikainen, and I. D. Petersen (eds), *The Nordic Countries and the EC*, Copenhagen: Copenhagen Political Studies Press, 1993.

NOTES

1 Denmark's EU policy is normally made by a broad coalition covering the Social Democratic Party (the largest and most important), the Radical Party (a small social-liberal party), the Conservative Party, the Liberal Party, the Centre Democrats and the Christian People's Party.

2 Between September 1982 and January 1993 Poul Schlüter (Conservative) led three subsequent government coalitions. The first one, from 1982 to 1988, was composed of Conservatives, Liberals, Centre Democrats and the Christian People's Party. The second one, from 1988 to 1991, consisted of Conservatives, Liberals and Radicals, while his last government (1991–93) was a coalition of Conservatives and Liberals. All the Schlüter cabinets were minority governments without a firm majority in the Folketing.

3 See: N.-J. Nehring, 'Parliamentary Control of the Executive', in: L. Lyck (ed.), *Denmark and EC Membership Evaluated*, London: Pinter, 1992, pp. 76–81. In October 1994 the Market Relations Committee changed its name to the Europe Committee [*Europa-udvalget*].

4 See: T. Worre, 'Den danske befolknings holdninger til EF i 1980erne' [The Danish Public's Attitudes towards the EC in the 1980s], in: B. N. Thomsen (ed.), *The Odd Man Out? Danmark og den europæiske integration 1948–1992* [The Odd Man Out? Denmark and European Integration, 1948–92], Odense: Odense Universitetsforlag, 1993, pp. 179–98.

5 See: N. Petersen and J. Elklit, 'Denmark Enters the European Communities', *Scandinavian Political Studies*, vol. 8 (1973), pp. 198–213; N. Petersen, 'Attitudes towards European Integration and the Danish Common Market Referendum', *Scandinavian Political Studies*, vol. 1 (new series) (1978), pp. 23–42.

6 See: T. Worre, 'Denmark at the Crossroads: The Danish Referendum of 28 [sic] February 1986 on the EC Reform Package', *Journal of Common Market Studies*, vol. 26 (1988), pp. 361–88.

7 See: J. H. Haahr, *Looking to Europe. The EC Policies of the British Labour Party and the Danish Social Democrats*, Aarhus: Aarhus University Press, 1993.

8 *Memorandum from the Danish Government*, 4 October 1990, reprinted in: F. Laursen and S. Vanhoonacker (eds), *The Intergovernmental Conference on Political Union. Institutional Reforms, New Policies and International Identity of the European Community*, Maastricht: European Institute of Public Administration, 1992, pp. 293–303.

9 See: F. Laursen, 'Denmark and European Political Union', in: Laursen and Vanhoonacker, pp. 63–78.

10 *Conference Document 1777/91*, 21 March 1991.

11 This formula was proposed by the Luxembourg Presidency in June 1991 and also included in the Dutch draft version prior to the Maastricht Summit.

12 This protocol allows Denmark to continue its ban on the sale of summer cottages to foreigners.

13 This problematic is dealt with in greater detail in N. Petersen, '"Game, Set and Match". Denmark and the European Union from Maastricht to Edinburgh', in: T. Tiilikainen and I. D. Petersen (eds), *The Nordic Countries and the EC*, Copenhagen: Copenhagen Political Studies Press, 1993, pp. 79–106.

14 K. Siune, P. Svensson and O. Tonsgaard, – *det blev et nej* [It Was a No], Aarhus: Politica, 1992, pp. 74 ff. See also: K. Siune, 'The Danes Said No to the Maastricht Treaty: The Danish EC Referendum of June 1992', *Scandinavian Political Studies*, vol. 16 (1993), pp. 93–103.

15 See: J. Iversen, *Det Nationale Kompromis. Danmark og det nye Europa* [The National Compromise. Denmark and the New Europe], Aarhus: SP-Forlag, 1992.

16 *Denmark in Europe*, 30 October 1992.

17 *Agence Europe*, 12 and 13 December 1993.

18 In Danish political parlance 'subsidiarity' [*subsidiaritet*] has become 'nearness' [*nærhed*]. Thus, subsidiarity is seen as a device for decentralization, while its centralizing aspects are de-emphasized.

19 See: P. Svensson, 'The Danish Yes to Maastricht and Edinburgh. The Referendum of May 1993', *Scandinavian Political Studies*, vol. 17 (1994), pp. 69–82.

20 *Politiken*, 18 May 1993.

21 *Politiken*, 13 December 1992.

22 See: S. Bulmer, 'Domestic Politics and EC Policy-Making', *Journal of Common Market Studies*, vol. xxi, no. 4 (1982–3).

23 See: R. D. Putnam, 'Diplomacy and Domestic Politics: The Logic of Two-Level Games', *International Organization*, vol. 43 (1988), pp. 427–59, and the articles in: P. B. Evans, H. K. Jacobson and R. D. Putnam, *Double-Edged Diplomacy: International Bargaining and Domestic Politics*, Berkeley, CA: University of California Press, 1993 (especially: A. Moravcik, 'Introduction. Integrating International and Domestic Theories of International Bargaining', pp. 4–42).

24 A. Moravcik, 'Preferences and Power in the European Community: A Liberal Intergovernmentalist Approach', *Journal of Common Market Studies*, vol. 31 (1993), pp. 473–524.

25 J. N. Rosenau, *The Adaptation of National Societies: A Theory of Political Systems Behaviour and Transformation*, New York: McCaleb-Seiler, 1970. For later developments of the theory, see: N. Petersen, 'Adaptation as a Framework for Foreign Policy Analysis', *Cooperation and Conflict*, vol. 12 (1977), pp. 221–50; and: H. Mouritzen, *Finlandization. Toward a General Theory of Adaptive Politics*, Aldershot: Avery, 1988.

26 See: M. Kelstrup, 'Small States and European Political Integration. Reflections on Theory and Strategy', in: Tiilikainen and Petersen (eds) (n. 13 above), pp. 136–63; and N. Petersen, 'Denmark and the European Community 1985–93', in: C. Due-Nielsen and N. Petersen (eds), *Adaptation and Activism: Danish Foreign Policy 1967–93*, Copenhagen: Danish Institute of International Affairs, 1995, pp. 189–224.

7   The crisis of the Italian state

Bruce Haddock

Governmental crises have been endemic in the post-war Italian Republic. Such crises in the past have served, however, to mask a deeper continuity. Individuals and interests had been able to consolidate their hold on crucial factions within the principal political parties, effectively preventing reforms which might have undermined or weakened their positions. The political parties in their turn, headed by the Christian Democrats (DC) and Socialists (PSI), had sought to control the crucial organs and interests of civil society through the control of patronage. This (essentially symbiotic) relationship between parties and interests involved mutual accommodation on such a scale that the political system has been described as 'blocked'.[1] It seemed that radical reform could not be countenanced because vested interests, including both capital and labour and a host of more specialized groups, would suffer. And if a significant interest were dislodged from the complex edifice which patronage had built up, some cautious commentators have argued that there is a real risk that the rest of the building could be brought down with it, threatening democracy itself.[2]

The crisis which has been developing over the last few years is of a quite different order. Conventional assumptions about relative electoral stability were overturned in the 1992 election. The DC and the reformed Communist Party (PDS) returned their worst results in the post-war period (29.7 per cent and 16.1 per cent respectively), while the PSI was also slightly down on its 1987 return (13.6 per cent from 14.3 per cent). The large fall in the old Communist Party (PCI) vote can in part be explained by the siphoning off of 5.6 per cent of the PCI vote to *Rifondazione comunista* when the Democratic Party of the Left (PDS) was formed in 1991. The emergence of the *Lega nord* as the fourth political force in Parliament, however, constituted a challenge to all the established political parties in Northern Italy. The increase in the *Lega* vote from 0.5 per cent in 1987 to 8.7 per cent in 1992 was unprecedented. Both the DC and the old Communist bloc had suffered at the hands of the *Lega*. Though it is generally seen as a right-of-centre party, it is clear that the *Lega* had an appeal in 1992 across the political spectrum. It could no longer be dismissed as an ephemeral protest movement. Emerging from Italy's economic heartland, it had made serious inroads into the positions of different political establishments. Its rhetoric, a curious blend of crude populism and constitutional analysis, had evoked an enthusiastic response from voters whose discontents had taken many forms. Most crucially, however, it had enabled voters who would never have dreamed of switching from the DC to the PCI or vice versa to come together, at least for the moment, in a common political party.[3]

The election of 1992 was described at the time as an 'earthquake'. Yet few can have anticipated the extent of the political changes that would be in store for Italy within the next two years. By the 1994 election the political landscape had altered so profoundly that commentators referred to a change of régime rather than a change of government, with casual reference in newspapers to the beginnings of a 'Second Republic'. The DC and PSI had both been disbanded. Significantly, however, their collapses followed corruption scandals and legal proceedings rather than a direct electoral reverse. The reformed electoral system had fostered new alliances, more or less effectively spatchcocked together, with a so-called *Polo delle libertà* (Freedom Alliance) opposing *Progressisti* (Progressive Alliance). A new political party, *Forza Italia*, had formed around the media magnate Silvio Berlusconi, capturing 21 per cent of the vote. Berlusconi's entry into politics had been spurred by the prospect of a left-wing victory following significant PDS successes in the municipal elections of December 1993. What was remarkable, in a country noted for the stability of its political subcultures, was that a party barely three months old could sweep to victory in a general election. The PDS and *Rifondazione comunista* improved upon their 1992 performances, especially in the South (20.4 per cent and 6 per cent respectively). But, with the demise of the DC, a gaping hole remained to be filled in the centre. In the event, what we see emerging is not reform in the centre but consolidation on the right. The National Alliance (AN), established as the acceptable face of the previously shunned neo-fascist Italian Social Movement (MSI), picked up a significant proportion of the southern DC vote (13.5 per cent). The *Lega* more or less sustained its 1992 position (8.4 per cent), though the party was felt to have lost ground significantly to *Forza Italia*. The *Lega*'s parliamentary position was, in fact, artificially inflated because of an early agreement on the division of seats struck with Berlusconi. Centre groupings suffered the most striking collapse in 1994. In a Chamber of Deputies of 630 seats, they ended up with only 46. This was an entirely novel situation for post-war Italy. Brokerage from the centre had given place to an appearance of polarized confrontation. Italians seemed to be faced with a new political game, played by new players, according to uncertain rules and conventions. Whether or not things are quite as they appear is, of course, quite another question.[4]

One expectation was disappointed in the very first months of the Berlusconi Government. It was widely held that the constitution and conventions of Italian political life had so refined the arts of *garantismo* (the stress on constitutional guarantees) that significant reform could be discounted. Frustrating though this state of affairs may appear to be in a political culture confronting major problems – massive public sector debt, systematic political corruption and organized crime – the stability of the system had nevertheless enabled the economy to flourish and guaranteed conventional civil rights. In 1948 it was by no means certain that democracy could be successfully rooted in Italy. We need only look to the political experience of Spain, Portugal and Greece in the post-war period to appreciate the enormity of the task facing the Italian political élite in the early years of the Republic. The maintenance of a broad anti-fascist consensus in the 1950s and 1960s must be seen as a major political achievement, opening Italy to the full benefits of economic renewal in Western Europe. If the price of stability was political stagnation, it might well have seemed to be a price worth paying in 1948.

The attractions of *garantismo* have faded somewhat in the public mind as urgent structural problems in the economy and administration demand attention. The more difficult economic situation in Europe after 1973 has also called for a clear sense of priorities in policy formulation. Part of the appeal of Berlusconi was clearly that he embodied the virtues of *decisionismo* (decisive government) rather than *garantismo*. He was identified with conspicuous success in a ruthlessly competitive world. In political terms he had the semblance of a new face with a ready smile, associated with the consumer rather than the array of producer interests, concerned more to project a plausible image than to accommodate factional interests. His governing alliance, however, never had any coherence in policy terms. The federalism of the *Lega* was starkly opposed to the state-centred rhetoric of the AN. Berlusconi was able to hold his coalition together by studiedly avoiding the substantive policy issues that divided his 'supporters', focusing instead on the presentation of an appearance of political and economic modernization.

Relations between coalition partners, in fact, continued in time-honoured fashion. Arguments in the first instance hinged upon the distribution of the most advantageous portfolios. Competition between the *Lega* and Berlusconi for the Ministry of the Interior very nearly brought the government down before it had been formally established. Nor did competition for the spoils of office stop with cabinet responsibilities. Some of the bitterest disputes have revolved around attempts to exert a measure of political control of the public radio and television service (RAI), the Bank of Italy and the judiciary. None of this should surprise us as hardened students of Italian politics. But the transparency of the political manipulation bodes ill for a lasting resolution of the problems that brought Italy to the brink of crisis in the first place.

In December 1994 tensions within the ruling coalition finally led to its demise. Relations between Berlusconi and Umberto Bossi, leader of the

Lega nord, had always been uneasy. Both were essentially competing for the support of the same group of disenchanted Northern voters – productively employed, often hostile to the traditional rhetoric of the left, but significantly excluded from the narrow circle of high financial and industrial interests that had dominated the politics of the Republic. Despite enjoying broad parity with *Forza Italia* in terms of parliamentary representation, the *Lega* found itself dangerously exposed. Berlusconi seemed to have profited more from the collapse of the old parties than the *Lega* and could offer a modernizing programme that did not run the risk of inflaming separatist sentiment. The *Lega*, by contrast, found itself compromised by the presence of the AN in government. Fini, leader of the AN, could claim (more or less plausibly) that his party had emerged with a new post-fascist identity. The dilemma for the *Lega* was that the grassroots reaction against both the establishment and the left was now split three ways. And in national political terms, both *Forza Italia* and the AN seemed better placed to convert that groundswell of opinion into cohesive political support.

Bossi's final break with Berlusconi can be interpreted as a desperate attempt to sustain an independent political identity for the *Lega*. He has tried to shift towards the centre, hoping to form a crucial component of a reconstituted middle ground. Discussions with the PDS and the Italian Popular Party (PPI), the reformed group of moderate and progressive Christian Democrats, have so far met with limited success. *Lega* proposals for far-reaching devolution are likely to be acceptable to a range of influential political groupings. What is less clear, however, is the resilience of *Lega* support in the light of a political realignment involving the PDS. *Lega* deputies and voters have generally regarded themselves as opponents of the left, even if they have been anxious to distinguish themselves from the far right. Much may depend on the capacity of the PDS to present itself as a modern left-of-centre alternative. For the moment, its historical baggage has proved a deterrent to the populist ethos dominating contemporary Italian politics. The *Lega* and the PDS can find common ground in their opposition to Berlusconi and the AN. Formulating a viable political programme or electoral alliance, however, remains a daunting task.

The roots of the current crisis are, in fact, obscure and hotly contested. In some quarters the democratic state, at least in its Italian version, had never been finally accepted. The De Lorenzo affair in 1964 highlighted the vulnerability of the state. During difficult negotiations between the President of the Republic, Antonio Segni, and Aldo Moro regarding the formation of a new government, General De Lorenzo, head of the *carabinieri*, was called in, unusually, for discussions with Segni. It subsequently emerged in 1969 that De Lorenzo had actually drawn up contingency plans for the arrest of key figures who could be seen as threats to public order, including prominent leaders on the left, together with the occupation of sensitive institutions. Precisely how far Segni was aware of the detail of De Lorenzo's plan remains unclear. Yet it is significant that discussions along these lines were held at all. We must assume that at least some political leaders on the centre and right, including presumably Moro himself, were informed that specific measures had been planned in the event of a deepening crisis. More importantly a distinction seems to have been drawn between the defence of the interests of the state and the defence of parliamentary institutions.

The pattern of the De Lorenzo affair was to be repeated in other projects that came to public attention in the 1980s. News of a secret masonic lodge (P2), bent upon the formation of an authoritarian alternative to parliamentary institutions within the political establishment, and headed by Licio Gelli, broke in 1981. Membership lists were discovered implicating politicians from the right and centre, together with leaders of the armed forces, Civil Service and the business community. It does not follow, of course, that all notional members of P2 were aware of the gamut of possibilities entertained by Gelli and his closest associates. Berlusconi himself, for example, claims not to have known anything of the specifically political thrust of the sect. But the fact remains that confidence in parliamentary institutions was sufficiently fragile for influential individuals to look to alternative means of securing their interests.

Counter-revolutionary contingency plans had, in fact, always been central to the thinking of the armed forces and secret services. NATO plans drawn up in the 1950s, at the height of the Cold War, involved provision in Western European states for emergency measures to be adopted in the event of a land offensive from the Soviet bloc. Italy, with its large 'communist' presence, seemed to some security analysts to pose special problems. Specific arrangements were made for Italy in 1966 under the NATO umbrella, described as the 'Gladio' connection, anticipating the assumption of emergency powers and the arrest of prominent PCI and trade-union leaders. Special training camps were established in Sardinia which Cossiga, among others, is known to have visited. The PCI, though it regarded itself as a principal guardian of the constitution, was thus ostracized both officially and unofficially.

In the context of these measures and attitudes, the terrorist offensives of the 1970s assume a larger and more alarming significance. They are indicative not only of deep-seated anti-democratic sympathies but also of a more sinister disregard for parliamentary institutions at the heart of the state. Some of the more spectacular terrorist atrocities, including the assassination of Aldo Moro in 1978, are now seen to have involved at least the connivance of the secret services and tacit political approval in some quarters. The so-called 'strategy of tension' on the far right, designed to provoke an authoritarian reaction on the part of the state, clearly played into the hands of those who doubted the long-term viability of parliamentary institutions in Italy. It remains a significant political achievement that the democratic state held firm in the face of these provocations, even if central groups within the political establishment were actually involved in subversive activities.

Opposition to the state more recently has been both more public and more vociferous. The emergence of the *Lega* is a symptom of growing resentment in the richer Northern regions regarding the corruption and inefficiency of the state. The immense sums which were pumped into the *Cassa per il Mezzogiorno* (Southern Development Fund), for example, are dismissed by the *Lega* as wholly counter-productive. They might have served to buttress the crucial DC clientèle networks in the South but, as a consequence, seriously distorted and restricted economic growth. All that happened in effect was that potential investment capital was channelled away from the North. Indeed by propping up established clientèle networks, including the *mafia*, state funds were seen as essentially perpetuating the *status quo*.

Nor is it difficult to appreciate the initial appeal of the *Lega*. They had focused their criticism specifically on the role of the parties, calling for an end to so-called *partitocrazia*. But clearly this could not be achieved without a wholesale remodelling of the Italian state. What is at issue here is not simply the reform of the Republic but the dismantling of the unitary state. Whether or not the *Lega*'s federal proposals should be taken seriously is not the central point. The polemical thrust of their rhetoric had targeted one of the sacrosanct foundation myths of the Italian state. The unification of the state in 1861 may have been contentious, but its celebration had been a crucial symbol in the cultivation of national identity. In the late 1980s, however, we have the spectacle of respected academics arguing not simply for a different interpretation of the *Risorgimento* but that unification was a mistake. Gianfranco Miglio, at the time regarded as a principal ideologist of the *Lega*, went so far as to describe the Italian nation as a 'myth', constructed by a particular élite in order to press its own advantage and interest.[5] Far from the state in 1861 reflecting the Italian nation, Miglio argued that the Piedmontese propagandists effectively fabricated the idea of the nation as a means of legitimizing the position of a conquering dynasty. These, clearly, are claims that strike at the heart of the political consensus that has underpinned the Italian state since 1861. In a political climate fraught with allegations of corruption and criminal collusion at the highest levels, they raise fundamental questions about obedience and obligation.[6]

Perhaps the most remarkable feature of the collapse of the (so-called) 'First Republic' is that its demise should have been hastened by the head of state. Article 91 of the constitution suggests that the President of the Republic should swear an oath of loyalty to the Republic, promising to uphold the Constitution. Francesco Cossiga interpreted his role somewhat differently. In 1991, in a series of declarations to the press and on television, he publicly questioned the integrity and independence of the High Council of the Judiciary (CSM), talked openly about the end of the

Republic, responded to criticism of the performance of his duties from the PDS by encouraging an investigation of their position by the secret services and the *carabinieri*, made open overtures to the *Lega* and the MSI at a time when the governing parties were anxious to keep them in the political wilderness, and finally broke clamorously with his own party. Nothing, it might be supposed, would more effectively undermine the legitimacy of a state and constitution than sweeping condemnation by the head of state. Short of the impeachment of the president, which in the circumstances would have precipitated precisely the crisis they were trying to avoid, there is really very little that a government can do in such a situation. There is a sinister precedent within the Italian tradition. The king and liberal leaders in 1921–2 were directly responsible for Mussolini's assumption of power. We must hope that Cossiga's indiscretions have less onerous consequences.

The charges levelled against the régime by the *Lega*, Cossiga and others were neither novel nor surprising. Allegations of systematic links between the DC and the *mafia*, for example, had been heard for more than twenty years, inspiring conspiracy theories of the most fanciful kinds. Some of these fancies, as it has turned out, are closer to the truth than many of us would have supposed. What we really have to ask ourselves is why the conventional wisdom on the Italian system took so long to become politically significant. Informed observers knew that Salvo Lima was both Andreotti's right-hand man in Sicily and a crucial link between the *mafia* and the Roman establishment long before his assassination in March 1992. Why had the elaborate clientèle networks which the DC had carefully cultivated over several decades suddenly become a political liability? The internal fissures which finally led to the collapse of the DC power machine are familiar to us. We must remember, however, that a deeply divided DC had always managed to maintain an effective control of power, despite a serious decline in the DC vote in the 1980s (a drop from 38.3 per cent in 1979 to 29.7 per cent in 1992).[7] To be sure, this had involved power-sharing on an unprecedented scale with the PSI. But in 1989 no one would have suggested that the DC would collapse within three years.

In this chapter I can offer no more than an outline of developments which will need to be explained in considerable detail in due course. Yet we should be clear from the outset that methods adopted in the past, focusing on the exercise and maintenance of power, will only tell a part of the story. What we have witnessed over the last three years is a crisis of legitimacy on a massive scale. It is quite different from the standard governmental crises that have bedevilled Italian politics, where arguments about patronage would be cloaked in the language of policy. In one sense, the crisis might be seen as a belated attempt to make Italian democracy more transparent. The concern has not been to show that representative democracy is a sham (as was the case with the terrorist groups of the

1970s) but rather that democracy Italian-style is a sham. Clearly a great deal of empirical work will be required before we can explain satisfactorily how and why the political parties lost control of the system. Attention to the question of the *de facto* distribution of power should be conducted, however, in the context of the profound normative changes that have underpinned Italy's political transformation. Nor should we lose sight of the limited impact that institutional reform can have on a political system. We can all devise constitutions on a Sunday afternoon in our armchairs; making them work is quite another matter.

Developments within the Italian state have clearly reflected wider upheavals in European and world politics. The collapse of the Soviet bloc left the DC ideologically exposed. It seemed to many observers that its claim to constitute the only reliable bulwark against creeping communism could no longer be plausibly deployed, even as a rhetorical device. It was left, along with the PSI, as a naked power broker in a game of political patronage that got out of control. Political patronage had been used throughout the history of the Republic to reinforce a state that had initially been regarded as vulnerable. It must be granted, too, that the DC, in particular, were remarkably successful in giving a solid foundation to the Republic. The isolation of the political élite in the liberal era was overcome by a systematic deployment of resources, giving millions of people a vested interest in the *status quo*. Adapting the practice of *trasformismo* to the demands of a mass society, however, is prohibitively expensive. The scale of transfer payments, both licit and illicit, far exceeded the productive capacity of the Italian economy. A public sector debt threatening to rise to 134 per cent of GDP by 1997 simply could not be sustained.[8] More significantly, perhaps, the distribution of spoils, which in the 1950s and 1960s had helped to consolidate popular support for the Republic, had by the 1980s exposed the political class as a whole to censure. The spectre of politicians making fortunes for themselves and their acolytes at public expense tipped a balance which had been precariously sustained in the earlier period. Public resources were treated by the parties as a private political perquisite. In a difficult economic climate, popular patience was finally exhausted. The political class seemed to have lost touch with the wider society, effectively severing the link between patronage and legitimacy.

In the European context, the further integration of the European economy has made political options available which would previously have been dismissed as too costly or disruptive. Italy's initial commitment to European integration, it must be remembered, was part of a sustained effort to legitimize the fledgling Republic. The policy has proved to be' strikingly successful. Italy's access to the growing European market in the 1950s was guaranteed, enabling the economy to enjoy a period of export-led growth which doubled GDP in little more than a decade. The emergence of a European Community was not necessarily the decisive factor in this development. But it became associated in the public mind with unprecedented well-being. Successive Eurobarometer soundings consistently show a level of support for European integration significantly above the European average.[9] Even politicians whose domestic political vision has been notoriously short-sighted (Andreotti may be taken as an example) have seen deepening European integration not simply as a means of furthering Italian interests but also as a possible strategy for radical structural reform of the Italian state.

Commitment to Europe thus constituted a solid foundation in an otherwise fragmented political culture. By 1970 the PCI had accepted EC membership and would later become enthusiastic advocates of integration. The point to stress in this context is not so much the tangible benefits which accrued from EC membership as the legitimizing function of Euro-enthusiasm. The European dimension has become more significant as the fragility of the national political consensus has become increasingly evident. A vote for radical or separatist parties, for example, need not necessarily be portrayed as a threat to the Italian economy, provided political innovation in Italy was seen to be compatible with Italy's wider commitment to the European Union.

Italy's declared enthusiasm for Europe, however, should not blind us to fundamental, and currently unresolved, problems which integration has posed for the Italian economy and public administration. A cumbersome administrative structure, coupled with weak Cabinet control, has meant that co-ordination of European programmes has proved difficult. Among all the member states of the European Union, implementation of the measures necessary for the establishment of the Single Market has been slowest in Italy. Disciplinary referrals to the European Court of Justice involving Italy have also been higher than for any other state, with no sign of improvement to a rising trend.[10] This situation should not surprise us. The relative administrative autonomy enjoyed by ministries has meant that co-ordination of domestic policy has often been inefficient. The additional requirements of European policy have simply exacerbated familiar difficulties.

Administrative problems have been compounded by structural features of the Italian economy. A patronage-based state has until recently had neither the administrative means nor the political incentive to control effectively public-sector finances. The terms of the Treaty of Maastricht, however, have significantly shifted political and economic priorities. Target figures of 3 per cent for the budget deficit and 60 per cent for the accumulated public-sector debt in relation to GDP have been set as necessary conditions for Economic and Monetary Union (compared with the current position of 10.2 per cent and 114 per cent respectively for 1993).[11] Cuts on this scale would be difficult for any political system in any circumstances. In the context of fragile recovery from recession and institutional implosion, the task may well be deemed impossible. The Amato and Ciampi governments both showed remarkable resolve in addressing the issue. The Berlusconi Government, committed as it was to fiscal ortho-doxy, might have been expected to continue on the same path. The record, however, was not encouraging. The political cost of decisive action was higher than the Berlusconi Government was prepared to pay, despite an apparently safe parliamentary majority in the lower house. The stronger nationalist tone of the Berlusconi Government also led to revision of the automatic assumption that European integration is a good in itself. In economic terms, however, Italy cannot afford to isolate herself from the mainstream in Europe. The urgency is now such that radical reform of the Italian state can be presented as a necessary prerequisite for full Italian involvement in economic and political union. At the very least, with the prospect of a two-speed Europe emerging, it is essential that inter-national investors retain a modicum of confidence in the broad thrust of Italian economic policy. The immediate convergence terms signified in the Maastricht Treaty may not be attainable; but there must be no doubt that those terms can be met in due course.[12]

Pressure for structural reform of the Italian state thus came to a head in the late 1980s. The inability of the state to provide acceptable levels of service, coupled with profligate and questionable use of patronage, led to almost universal acceptance that the *status quo* was untenable. Yet there was serious confusion regarding possible remedies. That government should be answerable to the electorate rather than the parties became an article of faith, though there was much less agreement on the appropriate role of parties in the new scheme of things. Where constitutional critics in the mature democracies have generally argued that executives have become too powerful, Italian commentators have claimed instead that the powers of the legislature should be constrained. What they have sought is more decisive decision-making. And this will only be achieved, so the argu-ment goes, if policy rather than patronage becomes the principal concern of government.

The major electoral reform of August 1993 was designed precisely to encourage the emergence of clearly designated electoral alliances which would present alternatives to the electorate for popular decision. The law itself was a compromise, adopting a simple majority system for 75 per cent of the seats, with a remaining 25 per cent of the seats elected accord-ing to the proportional system in order to defend the interests of smaller parties. The upshot in the 1994 election, however, was not clearly defined policy alternatives but loose right- and left-wing coalitions formed by the existing or new parties. The system may be regarded as more transparent in that coalitions were set before the electorate rather than concocted following tortuous negotiation after an election. Yet in earlier elections the broad character of a governing coalition had seldom been in doubt. Parties and factions would argue among themselves in the light of their relative electoral performances, expecting the distribution of cabinet responsibilities to be adjusted to reflect gains and losses. More notice *may* have been taken of policy issues in the final formation of the Berlusconi Government. But parliamentary strategy was far more significant than considerations of policy. And the electorate, in the nature of things, was scarcely involved at all.

Nor would it be realistic to suppose that a pure majority system would necessarily lead to decisive single party government, with clear executive control of Parliament. Despite the vast electoral upheaval since 1992, Italy has remained an amalgam of politically discrete subcultures. The *Lega*, the AN and the PDS each depend upon a regional heartland. And even *Forza Italia*, with unrivalled access to national television channels, remains a predominantly Northern party in ethos and organization. Much has been written in the last decade about the progressive homogenization of Italian culture in the post-war period. In terms of political and economic culture, however, practices are as diverse as ever. Recent research has convincingly linked political and economic performance in the regions to patterns of association and subordination that were first established in the thirteenth century.[13] The practical lessons to be gleaned from the burden of the past are many, varied and contentious. At the very least, we can assume that deeply entrenched cultural attitudes will resist the fizz of television. Political and economic change will be variously accommodated. In these circumstances, it is unlikely that any party or movement will have a consistent national appeal. For better or worse, Italians will have to live with one version or another of coalition government.

In the context of the wider sweep of modern Italian history, we should really ask ourselves why coalition government should be regarded as a problem. Successive governments since 1861 have encountered acute difficulties in bridging the gap between a narrow political élite and a regionally diverse society. Where a genuine national political culture is lacking, and arguably this is still the case today, attempts must necessarily be made to forge links between disparate groups. *Trasformismo* and *clientelismo* might be regarded as consensual means of manipulating interests in order to fashion workable governing alliances. Other strategies have been tried. Fascism can be taken as, among very many other things, an authoritarian attempt to manipulate national culture through the control of information, employment, forms of association, etc. In practice we know that consensual and authoritarian means have often been combined in Italy's different régimes. Nor should this surprise us. In intractable circumstances, the exigencies of government may well require ingenuity, and even legal laxity. The real lesson from Italy's recent past is that circumstances are always intractable. To suppose otherwise is to court disappointment and disillusion.

A system so delicately balanced is fraught with difficulties. Easy political solutions can be discounted. The key to the success of the First Republic is perhaps that an effective network of institutional checks and balances matched the practical difficulty of mobilizing a political constituency for radical reform of any kind. To be sure, such a system can only function smoothly if politicians exercise self-restraint and an electorate's political expectations are low. Both conditions, arguably, were met until the 1980s. Precisely why the situation altered so fundamentally is a complex story which cannot be told here. Suffice it to say that a fatal cocktail of impotence and contempt undermined the legitimacy of a régime which had always depended upon a discreet blind eye. High-profile political leaders are naturally encouraged to offer an electorate more than can possibly be delivered. We should not be surprised if an electorate, once disappointed, should heed the blandishments of new and unproven voices.

Part of the problem derives from the gulf that has for so long separated the rhetoric of politics from the business of day-to-day accommodation. Ideologically distinct subcultures cultivate an exclusive view of the political world which makes it difficult to legitimize the pragmatic adjustment to opposed interests. That mutual accommodation had in fact been reduced to a fine art is beside the point. Official political discourse persisted in excluding the PCI and the MSI from the establishment long after their legitimacy had been acknowledged in practice. An inability to talk openly about what actually happens leads to suspicion, which in turn leads to a politics of paranoia, where initiates are able to exercise their delightfully refined skills while the public is left without political bearings.

Nor is the formal constitutional theory that underpins the Republic any more helpful in explanatory terms. The supposition that a properly functioning representative democracy should display an alternation between government and opposition has been disappointed. But this is not simply a problem for the post-war Republic. Governments since 1861 have been based upon the exclusion of opposition parties and movements as threats to the various régimes.[14] Oppositions have never come to power in the orthodox way following an election. Appearances to the contrary notwithstanding, the 1994 election was not an exception to this rule. The implosion of the DC and PSI did not lead to victory for the opposition. Despite the fact that no one could seriously believe in a communist threat to Italian political freedoms, old-style anti-communist rhetoric was deployed with renewed abandon. What we see in the election is not a shift from government to opposition but an unlikely regrouping on the right. It is an alternation that offers no real alternative at all.[15]

In the light of established practice within the Italian tradition, it should hardly surprise us that the left failed to win the election in 1994. Complex factors are necessarily involved, stemming from Berlusconi's obvious advantage with the media, through his *apparently* fresh image, untainted by association with the discredited régime, to the failure of the left itself to adjust to the changing nature of Italian society.[16] It is worth stressing that employment patterns in Italy have changed markedly over the last twenty-five years, with a significant decline in numbers employed in both agriculture and industry throughout the country, balanced by a marked expansion of the tertiary sector.[17] A party which persisted in presenting itself as the natural focus of working-class political activity was thus bound to face an uphill electoral task. The point to stress here, however, is the oddity of regarding alternation between government and opposition as a criterion of political legitimacy. It would be foolish to insist that orthodox alternation will never occur in Italy. Yet the fact that it has not occurred should not be dismissed as accidental or perverse.

What we are touching upon here is a fundamental problem of political perception and self-understanding which has persistently bedevilled the politics of modern Italy. It emerged in acute form in the middle decades of the nineteenth century, as different groups and interests contended for the creation of an Italian state. It was one thing, however, for a narrow intellectual élite to agree that Italy should be autonomous and independent; and quite another to settle on an appropriate form for the new state. The intellectual argument between federalists and unitarists is among the most compelling in modern Italian history, extending from abstract consideration of the nature of the state to the most detailed constitutional and administrative arrangements. Yet, far from putting an end to the problem, the achievement of an Italian state actually exacerbated some of the difficulties that had surfaced in the course of the debate. The state in 1861 embodied the political triumph of Piedmont rather than a considered judgement of Italy's institutional identity. And the gulf between regional and national political cultures has continued to haunt a beleaguered élite.[18]

It is not simply that relations between centre and periphery have been peculiarly fraught in Italy. A deeper problem concerns the failure of the various constitutional schemes that have been imposed on the country to reflect a wider national political culture. The paradox here is that nineteenth-century nationalists were insistent that Italy should be unified precisely because Austrian domination distorted social, economic, cultural and political development. It quickly became apparent that Piedmontese domination was no solution. Once established, however, a new central authority gained a momentum of its own, forging complex links with local élites based upon mutual accommodation. But the practical measures which made government possible have never been reflected in formal constitutional procedures. What we have is a stark mismatch between 'dignified' and 'efficient' dimensions of the polity which risks rendering the relations between theory and practice incomprehensible to even reasonably well-informed citizens.

The founders of liberal Italy supposed that they were establishing a classic Westminster-style parliamentary system. And the fissures between the leaders of the *Risorgimento* were sufficient to suggest that an orthodox party system might emerge. That the liberal state did not develop in the expected fashion was seen by some disenchanted liberal leaders as a major shortcoming. De Sanctis, who had served as minister of education, wrote in 1877: 'We have now reached the point where there are no solidly built parties in Italy except those based on either regional differences or the personal relation of client to patron; and these are the twin plagues of Italy.'[19] Twin plagues they might be; but they also served to bind the state together in the absence of a national political consensus. The post-war Republic has no doubt pushed the manipulation of patronage for political ends beyond sustainable limits. It has also managed to secure for Italians the sustained enjoyment of civil rights and economic well-being.

Despite recurrent crises and acute instability, the continuity in modern Italian history is remarkable. Periods of precarious consensus have been interspersed with fundamental political turmoil which has effectively brought three régimes to a close. But in each circumstance, from the estab-lishment of the liberal state in 1861, through fascism, to the post-war Republic, little progress has been made in addressing the social, economic and cultural problems which undermined the particular régimes. Political innovation, even when it has appeared to be far-reaching, has often been reduced to a cosmetic adjustment to intractable structural difficulties. It would be naive to assume that the political turmoil of the last three years will result in a transition to a qualitatively different scheme of things.

Political and administrative life, in general, has been slow to accommo-date profound social, cultural and economic changes. But in dire situations political ingenuity has at least enabled alternative solutions to be found to problems which have resisted legislative resolution. To be sure, political ingenuity has often taxed the patience and the pockets of citizens. And the complexity of informal arrangements has made obfuscation a crucial political tactic. Yet a political class aware of the precarious nature of the state has managed to avoid the worst disasters by the finest of margins.

In the last resort, the fortune of the Italian state has been tied to the wider balance of political power in Europe. The state was initially formed as a consequence of fundamental political adjustment in Europe, accom-modating the retreat of the Austrian empire and the emergence of new states. Subsequent Italian régimes have also been sensitive to the prevailing European climate. The First World War can be seen as a European crisis which effectively undermined the liberal state, as indeed the economic crisis of the 1920s would make life difficult for parliamentary democracies throughout Europe.

In the post-war period the Cold War and its aftermath, coupled with the emergence of the European Union, have clearly dominated. What has unsettled the Italian state since 1989 is the pace of change. Political pos-sibilities which had previously been foreclosed are now at the top of the' agenda. Institutional innovations which would once have been dismissed as dangerously disruptive (such as radical devolution) are now regarded as not only possible but desirable. Yet change is never without a cost. And the pressures for closer economic and monetary union have exposed public finances to international scrutiny. The current crisis, which ostensibly began as a reaction against political corruption, must be set in the deeper context of the global integration of economies. The fate of institutional reform in Italy is likely to hinge on international financial confidence.[20]

FURTHER READING

C. Duggan, *A Concise History of Italy*, Cambridge: Cambridge University Press, 1994.

P. Furlong, *Modern Italy: Representation and Reform*, London: Routledge, 1994.

P. Ginsborg, *A History of Contemporary Italy: Society and Politics, 1943–1988*, Harmondsworth: Penguin Books, 1990.

P. Ginsborg (ed.), *Stato dell'Italia* [The State of Italy], Milan: Bruno Mondadori, 1994.

D. Hine, *Governing Italy: The Politics of Bargained Pluralism*, Oxford: Oxford University Press, 1993.

J. LaPalombara, *Democracy Italian Style*, New Haven and London: Yale University Press, 1987.

R. D. Putnam *et al.*, *Making Democracy Work: Civic Traditions in Modern Italy*, Princeton: Princeton University Press, 1993.

M. L. Salvadori, *Storia d'Italia e crisi di regime: Alle radici della politica italiana* [Régime Crises in the History of Italy: The Roots of Italian Politics], Bologna: Mulino, 1994.

D. Sassoon, *Contemporary Italy: Politics, Economy and Society since 1945*, London: Longman, 1986.

F. Spotts and T. Wieser, *Italy: A Difficult Democracy*, Cambridge: Cambridge University Press, 1986.

NOTES

1 P. Ginsborg, *A History of Contemporary Italy: Society and Politics 1943–1988*, Harmondsworth: Penguin Books, 1990, pp. 418–21.

2 J. LaPalombara, *Democracy Italian Style*, New Haven and London: Yale University Press, 1987.

3 R. Cartocci, *Fra Lega e Chiesa: L'Italia in cerca di integrazione* [Between the *Lega* and the Church: Italy in Search of Integration], Bologna: Mulino, 1994; R. Mannheimer (ed.), *La Lega Lombarda*, Milan: Feltrinelli, 1991; F. Rizzi (ed.), *Tra leghe e partiti* [Between Leagues and Parties], Milan: Shakespeare & Company, 1990; R. Leonardi and M. Kovacs, 'L'irresistibile ascesa della Lega nord' [The Irresistible Rise of the Northern League], in: S. Hellman and G. Pasquino (eds), *Politica in Italia: I fatti dell'anno e le interpretazioni*, Bologna: Mulino, 1993, pp. 123–41; and O. Schmidtke, 'The Populist Challenge to the Italian Nation-State: The Lega Lombarda/Nord', *Regional Politics and Policy*, vol. 3 (1993), pp. 140–62.

4 P. Ginsborg (ed.), *Stato dell'Italia* [The State of Italy], Milan: Bruno Mondadori, 1994, pp. 652–91.

5 G. Miglio, 'Le leghe regionali: Il mito della nazione' [The Regional Leagues: The Myth of the Nation], in his *Il nerbo e le briglie del potere*, Milan: Edizioni del sole 24 ore, 1988, pp. 303–6.

6 Note that Miglio sees the 'right of secession' as a 'natural right', essential to the preservation of cultural diversity. See Miglio's preface to G. Morra, *Breve*

storia del pensiero federalista [A Short History of Federalist Thought], Milan: Arnoldo Mondadori, 1993, pp. 5–6.

7 R. Leonardi and D. A. Wertman, *Italian Christian Democracy: The Politics of Dominance*, London: Macmillan, 1989.

8 F. Modigliani, 'A Partial Cure for Italy's Deficit', *Financial Times*, 21 October 1994, p. 17.

9 D. Hine, *Governing Italy: The Politics of Bargained Pluralism*, Oxford: Oxford University Press, 1993, pp. 286–7.

10 Ibid., pp. 288–90.

11 *Financial Times*, 7 July 1994, p. 34.

12 P. Daniels, 'L'Italia e il trattato di Maastricht' [Italy and the Treaty of Maastricht], in: Hellman and Pasquino, pp. 199–218; and Ginsborg (ed.) (n. 4 above), pp. 503–6, 643–51.

13 R. D. Putnam *et al.*, *Making Democracy Work: Civic Traditions in Modern Italy*, Princeton: Princeton University Press, 1993.

14 M. L. Salvadori, *Storia d'Italia e crisi di regime: Alle radici della politica italiana* [Régime Crises in the History of Italy: The Roots of Italian Politics], Bologna: Mulino, 1994.

15 L. Bobbio, 'Dalla destra alla destra, una strana alternanza' [From the Right to the Right, a Strange Alternation], in: Ginsborg (ed.) (n. 4 above), pp. 654–61.

16 For further discussion see: F. Sidoti, 'The Significance of the Italian Elections', *Government and Opposition*, vol. 29 (1994), pp. 332–47; and H. Partridge, 'The Italian General Elections: Something New or More of the Same Thing?' *Politics*, vol. 14 (1994), pp. 117–25.

17 Employment in agriculture in fact declined from 18.4 per cent nationally in 1971 to 7.9 per cent in 1991, with industry declining from 44.9 per cent in 1971 to 33.7 per cent in 1991. Tertiary-sector employment increased from 34.2 per cent in 1971 to 58.3 per cent in 1991. See: A. Perulli, 'Com'è cambiata l'occupazione' [Changing Patterns of Employment], in: Ginsborg (ed.) (n. 4 above), p. 445.

18 See: G. Galasso, 'Italia: una nazione difficile' [Italy: A Difficult Nation], *Nuova antologia*, no. 572 (1994), pp. 108–41; L. Riall, *The Italian Risorgimento: State, Society and National Unification*, London: Routledge, 1994; J. A. Davis, 'Remapping Italy's Path to the Twentieth Century', *The Journal of Modern History*, vol. 66 (1994), pp. 291–320; B. Haddock, 'Italy: Independence and Unification without Power', in: B. Waller (ed.), *Themes in Modern European History, 1830–1890*, London: Unwin Hyman, 1990, pp. 67–98; B. Haddock, 'Political Lessons of Italian Unification', in: E. Semanis (ed.), *The Transition towards Democracy: Experience in Latvia and in the World*, Riga: Latvia University Press, 1994, pp. 23–33; and for the wider perspective C. Duggan, *A Concise History of Italy*, Cambridge: Cambridge University Press, 1994.

19 Quoted from: D. Mack Smith, *Italy: A Modern History*, Ann Arbor: University of Michigan Press, 1969, p. 111.

20 I am grateful to Robert Leonardi, Gino Bedani, Mark Donovan, Remo Catani and Barry Jones for their comments on an earlier version of this paper.

8 The Southern enlargement of the EC

Greece, Portugal and Spain

Robert Bideleux

The restoration of liberal parliamentary democracy following the fall of the Greek military junta in July 1974, the overthrow of the Salazar/Caetano régime in April 1974 and the death of Franco in November 1975 cleared the way for Greece, Portugal and Spain to apply for full membership of the EC in June 1975, March 1977 and July 1977, respectively. In each case EC membership was seen as a means of reinforcing the return to democracy; as the culmination of a process of opening up the economy to international (and especially European) trade, competition and investment; as the consummation of a spiritual 'return to Europe', marking the end of their extra-European 'vocations', the final attainment of First World status and the reversal of centuries of marginalization in European affairs. Indeed, the Spaniards and the Portuguese have become rather more whole-hearted Europeans than the British, making cleaner breaks with their former imperial connections, delusions and ambitions. They now see their futures largely in European terms, despite their continuing cultural affinities with Latin America. The desire to join the EC was both cause and effect of economic, social and political change and a redefinition of national identities and orientations. Becoming more 'European' implied wide-ranging programmes of 'liberalization' and 'modernization', to use appropriately loaded terms. Starting in the 1960s, well before their formal applications for EC membership, the governments of Spain, Portugal and (less successfully) Greece began to make use of the explicit and implicit requirements of EC membership to overcome resistance to programmes of reform designed to bring their political, legal and business institutions and practices and social and educational provisions closer to the 'norms' of Northwestern Europe. Membership of the Council of Europe, EFTA, OECD, WEU or NATO may have played analogous roles in some instances, but none of those organizations could rival either the EC's capacity for deep and pervasive penetration of political systems or its potential for promoting political, institutional and economic change and liberalization.

On the economic front, aided by substantial cross-party support for deeper integration into the EC, Spain, Portugal and, to a much lesser degree, Greece have made similarly judicious use of the requirements of participation in the Single European Market (SEM), the Exchange Rate Mechanism (ERM) and the projected Economic and Monetary Union (EMU) to subject their economies to wide-ranging deregulation of labour, capital and product markets and unaccustomed levels of fiscal and monetary discipline, so as to reduce their inflation rates, strengthen their currencies, enhance their international competitiveness and accelerate industrial restructuring. There has been a reorientation of their external trade towards the EC, which has also incidentally promoted a quantum leap in Iberian economic integration, allowing Spain to take over Britain's former role as Portugal's major economic partner. Trade between Spain and Portugal increased ten-fold from 1985 to 1994, and Spain's share of Portuguese imports rose from 5.0 per cent in 1983 to 17.8 per cent in 1993, while its share of Portuguese exports rose from 4.0 per cent in 1983 to 15.1 per cent (exceeded only by Germany) in 1991. Spaniards became Portugal's most numerous foreign visitors, the fortunes of the peseta and the escudo became interlocked (they had to be devalued in tandem within the ERM in November 1992, May 1993 and again in February 1995) and in 1993 Spain overtook Britain as the leading foreign direct investor in Portugal, which received 25 per cent of Spanish foreign direct investment. Investors increasingly saw the Iberian peninsula as a unified economic area.[1]

Table 8.1 EC/EU shares of Greek, Portuguese and Spanish foreign trade[2]

	1973	1977	1983	1991
Exports (%)				
Greece	55	48	39	62
Portugal	49	52	58	75
Spain	48	46	48	71
Imports (%)				
Greece	50	43	47	59
Portugal	45	44	40	72
Spain	43	34	32	60

Furthermore, all three states have become large net recipients of EU structural and cohesion funds designed to reduce the substantial economic disparities between the richer and poorer regions of the EU and to make good the missing links in the SEM by enhancing their physical and social infrastructures. But there the similarities end. This chapter assesses the differing historical contexts, results and significance of their accessions to the EC. Above all, it seeks to explain why the effects of and responses to membership have been so much less positive for Greece than for Portugal and Spain.

GREECE AND EUROPEAN INTEGRATION

Greek attitudes to the EC have long been characterized by degrees of division, ambivalence and *Angst* which have been largely absent in the cases of Portugal and Spain. These attitudes, which have been to a considerable extent both cause and effect of Greece's relatively poor political and economic performance since joining the EC in 1981, are direct products of the still potent cultural and psychological legacies of the Byzantine and Ottoman Empires and of the inherently vulnerable, dependent, embattled and irredentist nature of the Greek national state that emerged in the nineteenth and early twentieth centuries. These legacies, kept alive by perceived 'threats' and demagogic manipulation of nationalist issues, provide the keys to understanding Greece's exceptionally fraught and ambivalent relationship with Western Europe.

For centuries, as a result of its nodal position at the meeting point between three continents, Greece stood at the confluence of three cultures (Byzantine/Eastern Orthodoxy, Ottoman Islam and Catholic/Western Christendom). It has continued to be torn between its Byzantine/Eastern Orthodox cultural roots and its more recent westward maritime, mercantile and intellectual orientations. From 1946 to 1989 the artificial East–West division of Europe engendered by the Cold War induced the West to treat Greece as part of Western Europe, in blatant defiance of cultural and geographical facts. But the termination of communist rule and the Cold War ended Greece's special status as a front-line NATO state and reduced Western Europe's willingness to indulge strident Greek nationalism, rule-flouting and special pleading. After 1990 Greece again began to look and behave less like a Western than an Eastern European state, as the break-up of Yugoslavia and the resurgence of old national and territorial disputes and alliances 'dragged Greece back into the Balkans'.[3] Indeed, as elsewhere in the Balkans, the modern Greek state concept was built around an exclusive 'ethnic' conception of the nation. In Western Europe most of the existing monarchical states had defined their modern nationhood in ways that included all (or almost all) their subjects, fostered inclusive 'civic' conceptions of the nation and facilitated the development of constitutional monarchies and liberal democracies. But in nineteenth-century Eastern Europe the emergence of nationalism within predominantly supra-national/imperial polities induced nationalist movements to engage in long and often bitter struggles to bring into existence new nations and national states conceived and defined in narrowly ethnic and cultural terms and in opposition to the existing territorial and state structures. This gave rise to chronic irredentist and 'national minority' problems, whose creation had to a large extent been avoided in Western Europe, mainly as a result of the cultivation of more inclusive 'civic' and territorial conceptions of the nation in that part of the world. Accordingly, as in the parallel cases of Serbia, Croatia, Albania, Bulgaria and Hungary, Greek nationalist mythology and the Greek 'state idea' have remained inherently 'ethnic', integral, irredentist and expansionist, hankering after the eventual inclusion of all the major ethnic Greek communities and most of the territories that had long been Hellenic and/or Byzantine (including northern Macedonia, 'northern Epirus' and Cyprus) in a united Greek polity. The Pan-Hellenic '*Megale Idea*' [Great Idea] and the integral 'ethnic' conception of the Greek nation have long had profoundly unsettling effects on the Balkans and on Greece's relations with Turkey. Significantly, the Greek monarch was always 'King of the Greeks', not 'King of Greece', and the name of the Pan-Hellenic Socialist Party (PASOK) is similarly irredentist. This, more than economic difficulties or institutional disagreements, is what has made Greece an inherently uncomfortable and often truculent member of the EC, which was founded in order to surmount and leave behind the nationalist issues and mentalities that are still the staple fare of Balkan politics. Compared with almost all its EU partners (including Portugal and multi-cultural Spain), Greece is a differently conceived nation and its national politics rest on different foundations. Hence the very nature of Greek politics and national self-definition has complicated all attempts to resolve the ancillary economic and institutional problems that have impaired its economic and political performance as an EC member.

Furthermore, from the 1950s until at least the 1980s, Greek academic and political attitudes to the EC and NATO were strongly influenced by Greece's long and divisive experience of British economic imperialism and political tutelage, followed by US military and economic assistance and tutelage after 1947. The small Greek national state established with Russian and British military support at the end of the Greek War of Independence (1821–9) soon became part of the British 'sphere of influence' in the Eastern Mediterranean. From 1833 to 1947, the implanted Greek monarchy owed its survival and/or restoration at various junctures to recurrent British imperialist interventions in Greek affairs. In the immortal words of Sir Edmund Lyons as British Minister to Greece in 1841, 'A truly independent Greece is an absurdity. Greece is Russian or she is English; and since she must not be Russian, it is necessary that she be English.'[4] The same British attitude to Greece was embodied in Churchill's 'percentages agreement' with Stalin in October 1944, which divided the Balkans into British and Russian 'spheres of influence'.[5] Greek socialists, communists and radical nationalists (including many academic economists and historians) have long felt that the explicit membership rules, unwritten codes of conduct and policy prescriptions that EC and NATO membership has involved (or 'imposed') have amounted to new forms of Western imperialism, in the sense that stronger and supposedly 'superior' Western states have repeatedly tried to inflict their ideas, practices, nostrums and institutions on a relatively small, underdeveloped and dependent Greece.[6] Indeed, the involuntary subordination of Greece to an International Commission of Economic Control from 1897 to 1941, America's control of the purse strings during the 1950s, and the stringent and didactic terms of the EC 'stabilization loans' of 1985 and 1991 and the EU 'convergence programme' adopted in 1993 have subjected Greece to prolonged periods of irksome and sometimes humiliating external economic supervision or control. Furthermore, Western economic dominance and political tutelage has long been seen by radical nationalists, 'dependency' theorists and the neo-Marxist left as being largely responsible for the relatively stunted and 'dependent' development of the Greek state, economy and bourgeoisie.[7] In these radical 'anti-imperialist' perspectives, Greece's EC accession and its subservience to EC dictates has amounted to a perpetuation of Western capitalist imperialism. These somewhat embattled perceptions, conjoined with the protracted struggle to develop a fully 'independent' Greek national state, economy and identity after centuries of Ottoman and Western domination, lie at the heart of any attempt to understand the reasons why the question of EC and NATO membership (and the strings attached to that membership) helped to divide politically conscious Greeks into two mutually hostile camps from the 1950s down to the 1980s (with significant 'after-shocks' in the 1990s). This ideological schism reinforced and was reinforced by the profound left–right polarization of Greek society bequeathed by the Second World War and the subsequent Greek Civil War of 1946–9. Parts of the Greek left, notably the 17 November Movement (named after the massacre of twenty students by the Colonels' régime in 1973) and the Left Movement Against the EC, remain violently opposed to EU membership and have been debarred from participating in elections for their refusal to renounce violence. In reply, they mounted terrorist bombing campaigns in Athens during the June 1994 Euro-elections, deliberately targeting West European tourists.[8]

An even older tradition of Greek Orthodox mistrust of the 'heretical' West, stretching back to the schism between Orthodox and Catholic Christendom in 1054 and the subsequent barbaric behaviour of West European Crusaders in the Byzantine domains, resurfaced in the early 1990s in two major forms: first, Greek sympathy and support for Serb co-religionists in the conflicts unleashed by the break-up of Yugoslavia; second, enormous Greek public demonstrations against Western recognition and support for the newly independent Republic of Macedonia, whose chosen title, flag and constitution (in the view of most Greeks) make offensive and illegitimate claims on the Greek region of the same name and on part of the Greek classical heritage. This also led to Greek trade sanctions against the new state in 1994–5. Behind the emotional clap-trap lurks the old geopolitical maxim that whoever controls Macedonia dominates the Balkans. West European hostility to the Serbs and to Greece's stand on the 'Macedonian question' aroused strong feelings that the West has never really understood the ways, values and outlook of the Balkan Orthodox states.[9] During the 1994 Euro-election campaign Dimitria Liani, the wife (and Head of Cabinet Office) of Greece's ailing

76-year-old Premier Andreas Papandreou, declared that 'Serbs are cousins in Orthodoxy' and urged Greeks to resist 'the European way of thinking', while opinion polls indicated that 55 per cent of Greeks wanted to emphasize their Orthodox as against their European identity.[10] Officially, 97 per cent of Greeks are Orthodox Christians and, in nationalist eyes, being Orthodox is still part of their 'Greekness'. According to Professor Richard Clogg, 'for all his modernizing rhetoric, Papandreou essentially represents the powerful anti-Western substratum in Greece's political culture. It has found its most recent expression in cross-party support for the Serbs, an oppressed fellow Orthodox people, who, as many Greeks see it, are the victims of a dastardly Western conspiracy masterminded by the Vatican.'[11] As reported by another close observer of Greek politics:

> Steeped in their different culture, history and set of values, Greeks, like their fellow Orthodox Christian Serbs, have increasingly come to see themselves as victims of the West. Obsessed with their 'lost homelands', many will . . . regale a *Frangos* [Westerner] with the litany of misdeeds and betrayals the West . . . has inflicted on their country. It is this underdog syndrome and the anti-Westernism of most Greeks that Andreas Papandreou knows and taps so well.[12]

On the other hand, Greek ties with stronger Western states have long enjoyed strong support from pro-Western sections of Greek society, most recently from the allies and supporters of Konstantinos Karamanlis, Greece's long-serving Prime Minister (1955–63, 1974–80) and President (1980–5, 1990–5). Indeed, the Greek state has often found itself dependent on Western support for the preservation or restoration of its independence and territorial integrity, and the Greek 'establishment' has long seen Western investment, companies (especially 'multinationals') and economic/cultural influence as the main agents and underwriters of Greek economic development and the deeper integration of Greece into the community of Western capitalist nations. West European moralizing and preaching can be deeply insulting, but the conservative 'establishment' has usually been prepared to put up with that as the 'price' of Western support and assistance, at least until the re-emergence of the 'Macedonian question' in the 1990s. In order to bind Greece more tightly to capitalist Western Europe, the conservative government headed by Karamanlis from 1955 to 1963 applied for associate membership of the EC in June 1959. The EC was in no hurry to conclude association agreements with Europe's less developed countries. Nevertheless, it reached agreement with Greece in July 1961. The Treaty of Association, which came into effect in November 1962, committed both sides to equal treatment of each other's products in each other's markets, to the harmonization of their agricultural policies and to common action on social and economic matters, with the prospect of full membership by 1984. By 1968 all Greek exports enjoyed duty-free access to the EC, although other provisions of the Treaty of Association were formally 'frozen' during the period of military rule from 1967 to 1974.[13]

With the collapse of the Greek Colonels' régime in July 1974 (following the Colonels' abortive attempt to take over Cyprus and the consequent pre-emptive Turkish invasion of the Turk-inhabited northern part of the island), Karamanlis returned from an eleven-year voluntary exile in Paris – where he had cultivated the friendship of President Giscard d'Estaing – and resumed the premiership of Greece until May 1980, when he was elected President. To his credit, Karamanlis swiftly restored civil liberties, released political prisoners, legalized the long-suppressed Greek Communist Party, imprisoned the leaders of the military junta, launched his own conservative (and pro-EC) New Democracy party, partially withdrew Greece from NATO (in protest at NATO's inaction over Turkey's military occupation of Northern Cyprus), held a popular referendum on the future of the self-exiled and rather discredited Greek monarch, proclaimed a republic and held free parliamentary and local elections, which his New Democracy Party comfortably won. The EC Association Agreement with Greece was hastily 'unfrozen' and in July 1975, counting on Giscard's good offices, Karamanlis applied for full membership of the EC. His main intentions were to regain international respectability for Greece, to reinforce the restoration of democracy, to offset the temporary rift with NATO and the US over their acquiescence in Turkey's invasion of Northern Cyprus and to try to win less ambivalent European support for Greece against Turkey. Economically, Greece was widely seen as not yet strong enough to be able to maximize its potential benefits from full membership of the EC, and the Greek Left was still voicing opposition to Greek membership of either the EC or NATO at that time. Despite well-founded EC misgivings and despite considerable opposition from the Mediterranean farmers' lobbies within France and Italy, a Treaty of Accession was signed in May 1979 and Greece became a full member of the EC from 1 January 1981. The Treaty established various five- to seven-year transitional arrangements, some of which were subsequently prolonged into the 1990s, in order to shield the Greek economy from exposure to the full blast of EC competition and to delay the (inflationary) introduction of value added tax until 1988. Nevertheless, by 1983 Greek import duties on EC manufactured goods had fallen to just 5.5 per cent and the 'rapidity of the full accession to membership produced an unpleasant shock for Greek producers. . . . All the old fears of "foreign domination" of the Greek economy were revived.'[14]

Greece joined the EC at almost the worst possible moment. Most of the European economies were in deep recession, the Greek economy was still reeling from the effects of the 1973–4 and 1979–80 oil price hikes (which had trebled Greece's fuel import bills to nearly $3 bn per annum or nearly half its total imports), inflation reached 24 per cent per annum, Greece was running large trade and budget deficits, many firms were on the verge of bankruptcy and unemployment was rising rapidly. This severe economic crisis, coinciding with a widely opposed Greek accession to the EC, helped Andreas Papandreou's PASOK to win a landslide victory in the October 1981 general election. A second PASOK election victory in June 1985 kept it in office until June 1989.

From 1975 to 1979 PASOK had been fiercely neutralist and critical of the application for full EC membership. It had also called for the withdrawal of Greece from NATO and of American military bases from Greece. The New Democracy slogan that 'Greece belongs to the West' was answered by PASOK's slogan that 'Greece belongs to the Greeks'. But when it became clear that PASOK would win the approaching election, Papandreou decided to keep Greece within the EC and NATO after all, provided it was granted more advantageous economic terms for doing so. In 1982 a Greek 'memorandum' presented a shopping list of demands for special funding to improve Greece's poor infrastructure and for EC competition rules to be bent in order to protect Greece's weak industries. The EC responded by offering longer transitional arrangements and various Integrated Mediterranean Programmes to promote regional development and co-operation in the Mediterranean area. Papandreou was able to present this as a famous victory. In 1984 he also successfully threatened to veto the accession of Portugal and Spain unless the EC further increased its indulgence and generosity towards Greece, although he angered his EC partners in doing so.[15] During the 1981–9 Papandreou premiership most of the Greek Left gradually came to accept Greek EC and NATO membership, while the Greek Government became a vociferous advocate of redistributive policies within the EC, especially enhanced CAP support for Mediterranean farm products, increased EC expenditure on regional, social and infrastructural projects in Europe's poorer regions, and further development of the 'social dimensions' of the SEM. As Margaret Thatcher pointedly remarked in her memoirs, 'Mr. Papandreou always proved remarkably effective in gaining Community subsidies for Greece.'[16]

Since joining the EC in January 1981, Greece has not fared well economically. From 1981 to 1990, Greece's real GDP grew by only about 1.7 per cent per annum; its annual inflation rate hovered around 18–20 per cent per year; its current account trade deficits amounted, on average, to about 5 per cent of its GDP; its annual public sector borrowing requirement rose to around 20 per cent of its GDP by 1990; and in 1990 its foreign debt stood at $20.7 bn. Greece took Portugal's place as the poorest member of the Community. In 1981 Greece's per capita GDP had been 58 per cent of the EC average, but by 1990 the ratio was 51 per cent.[17] Thus Greece became increasingly dependent on net fiscal transfers from the EC, which by 1991 amounted to nearly 5 per cent of its GDP.[18] Greece's poor economic performance after 1981 was not solely attributable to EC membership, but this did play a part. Within the context of lax economic policies, the prospect of full exposure to competition from more advanced EC producers encouraged Greek entrepreneurs increasingly to concentrate on labour-intensive 'down market' services, shipping, tourism, property development and low-technology/labour-intensive light industries, which had to contend with increasingly fierce competition from even lower-cost non-European producers (reducing the returns, remuneration and growth potential for Greece), instead of attempting to move 'up market' into potentially more remunerative high-technology and capital-intensive activities. By the early 1990s manufacturing industry accounted for a lower share of GDP and produced even less than it had in 1980.[19] Moreover, although in narrowly fiscal terms Greece became a net gainer from the CAP, any overall benefit was greatly reduced by the fact that Greece (like Portugal) had become a net importer of farm products, and consumers were paying much more for these than they would have done if Greece had remained outside the EC. Yet Greece's economic performance was also impaired by Papandreou's economic policies, which undoubtedly shielded and subsidized economic inefficiency, allowed personal incomes to rise somewhat faster than productivity, fuelled inflation and encouraged both the public sector and private consumers to live far beyond Greece's means through most of the 1980s, despite the vigorous implementation of a two-year austerity programme from October 1985 to October 1987. During the 1980s Greece attracted no more than $2 bn of foreign direct investment (compared with the $6.5 bn invested in similar-sized Portugal over the same period).[20] On the other hand, PASOK had inherited deep-seated structural and balance-of-payments problems from the Karamanlis governments and the junta. It is almost impossible to disentangle these three possible lines of explanation or to apportion 'blame'. What one can safely say is that the conservative New Democracy administrations headed by Konstantinos Mitsotakis (from April 1990 to October 1993) also inherited (but did little to strengthen) an ailing economy which was unable to reap the full potential benefits of EC membership and which was far from ready for a fiercely competitive SEM let alone the ERM (which Greece has been unable to join) or the putative EMU. By the end of 1993 Greece was in last place on all four of the 'convergence criteria' for participation in EMU laid down at Maastricht, with the EU's largest public sector deficit (13.2 per cent of GDP), the largest public debt (138 per cent of GDP), the highest annual inflation rate (12.1 per cent); and the highest long-term interest rate (19.25 per cent).[21] Indeed, even post-communist Poland, Hungary and the Czech Republic may be more eligible to participate in EMU than Greece. In other EU states, the economic recession of the early 1990s had followed a period of boom, partly attributable to the economically stimulating effects of 'preparing for 1992' (the forging of the SEM) but the enfeebled Greek economy largely missed out on the '1992 effect'.[22] The painful economic contraction experienced by Greece from 1990 to mid-1993 merely compounded the 'stagflation' under Papandreou. Constrained by paper-thin parliamentary majorities, the Mitsotakis governments were not strong enough to administer the harsh economic medicine that they and the EC prescribed and believed necessary. They waited too long before really grasping the nettles of retrenchment, debt reduction, stricter fiscal discipline, pay restraint, deregulation, privatization of over-manned and inefficient state enterprises, removal of subsidies, reduction of 'patronage appointments' in the public sector and cracking down on Greece's huge 'black economy' (around 40 per cent of GDP) and rampant tax evasion. Nevertheless, the lax and inflationary economic policies of the 1980s were no longer sustainable, so in 1991 and 1992 New Democracy belatedly set in motion fundamental economic reforms and 'structural adjustment' under the exacting terms of the EC 'stabilization loan' obtained in February 1991. But it all started too late and amid an already punishing economic recession. It drove many Greek firms into even deeper financial distress and/or liquidation, alienating New Democracy's natural constituency. As fresh elections approached Mitsotakis lost his nerve, loosened the incipient fiscal restraint and made thousands of new 'patronage appointments' in the public sector. Moreover, following the break-up of Yugoslavia in 1991, the New Democracy Party was increasingly distracted by the contentious 'Macedonian question'. With only a one- or two-seat majority in Parliament, Mitsotakis was easily 'held to ransom' on this issue by nationalists within his own party, headed by his sometime Foreign Minister, Antonis Samaras. Mitsotakis himself resorted to nationalist tub-thumping in an attempt to divert attention from his government's acute difficulties and shady financial dealings,[23] but these issues slowly paralysed the government, split New Democracy and ultimately forced an election in 1993.

Another PASOK government headed by Andreas Papandreou was elected in October 1993 with a comfortable parliamentary majority. PASOK's electoral success was partly a result of the division of conservative votes between New Democracy and the ultra-nationalist Political Spring party, founded and led by Antonis Samaras. This time round Papandreou studiously avoided the socialist rhetoric of the early and mid-1980s and maintained his pragmatic acceptance of Greek EC and NATO membership in exchange for large cash 'handouts'. After all, Greece was expected to be a net recipient of annual EU fiscal transfers amounting to $4–6 bn (6–9 per cent of its GDP) from 1994 to 1999.[24] Characteristically, Papandreou had voted in favour of the Maastricht Treaty in July 1992, while simultaneously declaring that it gave Greece an opportunity to compete in 'a difficult and unfair race. Unfair because we are last on the starting block and because the Treaty defines the interests of the rich North.'[25] Hopes initially ran high that he would use his considerable political acumen and 'clout' to play the role of elder statesman and work for peace, reconciliation and political stabilization in the Balkans, which would also have boosted Greece's political and economic standing in the region and in the international community. Instead, as if to compensate for his partial renunciation of PASOK's former socialism and anti-Westernism, in 1994-5 Papandreou played to the gallery and pandered to PASOK's innate nationalism: first, by unilaterally imposing a partial trade boycott on the Republic of Macedonia, without even consulting or forewarning his EU partners, after Greece had already delayed EU recognition of and aid to the fragile new state; second, by expelling tens of thousands of Albanian 'illegal immigrants' and partly blocking EU aid to Albania (admittedly in retaliation for Albanian state harassment of Albania's Greeks, who were, however, asserting Greek territorial claims on southern Albania, alias 'northern Epirus', reviving their links with Greece and, as a first step towards eventual secession, demanding autonomy for the disputed territory); and, third, by tolerating blatant violations of the human rights of Greece's Macedonian, Albanian and Turkish minorities, despite a chorus of protests from politicians, writers and human rights groups in other EU states. Indeed, like his predecessor, Papandreou largely threw away a golden opportunity to capitalize on Greek maritime, mercantile and locational advantages and the collapse of Balkan communism to revive Greece's erstwhile roles as the great emporium of the Balkans and as a natural clearing house for trade between Southwest Asia, the Balkans and the rest of Europe and to further develop the tourism sector. The once-great port of Salonica could again become the commercial gateway to the Balkans, opening up a whole new economic hinterland for Greece. But there was a failure to see that the stabilization of the fragile post-communist Republics of Macedonia and Albania was very much in Greece's own interests, both to prevent a spread of the Yugoslav conflicts southwards to its own borders and to relaunch the Greeks on a much-needed new economic career as the natural economic and political 'brokers' and 'middlemen' of the post-communist Balkans.

The EC was originally established in order to defuse and to sublimate the recurrent rivalry, tensions, conflicts and mistrust between two great nations, France and Germany. In admitting Greece, however, it inadvertently imported the pan-Hellenic conflicts with Turkey (over control of the Aegean and Cyprus) and, latterly, with the Republic of Macedonia and post-communist Albania (on ethnic and territorial issues).[26] By upholding an exclusive and intolerant 'ethnic' conception of 'Greekness' and of the Greek nation, by refusing to respect the distinctive identities and rights of self-expression of its Macedonian Slav, Turkish, Pomak and Albanian minorities (totalling 200,000-400,000 people), and by prosecuting and denouncing as 'traitors' those who publicize the existence and champion the rights of these maltreated minorities, Greece's conduct during the first half of the 1990s exposed troublesome differences between the basic values of the Greek state and those of the other EU member states. The prevailing 'ethnic' conception of the Greek nation (along with official and popular reluctance to safeguard rights and liberties that conflict with this) is profoundly at odds with the 'civic' and multi-cultural conceptions of nationhood that prevail in Western Europe and is much closer to that of its Balkan neighbours. Just as this inherently exclusive and intolerant conception of nationhood could become the most fundamental long-term obstacle to the eventual inclusion of the post-communist Balkan states in the EU, so it should raise thorny questions as to whether Greece really deserves to be a full member of the EU. In August 1994 the British Helsinki Human Rights Group pointed out that if the Badinter Commission's prudent preconditions for EC recognition of the former Yugoslav Republics were now to be applied to Greece as stringently as the Greeks insisted they had to be applied to the new Republic of Macedonia, Greece would not qualify for EU recognition, let alone membership.[27] However, according to Jonathan Eyal:

> Those who suggest that it was a mistake to accept Greece into the European Community are not only adding to the country's sense of insecurity, but also distorting the very purpose of the institution they wish to safeguard. The Community was conceived as an organisation that would transcend national rivalries; the reconciliation between France and Germany is constantly touted as its greatest achievement. . . . The Greeks may be difficult EC partners. But they changed their government peacefully and democratically . . . and their EC membership serves as the best reminder that a true Europe already extends to the Balkans.[28]

Such considerations would carry more weight if Greece were more willing to uphold the letter and spirit of an essentially tolerant, liberal, law-governed and 'civic' EU, i.e. only if Greece were truly 'European' in the sense that Eyal implies. Unfortunately, the analogy with Franco-German reconciliation is a false one. A desire to reconcile nations and transcend national rivalries and grievances was indeed the overriding motive for West European integration. Yet reconciliation can occur only when the parties involved really desire it. Sadly, Greece has been seeking unambiguous EU support *against* Turkey, Albania and the Republic of Macedonia, rather than an EU role in brokering national reconciliation and/or a judicious settling of differences. Moreover, when PASOK's former Deputy Finance Minister (Nikos Athanassopoulos) was successfully prosecuted by the EC in 1990 for his government's role in defrauding the EC of CAP funds, the Greek side was essentially unrepentant and unapologetic, reflecting 'a widely held perception that the EC is an alien authority whose rules no self-respecting Greek should take too seriously', while the former (and present) European Affairs Minister, Theodoros Pangalos, told the court that Greece was merely the victim of 'a kind of racism against the Greeks'.[29] In 1990–1, however, the scale of Greek CAP fraud grew alarmingly and since then the EU has had to subject Greece to ever-increasing fines for its laxity in enforcing controls and prosecuting known infractors.[30] On minority and human rights issues, it remains perfectly reasonable to apply to Greece the same criteria that it insisted had to be applied to the Republic of Macedonia, and it would be hypocritical to deny EU membership to Turkey or the post-communist Balkan states on the grounds that they display insufficient respect for minority or human rights while allowing Greece to violate such rights with impunity within the EU. Full respect and safeguards for minority and human rights and equal observance and application of the law are fundamental prerequisites for the transcendence of national grievances and rivalries, for the proper working of the EU and for the peace and prosperity of Europe, including Turkey and the Balkans.

PORTUGAL AND EUROPEAN INTEGRATION

Portugal formally applied for full membership of the EC in March 1977, four months ahead of Spain. The protracted negotiations on entry terms were completed in March 1985 and the Accession Treaties were signed in June 1985, with effect from 1 January 1986. However, Portugal had no large exportable farm surpluses nor any major industrial export capabilities. It was a net importer of food and its accession to the EC would only increase the EC's population by 3.7 per cent, its territory by 5.5 per cent and its GDP by 1.9 per cent. Thus it could neither 'threaten' any existing EC state nor make burdensome claims on the EC budget or the CAP. It was therefore unfortunate, albeit perhaps not inevitable, that the negotiations with Portugal got caught up with the much more problematic Spanish ones, delaying Portuguese entry.

One of the major consequences of Portugal's accession to the EC was an enhancement of its *de facto* independence through the rapid attenuation of its longstanding 'dependent' relationship with Britain. Portugal is often described as Britain's 'oldest ally', with political and commercial ties extending back to the Anglo-Portuguese trade treaty of 1294, the dynastic alliance of 1373 and the trade treaties of 1654 and 1703, which gave Britain preferential access to Portugal's domestic and colonial markets in return for British military protection of Portugal and its empire against Spanish, French and Dutch interlopers. Portugal and its dominions became in effect part of Britain's 'informal' empire, subject to a kind of British military protectorate, especially after the French occupation of Portugal from 1807 to 1812, which Britain helped to end. British companies and investors gained substantial control of the Portuguese economy, lasting well into the twentieth century, and until the 1970s Britain remained Portugal's major export market. But 'anti-imperialist' sentiments did not develop as tenaciously in Portugal as they did in Greece, partly because Portugal itself remained an imperial power until 1974. Throughout the Second World War, despite the fascist trappings of Salazar's régime (1928–68), Portugal supplied strategic metals to the Western Allies and, from 1943 onward, allowed them to develop strategic bases on the Azores in return for much-needed infusions of British and American capital into the languishing Portuguese economy. As a consequence, Salazar's Portugal, unlike Franco's Spain, was allowed to become a founder member of the UN in 1945, NATO in 1949 and EFTA in 1960.[31] Moreover, when Britain joined the EC, the Community negotiated a Special Relations Agreement with Portugal (as with other EFTA states) in 1972, even though Portugal still had an authoritarian régime. This agreement gave most Portuguese exports unrestricted access to EC markets by 1978 (the important exceptions being so-called 'sensitive products' such as textiles, clothing, footwear, agricultural produce and processed foods), while by 1980 80 per cent of all imports from the EC and EFTA were entering Portugal duty-free and tariffs on the remainder were low.[32] During the 1960s and 1970s, moreover, nearly a million Portuguese migrants took jobs in Northwestern Europe, while millions of Northwest Europeans took holidays in Portugal, fostering ever closer contact with and dependence upon Northwestern Europe. Hence, less than three years after the April 1974 coup against Salazar's 'anointed' successor Marcelo Caetano, Portugal applied for full EC membership. This historic step was taken both as a consummation of Portugal's deepening relations with EC states and as a reinforcement of Portugal's still fragile transition to parliamentary democracy. Opposition to membership came only from the hard Left and the far Right, both of which still hankered after Portugal's former colonial links with Angola, Mozambique and Guinea-Bissau, whereas the more European-minded Socialist and Social Democratic Parties were seeking a clean break with that past. The loss of those African colonies in 1974–5, at the end of protracted and costly colonial wars, had played an important psychological role in reorientating Portugal towards Europe. Moreover, the subsequent rapid growth of Spanish, German and French trade with, and investment in, Portugal finally ended the British ascendancy. Henceforth, no one country would dominate either the Portuguese economy or its external economic relations.

Contrary to initial fears that the Portuguese economy might be too weak to withstand the impact of full membership of the EC, it grew by 4.6 per cent annually from 1986 to 1990, as against an EC average of 3.1 per cent, helped by investment and export growth running at double the EC average. 'Each year, some 120,000 new jobs were created, halving unemployment to a mere 4.2 per cent, a quarter of the rates in neighbouring Spain or in Ireland, countries just above Portugal on the EC's development ladder.'[33] The real danger was that the boom (and inflation) might surge out of control.

The decline in Portuguese economic growth after 1990 was less severe and of shorter duration than the economic recession in other EC states. Overall, after contracting by 3.2 per cent between 1974 and 1985, the Portuguese economy grew by 3.17 per cent per annum from late 1985 to 1995, compared with 2.75 per cent for Spain and 2.29 per cent for the EU[34]

Table 8.2 The Portuguese economy, 1985–94 (%)[35]

	1985	1986	1987	1988	1989	1990	1991	1992	1993	1994
GDP growth	2.9	4.0	5.0	3.8	5.4	4.4	2.5	2.3	−1.0	1.1
Inflation	19.6	11.8	9.0	9.7	12.6	13.3	11.4	8.9	6.5	5.4
Unemployment	10.2	10.1	7.8	5.6	4.8	4.6	4.1	4.2	6.3	7.1

and near stagnation in Greece. Portugal's per capita GDP rose from 51.4 per cent of the EC average in 1985 to 64.5 per cent of the EU average by 1994 and, if Portugal's annual GDP growth continues to be 0.88 per cent above the EU-12 average, it should draw level with most of its EU partners by 2035.[36] The Portuguese trade deficits that emerged in 1990 and 1991 were more than offset by rising invisible earnings and large capital inflows. The IMF-backed stabilization programmes of 1978–80 and 1983–5, the new investment laws adopted in 1980 and 1985 and the knowledge that all Portuguese exports would soon enjoy unrestricted access to EC markets attracted large volumes of foreign direct investment to Portugal after 1986.

Table 8.3 Foreign investment in Portugal, 1980–92[37]

Amounts (billions)	1980–4	1985	1986	1987	1988	1989	1990	1991	1992
Escudos	68.4	42.3	24.5	61.6	138	353	509	–	–
US dollars	–	–	0.16	0.44	0.96	2.22	3.37	5.53	4.38

Origin, 1980–9	UK	USA	France	Spain	EFTA	Brazil	Japan	EC total
Percentage of total	23.1	12.6	11.4	10.9	10.5	4.9	1.1	64.5

As a proportion of GDP, foreign direct investment rose from 0.6 per cent in 1986 to 3.7 per cent in 1990 and 6.0 per cent in 1991.[38] (Partly for this reason, Portugal's gold and foreign currency reserves stood at $25 bn in 1992, comfortably exceeding its $16 bn foreign debt.) Although this foreign investment mostly went into tourism, real estate, banking and services, nearly one-third went into manufacturing. Portugal attracted multinationals from Northern Europe, the USA, East Asia and Brazil, both to serve the fast-growing Portuguese market and to develop production bases from which to export to other EC markets. EC membership transformed a small and introverted economy of ten million people into a 'low-cost launching pad into a market of 320 million consumers'.[39] The flagship project was a three-billion dollar 'state-of-the-art' Ford–Volkswagen car plant (AutoEuropa), won in the face of stiff European competition and expected to boost GDP by 1 per cent and Portugal's manufactured exports by 20 per cent in 1995, its first full year of production. Portugal's cheap labour, flexible working practices, 'tamed' trade unions, tax incentives, EC subsidies, political stability and a resolutely free-marketeering government under the right-wing Social Democrat Anibal Cavaco Silva (1985–95) also attracted a Ford car electronics plant, a General Motors ignitions system plant, a CofaEuropa car components works, a Neste petrochemicals plant and a Pepsico potato crisp factory, with many more projects in the pipeline. Overall, these projects were expected to enhance GDP by 2–3 per cent and to increase Portuguese exports by 20–30 per cent in 1995, reinforcing the economic recovery that began in 1994.[40] Large net inflows of foreign investment assisted Portugal to upgrade, equip and expand its potential growth industries, thus helping to offset the steady decline of Portugal's traditional, under-capitalized and over-manned textiles, footwear, metallurgical, shipbuilding, fisheries and agricultural sectors and to restructure the economy and workforce towards more dynamic, efficient, profitable and capital-intensive ventures, enabling it to begin to compete on the basis of increased productivity, quality and innovation, rather than simply on the demeaning basis of having Western Europe's cheapest labour. Foreign investment was also helping to modernize and expand much of Portugal's existing infrastructure and productive capacity, simultaneously infusing technological innovation and new methods of management.

The main limitation of this pattern of economic development, apart from its vulnerability to fluctuations in external conditions and foreign investment, was that it was concentrated mainly in the richer and more developed metropolitan region and in the Algarve rather than the relatively impoverished and increasingly depopulated interior or the industrially depressed North. Social, intergenerational and interregional inequalities widened. The propertied, professional and entrepreneurial classes prospered during the boom, as did many skilled workers, technicians and educated young people, but Portugal's poor probably became poorer and more numerous as a result of highish inflation, soaring rents and property prices, sharp contraction of agriculture and traditional light industries (especially textiles) and inadequate social provisions. Portugal still has Western Europe's lowest wage rates and highest illiteracy rates, and its cities are disfigured by extensive slums and shanty towns populated by former agricultural workers, redundant industrial workers and people displaced from the ex-colonies. The Left has maintained that education, housing, health-care, pensions and other social provisions were neglected in order to keep down taxation on private companies, foreign investors and the well-to-do, but this may have been the price to be paid for sustaining the recent pattern of economic growth, which enjoyed stronger electoral support than the redistributive programmes of the Left, even if the socialist and communist votes are added together.

By 1992, as the hitherto rapid growth of foreign direct investment in Portugal tapered off, the country had become a net recipient of large fiscal transfers from the EC: roughly $3 bn per annum or 4 per cent of Portuguese GDP in 1992 and 1993. By 1995 45 per cent of public investment was financed by the EU, and by 1999 the annual net transfer from the EU should rise to double the 1992-3 level. According to António Gueterres, the Socialist leader of the opposition, the ruling Social Democratic Party:

> has created a vast network of clients, partly through the way it distributes EU funds and other subsidies. . . . The government intervenes in the economy in the interests of these clients, who are political supporters, rather than on the basis of clear policies.[41]

However, some foreign observers have put a much more favourable gloss on Cavaco Silva's eleven-year premiership. In sharp contrast to the 1981–9 Papandreou Government in Greece, the tough Cavaco Silva Government liberalized the labour market, faced down the trade unions, implemented a moderate privatization programme (despite the major legal/constitutional obstacles bequeathed by the April 1974 Revolution), kept a relatively tight rein on public expenditure and did not permit pay rises regularly to outstrip productivity growth. Thus Portugal's cost advantages and international competitiveness were not eroded by soft budget constraints and uncontrolled cost inflation. Blessed with a solid Socialist–Social Democrat consensus on deeper integration into Europe and with no territorial distractions, Cavaco Silva was able to concentrate on 'good housekeeping'. He took himself and his role very seriously, perhaps too seriously, and his iron resolve to do what he believed to be necessary to make Portugal internationally competitive and attractive to foreign capital proved to be more popular than the softer options offered by the Socialist opposition. His Social Democrats gained over 50 per cent of the votes in the 1987 and 1991 general elections and could probably have done so again in October 1995, as another nicely timed cyclical economic upturn gathered pace in late 1994 and early 1995, had he not decided to stand down in 1995.

All in all, EC membership brought with it new stimuli, positive responses, massive capital inflows and a sense of belonging to a larger and more challenging world. The Portuguese became more confident, dynamic and 'modern'. The heady idealism of 1974–6 steadily gave way to more hard-headed economic realism, careerism and materialism, especially among the younger generations.[42] For many 'convergence' meant, above all, gradually catching up with wage levels in Northwestern

Europe. The efficient Portuguese Presidency of the EU in early 1992 advertised Portugal's enhanced status and self-assurance on the international stage.

SPAIN AND EUROPEAN INTEGRATION[43]

Spain's accession to the EC in January 1986 was the consummation of a political and economic transformation that had been taking place since 1959, when a group of Catholic Opus Dei technocrats began to open up the Spanish economy to foreign trade and investment, reversing the autarkic and isolationist policies pursued from 1939 to 1951, during the most fascist phase of Franco's dictatorship. Spain first requested associate EC membership in 1962. The more serious discussions which began abortively in 1964 and again in 1967 eventually led to a preferential trade agreement in 1970, but the EC was unwilling to enter a closer liaison as long as Franco ruled Spain.

The reforming conservative coalition government of Adolfo Suárez (1976–81) applied for full EC membership in July 1977, four months after Portugal and one month after winning a sweeping victory in the first democratic elections held since Franco's death. The government had hoped that entry terms could have been negotiated and agreed by 1980, in time for admission soon after Greece. But French, Italian and subsequently Greek fears of the economic consequences of Spanish entry – mainly for their own producers of Mediterranean farm products, but also for the CAP and for EC industries such as steel, coal, cars, textiles and footwear – and German concerns over the budgetary implications, dragged out the negotiations from late 1979 until March 1985. In the interim Spain concluded a free-trade pact with the EFTA in December 1978. When Spain finally entered the EC in 1986, it had a socialist government under Felipe González. Having won a landslide election victory in October 1982 on a programme of radical reform and modernization, González continued to enjoy comfortable working majorities until the June 1993 election, after which he headed an increasingly vulnerable and beleaguered government whose increasingly tough monetary, fiscal and deregulatory policies and alleged abuses of power had antagonized many of its former supporters at a time of deep economic recession and very high unemployment.

Spain's EC admission did indeed seem to pose a major challenge for its existing members, especially France, Italy and, from January 1981, Greece. Spain's accession was to increase EC territory by nearly one third (in terms of land area it was the second largest EC member), total population by 14 per cent, cultivated area by 30 per cent, agricultural population by 25 per cent and fishing fleet by 70 per cent – Spain had the EC's largest fishing fleet in terms of both tonnage and numbers of boats. Spain then accounted for over 40 per cent of the world's olive-oil production and 20 per cent of the world's citrus-fruit exports. It also had Europe's most extensive vineyards, although its grape yields were well below those of France and Italy. By 1985, over 85 per cent of Spain's fresh fruit and vegetable exports were destined for the EC-10 and Spain was the third largest exporter of farm produce to the EC after the USA and Brazil. By the early 1980s Spain's industrial and agricultural exports exceeded those of all the other Mediterranean states put together. Thus the admission of Spain to the EC would further disadvantage those Mediterranean states which were not members and add to EC surpluses of wine and olive oil and to CAP costs, although, as a net importer of grain and dairy produce, it would help to reduce EC grain and milk product surpluses. The perceived 'threats' were softened or mitigated by EC insistence on a ten-year transition period for Spanish agricultural exports, seven-year transitions toward freedom of movement and free trade in industrial goods (i.e. until the end of 1992), and a sixteen-year transition to full access to EC fishing grounds and the Common Fisheries Policy (later brought forward to January 1996 as part of a 'deal' on the EU's 1995 northern enlargement).

Unlike the British debates on joining the EC, which had concentrated on the economics of the 'Common Market' and the CAP, in Spain there was relatively little debate on the economic implications of EC membership until quite late in the day. That was another reason why the final phase of the negotiations was so difficult and protracted, as Spaniards belatedly woke up to the risks and consequences of the step they were taking. Hitherto, while France, Italy and Greece were baulking at the potentially detrimental effects of Spanish accession on their own producers of Mediterranean foodstuffs and on their established trade partners in North Africa and the Near East, Spaniards had, understandably, been more pre-occupied by the dramatic political changes and conflicts within Spain itself. Between Franco's death in November 1975 and the advent of Spain's first socialist government since the 1930s in December 1982, Spaniards had seen the legalization of political parties and trade unions, the restoration of the monarchy, the abolition of censorship, the secularization of the state and public education, the introduction of civil marriage and divorce, the promulgation of a new democratic constitution, several attempted coups (including the dramatic televised seizure of the Cortes [Parliament] by Francoist Civil Guards in 1981) and the establishment of a quasi-federal system of regional autonomies, all against a backdrop of severe economic recession, a war of attrition against Basque terrorism and a war of nerves against security forces who still hankered after the Franco régime and a free hand to deal with Basque terrorism and Catalan 'insubordination' once and for all. Thus Spaniards had bigger issues to think about than the price of butter.

In 1986, when the first contingent of Spanish officials arrived to take up their new posts in the Brussels bureaucracy, some of them must have ruefully reflected on the fact that four centuries earlier Brussels had been an important outpost of the Spanish Empire. But the Spanish state had spent the next four hundred years vainly trying to promote a not-so-splendid Spanish isolation, a sense of separateness from the rest of Europe, only to throw in the towel and seek the reintegration of a much weakened and humbled Spain into 'Europe' in the 1970s. For Spain, indeed, the importance of EC accession was primarily political and psychological, marking a 'return' to a Europe from which it had stood apart for too long and a concern to consolidate and enlist European support for the then still fragile restoration of parliamentary democracy and the rule of law. Accession to the EC and the long negotiations that preceded it provided Spain's post-Francoist governments with additional leverage to push through far-reaching measures of political and economic liberalization which brought Spain into line with the laws, procedures, standards and commercial practices of Northwestern Europe.

In Spain EC membership has enjoyed all-party support since the later 1970s. The only significant opposition came from some initially dangerous 'unreconstructed' Francoist elements in the security forces and from the small grain and livestock farmers of northern Spain, whose survival was threatened by increased exposure to competition from their bigger French, Dutch, Danish and British counterparts. In contrast to Portugal and Greece, EC membership was not opposed by a hardline communist party. The Spanish Communist Party under Santiago Carrillo was a leading proponent of Italian-style 'Eurocommunism' and, unlike the Portuguese Communist Party, had few connections with revolutionary liberation struggles in Africa. Similarly, the Right had weaned itself away from nostalgic attachments to Spain's imperial past, having forfeited the last important remnants of Spain's once-great colonial empire when Cuba and the Philippines were 'liberated' by the US in the Spanish–American 'War of 1898'. After 1900 all that remained were a few toeholds in North Africa. Furthermore, Spanish 'big business' and the big landowners or latifundists of southern Spain expected to be major net beneficiaries of Spanish accession to the EC, in contrast to the much smaller, weaker or less confident industrialists and agriculturalists of Portugal and Greece. Moreover, many of Spain's industrialists were members of the Basque and Catalan minorities, who expected EC membership to free them from the irksome tutelage of (predominantly Castilian) central governments in Madrid.

EC membership even became a means of holding together the several nations and regions that make up modern Spain. The perilous difficulties involved in modernizing twentieth-century Spain and at the same time holding it together had prompted the Spanish philosopher José Ortega y Gasset to utter his famous statement that 'If Spain is the problem, Europe is the solution.' This came to encapsulate the hopes that the intelligentsia vested in Spain's eventual EC accession. The EC commitment to a 'Europe of the Regions' thus acquired a particular resonance in post-Francoist Spain, which endeavoured to reconcile the rival aspirations of the Catalans, Basques, Galicians, Asturians, Andalusians and Castilians by devolving power to autonomous regions whose dealings with each other and with the rest of the EC would nevertheless continue to be co-ordinated and mediated by a central government in Madrid. In drawing up the quasi-federal December 1978 Constitution, Premier Adolfo Suárez and King Juan Carlos sought to avoid devolving power merely to Catalonia and the Basque Country, granting them a privileged position vis-à-vis the other historic regions of Spain, as any such move would have been a red rag to many Castilian bulls, especially those elements in the security forces who regarded the crushing of the Basques and Catalans as Franco's 'finest achievement'. Instead, power was gradually to be devolved to seventeen semi-autonomous regions, each with its own revenues and elected regional assemblies and governments, in the hope of averting both a Castilian centralist backlash or a potential Yugoslav-style disintegration of Spain into several separate states. Once established, the regional governments and assemblies naturally endeavoured to enhance their own powers, revenues, spheres of competence, external representation and direct relations with the EC. This was assisted by the concurrent pan-European resurgence of nationalism, increased freedom of speech and association and the vision of a 'Europe of the Regions', causing continuous haggling and bickering between the centre and the regions over budgetary powers, financial allocations, EC relations and representation, policing and the role of the security forces. Madrid nevertheless managed to maintain the preponderance of the central government and bureaucracy, the Cortes and the centrally controlled security forces, to reserve the right to determine the framework of centre–region relations and to preserve the Kingdom of 'all the Spains', successfully preventing the creation of a truly federal state. Indeed, having lost an empire, the centre found a new role as arbiter between the diverse regions of Spain and mediator between those regions and the EU, assisted by the fact that EU regional, social, agricultural, structural and cohesion funds are mainly distributed to the regions via Madrid, which in turn funnels the views, bids and demands of the Spanish regions back to Brussels. Holding Spain together has long been Madrid's major problem. Membership of the EU is what, for the time being, functionally unites the disparate communities that make up Spain.[44]

No sooner had Spain and Portugal joined the EC in 1986 than they were confronted by the challenge of gearing up for the advent of the Single European Market (SEM) in 1992. They had to enact and implement a huge volume of SEM legislation on top of the massive task of 'harmonization' of Iberian laws and practices (including some 'Spanish practices') with the large body of EC laws, taxes and commercial procedures that had developed between 1951 and 1986. But for most Spaniards (other than legislators) 'preparing for 1992' mainly meant the $8 bn spent on preparations for the 1992 Barcelona Olympics, the Seville Expo 92 World Fair and the Columbus five-hundredth anniversary celebrations, which, ironically, turned sour by precipitating embarrassing accusations of excessive extravagance and highly critical inquests into the Ibero-American heritage.

In June 1989, just three and a half years after joining the EC, González decided to take Spain into the ERM. Spain's decision to join was facilitated by the strength at that time of the peseta, which was buoyed up by the huge influx of foreign investment and private loan capital into Spain after its accession in 1986 and by the high interest rates adopted from mid-1988 onward in an attempt to restrain the ensuing economic boom and inflationary pressures. Spain's economy grew by 5 per cent annually from 1986 to 1989 inclusive and approximately $30 bn of direct foreign investment was pumped into the economy. However, while Spain became a major recipient of EC 'structural' and 'cohesion' funds, such transfers amounted to less than 1 per cent of its comparatively large GDP in the early 1990s.[45]

Table 8.4 The Spanish economy, 1985–94 (%)[46]

	1985	1986	1987	1988	1989	1990	1991	1992	1993	1994
GDP growth	2.3	3.2	5.5	5.3	5.2	3.7	2.3	0.8	−1.0	1.1
Inflation	8.8	8.8	4.6	5.8	6.9	6.7	5.9	5.9	4.6	4.7
Unemployment	23.0	21.5	20.8	20.6	16.2	16.1	16.3	19.6	23.4	24.0

Awash with foreign capital, Spain's per capita GDP rose from 72 per cent of the EC average in 1986 to 78 per cent by 1991.[47] However, while Spain's real GDP trebled between 1964 and 1994, recorded employment remained almost static at 11.7 million, despite a 25 per cent population increase over the same period. This left 3.7 million people, or 24.2 per cent of the workforce, without declared employment in June 1994. Even though up to a million of the registered unemployed were considered to have significant undeclared earnings from the sizeable 'black economy', Spain nevertheless continued to have the EU's highest unemployment levels and this is likely to remain the case throughout the 1990s. The essential problem has been that the expanding economic activities are mainly (and increasingly) capital-intensive, whereas the declining ones are mainly (and decreasingly) labour-intensive. Additionally, many employers have been gearing up to increasingly competitive global markets, not just the SEM, while Spain was still industrializing. Therefore, a resumption of rapid economic growth in the later 1990s would not necessarily lead to fuller employment before 2001. Employers have been further discouraged from taking on additional employees by the rigidity of the inherited Francoist labour laws, by the growing burden of social insurance contributions pay-able by employers (as governments built up a modern welfare state, social expenditure rose from 27 per cent of GDP in 1977 to over 50 per cent in 1993), by a mismatch between the changing manpower requirements of the Spanish economy and the available skills – reflecting both the rapidity of structural change and the continuing paucity of vocational training and retraining provisions – and by a 42 per cent leap in unit labour costs (in domestic prices) between 1987 and 1992, as a result of the rising expecta-tions and other pressures generated by EC entry and the ensuing boom, compared with an average 13 per cent rise in unit labour costs in France, Germany and Benelux over the same period.[48] It is therefore uncertain whether rapid economic growth will be resumed after the economic and political hiatus of 1992–4, in the increasingly competitive and deflationary environment of the SEM, the ERM and preparations for EMU.

CONCLUSIONS

During the 1960s and 1970s, especially on the left and in the 'dependency' and 'core–periphery' literature on Southern Europe,[49] it was widely assumed that the prevalent liberal, free-marketeering, capitalist forms of European integration would merely make it easier for the EC's more developed and centrally located 'core' areas to prosper at the expense of Europe's less developed peripheries. The results of the first decade of Spanish and Portuguese EC membership spectacularly confounded the pessimists' expectations. EC membership not only accelerated economic growth and structural change, but also brought tangible welfare gains to most of their inhabitants and 'progressive' changes in thinking, attitudes, institutions and practices. Consequently, the pessimistic assumptions of the neo-Marxist left and of the 'dependency' and 'core–periphery' literature lost much of their purchase on Spanish and Portuguese political and economic opinion, as it flew in the face of actual experience. On the other hand, the poor political and economic performance of Greece subsequent to joining the EC in 1981 seemed to vindicate the pessimistic presumptions of the 'anti-imperialist', neo-Marxist Greek left and radical nationalists. Indeed, 'dependency' and 'core–periphery' concepts seemed to offer convenient face-saving excuses and external scapegoats for Greece's poor performance, which could thus be seen as 'structurally predetermined' by the inherently unequal, asymmetrical and exploitative economic and power relations between the EC's less developed 'peripheries' and its highly developed 'core'. It is therefore scarcely surprising that such theories and concepts continued to hold sway on the left and among radical nation-alists in Greece, helping to perpetuate an 'underdog syndrome' which encouraged many Greeks to blame their economic, social and 'national' misfortunes on external forces beyond their control, instead of putting their own house in order with the resoluteness and dogged determination that has characterized the Portuguese Social Democrats, with the qualified support of Portugal's Socialist Party. The overwhelmingly positive experiences of Portugal and Spain since 1985 strongly suggest that Greece's poor showing was in fact neither inevitable nor 'structurally predetermined' and that, with different policies and attitudes, Greece could have achieved a happier outcome both for itself and for the EU. The Portuguese economic achievement since the mid-1980s is even more impressive than the Spanish because the initial 'raw materials' were far less promising and the processes of liberalizing the domestic economy and opening it up to foreign trade, investment and visitors started so much later. Spain embarked on such a course in 1959, unleashing a wave of industrialization, diversification and inward investment which lasted from 1963 until the quadrupling of OPEC oil prices in 1973–4. The Franco régime (paradoxically) ran down the armed forces, kept Spain free of debilitating foreign entanglements and distractions and reaped great benefits from the concurrent Western economic boom and liberalization. During that same period Salazar embroiled Portugal in costly colonial wars which drained the economy, incurred mounting international condemnation and ostracization and eventually precipitated the military overthrow of his successor in 1974, leading in turn to a decade of political instability and zero growth (1974–84). Thus, despite its participation in EFTA and the growth of migration and tourism, Portugal initially derived very limited benefits from the 1960s Western boom and liberalization.

> The Salazar régime promoted a handful of powerful business families by regulating which companies could operate in which sectors and closing the country off to foreign investment. This oligarchy sheltered business groups from competition, but also prevented them from developing entrepreneurial skills and a free market mentality.[50]

Whereas Franco bequeathed to his democratic successors an essentially sound, vibrant, outward-orientated capitalist economy, which only awaited a chance to 'take off' again after the economic doldrums of 1974–84, Salazar bequeathed a small, secluded, stagnating, obsolescent economy which had to undergo drastic surgery and 'opening up' in 1978–80 and 1983–5. However, precisely because Portugal is so much smaller (in every sense) than Spain, EC/EU 'structural funds' and foreign investment have had a much greater impact on Portugal, while the much greater size of the Spanish domestic market makes it less dependent on free access to external markets than Portugal. However, the major advantage that both countries had over Greece was that they had already embarked on major programmes of macroeconomic stabilization and structural adjustment *before* their accessions to the EC. Perhaps even more important than the programmes themselves was the creation of political coalitions or cross-party consensuses with the necessary degree of resolve to see such programmes through to fruition.

FURTHER READING

Occasional *Financial Times* and *Economist* surveys of Greece, Portugal and Spain.

D. Birmingham, *A Concise History of Portugal*, Cambridge: Cambridge University Press, 1993.

R. Clogg, *A Concise History of Greece*, Cambridge: Cambridge University Press, 1992.

A. Freris, *The Greek Economy in the Twentieth Century*, London: Croom Helm, 1986.

P. Heywood, *Spain's Next Five Years: A Political Risk Analysis*, London: Economist Intelligence Unit, Special Report no. 2136, 1991.

J. Hooper, *The New Spaniards*, Harmondsworth: Penguin, 1995.

R. McDonald, *Greece in the 1990s: Taking Its Place in Europe*, London: Economist Intelligence Unit Special Report, 1991.

K. Salmon, *The Modern Spanish Economy: Transformation and Integration into Europe*, London: Pinter, 1991.

NOTES

1 T. Burns, *Financial Times Survey: Portugal*, 28 October 1994, p. iii.

2 Compiled from information in: L. Tsoukalis, *The European Community and its Mediterranean Enlargement*, London: Allen & Unwin, 1981, pp. 37, 60, 85; A. Williams, *The European Community*, Oxford: Blackwell, 1991, p. 68; A. Freris, *The Greek Economy in the Twentieth Century*, London: Croom Helm, 1986, p. 211; and various *Financial Times Surveys* of Greece, Portugal and Spain.

3 R. Clogg, *A Concise History of Greece*, Cambridge: Cambridge University Press, 1992, p. 206.

4 Quoted in: L. Stavrianos, *The Balkans since 1453*, New York: Holt, Rinehart & Winston, 1958, p. 292.

5 The cavalier manner in which Churchill and Stalin divided up the Balkans is described with remarkable candour in: W. S. Churchill, *The Second World War*, Harmondsworth: Penguin, 1989, pp. 852–6, 876.

6 See, for example, the cogent analyses in: Freris (n. 2 above), pp. 181, 196 and 216–18 ff.

7 See, for example: N. Mouzelis, *Modern Greece: Facets of Underdevelopment*, London: Macmillan, 1978, *passim*; and M. Evangelides, 'Core–Periphery Problems in the Greek Case', in: D. Seers *et al.* (eds), *Underdeveloped Europe: Studies in Core–Periphery Relations*, Hassocks: Harvester Press, 1979, pp. 177–95.

8 L. Doyle, *Independent*, 13 June 1994.

9 Historically, Orthodox Christians have been 'profoundly hostile to the West . . . as the home of Catholicism and Protestantism and as the birthplace of the Renaissance. . . . In short, Balkan Orthodoxy opposed the West not only because it was heretical but also because it was becoming modern. The inevitable result of this opposition was the intellectual isolation and stagnation of the Balkan peoples', according to Stavrianos, p. 111.

10 L. Doyle, *Independent*, 9 June 1994.

11 *Guardian*, 13 October 1993.

12 H. Smith, *Guardian*, 22 February 1994.

13 Freris (n. 2 above), p. 202.

14 Ibid., pp. 203, 214.

15 A. Ierodiaconou, *Financial Times* (hereafter *FT*), 8 January 1985.

16 M. Thatcher, *The Downing Street Years*, London: HarperCollins, 1993, p. 337.
17 *FT Survey: Greece*, 25 April 1992, p. ii.
18 *FT*, 23 March 1993.
19 B. Beedham, 'Survey of Greece', *The Economist*, 22 May 1993, p. 6; and J. Rigos, *International Herald Tribune* (hereafter *IHT*), 2 June 1994.
20 K. Hope, *FT*, 13 October 1993.
21 The Greek Institute of Economic Research, quoted by V. Walker, *The Times*, 24 June 1994.
22 L. Tsoukalis, *The New European Economy*, Oxford: Oxford University Press, 2nd edn, 1993, p. 257.
23 In 1994 he and two colleagues were charged with accepting a $22.5 m bribe during the privatization of Heracles Cement in 1992, but the charge was dropped amid great controversy in January 1995 as part of a political deal with Papandreou.
24 Beedham (n. 19 above), p. 6.
25 K. Hope, *FT*, 30 July 1992.
26 François Duchêne impressed this point on me.
27 The Badinter Commission was established by the EC in December 1990 to ascertain whether the former Yugoslav Republics met the standard criteria for international recognition as independent states (a permanent population, a defined territory, and a government in effective control of that population and territory) and, in addition, whether they had adequate respect and constitutional safeguards for ethnic minorities. Greece exploited these criteria to delay EC recognition of the Republic of Macedonia and also its admission to the UN, thereby depriving it of desperately needed international support at a time when it was in great danger of disintegrating and sucking Albania, Bulgaria and Greece into the conflicts precipitated by the breakup of Yugoslavia. The Greek state has not only denied the rights of ethnic minorities, but has prosecuted as 'traitors' people with the temerity to champion their rights and/ or existence, to call them by their chosen names, or to publicise Greek violations of their human/cultural rights. See: *Macedonian Minorities*, London: British Helsinki Human Rights Group, 1994.
28 J. Eyal, *Independent*, 12 October 1993.
29 K. Hope, *FT*, 29 August 1990. In November 1993 Pangalos, once again European Affairs Minister, gratuitously referred to Germany as 'a giant with bestial strength and the brain of a child' and accused Turkey of 'dragging its bloodied boots across the carpets of Europe'.
30 P. Marsh and K. Hope, *FT*, 7 January 1995.
31 Portugal also allowed the RAF to use the Azores during the Falklands War in 1982.
32 Tsoukalis (n. 22 above), pp. 54, 60.
33 D. Gardner in: *FT Survey: Portugal*, 4 November 1991, p. ii.
34 P. Wise in: *FT Survey: Portugal*, 28 October 1994, p. i.
35 Compiled from *FT Surveys* of Portugal from 30 October 1987 to 28 October 1994.
36 P. Wise (n. 34 above).
37 Compiled from *FT Surveys* of Portugal, 23 April 1991, p. iv; 26 April 1993, p. iv; and *IHT*, 15 November 1990.
38 D. Gardner in: *FT Survey: Portugal*, 4 November 1991, p. iv.
39 Ibid.
40 *FT Surveys* of Portugal, 22 February 1994, p. iii, and 28 October 1994, p. ii.
41 *FT Survey: Portugal*, 28 October 1994, p. i.

42 Changes in social attitudes are perceptively analysed by P. Blum in: *FT Survey: Portugal*, 4 November 1991, p. i.
43 This section is generally indebted to twenty years of excellent *FT* reportage on Spain, mainly by Robert Graham and, latterly, Peter Bruce and Tom Burns.
44 P. Bruce, *FT*, 4 January 1992.
45 *FT Survey: Spain*, 1 June 1992, p. v; *Independent*, 2 December 1992.
46 Compiled from various *FT Surveys* of Spain, from 1986 to 1994.
47 *FT*, 19 November 1991.
48 This analysis is based on a report by ICAE, the Economic Analysis Institute of Madrid's Complutense University, as summarized by T. Burns in: *FT*, 30 September 1994; supplemented by P. Bruce in: *FT Survey: Spain*, 1 June 1992; T. Burns in: *FT Survey: Spain*, 11 May 1994; and P. Heywood, *Spain's Next Five Years: A Political Risk Analysis*, London: Economist Intelligence Unit, Special Report no. 2136, 1991.
49 See: Mouzelis (n. 7 above); Seers *et al.* (eds) (n. 7 above), especially chs 1, 5, 8 and 10; and: R. King, 'Southern Europe: Dependency or Development?', *Geography*, vol. 67 (1982), no. 4, pp. 221–34.
50 P. Wise, *FT*, 22 April 1994.

9 National identity in a united and divided Germany

Gareth Pritchard

In Germany, as elsewhere in Europe, the disintegration of the Soviet bloc and the ongoing integration of Western European states have unleashed a far-reaching debate on European and foreign policy issues. To some extent, this debate has covered the same terrain as in many of the other countries of the European Union. In Germany, as in Britain, France and Italy, there have been heated arguments between 'Eurosceptics' and 'Europhiles' over the economic and political implications of the Exchange Rate Mechanism (ERM), over the desirability of a single European currency, and over the Maastricht Treaty.

But, perhaps to a greater extent than in any other Western European country, the debate about a future role in Europe has been much, much more than simply a debate about the future of the European Union. As Timothy Garton Ash has pointed out, 'All European countries are having to re-examine their national interests after the end of the Cold War. But nowhere is the re-examination more fundamental, and in few places is it proving more difficult, than in Germany.'[1]

The intensity of the European policy debate in Germany has been partly due to the fact that, given its central economic and geographical significance, Germany is confronted by opportunities and perceived dangers that other Western European countries simply do not have to face. Unification and the collapse of the Soviet Empire have left Germany as the dominant political and economic power on the European continent. In particular, the whole of Eastern Europe and Russia now lie open to German economic penetration. All this inevitably raises difficult questions about the relationship between the Federal Republic and the other nations of Europe. Some politicians, both in Germany and in other European countries, have voiced the fear that the new-found pre-eminence of Germany is unhealthy, and that the Federal Republic is now achieving through peaceful means the hegemony that previous German régimes failed to achieve through force of arms. Others have argued that, on the contrary, the Federal Republic can and should play a leading role in integrating the two halves of Europe into a democratic and prosperous whole.

Germany is also unique amongst the nations of the European Union in the sense that the collapse of the Soviet bloc, and the construction of a post-Cold-War European order, are matters which have had a crucial bearing, not just on Germany's relations with her neighbours, but also on German domestic politics. The Iron Curtain that divided Western and Eastern Europe also sundered the Federal Republic of Germany from the GDR. Now that the Iron Curtain has been torn down, the Germans are confronted with the task of reuniting their own divided homeland. To this extent, the problems of re-integrating Eastern and Western Europe are mirrored on the smaller stage of German domestic politics.

The purpose of this chapter is to examine both the European and the domestic aspects of post-Cold-War reconstruction in Germany. Particular emphasis will be placed on the underlying problems of German history and national identity, which have rendered the debate so contentious and divisive. In West Germany, for example, it has never been possible to discuss the role of Germany in Europe without being drawn into the continuing debate about Germany's bloody and traumatic past. As Günter Grass has pointed out, 'whoever thinks about Germany and looks for answers to the German question must also think about Auschwitz'.[2] Equally, no discussion about German domestic re-integration can fail to overlook the fact that the East German people have a separate and distinct history, and, to some extent at least, a distinctive, specifically East German identity.

IN HITLER'S SHADOW: NATIONAL IDENTITY IN WEST GERMANY

Throughout the whole of post-war West German history, few important domestic debates, and almost no foreign policy ones, have failed to be influenced in some way by the continuing ideological battle between adherents of different interpretations of the Nazi period. All political tendencies in the Federal Republic have predicated their views on the present and the future on their various interpretations of the Nazi past. On numerous occasions, this debate has become an argument, not just about the details of German history, but about fundamental issues of German nationality and national identity. In West Germany since 1945 the struggle to determine the political future of the country, and the struggle to interpret its past, have been one and the same thing.

Thus, in the first months and years after the war, the political stage in West Germany was dominated by those who wanted to make a fundamental break with the Nazi past. Particularly amongst West German socialists and trade unionists, but also amongst progressive Christian circles, there was a widespread belief that Nazism had been no historical accident, but had sprung from the reactionary character of the German political establishment. In these radical and left-wing quarters, the finger of blame was pointed above all at the traditional political and social élites, such as the 'monopoly capitalists', the Junkers, and the German officer corps, which, it was believed, had paved the Nazis' road to power. In order to break the stranglehold of these reactionary groups on German society, the radical anti-Nazis advocated far-reaching political and economic reforms, such as land reform, nationalization, and sweeping de-Nazification.[3]

The reforming zeal of German anti-Nazis during the immediate post-war period was by no means restricted to domestic political matters. The overwhelming majority of socialists and trade unionists also wanted to see a fundamental revision of the role played by Germany in Europe. Germany, they argued, should abandon the imperialistic and expansionistic traditions of the past, and seek to build a Europe in which all nations would co-operate as equals. In particular, many anti-Nazis wanted to see Germany establish a close and friendly relationship with the Soviet Union. The goal, for many German socialists and trade unionists, was a united, neutral and unaligned Germany, which would be both socialist and democratic, and which would serve as a bridge between East and West. The leadership of the West German labour movement was rather more hostile than the rank-and-file towards the Soviet Union, but even fervent anti-communists such as Kurt Schumacher wanted post-war Germany to adopt a neutral foreign policy which would keep the country out of the incipient Cold War conflict between the United States and the USSR.[4]

In the immediate post-war period, the prospects for such a fundamental transformation of German society seemed to be good. The old state machine, which up till then had presented an insuperable obstacle to social progress, had disintegrated utterly during the last months and weeks of the war. In Germany in 1945, there was no army, no police force, no judiciary or civil service, to frustrate a radical overhaul of German politics and society. At the same time, the old political parties of the Centre and the Right were dispersed, demoralized, and discredited by the feeble resistance that they had offered to the Nazis. In 1945, socialists and progressive Christians constituted the only active force in West German politics, and they wanted to use this advantage, not just to push through a series of radical domestic reforms, but also to develop a neutral foreign policy orientation.

All such aspirations were to be disappointed. The British, French and American occupying authorities did not want to see any radical transformation of German society, and, during the early years of the occupation, they placed severe restrictions on the activities of West German anti-Nazis. In particular, the Western Allies were determined to deny a' political role to all German anti-Nazi organizations that were suspected of harbouring sympathies towards the Soviet Union. Thus the radical 'anti-fascist committees', which had sprung up in great profusion in the spring of 1945, were suppressed.[5] Trade unions were prohibited from organizing except on a purely local level.[6] A blanket ban was placed on open political activity, which in reality only affected the Social Democratic Party (SPD) and the Communist Party (KPD), because they were the only parties that existed on the ground.[7] Reforming legislation passed by the new German provincial authorities was vetoed.[8] At the same time, the Western military governments reconstructed the German state machine from the ground up, whilst covertly fostering the political organizations of the Centre and Right.[9] By 1949, the political balance between Left and Right had been restored, and the Western Allies felt confident enough to permit the resumption in West Germany of normal democratic politics.

But the greatest single obstacle to the plans of West German anti-Nazis was the apathy and passivity of Germans themselves. Twelve years of Nazism and war may have radicalized a minority of socialists and progressive Christians but, for the bulk of the population, the experience of the preceding twelve years had had precisely the opposite effect. Almost all contemporary accounts record that the majority of the German population emerged from the war in a state of profound exhaustion. Entirely absorbed by the pressing tasks of day-to-day survival, and still influenced by Nazi propaganda, these millions of Germans now had only one desire – to forget the past, and to concentrate on rebuilding their shattered personal lives. They wanted, not radical change, but the swiftest possible normalization of German society. They had no desire to engage in yet more political experimentation.[10]

At no point in the period 1945 to 1949 were the radical anti-Nazis able to win over this 'passive majority' of the West German population. On the contrary, this section of the German people provided a natural constituency for Konrad Adenauer's Christian Democratic Union (CDU), which promised, above all, a rapid return to stability, normality, prosperity and the status quo. Accordingly, in the first Bundestag elections of 1949, the SPD and KPD between them won only 34.9 per cent of the vote and, for the next twenty years, the Left were to remain in opposition. The elections of 1949 thus witnessed the decisive defeat of the 'active minority' at the hands of the 'passive majority', and marked a turning point in the development of West German politics.

There now began a long period during which the political scene was dominated by the conservative figures of Konrad Adenauer and Ludwig Erhard. Between them, they developed a political agenda which was to prove extremely popular with the West German electorate. On the one hand, they presided over an economic upsurge so vigorous that it became known as the *Wirtschaftswunder* [economic miracle]. On the other hand, although they naturally condemned the crimes of the Nazis, they argued that there was no need for the Germans to feel guilty about this till the end of time. The prevailing theory on the right of German politics was that the Nazi episode had been a tragic 'accident in the works' [*Betriebsunfall*], which, however regrettable, had no deep roots in German society, and therefore no implications for the conduct of present-day politics.

In short, according to the Adenauer régime, there was no pressing need fundamentally to transform German society, and no reason to listen to those who said that radical political action was necessary to extirpate the structural roots of Nazism. In the words of Ludwig Erhard: 'We cannot accept those who try to infer from previous cruelty a German hereditary sin and try to preserve this for political purposes.'[11]

The approach of the Adenauer and Erhard régimes to the Nazi past was also intimately connected to their foreign and European policies. Both men were profoundly hostile to communism, and, unlike their Social Democrat opponents, they believed that the only way to protect the newly born West German republic from Soviet encroachment was to establish the closest possible relationship between the Federal Republic and the various capitalist Western powers. Thus in April 1951 the Federal Republic joined the European Coal and Steel Community (ECSC), an organization proposed by the French Foreign Minister, Robert Schuman, with the aim of encouraging the interdependence of Western European nations in this crucial economic sector. In the following month, West Germany became a full member of the Council of Europe. In 1957 the Federal Republic became a founding member of the European Economic Community. Most importantly, in May 1955 the Federal Republic enlisted in the North Atlantic Treaty Organization (NATO).

All these steps and, in particular, West Germany's entry into NATO, provoked a great deal of controversy in the Federal Republic. By committing itself to joining a military alliance aimed at the Soviet Union, and by pledging to raise an army of 500,000 men, the Federal Government seemed, in the eyes of some, to be resurrecting the ghost of German militarism and imperialism. For many Germans on the left of the political spectrum, it was entirely inappropriate for Germany, with its bloody and militaristic history, to participate in such an alliance, and throughout the early and mid-1950s, the SPD, KPD and trades unions campaigned vigorously against West German rearmament. The Adenauer régime successfully countered such opposition by promoting a suffocating silence on the issue of the Nazi past. As Richard Evans points out: 'Very little was said about Nazism. Next to nothing was taught about it in schools. . . . Critical enquiry into the German past was discouraged.'[12] The régime, in short, constructed a wall of silence about the Nazi past, thereby undermining the effectiveness of the arguments put forward by the radical opponents of West German rearmament.

The period of West German history from the late 1940s to the early 1960s was thus dominated by a conservative régime which denied that Nazism had deep roots in German history and society, and which, on the basis of that denial, justified both its domestic and also its European policies. By the mid-1960s, however, the political and historiographical pendulum had begun to swing back towards a more critical evaluation of the Nazi period and the Holocaust. There now came to the forefront a new generation of young people, who had no recollection of the Nazi period, but who wanted to examine more thoroughly the role that their parents had played during those calamitous years. Declaring themselves heirs of the SPD and KPD resisters of the 1930s, they set up local history workshops 'to stimulate among "ordinary" Germans . . . the feeling that (self-)critical interpretations of one's own role and behaviour during fascism was both a moral duty and a political necessity'.[13]

To a considerable extent, this new and more critical temper spilled beyond the narrow confines of academia and the student movement, and began to influence wider public opinion. Throughout the later 1960s and 1970s, there emerged a flood of articles, books, films and plays, many of which exposed the degree to which the German people had known about the Holocaust, but had nonetheless supported and co-operated with the Nazi régime. This process reached its zenith in January 1979, when the screening of the American film 'Holocaust' provoked a huge wave of public interest and debate.[14] Though many radicals and left-wingers remained dissatisfied with the amount of progress that had been made, there can be no doubt that the whole climate of public political debate had shifted towards a more open approach towards the Nazi period and its legacy.

As always in post-war German politics, this change in approach to the Nazi past was closely related to a reorientation of Germany's foreign and European policy. In the early 1950s, the Adenauer régime had constructed a wall of silence about the Nazi past, thereby isolating the mass of the population from the opponents of West German rearmament. In the 1970s, by contrast, the new and more open approach to the Nazi past was part and parcel of Willy Brandt's policy of achieving better relations with the countries of Soviet-dominated Eastern Europe. Hitherto, the approach of the Federal Republic to the Nazi past had always been a source of tension between West Germany and her Eastern neighbours. The East Germans, for example, had denounced the attitude of Adenauer's Germany to the Nazi past as reactionary. The Poles, meanwhile, had worried that West Germany might still harbour ambitions on the so-called 'lost Eastern provinces', which had been annexed by Poland at the end of the Second World War. For the Soviets, the whole issue of the Nazi past was, in view of the enormous losses suffered by the USSR during the war, of particular sensitivity. Under these circumstances, the new approach of the Federal Republic to the problems of German history did much to reduce the suspicion with which West Germany was regarded by the countries of the Soviet bloc. When, in December 1970, Willy Brandt knelt at the memorial to the victims of the Warsaw ghetto, he was doing more than making a public gesture of German remorse and contrition. He was also laying the foundations for a better relationship between the Federal Republic and the countries of the Soviet bloc.[15]

The approach of the German left to the Nazi period influenced the policy of the SPD, not just towards the Soviet bloc, but also towards the Federal Republic's Western partners. In the 1950s, the Social Democrats had not been enthusiastic supporters of Western European integration, for they had regarded it as a policy that would institutionalize the division of Germany. By the 1960s, however, the left in general, and the SPD in particular, had become convinced of the merits of the EEC. By the 1970s, the Social Democrats had become fervent exponents of Western European integration. There can be little doubt that this enthusiasm for the European project was motivated, at least in part, by a genuine feeling that the Federal Republic, in view of Germany's bloody past, had a particular duty to foster peaceful co-operation amongst the nations of Europe.

But there was also a darker and often unspoken reason for the conversion of the German left to the cause of European integration. For that section of the German population which has an ingrained distrust of the German national character, the European Union had the great advantage that it bound Germany to the political and economic structures of a united Europe, thereby holding German nationalism in check, and ensuring that Germany could never again assert an unhealthy dominance over European politics and the European economy. European integration, in short, was for many left-wing or liberal Germans a means by which the German Gulliver could be securely tied down by the British, French, Italian and Spanish Lilliputians. According to Margaret Thatcher, such 'modern German politicians are so nervous of governing themselves that they seek to establish a European system in which no nation will govern itself'.[16]

The late 1960s and 1970s were thus a period when a new and more critical approach to the Nazi past was intimately bound up with a new conception of the role that Germany should play in Europe. During the 1980s, however, and especially after Helmut Kohl's assumption of power in 1982, a further change in the political climate became discernible. Conservative academics and politicians, obviously feeling that the more critical temper of the 1960s and 1970s had gone far enough, began to argue for a rehabilitation of German patriotism and national self-confidence. Revisionist historians such as Ernst Nolte and Michael Stürmer sought to 'relativize' the crimes of the Nazis, thereby leaving open the implication that, however appalling these crimes may have been, there is no reason why the Germans, more than any other nation, should feel burdened by their history. In a controversial article that appeared in the *Frankfurter Allgemeine Zeitung* in June 1986, Nolte, for example, argued that Nazism had been born out of a fear of Bolshevism, and that the barbaric methods of the Nazis were a reflection of, and response to, the barbarism that Lenin and Stalin had unleashed upon the world. Nazism was thus an essentially defensive response to Bolshevism, and was hence, in the view of Nolte, 'understandable, and up to a certain point, indeed, justified'.[17]

At the same time, politicians of the right began to argue that Germany had repented enough, and that the time had come, in the words of the leading CDU member Alfred Dregger, 'to step out of Hitler's shadow'.[18] In a famous speech made at Passau in 1988, Franz-Josef Strauß proclaimed that: 'We must once again become a people that does not walk with the stoop of a convict of world history, but with the upright stance of confident citizens who are proud to be Germans.'[19]

The theories put forward by the revisionist historians, coupled with the increasingly nationalist tone of certain CDU politicians, provoked in the 1980s a prolonged and vigorous debate. Many historians bitterly rejected the claims put forward by the likes of Nolte, and even many Christian Democrats displayed little enthusiasm for the nationalistic outbursts of their more bellicose colleagues. But, if the debates of the 1980s on the national question were heated, the tumultuous events of the years 1989 to 1994 rendered them yet more passionate and divisive.

To begin with, of course, there was the *Wende* [turning point] of 1989 and the German unification of October 1990. At a stroke, the Federal Republic gained five new *Länder*, sixteen million new citizens, and one economic disaster area. Almost immediately thereafter, the West German economy slid into the most serious and long-lasting recession since the founding of the Federal Republic in 1949. Simultaneously, the collapse of the Soviet bloc produced political and economic chaos throughout Eastern Europe and, in the case of Yugoslavia, civil war. Tens of thousands of refugees, seeking asylum under the Federal Republic's relatively liberal immigration laws, began to pour across the country's Eastern and Southern borders. On the domestic political scene, there was an upsurge of neo-Nazi violence, coupled with a rising level of electoral support for extreme right-wing parties such as the *Republikaner*. In the wider world, the end of the Cold War was followed, not by a 'new world order' of peace, stability and free-market democracy, but by global instability and uncertainty.

Given its central economic and geographical significance, Germany now found itself confronted by a whole series of difficult questions concerning the role that it should play in this confusing new world of dangers and opportunities. As always, the ensuing debate became bound up with arguments about German national identity and German history. Now, however, under the pressure of events, the divisions which for fifty years had sundered West Germans took on an almost unprecedented intensity.

Thus, by Germans of right-wing and nationalist predilections, the *Wende* was greeted as an opportunity to re-establish the national unity and territorial integrity of Germany. Accordingly, Helmut Kohl and the CDU campaigned successfully in 1990 for the swiftest possible assimilation of East Germany into the Federal Republic. But, for Germans of nationalist inclinations, the unification also had a deeper historical significance. The division of Germany had, after all, been a direct and painful legacy of the Nazi period. Now that the division had been finally overcome, they argued, this whole traumatic period of German history had been brought to a definitive conclusion. Now, at last, Germany could once again become a 'normal nation', which could take a 'normal' and 'healthy' pride in its own history and national identity. In September 1993, Steffan Heitmann, the then CDU presidential candidate, made a speech in which he argued that too much had been made of:

> the Nazi episode. The organised death of millions of Jews in gas chambers was just a one-off incident . . . very similar to other singular incidents throughout history. There is no reason why Germany should worry about it until the end of time.[20]

In the same month, Wolfgang Schäuble proclaimed that: 'Patriotism is not old-fashioned. Our fatherland could do with more patriotism.'[21]

The politicians of the CDU, whilst condemning the numerous neo-Nazi outrages, nonetheless argued that far-right extremism was grounded in the legitimate concern of the German people about a tide of asylum seekers pouring in from the East. In November 1992, three months after the Rostock pogrom, Helmut Kohl referred to a 'state of emergency' caused, not by neo-Nazi violence, but by the 'flood of refugees'.[22] The Christian Democrats accordingly argued that the liberal immigration laws of the Federal Republic should be significantly tightened and, after a fierce public debate, they succeeded in implementing their proposals.

Perhaps most striking of all was the shift in the rhetoric of right-wing politicians on foreign policy and European issues. In his official Chancellor's address in January 1991, Kohl argued that 'Germany has now come to terms with its history. From now on it can openly assume, and even expand, its role as a world power.'[23] In the spirit of this declaration, Germany applied for a permanent seat on the Security Council of the United Nations, and generally tried to raise its profile on the world stage.

In particular, the German Parliament amended the Basic Law to allow the active deployment of German troops in non-Nato countries, and units of the *Bundeswehr* were subsequently dispatched to Cambodia and Somalia to participate in United Nations 'peace-keeping' operations. Wolfgang Schäuble, meanwhile, proclaimed in 1992 that the *Bundeswehr* should be prepared to intervene all over the world to 'defend German interests' and to ensure the 'maintenance of free trade and unrestricted access to markets and raw materials the world over'.[24] According to Schäuble, the possibility of the world-wide participation of German troops was '*the* question of destiny of our country'.[25]

The new, more assertive temper of right-wing politicians has even caused them, to some extent at least, to attack that most sacred of German foreign policy cows – West European integration. On the extreme right of the political spectrum, the neo-Nazis and the *Republikaner* maintain that the European Union is little more than a conspiracy against the German nation. In a rather less outspoken fashion, this suspicion of European integration is also shared by people on the far right of the CDU. In particular, the Bavarian sister party of the CDU, the so-called Christian Social Union (CSU), has shown a marked lack of enthusiasm for the European policy currently being pursued by the Federal Government. In September 1993, the leader of the CSU, Edmund Stoiber, published a controversial article in a leading German newspaper in which he attacked the whole notion of a federal Europe.[26] Instead, Stoiber argued that the European Union should be a loose confederation of sovereign states, to which the countries of Eastern Europe should be admitted as rapidly as possible. From Stoiber's point of view, this would not only protect the sovereign power of Germany, it would also help to encourage and consolidate German economic hegemony in Eastern Europe. Though Stoiber was promptly denounced by his more mainstream Christian Democratic colleagues, his outburst was nonetheless symptomatic of an increasing level of 'Euroscepticism' on the right of the CDU and CSU.[27]

For those West Germans who have an ingrained distrust of any form of German nationalism, all these developments have been a source of both anger and concern. During the *Wende*, for example, such individuals tended to view the unification as being, at best, premature, and at worst, as something to be opposed on principle. Günter Grass argued at the time that:

> there can be no demand for a new version of a united nation that in the course of barely seventy-five years, though under different managements, filled the history books . . . with suffering, rubble, defeat, millions of refugees, millions of dead, and with the burden of crimes that can never be undone.[28]

Nor did anything happen in the ensuing four years to assuage the gloomy anxieties of people such as Grass. The new assertive approach to foreign policy issues was, for these individuals, no more than a recrudescence of old-fashioned German militarism and imperialism. The claim that Germany was now a 'normal nation' was denounced as a *Lebenslüge* [a life-long illusion].[29] The policy of the government towards asylum seekers was seen as a craven capitulation to neo-Nazi violence which could only inflame the racist climate which had spawned the neo-Nazi violence in the first place. Above all, the massive upsurge in the level of racist violence, coupled with the abject failure, as the left saw it, of the establishment to confront the neo-Nazis, confirmed many radical West Germans in their darkest suspicions of German culture and society. Their view that there exists in German history and politics a dark thread of xenophobia and of reaction was succinctly encapsulated by a slogan which appeared during this time on a railway bridge in Frankfurt:

> *Auschwitz, Hoyerswerda, Rostock, der deutsche Ungeist lebt! Wehrt Euch!* [Auschwitz, Hoyerswerda, Rostock, the German spirit of evil lives! Be on your guard!]

This deep-seated but often unspoken suspicion of German nationalism on the part of Germans of radical or left-wing sympathies also permeates the debate about the future of the European Union. For many Germans of radical or liberal proclivities, the 'Eurosceptical' outbursts of Stoiber, and of politicians even further to the right, are viewed with fear and anxiety. If European federalism is a means by which the dragon of German nationalism can be securely tied down, then Stoiber and his ilk, by attacking the very concept of European federalism, are threatening to cut the economic and political ropes that bind Germany to the rest of Europe.

The turbulent years that followed the unification thus emphasized and exacerbated the gulf between the minority that is aggressively proud to be German and the minority that is ashamed of it. The battle between the two groups, which has coloured the whole history of the Federal Republic, will indubitably continue into the future. Whichever side gains ascendancy over the German population as a whole will use its advantage to determine the domestic and foreign policy agenda. The future of Germany in Europe, and the ideological struggle over Germany's past, will remain inextricably intertwined.

IN HONECKER'S SHADOW: NATIONAL IDENTITY IN EAST GERMANY

When the Red Army marched into Eastern Germany in the spring of 1945, it found, just as the Western Allies did, that the population had been polarized by the experience of war and dictatorship into a 'passive majority' and an 'active minority'. As in the Western zones, the greater part of the population was exhausted, passive, cynical about politics, and entirely absorbed with day-to-day survival. As in the Western zones, a minority of the population had by contrast been radicalized by the previous twelve years, and was eager to begin the construction of a new and better Germany on the de-Nazified rubble of the old.

In the Western zones, the policy of the occupying authorities was to hold back those elements that wanted a thorough reckoning with the Nazi past, whilst simultaneously fostering a new state machine and a new range of centre and right-wing organizations as a counterweight. The policy of the Soviets, by contrast, was to harness the energies of the 'active minority' and to direct these energies into channels of the Soviets' choosing. To this end, the Soviets pursued a two-track policy in Eastern Germany. On the one hand, they attacked and suppressed any independent, grass-roots initiatives of the working class such as the anti-fascist committees[30] and the factory councils.[31] On the other hand, they encouraged anti-Nazi activists to participate in those organizations, such as the official trade unions and the Socialist Unity Party (SED), which could be securely controlled from above.

At the same time, the Soviet authorities and their communist allies pushed through a whole series of social and political reforms, such as nationalization, sweeping de-Nazification, and land reform. At every step along the way, they argued that these measures were objectively necessary if the material roots of Nazism in Germany were to be destroyed. By 1949, when the GDR was officially brought into being, the 'anti-fascist democratic transformation' was largely complete. The basic outlines of the state that emerged from this process were to remain essentially unchanged for the next forty years.

The attitude of the 'active minority' to this process of transformation was highly ambiguous. The authoritarianism and undemocratic methods of the communists aroused a deep resentment, as did the enormous reparations and territorial losses that were inflicted on East Germany by the victorious Soviets.[32] There was also, however, genuine and widespread support for the programme of reforms, and many tens of thousands of East German socialists, trade unionists and progressive liberals participated in its implementation. The Soviets and communists, moreover, possessed a trump card, which they consistently and successfully employed throughout the critical early years of East Germany's development. The prime objective and duty of German anti-fascists, the argument ran, was to ensure that Nazism could never again flourish on German soil. Any socialist or trade unionist who, on the basis of relatively minor 'sectarian' disagreements with the new régime and its policies, abstained from or opposed the process of 'anti-fascist democratic transformation', was, according to the communists, merely repeating the mistakes of the early 1930s. Then, German anti-Nazis had been defeated because they were disunited. Now, unless all German anti-Nazis united to push through the necessary changes, German reaction would recover from the setback of the Second World War, just as it had recovered after the half-hearted German Revolution of 1918 to 1921.[33] For many East German anti-Nazis, still traumatized by their experiences of the previous twelve years, and inspired by a sense of historic responsibility to ensure that Nazism never happened again, such arguments proved difficult to counter. Many thousands of German socialists and trade unionists swallowed their doubts and resentments, and co-operated with the new régime.

The significance of all this is simply that, from the very beginning in East Germany, there was a small but politically active section of the population that believed in the anti-Nazi principles that the new régime purported to represent, and which approved, albeit with qualifications, of the régime's policies. The exact size of this minority is difficult to determine, but in the free elections held in Berlin in 1946, the SED received 20 per cent of the vote. In places such as 'red' Saxony, a traditional heartland of radical working-class politics, the level of support for the SED at this time was probably much greater.[34]

Throughout the whole of the ensuing forty years, the SED régime continued to enjoy the active if qualified support of a minority of the East German population. The extent of this support is difficult to gauge, for, after 1946, the SED never again thought it expedient to allow free elections. However, in a survey carried out in the autumn of 1993, 37 per cent of those questioned claimed that, before 1989, they had been broadly in favour of the social system prevailing in the GDR, even though they had been critical of certain aspects.[35] Many such individuals would agree with Gregor Gysi's assessment of the positive aspects of the German Democratic Republic:

> I believe that the positive element was the attempt to follow a non-capitalist path. Positive, as well, was an antifascist state which developed something which I still today maintain as important: one thinks of the minimal social differences, of the fact that the line between rich and poor was very small compared to that which occurs in all capitalist states.[36]

During the momentous events of 1989 and 1990, East Germans such as Gysi generally regarded the collapse of the Berlin Wall as an opportunity to rid the GDR of what they believed were its bureaucratic and authoritarian distortions. There was much talk of a so-called 'third way' which East Germany could now tread – neither capitalism nor Stalinism but genuine and democratic socialism. What they emphatically did not want was for the GDR to be simply incorporated into the Federal Republic. Stefan Heym, for example, a well-known East German writer and dissident, made the following plea:

> And I ask, from the bottom of my heart: is the noble experiment of Socialism here in the heart of Europe to be abandoned altogether simply because it has been run for so long with poor equipment and the wrong ingredients? There are, of this there is no doubt, enough people in the country who would stay in order to attempt the experiment again under new, democratic conditions.[37]

In the years following the unification there remained a minority of people in East Germany who refused to write off forty years of GDR history, and who continued to insist that the best features of the East German past could be combined with democracy to produce a new sort of German society. Overwhelmingly, such elements of the population looked for political leadership to the Party of Democratic Socialism (PDS), the successor to the SED. This organization, which in December 1993 had some 145,000 members,[38] was by far the largest political party in East Germany during the post-unification period, and represented a very different vision of Germany's future from that put forward by the traditional West German political parties.

So far we have discussed only the minority in East German society that was more or less sympathetic to the declared aims of the GDR. The majority of the population was probably never won over by the SED's rhetoric. It is unlikely that the SED could have won a genuinely democratic election at any point between 1949 and 1989. But, even for these people, the forty years of SED rule were not without effect upon their attitudes and aspirations. In particular, even amongst East Germans who were generally hostile towards the SED régime, there was a broad acceptance of the policy of full employment and comprehensive welfare provision. In the late 1950s, surveys conducted among East Germans who had fled the GDR revealed that the majority of workers regarded the numerous East German convalescent homes and polyclinics as 'positive achievements' [*Errungenschaften*].[39] In a survey conducted in the autumn of 1993, 96 per cent of East Germans questioned believed that security of employment had been a 'special strength' of the GDR, 94 per cent approved of the comprehensive child-care facilities, 83 per cent regarded the comprehensive system of social security benefits in a positive light, and 80 per cent maintained that the free and universal education system had also been a 'special strength' of the German Democratic Republic.[40]

Thus, when unification came in 1990, a significant minority of the population either did not want it at all, or wanted it to take a very different form. Most were enthusiastically in favour, but they brought to the new and enlarged Federal Republic a set of assumptions and attitudes very different from those prevailing in West Germany. In the period 1990 to 1993, moreover, a number of circumstances conspired to widen the gulf between East and West Germans yet further.

To begin with, of course, there was the collapse of the East German economy. In 1989 and 1990, a great number of East Germans had believed Helmut Kohl's promises that a swift unification would lead to a rapid increase in their standards of living. This mood of naive hopes and high expectations was summed up by a placard unfurled at a CDU election rally in Leipzig in 1990:

> *Helmut, nimm uns an der Hand, zeig uns den Weg ins Wirtschaftswunder-land!*
> [Helmut, take us by the hand, show us the way to economic-miracle-land!][41]

In the ensuing three years, such unrealistically high expectations were doomed to be disappointed. Rather than experiencing a rapid economic upturn, the rickety and uncompetitive East German economy was exposed, overnight, to the chill winds of free-market capitalism. The result, unsurprisingly, was a widespread collapse of the East German manufacturing base. The number of people involved in the textile industry shrank from 100,000 to 19,000, in the chemical industry from 150,000 to 50,000, in machine engineering from 660,000 to 110,000.[42] By October 1993, 15 per cent of the East German workforce was registered as unemployed. Taking account of work-creation schemes and early retirement, the real figure was at least 35 per cent.[43]

Nor did the standards of living of those East Germans still in employment increase as rapidly as they had hoped. Wage levels did improve considerably, but they still remained significantly below those of West Germany. Thus, in 1990, the average worker in East Germany earned DM 1,223 per month, compared to DM 3,705 in West Germany. By 1993, the average Eastern wage had increased to DM 2,753, but this still remained significantly below the Western average monthly wage of DM 4,305.[44]

The sense of grievance generated among East Germans by their relatively poor wage levels was compounded by the humiliating fashion in which they believed they had been treated by their Western compatriots. It was certainly true that West Germans took over almost all important positions in the political, economic and educational structures of East Germany. In the view of many East Germans, their new Western masters behaved with arrogance, treating their East German subordinates as backward and ignorant provincials. In a survey conducted in Rostock in September 1993, 60 per cent of those questioned saw East Germany as a 'colony' of the West.[45] In a survey carried out in January 1993, 77 per cent of East Germans said they felt like 'second-class citizens' in the new Federal Republic.[46] In the same month, another survey revealed that 74 per cent of those questioned agreed with the statement: 'The wall is gone, but the wall in people's heads is growing.'[47]

Taking all these factors into consideration, it would be foolish to argue that unification was followed by the rapid emergence of a new sense of national unity between East and West Germans. On the contrary, East Germans retained a distinct and separate identity – a fact that was exacerbated by their assorted grievances. The political consequences of all this in the period following unification were numerous and unpredictable.

On the lighter side, the period witnessed a discernible growth in 'GDR nostalgia'. This manifested itself in, for example, an increased demand for commodities which proclaimed their East German origin. In 1991, 67 per cent of East Germans preferred to buy home-produced groceries. By 1993, this figure had grown to 82 per cent. There was also a renewal of enthusiasm for old GDR films and entertainment personalities.[48] Discos were organized specifically to celebrate the 'good old days', complete with Ostmarks and uniforms of the old GDR youth organization.[49] According to *Der Spiegel*: 'The new pride of the "Ossis" is a symptom of deep-seated fears and inferiority complexes.'[50]

A more politically significant consequence of East Germany's separate identity was a solid and increasing level of support for the PDS. Many East Germans in the post-unification period felt that the other major parties were dominated by Westerners, and that only the PDS could understand and represent the interests of the population of the former GDR. In the words of one female PDS voter in Potsdam, 'I feel at home with the PDS. It is familiar to me.'[51] Thus, the PDS share of the vote in Brandenburg increased from 11 per cent in December 1990 to 21 per cent in December 1993.[52] In Potsdam, the PDS candidate for the post of mayor received 43.5 per cent of the vote, despite having been revealed as a Stasi informer.[53] In the Federal election of October 1994, the PDS secured 17 per cent of the vote in East Germany, up from 10 per cent in the Federal election of 1990.[54]

The specific frustrations and grievances that prevailed in East Germany during the period also found more extreme outlets. On the one hand, the level of industrial militancy in East Germany was considerably higher than in the West. In 1993, for example, 84,308 days were lost through strikes in West Germany, whereas the figure in East Germany was 508,737.[55] Thus, despite the fact that it contains only one fifth of Germany's population, more than six times as many days were lost through strike action in East Germany as compared with West Germany. More disturbingly, the level of racist violence was also much higher than in the West. In 1992, there were 2.4 racist attacks per 100,000 inhabitants in West Germany, whereas in East Germany the number was 5.7. Of the seven worst *Länder* for racist violence in 1992, five were the *fünf neuen Bundesländer* [five new federal provinces] of the former GDR.[56]

To some extent, the economic upturn beginning in 1993 seems to have alleviated the social tensions apparent in East Germany and brought with it a partial reconciliation of the East and West German peoples. Particularly in 1994, the East German economy grew vigorously, and the prosperity this generated has done much to assuage East German grievances. Between November 1992 and August 1994, the proportion of East Germans who felt that their economic situation was 'good' or 'very good' increased from 38 per cent to 54 per cent. This marked improvement in people's economic circumstances seems to have had a dramatic effect on their view of the East–West divide. In a survey of November 1992, 54 per cent of those questioned said they regarded themselves primarily as *East* Germans, whereas by August 1994 this figure had sunk to 36 per cent.[57]

The economic upturn has thus tended to alleviate the particular frustrations and grievances of the East Germans. Nonetheless, there are certain underlying structural problems in the East German economy which have yet to be solved. In East Germany, for example, unit labour costs are still significantly higher than in West Germany. Moreover, since wage rates in East Germany have been rising faster than productivity, East German industry is actually becoming less competitive![58] This simple fact creates a long-term problem of significant proportions. As long as the East German economy remains so inefficient in comparison to West Germany, the Federal Government will have to continue subsidizing East German living standards. Since East German domestic output can only pay for approximately half of domestic demand, the amount of money involved is enormous.[59]

In the absence of a long-term investment policy, the only other way to solve the problem of high unit-labour costs would be dramatically to cut wage levels in East Germany. But East German workers are already unhappy that their wages are so low compared to those of their West German colleagues, and would be unlikely to accept any wage reductions without putting up considerable resistance. If that were to happen, all the underlying differences of mentality and outlook in East Germany would once again be transformed into resentment and bitterness. On the other hand, if there is no attempt to hold down East German wage levels, then the economy of the former GDR will remain uncompetitive and inefficient, in which case a new recession at some point in the future would punish it as severely as the recession of 1990 to 1993. Under such circumstances, the East Germans' sense of separate identity would probably be inflamed once again by their economic privations.

CONCLUSION

In Germany, as in the other countries of Europe, foreign and European policy is not determined solely on the basis of hard-headed calculations of political and economic self-interest. In Germany, as elsewhere, the debate about post-Cold-War reconstruction is also bound up with questions of nationality and national identity. The debate about the role that Germany should play in the new, emerging European order has thus become enmeshed in the continuing ideological battle between those who are proud to be German and those who are ashamed to be German. In a similar vein, the integration of the former GDR into the Federal Republic is inevitably influenced by the fact that the population of East Germany possesses a separate and distinct East German identity.

The ideological gulf between West German nationalists and 'anti-nationalists', and the continuing division between West Germans and East Germans, can both be traced back to 1945, when the differing occupation policies of the Soviets and the Western Allies threw the development of East and West German national identities on to different trajectories. In the West, a régime came to power which defended its legitimacy by erecting a wall of silence about the Nazi past. Ever since, the question of Nazism and the Holocaust has been the single most divisive issue in West German politics, as West Germans battle with each other either to break down the wall or to maintain it. In East Germany, by contrast, the communist régime based its claim to legitimacy on the argument that the

GDR was an overtly anti-fascist state which, unlike West Germany, had been thoroughly purged of the canker of Nazism. Rightly or wrongly, many East Germans were at least partially convinced by this argument, thereby creating a pool of support for the declared aims and principles of the GDR Government. Even after 1989, the different ideological orientation of sections of the East German population has continued to be a divisive factor in German politics.

Germany, in short, continues to be a divided nation, and these divisions will continue to influence both the role that Germany plays in Europe, and also the re-integration of the former GDR into the Federal Republic.

FURTHER READING

R. Evans, *In Hitler's Shadow*, London: I. B. Tauris, 1989.

M. Fulbrook, *The Two Germanies, 1945–1990*, London: Macmillan, 1992.

H. James and M. Stone (eds), *When the Wall Came Down*, London and New York: Routledge, 1992.

B. Marshall, *The Origins of Post-War German Politics*, London: Croom Helm, 1988.

G. Sandford, *From Hitler to Ulbricht*, Princeton: Princeton University Press, 1983.

H. Turner, *Germany from Partition to Reunification*, New Haven and London: Yale University Press, 1992.

H. Weber, *Geschichte der DDR* [History of the GDR], Munich: DTV, 1985.

NOTES

1 T. Garton Ash, 'United Germany Seeks Common Voice', *The Times*, 18 October 1993, p. 3.
2 Quoted in: M. Schmidt, *The New Reich* (trans. by D. Horch), London: Hutchinson, 1993, p. 119.
3 For an excellent insight into the thinking of German anti-Nazis in 1945 see: *Gemeinsam begann es 1945: 'Der Aufbau' schrieb das erste Kapitel* [It Began as a Collective Enterprise in 1945: 'Der Aufbau' Wrote the First Chapter], Frankfurt am Main: Röderberg, 1978.
4 H. Turner, *Germany from Partition to Reunification*, New Haven and London: Yale University Press, 1992, pp. 117–21.
5 For detailed information on the anti-Fascist committees, see: L. Niethammer *et al.*, *Arbeiterinitiative 1945* [Workers' Initiatives 1945], Wuppertal: Peter Hammer, 1976.
6 B. Marshall, *The Origins of Post-War German Politics*, London: Croom Helm, 1988, ch. V.
7 Marshall, pp. 74–5.
8 For example, in Hessen in 1946, and in Schleswig-Holstein and North Rhine Westphalia in 1948.
9 The British, for example, worked closely with the Chambers of Commerce. The Americans developed a close relationship with the Catholic Church and the emerging CDU/CSU. The French tried to promote right-wing Rhineland separatists.
10 See, for example: M. Fulbrook, *Germany 1918–1990: The Divided Nation*, London: Fontana, 1991, pp. 134–5; L. Krieger, 'The Inter-regnum in Germany:

March–August 1945', in *Political Science Quarterly*, vol. 64 (1949), no. 4, p. 512; F. Willis, *The French in Germany*, Stanford: Stanford University Press, 1962, pp. 182–3.

11 Quoted in: A. Lüdtke,' "Coming to Terms with the Past": Illusions of Remembering, Ways of Forgetting Nazism in West Germany', *Journal of Modern History*, September 1993, p. 570.

12 R. Evans, *In Hitler's Shadow*, London: I. B. Tauris, 1989, p. 11.

13 Lüdtke, pp. 556–7.

14 Lüdtke, pp. 543–6.

15 M. Postone, 'After the Holocaust: History and Identity in West Germany', in: K. Harms *et al.* (eds), *Coping with the Past: Germany and Austria after 1945*, Madison and London: University of Wisconsin Press, 1990, pp. 236–7.

16 Quoted in: 'Reunited Germany Reviving Extremism', *Guardian*, 18 October 1993, p. 3.

17 Quoted in: Evans (n. 12 above), p. 28.

18 Quoted in: Schmidt (n. 2 above), p. 122.

19 Quoted in: ibid.

20 Quoted in: *Searchlight*, October 1993, no. 220, p. 15.

21 Quoted in: 'German Parties Urge Patriotic Revival', *Guardian*, 14 September 1993, p. 8.

22 Quoted in: Schmidt (n. 2 above), p. 248.

23 Quoted in: ibid., p. 153.

24 'Eine Truppe für alle Fälle' [An Army for all Seasons], *Der Spiegel*, 10 January 1994, pp. 21–3.

25 Quoted in: *Searchlight*, October 1993, no. 220, p. 15. Emphasis in the original.

26 *Süddeutsche Zeitung*, 2 November 1993.

27 'Dispute on EC's Future Puts Kohl's Coalition at Risk', *The Times*, 2 November 1993, p. 13; and 'Bavarian Leader Rejects Vision of Federal Europe', *Independent*, 3 November 1993, p. 12.

28 G. Grass, 'Don't Reunify Germany', in: H. James and M. Stone (eds), *When the Wall Came Down*, New York and London: Routledge, 1992, pp. 57–8.

29 Jürgen Habermas, quoted in: F. Stern, 'Freedom and Its Discontents', in: *Foreign Affairs*, September/October 1993, p. 122.

30 W. Leonhard, *Die Revolution entlässt ihre Kinder* [The Revolution Dismisses Its Children], Frankfurt am Main, Ullstein, 1961, pp. 313–20.

31 For more information on the East German factory councils, see: S. Suckut, *Die Betriebsrätebewegung in der sowjetisch besetzten Zone Deutschlands* [The Factory Council Movement in the Soviet Zone of Occupied Germany], unpublished dissertation, Hanover, 1978.

32 See, for example, the speech given by Otto Grotewohl, leader of the East German SPD, in Leipzig on 26 August 1945: Sächsisches Staatsarchiv Leipzig, Bezirksvorstand der SPD Leipzig, II/1/01.

33 Sächsisches Staatsarchiv Leipzig, Aktions- und Arbeitsgemeinschaft KPD-SPD, III/01.

34 It was certainly the perception of the SED leadership that the level of support for the party's policies was greater in Saxony than elsewhere in the Soviet zone. For this reason, a referendum was held in Saxony in June 1946 in order to provide some degree of legitimacy for the régime's policy of nationalization. In the referendum 77.7 per cent of voters supported the régime's policy; see: G. Sandford, *From Hitler to Ulbricht*, Princeton: Princeton University Press, 1983, pp. 210–14.

35 *Die Zeit*, 1 October 1993, p. 20.

36 S. Vastano, 'Germany United and Divided: Interview with Gregor Gysi', in: James and Stone (eds) (n. 28 above), p. 149.
37 S. Heym, 'The Forty Year Itch', in: James and Stone (eds), p. 138.
38 'Communists defeated in German poll', *Independent*, 20 December 1993, p. 8.
39 H. Weber, *Geschichte der DDR* [History of the GDR], Munich: DTV, 1985, p. 297.
40 *Die Zeit*, 1 October 1993, p. 20.
41 *Der Spiegel*, 27 September 1993, p. 51.
42 'Geld sinnlos verpulvert' [Money Uselessly Squandered], *Der Spiegel*, 3 January 1994, pp. 60–2.
43 'A Painstaking Restoration', *Financial Times*, 14 October 1993, p. 15.
44 'Eine Politik der Strenge' [A Policy of Austerity], in *Der Spiegel*, 10 January 1994, pp. 90–7.
45 'Helmut Kohl's Consumer Colony', *Guardian*, 17 September 1993, p. 13.
46 *Der Spiegel*, 18 January 1993, p. 56.
47 Ibid., p. 52.
48 'Wehre dich täglich' [Be on Your Guard Every Day], *Der Spiegel*, 27 December 1993, pp. 46–9.
49 'An Ersatz East Germany Rears Its Fanciful Head', *International Herald Tribune*, 12 October 1993, p. 1.
50 'Wehre dich täglich' (n. 48 above).
51 Ibid.
52 'Further Polls for German State', *Financial Times*, 7 December 1993, p. 2.
53 'Communists Defeated in German Poll', *Independent*, 20 December 1993, p. 8.
54 'Former Communists Bounce Back', *The Times*, 17 October 1994, p. 10.
55 Figures supplied by the London office of the British–German Chamber of Industry and Commerce.
56 *Der Spiegel*, 11 January 1993, p. 16.
57 *Der Spiegel*, 15 August 1994, p. 111.
58 See, for example: 'Dream of German Pay Parity Dims', *Guardian*, 25 October 1993, p. 8; 'Eine Politik der Strenge' (n. 44 above), pp. 90–7.
59 'A Painstaking Restoration' (n. 43 above), p. 15.

10 The Comecon experiment[1]

Robert Bideleux

From 1955 to 1990 the international economic relations of the East
European states were dominated by the Council of Mutual Economic
Assistance (CMEA, alias Comecon), which had been formally established
in 1949 at the height of the East–West confrontation and Cold War division of Europe. In parallel with the Inter-Party Communist Information
Bureau or Cominform (founded in 1947) on the ideological front and the
inter-governmental Warsaw Pact (1955–91) on the military/political front,
Comecon enhanced the cohesion and 'international proletarian solidarity'
of the Soviet bloc. Although Comecon disintegrated in 1990–1, the
Comecon experiment still merits attention for two main reasons: by 1984
its member states purportedly accounted for one-third of the world's
industrial production and, with 455 million inhabitants (385 million within
the European member states), 10 per cent of its population;[2] second, as
Europe's only major attempt at non-capitalist integration, Comecon threw
considerable light on the respective advantages and disadvantages of
capitalist and non-capitalist approaches to international integration. Even
if it was never genuinely socialist, many of the inherent problems and
barriers that it encountered would also have been experienced by any
realistic attempt at supranational integration between centrally planned
economies (CPEs), no matter how these were conceived. Socialists must
not simply 'assume' such problems and barriers out of existence by confin-
ing their attention to ideal types. In any conception of socialism involving
the erection of CPEs, attempts to promote supranational integration
would fall foul of many of the same fundamental difficulties as Comecon,
even if they were guided by angels rather than tyrants and thugs.

THE BIRTH OF COMECON

The victories of the USSR and certain communist-led resistance movements over fascism by the end of the Second World War ended the
former isolation of Soviet 'socialism in one country' by extending Soviet
ascendancy into Eastern Europe, which by early 1945 had been recognized
by both Britain and the US as a legitimate Soviet 'sphere of influence'. The

precise consequences for Eastern Europe were not immediately obvious or clearcut, however. British and American strategists mainly understood 'spheres of influence' to mean informal, non-exclusive hegemony. However, the innate characteristics and war-ravaged condition of the Soviet economy after the Second World War made it hard for Stalin to dominate his newly gained 'sphere of influence' primarily by informal economic means. The prevalence of state ownership and central planning in the USSR was bound to politicise its relations with its new 'satellites'. Since the 1930s, moreover, Stalin had been grooming hand-picked (and often little known) Communist Party leaders from many parts of Europe to take power in various European states in the wake of the eventual overthrow of fascism. In Stalin's eyes, the liberal capitalist states were inherently 'soft' on fascism, which they had often 'appeased' and always regarded as a potential ally or weapon in the 'containment' of communism. Therefore, notwithstanding the various temporary deals that he struck with European fascist powers during the 1930s, Stalin saw the Second World War as essentially a struggle between communism and fascism, not between fascism and the supposedly moribund capitalist democracies. Consequently the comprehensive defeat of fascism in 1944–5, mainly at the hands of the USSR and a number of communist-led resistance movements, was expected *ipso facto* to 'deliver' most of Europe to the victorious communists.

The formal establishment of Comecon was at least partly a consequence of Stalin's decision to veto East European participation in the European Recovery Programme (ERP) announced by US Secretary of State George Marshall in June 1947. The US seemingly offered Marshall Aid to all the European states that were struggling to recover from the war, including the USSR and the young 'people's democracies' in Eastern Europe. In those East European states that were not yet fully under communist control in mid-1947 (Czechoslovakia, Hungary and Poland), communist parties were still formally espousing gradualism and a 'middle way' between Soviet 'socialism' and Western capitalism, for fear of frightening the numerous peasant and middle-class voters. Their increasingly communist-dominated coalition governments initially signalled their interest in receiving Marshall Aid, even though the conditions attached to it would commit the recipients to a full restoration of market economies with convertible currencies and to multilateral integration of their economies with those of the other members of the Organization of European Economic Co-operation (OEEC). The latter was to be responsible for allocating Marshall Aid and for upholding the liberal integrationist economic conditions on which it was to be granted. Recipients would thus be drawn into the economic orbit of the richer Western capitalist economies. To prevent this happening in Eastern Europe, in July 1947 Stalin ordered the Czechoslovak and Polish governments to reverse their earlier decisions to participate in the ERP. The communist and socialist ministers in these governments meekly complied, thereby precipitating serious crises in relations between them and the so-called 'bourgeois' ministers within the Popular Front coalition governments. This was the moment of truth, the signal for the communist parties rapidly to establish more complete control of the people's democracies during late 1947 and early 1948. East European states were thus forced to retreat into economic self-reliance and crude, coercive methods of resource allocation and mobilization modelled on those employed in Stalin's USSR.

On 25 January 1949 most communist newspapers and news agencies published a brief communiqué announcing that an 'economic conference' representing the USSR, Czechoslovakia, Poland, Hungary, Romania and Bulgaria had met in Moscow and, 'in order to establish still broader economic co-operation among the countries of people's democracy and the USSR', had instituted a Council for Mutual Economic Assistance:

> on the basis of equal representation, and having as its tasks the exchange of experience in the economic field, the rendering of technical assistance to one another and the rendering of mutual assistance in regard to raw materials, foodstuffs, machinery, equipment etc.[3]

Albania joined Comecon in February 1949 (although its active membership lapsed in 1961) and the new GDR followed suit in 1950.

At the height of the Cold War it was widely believed that the creation of Comecon was part of a slowly unfolding plan for Soviet domination of post-war Europe. But we still have no windows into Stalin's inscrutable mind and it is conceivable that Stalin was merely reacting defensively to unforeseen events and Western challenges and provocations, improvising *ad hoc* 'plans' as he went along. The Soviet leadership correctly perceived that Marshall Aid was partly an anti-Soviet stratagem, an indirect attempt to subvert or renege upon the apportionment of Soviet and Western 'spheres of influence' agreed in Moscow, Yalta and Potsdam in 1944–5, as the strings attached to it were bound to enmesh the recipients firmly in the Western sphere. Indeed, the Truman administration presented the Marshall Plan as an anti-communist programme and, had it not done so, the parsimonious and instinctively isolationist US Congress might well have voted down the requisite budget appropriations. Just as Stalin has sometimes been seen as the true 'father' of the EC, so one could regard President Truman and General Marshall as the real 'parents' of Comecon. Significantly, the communiqué announcing the formation of CMEA stated that the USSR and the people's democracies 'did not consider it possible to submit to the Marshall Plan dictate, as this plan violated the sovereignty of the countries [in question] and the interests of their national economies'.[4] However, having prohibited the people's democracies from participating in the OEEC, the Soviet leadership may have felt obliged to offer them a surrogate for the OEEC and Marshall Aid, both by way of compensation for the opportunities forgone and as a means of propping up their economies, which had been damaged by the subsequent collapse of their trade with the West.

Nevertheless, the motives for the creation of Comecon were

> not reducible to the Soviet desire to oppose to the OEEC an East European organization. The establishment of the OEEC certainly served as an incentive, but it seems to have provided no more than an occasional prompting for the establishment of a multilateral co-operation body, the need for which was already felt.[5]

Indeed, ever since the mid-nineteenth century there had been dozens of projects for customs unions and political federations or confederations in East-Central Europe and the Balkans. From 1848 onward there were various schemes for 'federalizing' the Austro-Hungarian Empire (which became a customs union in 1850), or for transforming it into an 'Austro-Slav' federation. From 1862 onward the Hungarian nationalist Lájos Kossuth urged his compatriots to repair their relations with their Croatian, Serb and Romanian neighbours and foster an anti-Habsburg Danubian Confederation under Hungarian leadership. During the interwar years the major Slav peasant parties in Bulgaria, Yugoslavia, Czechoslovakia and (to a lesser extent) Poland toyed with various proposals for Balkan and/or East-Central European federations and countless East European economists put forward schemes for various Danubian customs unions and confederations, in the hope of recreating (on an expanded and more equitable basis) the large unified and protected regional market and political bulwark against German and/or Russian encroachment that had formerly been provided by the Austro-Hungarian Empire. From 1923 onward, the Hungarian Count Richard Koudenhove-Kalergi emerged as Europe's best known campaigner for a Christian, anti-Soviet pan-European confederation. The economic and political crises of the 1930s and 1940s also elicited various proposals for a Western Slav (Polish-Czechoslovak) customs union and confederation, as well as a Balkan federation that would bring together Bulgaria, Yugoslavia and possibly Romania or even Greece. Thus, at least among the 'chattering classes', there was a widely perceived need for supranational and confederal arrangements, economic co-operation and regional institutions in Eastern Europe, long before the creation of Comecon. However, most of these antecedents differed from the Comecon project in two crucial respects: first, none of them envisaged the inclusion of Russia, as the Russian/Soviet colossus could have dominated or overwhelmed any Eastern European club of which it became member; and, second, few of them were explicitly socialist or étatist. On the contrary, quite a few were expressly directed against the Russian/Soviet 'menace'.

Nevertheless, the emergence of CPEs and communist dictatorships obliged Eastern Europe's new rulers to place the economic and political relations between their states and between themselves and the USSR on a new and more coherent footing, not least because Western economic sanctions were rapidly freezing them out of their previous export markets and cutting them off from many former Western suppliers. The new East European régimes were bonded by common political systems and precepts, similar patterns of lopsided industrialization ('steel chains'), geographical proximity and provisions for collective security. More fundamentally, however, the new international trade and payments systems that were emerging in the increasingly US-dominated capitalist world were incompatible with neo-Stalinist forms of CPE.[6] In establishing Comecon, the member states sought to create 'an alternative international régime' better suited to their own possibilities and requirements. As argued by Brada:

> planned economies require an international régime to mediate trade among them more than do market economies. . . . Among planned economies international trade is a state monopoly. Therefore markets cannot function, since each transaction confronts a monopolist with a monopsonist. As a result . . . there is less information, transactions are much costlier to negotiate, and states must interact with each other directly as parties to each transaction rather than merely as creators and guarantors of the rules of the game.[7]

The pricing formulae employed by Comecon fixed intra-CMEA prices for one or more years at a time, but took recent world market prices as their reference point. (Hence the old adage that Comecon could never have taken over the whole world, because then it would no longer have known what prices to charge.) In the absence of stable pricing formulae, the CPEs would have had to undertake more frequent trade negotiations with 'no starting point for the prices at which trade would take place' and no certainty that 'prices obtained in negotiations with one country would resemble those achieved with other countries', thus making trade negotiations exceedingly costly and time-consuming. Moreover, the use of stable pricing formulae in international transactions helped to maintain stable contexts for central planning, while the systematic over-pricing of manufactured goods relative to fuels and raw materials offered the East European members of Comecon higher guaranteed returns on their production of manufactures which were often 'not up to world standards'. This gave them considerable protection against risk and competition as well as compensation for 'the high investment costs of modernizing and developing industries to serve the Soviet market'. Conversely, it provided the Soviet Union with substantially larger supplies of manufactured goods from Eastern Europe than would otherwise have been the case, but at overall costs that were lower than those of producing them itself.[8] These arrangements also economized on the Comecon states' perennially scarce earnings of hard currency.

Inevitably, some member states would derive larger benefits from the intensification of intra-CMEA relations and cohesion than others, just as some would incur larger costs than others. The most tangible and measurable costs of the collective benefits that Comecon could confer on its participants would mainly be borne by those member states who could have either sold their main exports much more dearly or purchased their import requirements more cheaply in non-CMEA markets (to the extent that they actually refrained from doing so). Nevertheless, even if the individual balance sheet of costs and benefits varied considerably between members and over time, there was a basic presumption that all members would reap net benefits from Comecon membership, not only in narrow economic terms, but also in terms of increased internal and external legitimacy, stability and room for manoeuvre, always bearing in mind that increases in the economic strength, political stability or international standing of the Soviet state could also enhance the standing of its East European acolytes. Intra-CMEA co-operation represented a positive-sum game (rather than a zero-sum game) in most respects. Member states would benefit not only from their individual gains vis-à-vis other members, but also from increases in the economic strength, political stability and international standing of CMEA as a whole. Brada even claimed that, for some East European states, Soviet hegemony 'represented an important psychological counter-weight to traditional fears of a resurgent Germany' and, for others, 'kept longstanding tensions over disputed territories and treatment of ethnic minorities relatively dormant'.[9]

In his classic analysis of the emergence and inherent problems of Comecon, Kaser argued that Nikolai Voznesensky, who was the able and influential chairman of the Soviet State Planning Commission (Gosplan) from December 1937 to March 1949, wanted to put economic relations within and between the USSR and Eastern Europe on a more regular, law-governed and impersonal economic footing, effectively removing them from the jurisdiction and interference of capricious communist politicians and enhancing the roles of more 'rational', impersonal and predictable economic mechanisms and of economic planners like himself.[10] In Kaser's view, the dismissal and arrest of Voznesensky in March 1949, not long after the death of his 'protector' Andrei Zhdanov in August 1948, eliminated the crucial Soviet proponent of (and the systemic basis for) a more far-reaching and 'rational' conception of Comecon and facilitated its subsequent emasculation by Stalin. The continuing absence of criteria whereby economic goals, performance, output, inputs, costs and demand could be adequately measured, compared, evaluated and aggregated would become the rock on which Comecon integration would eventually founder.[11]

In the year Comecon was formed, the eastern European states were consummating their transitions to Soviet-type practice, but they took over not the macro-economic value planning which Voznesensky was beginning to introduce, but the principle of instruction to enterprises in terms of physical goals of production. The consistency of these goals was effected . . . by a complex of 'material balances', but because the units of each were physical (tons, metres, boxes, bales), there was no aggregation, and hence no procedure to reach an optimum, that is, a set of plans that would maximize output and minimize input. More importantly – for the effect on Comecon – the prices of goods balanced in physical terms were all but irrelevant.[12]

In the absence of prices that could meaningfully reflect relative costs, scarcities and consumer preferences, and without any real means of economic aggregation and calculation, there could be no valid comparisons of economic costs and returns either within or between Comecon members. Nor could there be convertible currencies and multilateral trading. Economic exchanges between members of Comecon could only be based on forms of barter regulated by 'material balances', as was also the case in domestic resource allocation. While this could in principle be used to achieve a rough and ready consistency of centrally planned production goals between member states, 'balances do not in themselves gravitate towards an optimal solution, as would an international market mechanism'.[13] Voznesensky, by contrast, was trying to inject greater calculability and rationality into the Soviet economic system.

> The implications for Comecon of the Voznesensky approach were, it may be suggested, trade arrangements based on the analysis of comparative costs and permitting the evaluation of multilateral exchanges. . . . A 'law of value' operating between Comecon members would have furnished criteria for . . . rational specializations undertaken in the context of co-ordinated long-term planning.[14]

But in order to be able to analyse comparative costs and maximize economic returns, there would have to be economic systems that could generate the information on the basis of which such costs and returns could be calculated, compared and aggregated. The neo-Stalinist economic systems were to prove incapable of generating such information. In the short run Stalin could ignore the message and shoot the messengers, including Voznesensky. In the long run, however, this was to be the undoing of the neo-Stalinist economic systems.

If the ideas, policies, procedures and supranational institutions and mechanisms discussed by CMEA officials, economists and technocrats in 1949–50 had actually been implemented at that time, when the new CPEs were still inchoate and malleable, it is conceivable that Comecon could have developed much more strongly and advantageously and that East European centrally planned industrialization, inter-state specialization and industrial location could have been placed on a less arbitrary, less autarkic and more 'rational' footing from the outset. This could certainly have avoided a lot of wasteful duplication and would have been far more efficacious than the belated attempts to pull these processes back on to more efficient and 'rational' paths in the 1960s and 1970s, by which time the autarkic tendencies of the East European CPEs were set in concrete and difficult to correct.[15]

However, fuller integration of the East European CPEs could only have been achieved *either* through the adoption of market principles, sweeping economic decentralization, prices broadly reflecting relative costs and scarcities, convertible currencies and multilateral trading, *or* by erecting (under Comecon auspices) supranational agencies with the capacity and the authority to plan production, control trade, direct investment and assign specializations for the whole Comecon territory, from Prague to Vladivostok. The first option, which was persistently canvassed by liberal economic reformers (especially in Hungary and, to a lesser extent, Czechoslovakia and Poland) was never really politically feasible, as its inherent logic pointed to the gradual abandonment of central planning and Communist Party control of (and interference in) production, with the eventual adoption of an unalloyed market system. This prospectus was ultimately as unacceptable to most communist *apparatchiki*, who stood to lose power, status and control, as it was attractive to most reformers. While it would have 'relieved' the communist parties of economic responsibilities which they were ill fitted to discharge, it would also have removed the central *raison d'être* of communist rule. The second option was seriously considered and explored. It seems that on 18 January 1949 the six founder members of CMEA signed (but never ratified) a protocol on the establishment of a common economic organization and a supranational economic institution that would 'formulate a common economic plan for the harmonious development of the entire region, including the USSR'. It would have been 'endowed with plenipotentiary economic powers' in order to 'help dovetail the member economies'. The organization would have had a General Secretariat based in Moscow, with its own resources, half of which would have been contributed by the USSR, the other half coming in equal shares from the other members.[16]

However, while this more centralized and pro-active option was superficially compatible with the retention of CPEs and the 'guiding roles' of the communist parties, in practice it would have caused ultimate control of economic processes to pass from *national* economic planners and industrial ministries to *supranational* planners and Comecon industrial directorates and, more fundamentally, from communist politicians and *apparatchiki* to economic planners and technocrats. The long-term implications of this option would have been as unwelcome to national economic planners and industrial ministries as they were to national Communist Party bosses and their henchmen, all of whom would have suffered major losses of power, function and status within an increasingly centralized, supranational Comecon. They could most effectively protect their very considerable new powers and perquisites by defending the principle of national economic sovereignty. Indeed, it is very likely that Stalin vetoed the entire project for a thoroughgoing supranational integration of the Comecon countries (along with the more 'rational' and technocratic system of central planning that such a project would have required), not merely out of uncharacteristic regard for the particular interests and sensibilities of his communist vassals in Eastern Europe, but also because the whole process could have developed a momentum and power base of its own, beyond the control of the Soviet political leadership. In the words of Sándor Ausch, who was Hungary's official economic representative at Comecon headquarters in Moscow in 1949 and again from 1962 to 1964:

> Stalin . . . intervened and, by referring to the principle of national sovereignty . . . put an end to the activities of the CMEA apparatus in this field. He proposed a different solution, resting partly on autonomous national decisions and partly on bilateral agreements. Both tended to favour decisions pointing to economic autarky.[17]

As the supreme communist *apparatchik*, Stalin evidently preferred more informal, direct, *ad hoc* methods of Soviet intervention in the affairs of the East European states through Soviet embassies and the legions of Soviet agents attached to them. By 1950 the USSR was directly supervising East European policies, and 'substantial components of national economic planning were entrusted to Soviet advisers and technicians, primarily through the so-called Soviet embassy system'.[18] This system prevailed at least until November–December 1989, when Soviet agents helped to engineer the downfalls of the more hardline anti-Gorbachev régimes, precipitating East European revolutions that soon escaped Soviet control and went beyond what Moscow had intended.

Partly as a result of the outbreak of the Korean War in June 1950 and the increased priority for Stalinist methods of resource mobilization and industrialization, the USSR 'abruptly ceased active participation in the CMEA's Bureau' and it was decided to confine Comecon to 'practical questions of facilitating mutual trade', at least for the time being.[19] Nevertheless, partly as a result of the severity of Western economic sanctions, by 1953 intra-CMEA trade accounted for nearly 80 per cent of the foreign trade of Comecon's member states, who had conducted less than 15 per cent of their trade with one another in 1938 and would transact only 54 per cent of their foreign trade within CMEA by 1983, after the revival of East–West trade.[20]

In Kaser's judgement, the Soviet leadership had made a (bogus) virtue of national sovereignty in an endeavour to justify its suppression of Georgi Dimitrov's project for a Balkan federation, initiated in the Bulgarian–Yugoslav Treaty of 1947, and the economic union proposed in the Polish–Czechoslovak Treaty of that same year.[21] From the outset, Stalin viewed his new East European 'allies' with considerable suspicion. They were too 'Westernized', untested and unstable for his liking. He therefore endeavoured to restrict their contacts not only with the West, but also with each other and with the USSR, in order to insulate the Comecon states more completely from the outside world and from the hazards of cultural and ideological 'contagion'. He did not trust them enough to allow Comecon to realize more than a fraction of its true potential, and it would remain permanently scarred by this early experience. Instead of using the expansion of communist power to bring the stultifying autarky, paranoia and siege mentality of Stalinist 'socialism in one country' to an opportune end, the Soviet leadership in effect replicated most of its maladies, deformities and constraints in each of the new communist states.

Nevertheless, all was not lost. At its August 1949 Council Session in Sofia, Comecon took a seminal decision on the 'pooling' or 'sharing' of technology among its member states (the 'Sofia principle'). They would transfer or make technologies freely available to each other, at a nominal charge, instead of setting up an elaborate patents system and scientific protectionism to safeguard the advantages of technological leaders, as has been standard Western practice. This was not much liked by the more highly industrialized members of Comecon, who at least initially stood to gain very little in return for the technologies they passed on to their less developed partners, especially the USSR, Bulgaria and Romania. By the mid-1940s the increasingly isolated Soviet economy had largely exhausted the potential of its now obsolescent 1920s–30s technologies and it stood in desperate need of large new 'injections' of foreign technology in order to ward off technological stagnation. These were obtained partly through the heavy-handed removal of plant, equipment, prototypes, blueprints and even scientific personnel from Soviet-occupied Eastern Germany, on a scale which imparted new meaning to 'technology transfer', and partly by obliging Czechoslovakia, Hungary and Poland to 'share' their techno-logical know-how with the USSR, Bulgaria and Romania, under Comecon rules. Similarly, some of the Western technologies acquired or 'imported' by individual East European states and enterprises up to the 1960s were passed on to their partners under Comecon's scientific and technical co-operation (STC) arrangements. This was what 'co-operation' in CMEA really meant. In return, Eastern Europe received 'dirty' and/or environ-mentally hazardous Soviet power stations and metallurgical technologies, rickety Soviet aircraft and lethal Soviet weapons, for which they were supposed to be exceedingly grateful.[22]

THE FIRST 'RELAUNCH', 1954–6

Following Stalin's death in March 1953, there were various attempts to 'relaunch' Comecon on a more equitable and propitious footing and to use it as a substitute for more invidious direct methods of Soviet dominion over Eastern Europe. The Council Sessions of March and June 1954 established a permanent Comecon Secretariat and a standing Conference of Representatives of Member Countries. They also initiated a series of 'specialization agreements' designed to curb costly industrial duplication and import substitution, while in 1956 ten permanent Standing Commissions were established to co-ordinate specialization and co-operation in particular sectors,[23] partly in response to an extension of the range of economic tasks and challenges confronting the USSR under its frenetic new Party leader, Nikita Khrushchev. The USSR wanted the East European members of Comecon to serve as suppliers of manufactures and foodstuffs that were in short supply internally and to provide 'soft' markets for Soviet-produced plant, machinery, armaments and oil, especially as Soviet planners were now paying increased attention to comparative costs, economic returns, location of production and the scope for specialization.[24] The December 1955 and May 1956 Council Sessions attached great importance to the co-ordination and synchronization of national five-year plans. In practice, however, most attempts at plan co-ordination at that time were bilateral and confined to subsequent harmonization of the trade implications of national economic plans, rather than prior reconciliation of either trade intentions or planned production, and the 'specialization agreements' of 1954–6 were largely nullified by the social and political upheavals of 1956, which led to the hasty imposition of new *ad hoc* production and trade priorities in the hope of defusing economic discontents, while plan synchronization was derailed by Khrushchev's abandonment of the 1956–60 Soviet Five-Year Plan in 1957.[25]

THE SECOND 'RELAUNCH', 1957–60

Comecon underwent a second 'relaunch' in the wake of the November 1956 Warsaw Pact invasion of Hungary. By fostering higher living standards, less costly patterns of economic growth and stronger economic bonds within Comecon, the USSR and its East European vassal régimes hoped to obviate a repetition of anything as drastic as invading an 'allied' state, as this had damagingly exposed the lack of legitimacy and popular support of the East European communist régimes. The June 1957 and June 1958 Council Sessions of Comecon initiated preparations for the introduction of multilateral clearing, the 'transferable rouble' (a unit of account to be used in intra-CMEA clearing) and a CMEA clearing bank, while in May 1958 a special Comecon 'economic summit' launched preparations for more far-reaching production specialization, which was to be achieved by multilateral, supranational, prior co-ordination of plan, with enhanced roles for fifteen sectoral and two functional Standing Commissions. Moreover, the June 1958 Council Session approved uniform rules on the pricing of goods traded within Comecon, in an endeavour to promote more equitable multilateral trading and to insulate intra-CMEA trade from the vagaries and fluctuations of world market prices, while that of December 1959 belatedly adopted a constitutional Charter for Comecon, no doubt spurred on by the shining example of the 1957

Treaties of Rome.[26] The Charter defined the status and functions of the Council Session ('the highest organ'), the Executive Committee ('the principal executive organ'), the Standing Commissions and the Secretariat. It also committed them to 'the consistent implementation of the international socialist division of labour' (ISDL).[27] The supranational 'integrationist' implications of ISDL opened a more substantive chapter in Comecon's development, while also sowing seeds of dissension and acrimony.

INTERNATIONAL SOCIALIST DIVISION OF LABOUR, 1960–8

During the 1960s East European economists and reformers increasingly viewed foreign trade as an important means of increasing economic specialization, economies of scale, factor productivity and the returns on investment and hence as a basis for more 'intensive' economic growth, making more productive use of more slowly growing resource inputs. Partly in an endeavour to keep up with surging West European economic growth and integration, but mainly at Soviet behest, the December 1961 Council Session of Comecon approved 'The Basic Principles of the International Socialist Division of Labour'. The explicit objectives of ISDL were:

> more efficient social production, a higher rate of economic growth, higher living standards, . . . industrialization and gradual removal of historical differences in economic development levels of the socialist countries, and the creation of a material basis for their more-or-less simultaneous transition to communism.[28]

It was emphasized that 'the principal means' of realizing these objectives would be 'the co-ordination of economic plans'. This would have to be 'strong and stable' since 'any deviation, even by a single country, would inevitably lead to disturbances in the economic cycle in the other socialist countries'.[29] Even more controversially, the document talked of 'concentrating production of similar products in one or several socialist countries' because 'specialization and co-operation are potent factors in the development of all industries, especially engineering, chemicals, ferrous and non-ferrous metallurgy'. Moreover, 'socialist countries differ in per capita farm land and in soil and climatic conditions. . . . This makes it necessary to explore the possibilities for further specialization in agricultural production.'[30] It also alluded to 'resultant recommendations for specialization and co-operation',[31] implying that some states could be asked to specialize in agriculture while others specialized in engineering, chemicals and metallurgy, and in November 1962 Khrushchev proclaimed the need 'to go quickly to the establishment of a common single planning organ for all countries, which would be composed of representatives of all countries coming to CMEA'.[32]

In practice, however, the Comecon states did little to implement these Basic Principles, which soon encountered resistance from Czechoslovakia, Hungary, Poland and, most famously, Romania.[33] Romania's increasingly nationalistic communist élite was committed to headlong industrialization and hotly denied Comecon's right to 'assign' specializations to sovereign states. In April 1964 the Central Committee of Romania's ruling party issued a public declaration that industry, not agriculture, held the key to 'balanced' and 'ever-ascending as well as rapid growth of the whole national economy'; and that the proposed transfer of some 'national' economic prerogatives to supranational agencies was unacceptable because: (i) 'The planned management of the national economy is one of the fundamental, essential, inalienable attributes of the sovereignty of the socialist state' and the 'chief means' by which it 'achieves its political and socio-economic objectives'; and (ii) 'The state plan is one and indivisible', as centrally planned 'management of the national economy as a whole is not possible if the questions of managing some branches or enterprises are . . . transferred to extrastate bodies'.[34] Beyond the nationalist claptrap, there were some substantive operational considerations: comprehensive, mandatory national economic planning really did rest upon untrammelled national economic sovereignty. Indeed, East European economists increasingly realized that the proposed surrender of various planning and co-ordinating functions to Comecon agencies and fora would not only further impair national economic planning, but also reproduce at the supranational level (and in much magnified forms) most of the rigidities and malfunctions that already dogged central planning at the national level, while leading to an even greater predominance of the priorities and predilections of the Soviet colossus over those of the smaller East European states.

Paradoxically, the emergence of major East European reform movements between 1961 and 1968, along with the more enduring expansion of bilateral East–West trade and co-operation, somewhat diminished the need and the pressure to increase intra-CMEA co-operation and integration, which could indeed have reduced the individual state's room for manoeuvre both in the pursuit of domestic economic restructuring and in the cultivation of West European economic partners. It was in many ways easier and more immediately rewarding for the CPEs (including an oil-exporting USSR) to expand their links with the West than with each other. This was not merely the line of least resistance, but also the avenue of maximum advantage, as East–West trade offered increased access to much-needed Western products, technology, finance and know-how.

Co-operation, specialization and integration did nonetheless make some headway within Comecon during the 1960s, partly by instituting round-about means of circumventing the objections and resistance of recalcitrant 'national' vested interests and central planners. There were expanded roles for Comecon's sectoral and functional Standing Commissions, mirroring sectoral and 'neo-functionalist' approaches to West European integration. Six new Standing Commissions were established, including four to deal with standardization, STC, statistics, and currency and finance, respectively. There was also increased reliance on joint-ventures, STC and the exchange of East European manufactures, equipment and foodstuffs for Soviet fuel, metals and nuclear technology. Comecon's physical cohesion was enhanced by the construction of the *Druzhba* [Friendship] oil pipeline and the *Mir* [Peace] electricity grid. In 1963–4 an International Bank for Economic Co-operation was founded, in order to regulate and facilitate multilateral 'clearing' via a new 'transferable rouble', which, however, never fulfilled its potential to develop from a mere unit of account (like the ECU) into a convertible 'single currency'. In 1967, moreover, Comecon adopted the so-called 'interested party principle', under which individual member states could simply 'opt out' of any Comecon project they did not like,[35] allowing the rest to go ahead unencumbered by awkward or reluctant partners. In principle, however, a member state could still veto a Comecon project or policy that was deemed to threaten its vital national interests, since Comecon's joint decision-making still rested ultimately on unanimity or consensus between 'equal' and 'sovereign' member states. Thus, while the 1962–7 crisis in CMEA relations bore some resemblances to the 1965 'empty chair' crisis in EC relations with de Gaulle's France, the chosen means of overcoming it combined elements of the 1966 Luxembourg Compromise (allowing EC member states to exercise a national veto to safeguard 'vital national interests'), neo-functionalism, variable geometry and the opt-outs obtained by Britain and Denmark in 1991 and 1992 respectively.[36]

Within Comecon, however, the continuing predominance of bilateralism over multilateralism could only have been overcome either by supranational central planning of Comecon as a single economy or by the adoption of convertible currencies, market mechanisms and realistic pricing. The former was naturally opposed by the more nationalistic and/or market-orientated East European régimes, while the latter would have allowed the more market-orientated member states to draw away from their Comecon partners and closer to the West, which was clearly unacceptable to the USSR and its 'hardline' allies. Comecon was therefore destined eventually to fall between two stools. Meanwhile, it had to settle for 'sub-optimal' or 'second best' solutions.

SOCIALIST ECONOMIC INTEGRATION, 1969–89

Integration only became the officially declared goal of Comecon after the 'special' Council Session of April 1969, at which communist leaders and governments discussed ways and means of keeping member states 'in line' and 'on side' in the aftermath of the August 1968 Warsaw Pact invasion of Czechoslovakia. Until then 'integration' was virtually a taboo word in communist circles, carrying connotations of 'monopoly capitalist' collusion against workers and consumers in the hope of postponing the (elusive) 'terminal crisis of capitalism', and the intraregional projects and policies of the European members of Comecon were largely confined to 'fraternal' inter-party and inter-governmental co-operation, modest 'mutual economic assistance' and minimal subsequent harmonization of national economic plans.[37] However, the very limited progress toward greater integration between the European members of Comecon from 1969 to 1989 was not attributable to any lack of official declarations, commitments and blue-prints, but rather to the existence of deep-seated impediments to integration between CPEs. It was almost impossible to integrate countries that were under such all-embracing national state control. It was possible to achieve 'hyperintegration' between the Soviet republics, because they were components of a single state, tightly controlled by a single centre of power. (Hence the economic consequences of the disintegration of the Soviet Union in 1991 were to be even more severe than those of the preceding disintegration of Comecon.) But, by the same token, integration between separate CPEs was virtually a contradiction in terms. Integration within Comecon was also hindered by the extremely disparate nature of its membership, exacerbated by the admission of underdeveloped and non-European Mongolia in 1962, Cuba in 1972 and Vietnam in 1978, and by the overwhelming asymmetry between the USSR, a real 'superstate', and the motley assortment of small and medium-sized members. Some of these became in a sense merely extra-territorial appendages of the USSR. For example, Bulgaria was often described as the sixteenth Soviet republic. Indeed, for many purposes, it was more meaningful to think of Comecon as an imposed monolith, as the economic arm of the Soviet bloc, rather than as a vehicle or forum for voluntary co-operation and (belatedly) integration between 'equal' and 'sovereign' member states. In 1983 the USSR accounted for 88 per cent of Comecon's territory and 60 per cent of its population.[38] Thus it was in a sense only natural that Soviet priorities and preferences predominated and that the vast economic, military and demographic disparities between the USSR and the rest should have fostered more suspicion, rivalry and animosity than mutual trust. Intra-CMEA co-operation and integration increasingly became 'a contest in which each participant endeavoured to extract the maximum advantage at the minimum price'.[39] Hence the Soviet bloc was never quite as monolithic as its leaders would have liked us to believe.

By 1989 the East European members of Comecon (excluding the USSR) accounted for no more than 4 per cent of world trade. They were 'trade' averse' for a whole host of reasons.[40] In addition to the autarkic bias of the initial neo-Stalinist industrialization strategies, central planning was found to be less fraught with difficulty in relatively self-sufficient or hermetically sealed economies than in ones that depended heavily on foreign trade, whose volume and composition lay largely outside the control of national economic planners. These therefore tended to treat foreign trade as an annoying 'residual' which had to be 'tacked on' to their laboriously constructed and 'balanced' national economic plans. In most cases foreign trade was a state monopoly. It had to be channelled through cumbersome, bureaucratic and often corrupt state agencies or foreign trade corporations and was limited to what these were willing and able to handle. This extreme institutional separation of domestic producers from foreign customers also increased the unresponsiveness of the former to the needs and desires of the latter, compounding the 'consumer resistance' caused by the characteristic inferior quality, limited assortment, restricted specifications or 'clunky' design of the products of East European state enterprise. In addition, the use of complex and arbitrary multiple exchange rates and foreign trade 'coefficients', combined with the deliberate overvaluation of Comecon currencies, meant that industrial, extractive and agricultural enterprises habitually made formal accounting 'losses' on their exports, even if importers and foreign trade agencies usually made profits. This effectively ruled out any meaningful calculation of relative costs, economic returns, and gains from trade, whether for individual enterprises or for the central authorities. The overwhelming preponderance of bilateral trade relations, caused by the endemic shortages of 'hard' currency, the inability of most of the enterprises and unappetizing products of the planned economies to penetrate and hold their own in internationally competitive markets, and the failure to develop convertible currencies and rational price mechanisms that could have facilitated multilateral trading, effectively restricted the volume of any bilateral trade to the quantities and types of products that the weaker partner could manage to export; and, by discouraging either partner from running a trade surplus, acted as a further disincentive to increase intra-CMEA exports. Moreover, many of the best products of any CPE were pre-emptively assigned to particular domestic projects or planned uses, since producers and planners were essentially judged and rewarded in accordance with the domestic performance of strategic industries and projects. Therefore, the products available for export were to a large extent the 'left-overs' that nobody particularly wanted. The Comecon states thus found it almost as difficult to trade with one another as with market economies, and this severely restricted the scope for intra-CMEA integration.

Moves towards market mechanisms, multilateralism and currency convertibility, which would have increased the latitude for autonomous integrative forces, were strongly resisted by Communist Party and central planning hierarchies, not only because such moves would have reduced the degrees of centralized political and economic control over the CPEs and the power, status and *raison d'être* of the Communist Parties and central economic agencies, but also because they would have weakened the absolute priority accorded to defence and heavy industry (the 'military-industrial complex'), while enabling the more successful and consumer-

and market-orientated CMEA members to reduce their dependence on the USSR. There would also have been a loss of 'captive' markets and suppliers, and the increased exposure to international competition and market forces would have threatened the survival of many obsolete, inefficient or feather-bedded industries and enterprises, as indeed came to pass after 1989. Furthermore, increased commercialization and monetarization would have given rise to acute liquidity problems and to heightened risks of bankruptcy and default at enterprise, national and Comecon levels, as also arose after 1989. Yet, while it was obvious to all that the so-called 'full market solution' to Comecon integration would depend on convertibility, multilateralism, and prices reflecting relative costs, returns and scarcities, it was still insufficiently appreciated that supranational central planning, specialization and division of labour within Comecon as a whole had remarkably similar prerequisites since, without convertibility and realistic prices and exchange rates, the supranational central planners would not have been able to calculate, compare and aggregate costs, returns, productivity, optimal locations, gains from trade or even total outputs across 'national' boundaries and price-structures.

However, except in the cases of Hungary and Yugoslavia, East European moves towards 'market socialism' were unceremoniously halted by the August 1968 Warsaw Pact invasion of Czechoslovakia and the subsequent suppression of reform movements. For a time even the Hungarians had to tread carefully, referring merely to a New Economic Mechanism (inaugurated in January 1968), rather than to 'reform' or to 'market socialism' as such. Yet the communist régimes still had to try to surmount the tightening resource constraints and the deteriorations in economic performance that had contributed to the emergence of 'reform' movements in the first place. Therefore, despite (or even because of) the 1968 invasion, the resultant brake on fundamental systemic change or 'reform' and the temporary setback to East–West trade prospects, it became all the more necessary to increase intra-CMEA trade, assistance, co-operation and cohesion, in the hope of enhancing economic performance and reducing the likelihood of another traumatic Warsaw Pact intervention in the internal affairs of a 'fraternal' state in the near future. This was certainly the major impetus behind the convocation of a 'special' Council Session of Comecon in April 1969, ostensibly to celebrate the organization's twentieth anniversary, and the proclamation of a new panacea: Socialist Economic Integration (SEI).[41] However, it was one thing to proclaim SEI and another to agree on what it meant and how to achieve it. Having decided in the late 1950s that each communist régime would have to chart its own 'national road to socialism' (even if the USSR reserved the right to prescribe or even change the 'driver' and the final destination), by 1969 the range of systemic and policy preferences of the communist despots had become too diverse, entrenched and mutually incompatible to lend themselves to a common conception and mode of integration. *The Complex Programme for the Further Extension and Improvement of Co-operation and the Development of Economic Integration by the CMEA Member Countries*, published by Comecon in 1971, was an incoherent hotchpotch of disparate ingredients cooked up by seventeen different committees.[42]

It may be objected that the EC and the EU have never had a coherent, comprehensive and generally accepted concept of integration either, yet Western Europe has made impressive progress towards 'ever closer union' since the 1950s. The crucial difference is that, once 'national' barriers to the free movement of goods, capital, labour and services have been largely eliminated and a permissive framework of institutions and ground rules has been established, integration between market economies can proceed autonomously and impersonally, even while the politicians and bureaucrats are asleep. 'Capitalist' integration is essentially a market-driven, decentralized, self-propelling process, once the politicians and bureaucrats have erected the necessary legal, commercial and institutional structures. It spontaneously creates cross-border or transnational links, mainly at the 'micro' rather than the 'macroeconomic' level. For the most part, it has not depended upon the willingness and ability of prickly, querulous or mutually suspicious national politicians and civil servants to reach coherent and comprehensive agreements on joint projects and common precepts. It has thus side-stepped and surmounted the rivalries, anxieties and animosities bequeathed by the interwar years and two world wars to both Western and Eastern Europe. Integration within Comecon, however, depended on the continuous active intervention of economic planners and politicians and on an agreed coherent conception of what they were striving to achieve, if they were not to pull in many different directions. In practice, it was largely restricted to what could be agreed in advance between mutually mistrustful communist states and incorporated into their prospective annual and five-year economic plans. Indeed, until they ceased to be CPEs, they could not easily generate or accommodate spontaneous, decentralized, cross-border or transnational trade, investment, migration or joint-ventures. This constraint mainly arose because, once their laboriously negotiated and elaborated national economic plans were finalized, almost all their available resources were 'committed' to preordained economic activities and projects, leaving little or no spare capacity with which to respond to unforeseen opportunities for transnational co-operation, etc., unless this had been built into the plans from the outset.

Integration between the Comecon states was restricted not only by the limited powers of clairvoyance of central planners and economic ministries, but also by the normal rivalries and animosities that arise between neighbours and by the abnormal mutual suspicions and mistrust generated by the extremely intrusive and all-pervasive hegemony of the USSR over its East European vassals, by the odd 'fraternal' invasion of an 'errant' East European 'ally' by its 'socialist' neighbours, and by the occasional 'comradely' removal of a communist potentate who had blotted his copy-book. Indeed, whereas 'capitalist' integration has helped West Europeans to overcome, to side-step and even to unite against the bitter legacies of the 1930s and the two world wars, East Europeans have had the opposite experience. They came out of the Second World War at least as disunited, aggrieved, suspicious and resentful as they had been before it. Soviet hegemony was able to muzzle many of the mutual enmities between its East European 'partners', but it did little to dissipate or defuse the under-lying sentiments. There was no comprehensive post-war settlement or reconciliation between former belligerents in Eastern Europe, comparable to that achieved by the ERP and the ECSC in Western Europe, nor did the East Europeans ever attain the peaks of prosperity and hedonistic materialism and/or oblivion that helped to soothe, dissipate and divert attention from inherited enmities and resentments in Western Europe.

In view of all these obstacles, SEI had to assume roundabout and limited forms, rather than 'head-on' comprehensive ones. Since it was impossible to agree on common approaches to pricing, economic reform, multilateral-ism, currency convertibility and intra-CMEA capital and labour mobility, Comecon had to limit itself to specific half-measures and sectoral pro-grammes that all its disparate members could accept but in which not all would participate. Thus in 1971 an International Investment Bank was established to finance and facilitate intra-CMEA co-operation on trans-national investment projects. In 1975, 1980 and 1985, moreover, the Comecon states formulated a series of five-year Concerted Plans for Multi-lateral Integration Measures, synchronized with their national five-year plans, designed to resource and co-ordinate transnational projects in key sectors such as energy and extractive industries. These were increasingly seen by the USSR as a means of getting the East Europeans to bear part of the increasing investment and production costs of the fuels and other 'hard' commodities that they imported from the Soviet Union at consider-ably less than world market prices (and sometimes re-exported to the West to make a nice hard-currency profit). But, from their own very differ-ent standpoint, most East Europeans resented being expected to bear some of the costs of developing the economy of their overlord and/or oppressor. It is possible to see both points of view. In 1975 it was also proposed that CMEA members should adopt a cluster of binding, collective Target Programmes to relieve critical deficiencies and bottlenecks in the areas of energy, raw materials, foodstuffs, industrial consumer goods and transpor-tation and to increase specialization and reduce duplication in engineering, but these did not become operational until the 1980s and trade flows linked to specialization agreements never exceeded 25 per cent of intra-CMEA trade in engineering products or 10 per cent of all intra-CMEA trade.[43]

From the early 1970s onward, the USSR and most East European members of Comecon began to devolve some of their economic planning, allocation and decision-making tasks to giant industrial 'combines' and/or 'industrial associations'. This was done partly in the hope of reducing the so-called 'operational and informational overload' on central planners in increasingly complex and industrialized CPEs through the creation of intermediate tiers of economic decision-making and of replicating the dynamic roles of gigantic, highly integrated and increasingly science-based industrial combines and conglomerates in the major capitalist economies. It was envisaged that the new industrial associations and combines would develop strong research, development, design and supply capabilities, reap increased economies of scale, and 'internalize' the more detailed planning and allocation functions, by transforming these into managerial tasks performable within giant enterprises or groups of enterprises. In theory, this would enable the overloaded central economic organs to concentrate on their overarching macroeconomic roles. It was also hoped that these industrial associations and/or combines would foster decentralized 'horizontal' contractual links with one another to supplement (and partly supplant) the 'vertical' chains of command extending from the central planning and supply agencies and industrial ministries to the myriad industrial enterprises. All this was expected to have a major impact on intra-CMEA integration, by facilitating the autonomous development of direct transnational links, investment, joint-ventures and STC between industrial associations and/or combines in different CMEA economies. In practice, however, the new conglomerations or groupings of enterprises were generally unenterprising, unwieldy, risk-averse and bureaucratic. They tended to reproduce most of the rigidities and other deficiencies of the central planning and supply organs which they were supposed to relieve. Frequently, they were little more than additional intermediate tiers in the 'vertical' central planning hierarchies. Inasmuch as they did spawn new ventures and initiatives at lower or intermediate levels, these were liable to disrupt or divert resources from centrally planned activities and, unless prepared well in advance, were difficult to incorporate into national economic plans.

It was never clearly explained how the 'horizontal' links which the industrial associations and combines were expected to foster would intermesh with the 'vertical' chains of command radiating from the central planning and supply organs and economic ministries. It can be argued that, in order to have any chance of functioning smoothly and in accordance with some idealized (or Orwellian) cybernetic vision, a command economy needs to have clearly defined and free-standing chains of command. Any 'cross currents' are more likely to generate disorganization and malfunctions than increased efficiency and productivity. In any case, the 'actually existing' CPEs lacked most of the financial, commercial, legal and distributive infrastructure that sustained or facilitated autonomous 'horizontal' links between industrial enterprises in capitalist economies. Not surprisingly, therefore, the industrial associations and combines were unable to foster many direct 'horizontal' links either within or between different members of Comecon.

The quadrupling of OPEC oil prices in 1973–4 and the ensuing economic recession in the capitalist world greatly increased East European dependence on the relatively 'soft' Soviet market and on imports of lower-priced Soviet oil and gas, which were largely to be paid for by increasing East European manufactured and agricultural exports to the USSR, often on a barter basis. These forms of Soviet 'assistance' helped both to cushion most of the East European economies against the adverse trends in their terms of trade and to allow them to continue to grow (albeit at diminishing rates) through most of the 1970s (see Table 10.1). However, while increased integration with the USSR helped to insulate them from the damaging effects of recession and higher oil prices in the capitalist world, in the longer term it further impaired their capacity to export successfully to the West. The size, direction and significance of the implicit transnational subsidies that emerged within Comecon raised complex and emotive issues

Table 10.1 Annual rates of economic growth in Eastern Europe, 1971–94 (% real GDP)[44]

	1971 –80	1981 –5	1986 –8	1989	1990	1991	1992	1993	1994
Poland	3.6	0.6	1.0	0.2	−11.6	−7.6	1.5	3.8	5.0
Hungary	2.6	0.7	1.5	0.7	−3.5	−11.9	−4.3	−2.3	3.0
Czecho-slovakia	2.8	1.2	1.5	1.4	0.4	n/a	n/a	n/a	n/a
Czech Republic	n/a	n/a	n/a	n/a	n/a	−14.2	−7.1	−0.3	3.0
Slovakia	n/a	n/a	n/a	n/a	n/a	−14.5	−7.0	−4.0	4.0
Romania	5.3	−0.1	0.1	−5.8	−5.6	−12.9	−13.6	1.0	2.0
Bulgaria	2.8	0.8	1.9	0.5	−9.1	−11.7	−5.6	−4.2	0.0
Albania	4.7	2.0	1.7	9.8	−10.0	−27.1	−9.7	11.0	7.0
Yugoslavia	5.1	1.3	0.9	−0.8	−7.5	−15.0	−20.0	n/a	n/a
Serbia	n/a	n/a	n/a	−8.0	−11.0	−26.0	−30.0	n/a	n/a
Croatia	n/a	n/a	n/a	−1.6	−9.0	−14.0	−9.0	−3.0	1.0
Slovenia	n/a	n/a	n/a	−1.8	−4.7	−8.1	−5.4	−1.0	−5.0
Macedonia	n/a	n/a	n/a	n/a	−10.0	−12.0	−14.0	−14.0	−7.0
Estonia	n/a	n/a	n/a	−1.1	−8.1	−11.0	−26.0	−8.0	4.0
Latvia	n/a	n/a	n/a	6.8	2.9	−8.3	−34.0	−12.0	3.0
Lithuania	n/a	n/a	n/a	1.5	−5.0	−13.0	−38.0	−16.0	4.0
USSR/ CIS*	3.1	1.7	2.3	3.0	−4.0	−12.0	−19.0	−12.0	−17.0
Russia	n/a	n/a	n/a	3.0	−4.0	−13.0	−19.0	−12.0	−15.0
Ukraine	n/a	n/a	n/a	4.0	−3.0	−12.0	−17.0	−14.0	−23.0
Belarus	n/a	n/a	n/a	8.0	−3.0	−1.2	−9.6	−12.0	−26.0

* Figures for USSR include Estonia, Latvia and Lithuania up to and including 1991.

to which it is impossible to do justice within the confines of the present chapter. Despite the considerable assistance granted to Cuba, Vietnam and Mongolia from the 1960s onward, Comecon never engaged in large explicit fiscal transfers between its European members comparable to those under the EC's CAP and structural and cohesion funds. The real bones of contention within Comecon concerned the implicit transfers generated by systematic deviations of intra-CMEA prices from world market prices, especially the supply from 1973 onward of large quantities of Soviet oil and gas to Eastern Europe at substantially lower prices. The dominant Western view was that this apparent Soviet 'subsidization' of Eastern Europe was politically motivated, representing conscious endeavours to underwrite the further development of their shaky CPEs, to reward political loyalty and to maintain the Soviet imperium without recurrent recourse to coercion. Others, notably Holzman and Brada, have put forward essentially economic explanations of the implicit subsidies, arguing that within *any* trade bloc whose prices systematically deviate from world market levels, some will gain and some will lose out, and this is not necessarily the result of a conscious plan to reward some and penalize others on political grounds. The CAP produces similar effects within the EU, and the growth of intra-CMEA 'subsidies' after 1973 was a largely fortuitous consequence of external factors, primarily the 1973 and 1979 OPEC oil-price rises. Moreover, the distribution of gains and losses can be explained by the fact that, within Comecon as a whole, capital was scarce, while fuels and raw materials were *relatively* abundant. Therefore, the comparatively capital-rich states (GDR, Czechoslovakia and Hungary) were bound to benefit at the expense of the more mineral-rich USSR and Romania. However, most East Europeans resented any suggestion that they were being subsidized by the USSR. In their eyes, they were entitled to *compensation* from the USSR for the *imposition* of economic systems and development strategies that were neither of their own choosing nor appropriate to their particular economic needs and that therefore kept them much poorer than they would otherwise have been.[45]

The increasingly nationalistic and independent-minded Romanian and Albanian communist régimes had to manage without such Soviet 'assistance', but they had significant (albeit rapidly declining) oil resources of their own, while Albania received Chinese economic assistance until the mid-1970s in return for its support for China in the Sino-Soviet disputes of the 1960s and early 1970s.

In the short term, the 1970s East–West détente facilitated increased inflows of Western capital and technology into the still expanding East European economies. There was an uncontrolled proliferation of East–West joint-ventures, production licensing agreements and imported 'turn-key' installations, partly financed by recycled 'petrodollars', as Western banks were somewhat incautiously re-lending to Eastern Europe some of the oil 'windfalls' deposited by the newly rich oil states. The East European dictatorships eagerly accepted Western capital, joint ventures and 'technology transfers' as substitutes for more fundamental reforms in their socio-economic systems although, in the absence of far-reaching systemic reforms to increase their economic efficiency, they would be unable to reap in full the potential benefits that could have been obtained from these transfers. However, in the wake of the ill-fated 'Prague Spring' (1963–8), most of the East European dictators perceived radical reforms to be politically dangerous. 'Technology transfer' and 'import-led' growth, financed by inflows of foreign capital, seemed to offer politically safer means of modernizing the East European economies. Nevertheless, increased reliance on Western capital, technology and firms resulted in the accumulation of uncomfortably large hard-currency debts and had unanticipated political and social consequences. Increased contact with Western visitors (including businessmen), together with the proliferation of amenities catering to their needs, helped to diffuse Western values, comparators, consumerism and pop culture, especially among the young. The ensuing Westernization of East European attitudes, values, dress and leisure activities was, in the end, just as corrosive of communist influence on the minds of the young as any radical systemic change.

Excessive reliance upon Western capital and technology transfers posed equally serious economic hazards. Debt service payments became very burdensome (see Table 10.2) and began to exceed fresh inflows of Western capital by the late 1970s. The East European states found themselves having to expand their exports to the West to service their $60–70 bn hard-currency debt at the same time as the doubling of OPEC oil prices in 1979 plunged most of the capitalist world into another economic recession which further depressed demand for (and raised trade barriers

Table 10.2 Eastern Europe's accumulated hard-currency indebtedness, 1989[46]

	Gross debt (bn $)	Net debt (bn $)*	Ratio of net debt to exports (%)	Debt service ratio**	Per capita gross debt ($)	Per capita net debt ($)
Poland	40.8	37.0	433	88	1,077	976
Hungary	20.6	15.6	278	45	1,925	1,458
Czechoslovakia	7.9	0.2	6	17	510	13
Romania	0.5	−1.2	−21	15	22	−52
Bulgaria	10.2	9.2	347	57	1,133	1,022
Albania	0.4	n/a	n/a	n/a	125	n/a
Yugoslavia	16.5	9.6	91	28	697	405

*   Gross debt minus hard-currency reserves.
** Annual interest and repayments as a percentage of the value of annual exports.

against) imports from Eastern Europe. This time, however, the Soviet Union was less able to come to Eastern Europe's rescue. The 1979–82 world recession coincided with the nadir of the Brezhnev 'years of stagnation', during which Soviet economic growth sharply decelerated and key sectors such as oil, coal, iron and steel stopped growing altogether. The USSR's inability to go on supplying ever-increasing quantities of fuel and raw materials to Eastern Europe on 'soft' terms also reduced its capacity to absorb (in return) ever-increasing quantities of obsolescent and/or poor quality East European manufactured consumer goods and equipment, some of which must have contributed to poor Soviet economic performance. Eastern Europe was therefore caught in a 'two-way squeeze' between a stagnating Soviet economy and a recession-bound West. This was compounded by the simultaneous termination of East–West détente and the start of the 'new Cold War', precipitated by Western escalation of the nuclear arms race from 1978 to 1983, the Soviet invasion of Afghanistan in December 1979, the accession of Ronald Reagan to the US Presidency in 1980 and the imposition of martial law in Poland in December 1981. Thus, from 1979 to 1983 the East European economies were pushed into severe economic recessions from which they still had not recovered in 1989, when the 'iron curtain' finally lifted. Between 1979 and 1989, with the possible exceptions of the GDR and Bulgaria, the East European economies hardly grew at all in real per capita terms and, at least in the extreme cases of Romania, Albania and Poland, experienced serious economic contractions (see Table 10.1).

There were some last-ditch attempts to breathe new life into Comecon during the 1980s, however, in the vain hope of revitalizing the moribund CPEs. The major CMEA 'economic summit' in Moscow in June 1984 essentially decided on more of the same: accelerated transition to 'intensive growth' through more 'rational' use of Comecon's resources, closer and more sharply focused co-ordination of national economic plans, a strengthening of *bilateral* ties between CMEA states and recognition of the need for 'active utilization of commodity–money relations' in addition to co-operation and plan co-ordination, while the USSR warned that low-priced deliveries of fuel and raw materials to its 'allies' would only be increased if they would upgrade their very substandard exports to the USSR.[47]

Much was expected of Mikhail Gorbachev, who became Soviet leader in March 1985. The December 1985 Council Session of Comecon approved a Comprehensive Programme to Promote Scientific and Technological Progress of the Member Countries of the CMEA up to the Year 2000, calling for increased STC in the fields of electronics (including data-processing technologies), automation, nuclear energy, new materials and biotechnology, with the aim of doubling output per worker by 2000. As a surrogate for more fundamental systemic change, which would have run up against fiercer opposition from powerful vested interests, Gorbachev and his chief economic mentor, Abel Aganbegyan, were essentially gambling on a quick technological 'fix' for the problems of the Soviet economy and Comecon:

> Especially important is the preferential development of external economic ties within the framework of the CMEA. . . . Of key significance here is the implementation of programmes of scientific technological progress with these countries. . . . Since we must overcome the current trends and achieve a qualitative breakthrough in the development of the forces of production, we can no longer rely on the evolutionary form of scientific and technological progress. It cannot guarantee radical increases in economic efficiency. Such radical increase can only be assured by *revolutionary changes* in scientific and technological progress, with the transition from the old generation of technology, to fundamentally new technological systems. . . . Virtually no machinery that is now in use will then remain. . . . This is to be assured by trebling the machine-building output over the fifteen years.[48]

This new STC programme reflected Gorbachev's essentially voluntarist and directive approach to the economic 'acceleration': imposing new priorities and technologies 'from above' on a largely unchanged economic system. The programme had little impact because: (i) it grossly underestimated the extent and the negative consequences of the institutional isolation of the CPEs and their scientific communities and the inability of CPEs to match the continuous and all-pervasive pressures on capitalist economies to innovate in order to survive in increasingly competitive environments; (ii) Gorbachev made too many commitments on too many fronts, thereby overstretching and overheating the Soviet economy and exacerbating its bottlenecks and shortages; (iii) the East European members of Comecon resented being asked to contribute to projects that were chiefly of interest to the USSR, all of which were to be placed under the overall direction of Soviet institutions; and (iv) it was hastily cobbled together, just too late to be incorporated in the 1986–90 five-year plans.

SOCIALIST ECONOMIC DISINTEGRATION, 1989–91

Gorbachev did, however, authorize a step that marked the beginning of the end of Comecon. If he had understood its full implications, he might have acted differently. In June 1985 Comecon's Secretary General, Vyacheslav Sychov, sent a letter and a draft Joint Declaration to the new President of the EC Commission, Jacques Delors, proposing reciprocal recognition and relations between the EC and Comecon, 'in the context of their respective competences'.[49] This signalled implicit acceptance that the EC could directly negotiate trade agreements with individual CMEA states (bypassing Comecon), because, unlike the EC, Comecon was not a supranational legal entity and its members had never empowered it to negotiate trade treaties on their behalf. In October 1985 the EC Commissioner for External Relations informed the European Parliament that the draft Joint Declaration would be acceptable in principle, provided that it was linked to a normalization of relations between the EC and Comecon's individual member states, who would therefore accredit diplomatic representatives to the EC, negotiate trade agreements with the EC and cease to oppose EC representation in international organizations. He sent Comecon and each of its members a letter to this effect in February 1986, and by May all had formally accepted this twin-track approach to 'normal relations' between the two groups and their individual member states, clearing the way for the formal commencement of negotiations between Comecon and the EC in September 1986.[50] These were prolonged by wrangling over the status of West Berlin, which in Western (but not Soviet) eyes was already in the EC, but a Joint Declaration of reciprocal recognition, relations and co-operation on matters of mutual interest was finally signed in June 1988. This gave the green light for the EC to conclude trade and co-operation agreements with the European members of Comecon, starting with Hungary in December 1988, Poland in December 1989 and the USSR, Czechoslovakia, Romania and Bulgaria in 1990, followed by treaties of association in 1991–2.[51]

Significantly, there was no Council Session of Comecon during the *annus mirabilis* of 1989. But in July 1989, on the eve of the East European revolutions, Mikhail Gorbachev told the Council of Europe:

> The political order of one country or another changed in the past and may change in the future. This change is the exclusive affair and choice of that country. Any interference in domestic affairs and any attempt to restrict the sovereignty of states, both friends and allies or any others, is inadmissible.[52]

The so-called 'Sinatra doctrine' (on doing it 'their way') reversed the 'Brezhnev doctrine' on the 'limited sovereignty' of 'fraternal' East European states, in whose name Czechoslovakia had been invaded in 1968. In December 1989 Soviet Premier Ryzhkov proposed that from 1991 onward intra-CMEA trade should be conducted in hard currencies and at full world market prices, signalling the end of Soviet readiness to meet on concessionary terms Eastern Europe's voracious fuel and raw material requirements. Allowing the East European states to go their own ways was seen as absolving the USSR of any further economic responsibilities towards them. They would have to 'stand on their own feet', unconstrained but also unsupported by the Soviet Union. On the eve of the January 1990 Council Session of Comecon, the Czechoslovak Finance Minister Václav Klaus threatened that his country would unilaterally withdraw from the organization if the other members did not support his motion to put it into liquidation.[53] In the event, a commission was established to assess the options and in March a Comecon meeting in

Prague proposed a rapid switch from multilateral co-operation and plan co-ordination to bilateral trade and co-operation and the downgrading of Comecon's Secretariat to an 'information centre'. In any case, the widespread abandonment of central planning left little to co-ordinate. However, the pains and tribulations of the East European transitions to market systems and untrammelled sovereignty were greatly magnified by the over-hasty abandonment of the intra-CMEA economic interdependencies, 'division of labour' and trade links that had been nurtured (albeit artificially) during Comecon's 41-year existence, and intra-CMEA trade contracted by about 15 per cent in 1990.[54]

From 1 January 1991, all intra-CMEA trade was officially to be conducted in hard currencies and at full world market prices, although the change began earlier and some bilateral barter arrangements survived into the mid-1990s. The effects were cataclysmic. The OECD estimated the cost of the implicit changes in Eastern European terms of trade to be, as percentages of GNP, 4 per cent for Bulgaria, 2 per cent each for Hungary and Czechoslovakia, 1.5 per cent for Romania and slightly below 1 per cent for Poland.[55] The USSR was the immediate beneficiary of this *de facto* disintegration of Comecon, which wrought a dramatic improvement in its terms of trade with Eastern Europe. In 1991, however, intra-CMEA trade more than halved and the OECD estimated that this, combined with the costs of the switch to trading in hard currencies and at world prices, accounted 'for as much as two-thirds of the output decline' during Eastern Europe's *annus horribilis*.[56] Tables 10.1, 10.3 and 10.4 demonstrate the magnitude of the crisis that attended the disintegration of Comecon.

With the collapse of intra-CMEA trade in 1990–1, trade with the EC came to constitute about half the foreign trade of the East European states in 1992 (compared with a mere 25 per cent in 1989), even though trade with Eastern Europe (excluding the Commonwealth of Independent States (CIS)) still only accounted for 1.7 per cent of EC foreign trade in that year, that is less than EC trade with either Sweden or Austria. A new asymmetrical relationship was emerging.[57] Conversely, the share of other ex-members of Comecon in the foreign trade of the East European states fell to less than 25 per cent in 1993, from an average of just over 50 per cent in 1988. The EC and the former CMEA had effectively swapped roles in the foreign trade of the region.

The final Council Session of Comecon was held in Budapest on 28 June 1991. The CMEA was to be disbanded within 90 days (by 28 September 1991), allowing its members time for one last squabble over the disposal of its physical assets, especially its grandiose offices in Moscow. Comecon was probably beyond redemption, but its passing would have been less painful if it had been more gradual and dignified. As the *Financial Times* remarked on 11 January 1990, its members 'may have hated being tied together, but they still need the bonds'. The dowries that its members could have offered the EC, the export niches they had carved as suppliers

Table 10.3 Officially recorded unemployment in Eastern Europe, 1989–94 (% of workforce at end of year)[58]

	1989	1990	1991	1992	1993	1994
Poland	0.1	6.1	11.8	13.6	15.7	15.0
Hungary	0.3	2.5	8.0	12.3	12.1	11.0
Czech Republic	0.0	0.8	4.1	2.6	3.5	3.0
Slovakia	0.0	1.5	11.8	10.4	14.4	14.0
Romania	n/a	n/a	3.0	8.4	10.2	15.0
Bulgaria	n/a	1.5	11.1	15.3	16.4	18.5
Albania	9.0	13.0	11.0	39.0	18.0	17.0
Serbia	18.7	21.3	22.4	24.6	24.6	n/a
Croatia	8.0	9.3	15.5	17.8	17.5	18.0
Slovenia	2.9	4.7	8.2	11.1	14.5	14.0
Macedonia	22.0	23.5	25.7	27.9	28.7	n/a
Estonia	0.0	0.0	0.1	1.9	2.6	4.5
Latvia	0.0	0.0	0.1	2.1	5.3	6.5
Lithuania	0.0	0.0	0.3	1.0	1.4	7.0
Russia	0.0	0.0	0.1	0.8	1.1	3.5
Ukraine	0.0	0.0	0.0	0.3	0.4	n/a
Belarus	0.0	0.0	0.0	0.5	1.5	n/a

Table 10.4 Average annual inflation rates in Eastern Europe (%)[59]

	1988	1989	1990	1991	1992	1993	1994
Poland	61.0	251.0	586.0	70.0	43.0	35.0	30.0
Hungary	16.0	17.0	29.0	35.0	23.0	23.0	21.0
Czechoslovakia	2.2	2.3	10.8	n/a	n/a	n/a	n/a
Czech Republic	n/a	n/a	n/a	57.0	11.0	21.0	10.0
Slovakia	n/a	n/a	n/a	62.0	10.0	23.0	15.0
Romania	0.5	1.1	5.1	175.0	211.0	256.0	150.0
Bulgaria	5.0	6.4	24.0	334.0	82.0	73.0	120.0
Albania	0.0	0.0	0.0	36.0	226.0	85.0	16.0*
Yugoslavia	194.0	1,256.0	121.0	164.0	n/a	n/a	n/a
Serbia	n/a	n/a	124.0	231.0	19,830.0	35 bn	n/a
Croatia	n/a	n/a	136.0*	122.0	578.0	1,501.0	98.0
Slovenia	n/a	n/a	550.0	117.0	201.0	32.0	24.0
Macedonia	n/a	n/a	608.0*	115.0*	1,691.0*	244.0*	54.0*
Estonia	n/a	6.1	23.0	211.0	1,076.0	90.0	47.0
Latvia	n/a	4.7	11.0	124.0	951.0	109.0	36.0
Lithuania	n/a	2.1	8.4	225.0	1,021.0	390.0	70.0
USSR	2.0	2.0	5.0	91.0	n/a	n/a	n/a
Russia	n/a	2.0	5.6	93.0	1,354.0	896.0	300.0
Ukraine	n/a	n/a	4.5	125.0	2,384.0	3,962.0	276.0*
Belarus	n/a	1.7	4.5	94.0	969.0	1,188.0	1,175.0*

* Denotes end-of-year (i.e. December to December) figures where average annual inflation figure is not available.

of highly specific products to the former Soviet republics, were incautiously thrown away. Professor Stanislav Shatalin's September 1991 proposal for the establishment of a looser economic community embracing all the former Soviet republics and former European members of Comecon sank without trace. Much as they needed a mechanism for the resuscitation of intraregional trade and co-operation, few non-Russians (or even Russians) wished to create new frameworks for Russian domination of Eastern Europe – at least, not yet.

FURTHER READING

J. van Brabant, *Economic Integration in Eastern Europe*, Hemel Hempstead: Harvester-Wheatsheaf, 1989.

J. Brada, 'Interpreting the Soviet Subsidization of Eastern Europe', *International Organization*, vol. 42 (1988), no. 4, pp. 639–58.

F. Holzman (ed), *The Economics of Soviet Bloc Trade and Finance*, Boulder, CO: Westview Press, 1987.

M. Kaser, *Comecon: Integration Problems of Planned Economies*, Oxford: Oxford University Press, 2nd edn, 1967.

A. Korbonski, 'CMEA, Economic Integration and Perestroika, 1949–1989', *Studies in Comparative Communism*, vol. 23 (1990), no. 1, pp. 47–72.

D. Rosati, 'The CMEA Demise, Trade Restructuring, and Trade Destruction in Central and Eastern Europe', *Oxford Review of Economic Policy*, vol. 8 (1992), no. 1, pp. 58–81.

NOTES

1 I wish to thank Ian Jeffries for generously supplying some of the statistical data used in this chapter, and Eleanor Breuning for her helpful comments.

2 Tsentralnyi Statisticheskoe Upravlenie SSSR, *Narodnoe khoziaistvo SSSR v 1983 g.* [Statistical Yearbook of the USSR in 1983], Moskva: Finansy i statistika, 1984, pp. 55–6; and Sekretariat SEV, *Statisticheskii ezhegodnik stran-chlenov Soveta ekonomicheskoi vzaimopomoshchi, 1984* [Statistical Yearbook of the Member-States of the CMEA, 1984], Moskva: Finansy i statistika, 1984, p. 7.

3 Reprinted in: R. Vaughan (ed.), *Postwar Integration in Europe*, London: Edward Arnold, 1976, pp. 132–3.

4 Ibid.

5 G. Schiavone, *The Institution of Comecon*, London: Macmillan, 1981, p. 16.

6 J. Brada, 'Interpreting the Soviet Subsidization of Eastern Europe', *International Organization*, vol. 42 (1988), no. 4, p. 654.

7 Ibid., p. 655.

8 Ibid., pp. 656–7.

9 Ibid., pp. 645, 657.

10 M. Kaser, *Comecon: Integration Problems of Planned Economies*, Oxford: Oxford University Press, 2nd edn, 1967, pp. 21–6, 32–5.

11 Ibid., pp. 26, 32–8.

12 Ibid., p. 32.

13 Ibid., p. 36.

14 Ibid., p. 35.
15 S. Ausch, *Theory and Practice of CMEA Cooperation*, Budapest: Akadémiai Kiadó, 1972, p. 44; and: J. van Brabant, *Economic Integration in Eastern Europe*, Hemel Hempstead: Harvester-Wheatsheaf, 1989, pp. 26, 40–1.
16 Brabant (n. 15 above), pp. 20–1, 34.
17 Ausch (n. 15 above), p. 44.
18 Brabant (n. 15 above), p. 22.
19 Ibid., p. 39.
20 P. Robson, *The Economics of International Integration*, London: Unwin Hyman, 1987, 3rd edn, pp. 225–6.
21 Kaser (n. 10 above), p. 14.
22 A. Sutton, *Western Technology and Soviet Economic Development*, Stanford, CA.: Stanford University Press, 3 vols, 1968–72.
23 Brabant (n. 15 above), pp. 46–7, 52–4.
24 R. Mellor, *Comecon: Challenge to the West*, New York: Van Nostrand, 1971, p. 14. Soviet oil initially experienced difficulties in entering Western markets, which were being over-supplied with cheap Arab oil at that time.
25 Brabant (n. 15 above), pp. 47, 51; Mellor (n. 24 above), p. 15.
26 Brabant (n. 15 above), pp. 54–60.
27 The Charter is reprinted in Vaughan (n. 3 above), pp. 138–44.
28 Quoted in Kaser (n. 10 above), pp. 249–50.
29 Quoted in ibid., p. 251.
30 Ibid., p. 252.
31 Ibid., p. 254.
32 Quoted in: A. Smith, *The Planned Economies of Eastern Europe*, London: Croom Helm, 1983, p. 183.
33 Brabant (n. 15 above), pp. 69–70.
34 Reprinted in: Vaughan (n. 3 above), pp. 148–50.
35 I. Jeffries, *The Socialist Economies and the Transition to the Market*, London: Routledge, 1993, p. 29.
36 See also Chapter 6.
37 Brabant (n. 15 above), p. xxi.
38 Sekretariat SEV (n. 2 above), p. 7.
39 J. van Brabant, *Socialist Economic Integration*, Cambridge: Cambridge University Press, 1980, p. 4.
40 Jeffries (n. 35 above), pp. 24–9.
41 Brabant (n. 15 above), pp. 78–9.
42 Commonly known as the Complex Programme for short. It is also known as the Comprehensive Programme, as the word *kompleksnyi* can mean 'comprehensive'. However, this programme was far from comprehensive. For further details, see: Brabant (n. 15 above), pp. 85–9, and the English-language editions of the document itself.
43 Robson (n. 20 above), p. 225.
44 Sources for 1971–88: OECD data in *Financial Times* (hereafter *FT*), 24 September 1990, except for Albania (NMP) and Yugoslavia (GNP), taken from Jeffries (n. 35 above), pp. 229, 319, 472. Sources for 1989–94: EBRD data from *Transition Report*, London: EBRD, October 1994, pp. 148–73; *Economics of Transition*, vol. 2, no. 4, December 1994, pp. 513–20; and *FT*, 7 March 1995, except for Serbia and Yugoslavia; miscellaneous *FT* reports and surveys.
45 See, among others: F. D. Holzman, 'The Significance of Soviet Subsidies to Eastern Europe', *Comparative Economic Studies*, vol. 28 (1986), no. 1, pp. 54–65 and no. 3, pp. 59–63; M. Marrese and J. Vaňous, *Soviet Subsidisation of Trade with Eastern Europe*, Berkeley, CA.: Institute of International Studies,

1983; M. Marrese, 'CMEA: Cumbersome but Effective Political Economy', *International Organisation*, vol. 40 (1986), no. 2, pp. 111–51; P. Desai, 'Is the Soviet Union Subsidising Eastern Europe?', *European Economic Review*, vol. 1 (1986), pp. 107–16; and J. Brada, 'Soviet Subsidisation of Eastern Europe: The Primacy of Economics over Politics', *Journal of Comparative Economics*, vol. 9 (1985), no. 1, pp. 80–92.

46 Compiled or calculated from: *FT*, 24 January 1990, 4 February 1991, 19 August 1991; *South*, April 1990, p. 16; Jeffries (n. 35 above), pp. 229, 319.

47 Brabant (n. 15 above), pp. 114–16.

48 A. Aganbegyan, *The Challenge: Economics of Perestroika*, London: Hutchinson, 1988, pp. 38, 84, 220. See also: pp. 76, 105, 153, 208–10 and 219.

49 J. Pinder, *The European Community and Eastern Europe*, London: Pinter, 1991, pp. 24–5.

50 Ibid.

51 See Chapter 12.

52 *Guardian*, 20 August 1991.

53 *FT*, 5 January 1990.

54 Jeffries (n. 35 above), pp. 33–4.

55 *FT*, 21 December 1990.

56 *OECD Economic Outlook*, no. 51, June 1992, p. 43.

57 D. Marsh and L. Barber, *FT*, 7 June 1993.

58 Figures from the same sources as Table 10.1, but supplemented by Deutsche Bank Research, *Focus: Eastern Europe*, no. 125, 15 February 1995, pp. 10–17, national data and press reports.

59 Ibid.

11 Poland's 'return to Europe', 1989–94

Frances Millard

Discussion about 'Europe' pervaded numerous issues in both the foreign and domestic arenas in Poland after 1989, as well as conveying a powerful symbolic resonance, even when Europe was not consciously at the forefront of Polish politics. Indeed, after the mass opposition movement Solidarity came to power in September 1989, both élites and public shared a broad consensus on the general postulate of a 'return to Europe', an aspiration shared with the neighbouring states of Hungary and Czechoslovakia. By 1991 the broad consensus had begun to unravel. A '"post-revolutionary hangover" could be detected in Poland, this now being explicitly linked with the return to Europe'.[1] The process of 'return' was proving complex; the yearned-for normality appeared remote as policies endorsed by Western governments and advisers generated unforeseen consequences. Europe itself had laid a welcome mat before the door but littered the front path with obstacles.

For a brief period in 1992 a right-wing nationalist government was in office, but it offered few alternative policies, and its preoccupation with alleged continuing communist conspiracies diverted it from the major problems besetting the country. In July it was succeeded by a new seven-party 'Solidarity' coalition, again firmly committed to 'Europe' and to liberal models of economic change. For much of 1992 and 1993 social discontent continued to grow, and embraced some distinctly xenophobic traits; some observers saw signs of a deepening political crisis.[2] Nonetheless élite commitment to Europe remained generally strong, and in the September 1993 election the electorate preferred 'respectable' left-wing parties, despite their previous links to the communist régime.

The victory of the successor parties, the Social Democrats [*Socjal-Demokracja Rzeczpospolitej Polskiej*, SDRP] and the Polish Peasant Party [*Polskie Stronnictwo Ludowe*, PSL], raised questions in the minds of some domestic and foreign observers about the democratic credentials and economic reliability of their new governing coalition. The parties that had most ardently endorsed Western strategies of transformation had been soundly defeated in the election.

These fears appeared largely unjustified, however. The differences between the parties were often exaggerated. No significant political formation favoured the 'Eastern option', that is close political and military association with Russia. All were (Western-oriented) 'Europeans', albeit with differences of emphasis. This meant that the foreign policy direction of the new government did not change, although the new government's orientation regarding domestic issues was somewhat different. The tempo of privatization slowed considerably, and the PSL successfully engineered greater support for agriculture. However, by late 1994 the deteriorating relationship between government and President increasingly affected the position of the Foreign Minister. Yet there remained strong, deep-rooted historical and cultural reasons, buttressed by current political and economic desiderata, for a continuing westward orientation of Polish policy.

POLAND AND EUROPE: THE HISTORICAL DIMENSION

After 1989 the Europe of the 'return to Europe' represented a political concept referring to *Western* Europe, just as the concept of *Eastern* Europe in the post-war period had signified those countries on the Soviet side of the Iron Curtain. 'Europe' in this sense was both a political and a symbolic term, representing the incarnation of the twin goals of political democracy and economic affluence; for many, being part of Europe meant being free and being rich. However, for significant elements of the creative intelligentsia (including former dissidents), Europe served as a shorthand for Western historical, philosophical and cultural traditions as well as contemporary political practices. Affirmation of Europe meant rejoining the mainstream of European civilization, from which these countries had been detached by processes of more or less forced subordination to the Soviet Union and its particular version of socialism.

The communists in Poland (1944–1989) never succeeded in establishing the legitimacy of the political system of single-party rule. They enjoyed power and privilege but lacked authority. Perceived divisions between rulers and ruled, between 'us' and 'them', appeared an entrenched element of Polish political culture. Widespread animosity to the political system was also a consequence of official ideological and institutional links to the USSR. The communists failed to eradicate traditional anti-Russian and anti-Soviet attitudes; indeed, strong pro-American sentiments reinforced these, especially in periods of deteriorating superpower relations. The Poles developed a variety of reference points to judge their politics and economics. Western influences penetrated Poland more easily than elsewhere in Eastern Europe, through widespread access to external radio broadcasts, foreign travel and extensive family ties abroad, particularly in the United States, which the Communist Party came increasingly to encourage for economic reasons.

Furthermore, a strong historical sense of civic identity pervaded the intelligentsia, which transmitted this to wider circles. The central myths of Polish history stressed Poland's links with Western Europe. The patriotic fervour of the last days of the eighteenth-century republic before its dismemberment by predatory neighbours, its reforming zeal, its traditions of independence and active citizenship were valued as a Polish contribution to the European Enlightenment; such traditions continued to influence the development of Polish national consciousness.[3] Heroic resistance to foreign domination by neighbouring powers took not only the form of uprisings against Russian tsardom and a mass resistance movement against Nazi occupation but also Polish participation in European liberation movements from the Napoleonic legions through 1848 to the Battle of Britain. The Polish oppositional intelligentsia took history and literature very seriously as mechanisms for the transmission and preservation of national identity. After 1956 there was a steady growth in the availability of a wide range of prohibited materials, disseminated by dissident elements. By the 1980s a vast parallel press and publishing network existed, while numerous journals were also smuggled in from Western Europe. Debate was multi-faceted, diverse and well acquainted with Western European thinking. There was no sign of either the national inferiority complex or the paro-chialism so often characteristic of (say) Serb or Romanian intellectuals.[4]

The situation was obviously aided by the relative tolerance of the communist authorities, and indeed, the Communist Party itself was not immune to diverse influences. Reformist strands waxed and waned with circumstances, but the Polish Party was virtually a perpetual battleground of factions. It had its fair share of unimaginative hacks and fanatical ideo-logues, but it did not lack competent, informed cadres; and its appoint-ments, especially of academics, were often surprisingly enlightened. (A 1984 report prepared for the Politburo described the Polish Academy of Science as a hotbed of opposition.[5]) Many, especially younger cadres, were increasingly exposed to foreign milieux. Włodzimierz Cimoszewicz, later leader of the Democratic Left Alliance and Minister of Justice after the 1993 election, studied in the United States; he was not an isolated case.

By the late 1980s the Party had come to permit an expanded role for private enterprise. The legal private sector began to grow and the illegal (but tolerated) second economy continued to thrive on the system's persistent shortages. This expansion changed the quality of the system from a socialist one to an emerging 'mixed' economy.[6] Many economists were well informed about Western debates concerning the nature of the capitalist economy and ready to incorporate Western ideas into strategies for economic reform.[7]

Finally, one must stress the role of the Catholic Church, not only because it was an autonomous institution functioning under the communist régime, but also because of its close association with the preservation of Polish national identity under the partitioning powers. The Church too was an enduring symbol of Poland's 'natural' association with Western Europe. The dividing line between Catholic and Orthodox Christianity ran roughly along Poland's contemporary eastern border, where religious affiliation constituted a distinctive aspect of social identity long before the emergence of mass national consciousness. In the modern period the Church provided an alternative focus of loyalty and, often, a haven for the political opposition. It played a mediating role in times of crisis, providing an avenue of communication between the régime and its opponents. The significance for the largely Catholic population of the election of the Polish Pope John Paul II in 1978 was inestimable.[8]

Thus there were historical factors impelling Poland towards Western Europe, and the 'return to Europe' was in that sense unproblematic. The link with the East had been an unhappy experience, both under the Russian tsars and their communist successors. The political model imposed from Moscow had been stifling, and the economic system had proved a disaster. Gorbachev's reforms in the Soviet Union pulled the rug out from under the hard-line, conservative Polish communists, who could no longer rely on Moscow for support. Western ideological influences were powerful, and the West promised assistance to those who moved rapidly to ensure irreversible régime change. Given the high levels of external debt bequeathed by the communists, such aid appeared vital; accepting the dominant economic ideas of Western governments was one means of gaining their advocacy with Poland's creditors and with the International Monetary Fund. Once free of communist rule, Poland, along with Hungary and Czechoslovakia, indicated its desire to join the Council of Europe, the European Community and the North Atlantic Treaty Organization (NATO).

Eastern Europe, on the other hand, became a more problematic term. Poland, Hungary and Czechoslovakia signalled their rejection of Eastern Europe by redefining their own geographical position as Central European.[9] Post-communist governments hastened to dismantle the structures which had bound them to the Soviet Union, notably the Warsaw Pact and the CMEA (Comecon), with little thought of the consequences or of filling the resulting vacuum. The Warsaw Pact was already 'gradually withering away'[10] with the loss of the defunct German Democratic Republic. However, the process of dissolution was accelerated to a greater degree than originally anticipated; military activities ceased in April 1991. It was also at the insistence of the East European states and 'with an eagerness bordering on naïveté'[11] that agreement was reached to trade in convertible currency from January 1991; Comecon was dissolved at its final session in June. This haste was to prove profoundly disruptive of economic relationships, for trade with the Soviet Union suffered a drastic and sudden collapse.

Although turning westwards, these countries could not turn their backs on the relationships forged under Soviet supremacy. The new governments could not ignore the Soviet Union or, after December 1991, its successor states. They also needed to establish the basis for a new relationship with other former fraternal allies, with whom they shared borders, a legacy of common experience, similar problems and common aspirations. In some cases the new leaders of Poland, Czechoslovakia and Hungary had also been friends and helpmates since their days of illegal opposition. Václav Havel, President of Czechoslovakia and then of the independent Czech Republic, urged their continuing co-operation 'to transform Central Europe from a phenomenon that has so far been historical and spiritual into a political phenomenon'.[12] One concrete achievement was the establishment of the Visegrad Triangle (later Quartet) of Poland, Hungary and Czechoslovakia and the co-ordination of the three countries' (four countries' after the splitting of Czechoslovakia) negotiations with the European Community.

Such developments enjoyed wide public support. At base, however, the concept of 'Europe' still remained unclear. It meant many things to different people. To some it meant willingly succumbing to the embrace of Western European values and institutions. To others it was primarily anti-Russian in cast or anti-communist or both. For some it offered a new opportunity to generate a Central European identity. Still others hoped for long-term peaceful integration of the wider, geographical Europe, including Russia itself. For some it provided conditions in which Poland would thrive; for others its embrace was a double-edged sword, offering security but also constituting a potential threat to Polish national identity. Combinations of such attitudes, often ambiguous and contradictory, were also common. The political parties aggregated these attitudes in distinctive ways, signifying differences of emphasis regarding the concept of Europe, Poland's place within Europe, and the meaning of Poland and Polishness. We shall attempt below to illustrate these differences with respect to particular policy areas. First, however, it seems appropriate to comment on the parties themselves.

POST-COMMUNIST POLITICAL PARTIES

After the breakup of Solidarity in 1990–1 a myriad of new political parties emerged to create a highly fragmented party system in the Parliament of 1991–3. There were right-wing nationalist and populist parties, liberal parties, peasant parties and social democratic parties. Perhaps surprisingly, given the importance of the Catholic Church to Polish political culture, there was no significant Christian Democratic party. In regard to 'Europe' the liberal parties were internationalist, actively seeking economic, political and defence co-operation, association, and integration with Western Europe, while also aiming to cement good relations with Poland's immediate neighbours. They saw accession to the EC as a means of enhancing Poland's status, security and economic position. It would reaffirm Poland's

historic affinity with European 'civilization', and it would assist the establishment of democracy in Poland itself by setting European yardsticks in
areas such as civil liberties. Integration with the Community would not
sacrifice Poland's sovereignty but acknowledge the changes to the concept of sovereignty wrought by processes of increasing globalization; there
was no conflict in simultaneously asserting a 'Polish' and a 'European'
identity.

The Democratic Union [*Unia Demokratyczna*, UD] of Tadeusz
Mazowiecki, the first non-communist Prime Minister in Eastern Europe,
belonged firmly in this category, as did the Liberal Democratic Congress
[*Kongres Liberalno-Demokratyczny*, KLD] of Mazowiecki's successor
as Prime Minister, Jan Krzysztof Bielecki. The Liberals were the most
integrationist of all, and many members strongly favoured a 'Europe of
regions' rather than of states. The origins of both parties lay with
Solidarity, and the two parties largely controlled governments from
1989–93. The Foreign Minister throughout this period was Krzysztof
Skubiszewski, a non-party academic lawyer who vigorously endorsed the
view that European integration 'is no threat to national identity but
rather enhances its fuller development'.[13] After their failure in the 1993
elections, the two parties merged into the new Freedom Union [*Unia
Wolności*].

The nationalist-populist parties were more insular. They saw Western
Europe as potentially threatening the erosion of Polish national identity.
Their attitudes to future political integration within the European Community were at best ambivalent. They opposed a federal community as entail-
ing loss of sovereignty, but favoured a community of states (or 'nations')
so long as Poland could protect her own 'national interests'. They also
tended to favour economic protectionism, and they viewed critically the
association agreement negotiated with the Community. Fears of Western
exploitation were widespread, including anxiety over the role of foreign
capital. Increasingly they argued that the liberal economic policies
endorsed by Western governments (and international institutions) were
inappropriate, failing to understand or take account of the socio-economic
conditions resulting from the communist system of central planning. There
was a strong emphasis on 'Christian values', and several, notably the
Christian Nationalists, were anxious about the negative impact of Western
commercialism. There was also a philosophical dimension which opposed
European liberalism because of its perceived moral relativism.

However, anxieties about Europe were more than outweighed by
considerations of national security. All these parties were intensely pro-
NATO, despite NATO's obvious reluctance to extend its membership.
They expressed traditional Polish fears of Russia and saw a close relationship with the European Community and the United States as constituting
a bulwark against potential instability in or aggression from the former
Soviet Union. Two elements of this group dominated government for six

months in 1992: the Centre Accord [*Porozumienie Centrum*, PC] of Prime Minister Olszewski, and the Christian National Union [*Zjednoczenie Chrześcijańsko-Narodowe*, ZChN]. The nationalist Confederation for Independent Poland [*Konfederacja Polski Niepodległej*, KPN] shared most of their views, though it was more secular, but it remained outside government. The KPN was also more sensitive to the need for developing good economic relations with Russia than its nationalist rhetoric often implied.

Of course, every party had its dissident elements. One angry member of the ZChN executive found the whole notion of the 'return to Europe' demeaning, because it suggested that Poland was in need of a new protector to replace the USSR; and unnecessary, because Western Europe was ageing, conservative, lacking dynamism and subject to increasing numbers of 'coloured peoples'.[14]

The social democratic group embraced the SDRP and the small Solidarity-inspired Labour Union [*Unia Pracy*]. As Adam Michnik put it, the former Communists were transformed by quickly absorbing 'the atmosphere of freedom, money, and Europe'.[15] That such perceptions were widely shared was confirmed by the SDRP's considerable success in attracting votes from private-sector business in the 1993 election.[16] In a joint statement shortly after the 1993 election the two parties (with the Polish Peasant Party) expressed their determination to continue to seek NATO's acceptance of Polish membership,[17] but they also favoured the development of a comprehensive European security system which would not leave Russia isolated. The social democratic parties viewed Europe positively from a political point of view and vigorously endorsed Polish membership of the EU, but still shared some of the nationalists' fears of exploitation by the industrialized Western states, as well as a traditional preoccupation with workers' rights. A social democratic Europe would be ideal, firmly grounded in the social chapter of the Maastricht Treaty.

The Polish Peasant Party, the PSL, and a number of ephemeral peasant parties of Solidarity provenance were less enthusiastic about Europe. They favoured gradual economic integration, but endorsed a degree of protectionism, especially in regard to agriculture. Of the entire Polish population, the peasants were the most disaffected and angry over the economic policies pursued after 1989. They continually manifested their collective outrage at the influx of foodstuffs from Western Europe after 1990; their demands included restrictions on 'unfair competition', easy credit and minimum agricultural prices. The PSL, which attracted the vast share of the peasant vote in 1993, clearly needed to offer some concrete gains to its rural constituents.

Thus a high degree of consensus characterized the first years of post-communist government. Despite their differences, the parties shared the view that there was no alternative to the European road. All serious political parties endorsed the transition to capitalism, albeit at varying rates and with varying degrees of state interventionism. All claimed adherence to the rule of law and democratic procedures. All sought admission to European political and military structures, though often for different reasons. We shall illuminate these differences below with reference to the areas of security policy, the European Community, and the 'Euroregions'.

POST-COMMUNIST FOREIGN POLICY

When Tadeusz Mazowiecki became Prime Minister in autumn 1989, there were few political parties. The Communist Party and its former satellite Peasant Party were in the throes of identity crises following the victory of Solidarity in the June election. Solidarity functioned as an umbrella movement embracing numerous different viewpoints. There was little public debate over foreign policy issues and Foreign Minister Skubiszewski ranked consistently high in surveys of politicians' public standing. After the 1991 election some sixteen different clusters were represented in Parliament; this created severe problems of government formation. However, the 1993 election result sharply reduced the number of parliamentary parties.[18] This was in great measure the result of an electoral system designed to penalize smaller parties. Largely because of the fragmentation of the right wing, only six parties achieved representation. The Liberals, the Centrum, the Christian Nationalists, Olszewski's Movement for the Republic and numerous other small parties failed to cross the five-per-cent threshold. In October 1993 the SDRP and the PSL formed a coalition which dominated Parliament with virtually a two-thirds majority.

Despite government instability, with five governments between 1989 and 1994, underlying élite consensus on foreign policy was enhanced by considerable continuity of personnel. Skubiszewski remained Foreign Minister from September 1989 to September 1993. Finance Minister Balcerowicz held his post for two years, and his successors were cast in similar mode. When Suchocka acceded in July 1992, following the short-lived Olszewski coalition, previously experienced ministers returned to government. For example, former Prime Minister Bielecki became Minister without Portfolio for Relations with the European Community, and Janusz Onyszkiewicz of the Democratic Union, Deputy Minister of Defence in the Mazowiecki and Bielecki Governments, now became Minister. When the Pawlak Government took office in October 1993 the new peasant/social-democratic coalition acknowledged the sphere of presidential powers by accepting President Wałęsa's nominees for Foreign Affairs, Defence, and the Interior. The new Foreign Minister was the President's economic adviser, Andrzej Olechowski, who stressed his agreement with the general policies of his predecessor.[19]

Skubiszewski developed and orchestrated the general foreign-policy line of the Mazowiecki Government. Balcerowicz dealt with economic relations, especially negotiations with international economic organizations and foreign creditors. Skubiszewski's policy goals were: the development of co-operative relations with all Poland's neighbours; the gradual integration of Poland into the structures and networks of mutual European interdependence, such as the Council of Europe and the Conference on European Security and Cooperation and including accession to the European Community; developing mechanisms of regional co-operation such as the Baltic Council and the Visegrad Triangle with Hungary and Czechoslovakia; and gaining support for the economy through international organizations such as the IMF and World Bank. In all these areas tensions surfaced, but a remarkable measure of consensus remained, not least because of the growing sense of physical security derived from the perceived absence of external threat.

In the few months from Mazowiecki's assumption of the premiership to the early part of 1990, Poland affirmed its alliance with the Soviet Union. Indeed, Poland continued to envisage the USSR as a guarantor of its western border, a topic reopened by Chancellor Kohl's ambiguous statements about the Oder-Neiße border in the context of impending German unification. Kohl briefly stimulated resurgent fears of German designs on territory awarded to Poland after the Second World War.

A second brief period lasted from the spring of 1990, by which time the demise of communism in Eastern Europe appeared assured, to the disintegration of the USSR in December 1991. In September 1990 Poland formally requested the USSR to negotiate the withdrawal of Soviet military units. The resolution of the border with Germany by a new treaty in November freed the Polish Government to pursue a more determined line with Moscow, as well as to develop good relations with the westernmost Soviet republics, the so-called 'two-track' policy. Both Comecon and the Warsaw Pact were dissolved in this period. Then, after December 1991, the Soviet/Russian relationship ceased to be the paramount element of Polish foreign policy, whose nature became at once more multi-faceted, but also more explicitly oriented towards Western Europe. However, the Soviet dimension continued to exert a profound influence on Polish defence policy during the tenure of the Olszewski Government, and the development of good relations with all Poland's eastern neighbours was an abiding concern of Skubiszewski's orientation. Olechowski, his successor in 1993, likewise favoured the entrenchment of multi-layered political, diplomatic, economic and security links with all of 'Europe', including strengthening the now troubled Visegrad Quartet. The record of achievement for his first year in office was rather thin; certainly he made no impact in his attempts to improve relations either with Russia or within the Visegrad Quartet.[20] Increasingly, Olechowski's position came under attack, first because of confusion arising from anti-corruption legislation, and then as a result of worsening relations between President Wałęsa and Prime Minister Pawlak.

ISSUES OF DEFENCE

There was limited reaction to the Mazowiecki Government's rather gentle line with the Soviet Union, but in 1990 Poland's geopolitical position briefly seemed once again the dominant factor in its international relations. Many, terrified at the prospect of a reunited, irredentist Germany, welcomed the continuing Soviet presence. A poster issued in Silesia by the ephemeral National Independence Action group portrayed the 1990s' version of the German Drive to the East (*Drang nach Osten*) as a dragon's head surging hungrily eastwards, accompanied by the words 'Today the unification of Germany, tomorrow the fifth partition of Poland!'[21] At the same time, groups such as the Confederation for Independent Poland (KPN) organized numerous protests and demonstrations against the Soviet military presence. The Soviet role became a factor in the deteriorating relationship between Mazowiecki and Lech Wałęsa, then still leader of the Solidarity trade union but holding no formal political office. Wałęsa embarrassed the government with his peremptory demand to the Soviet ambassador in January 1990 that all Soviet troops must withdraw that year. By the spring his demands for the acceleration of the reform process and for 'de-communization' had helped split Solidarity into two camps, one supporting Wałęsa and the other Mazowiecki.

The most acute conflicts over Polish defence policy, however, arose during Olszewski's premiership (December 1991 to June 1992). Although the parties of Olszewski's coalition had formed from the pro-Wałęsa Solidarity bloc and helped orchestrate Wałęsa's presidential candidacy, Olszewski's Government was at loggerheads with the President from the outset. The most important glue binding together the parties of the coalition was their anti-communist sentiment, their view that communism was still a relevant issue, and the desperation with which they pressed for Polish admission to NATO. By contrast Wałęsa was already in bridge-building mode, pursuing reconciliation and castigating witchhunts. Although he shared the pro-Western orientation of the government, he rejected its analysis of the current situation. Nor was he willing to suffer an erosion of his own power, which in any case he regarded as too limited.

Conflict over the respective jurisdiction of the President and Minister of Defence was a constant feature of the presidential–government relationship. In vain Wałęsa had opposed Olszewski's decision to retire the former minister, a military professional. The government saw this as confirmation that the President was soft on the old communists of the officer corps. The new minister, Jan Parys, also opposed Wałęsa's plans to re-organize the security organs. Parys favoured the concentration of defensive capability in the east, which he saw as the likeliest source of threat to Polish national security. Parys challenged the President's jurisdiction as Commander-in-Chief by claiming the right to exercise effective control of the armed forces as a whole.[22]

In April 1992 Parys issued a veiled attack, accusing the President of plotting with elements of the officer corps. Under pressure from Wałęsa, Parys finally resigned in May, calling publicly for the formation of 'state defence committees' by 'those with clean hands' to defend Polish independence in the event of a powerless government.[23] These committees subsequently formed the nucleus of a new right-wing political formation led by Parys. A parliamentary investigative commission found Parys' accusations unfounded and highly damaging.

Suspicion of Russia pervaded Olszewski's Government. Lack of foreign-policy co-ordination was manifest when Wałęsa, in Moscow in May 1992 to sign a treaty with Boris Yeltsin, was deeply embarrassed by the arrival of a coded telegram detailing government reservations to a clause in the treaty dealing with Soviet troop withdrawals. This was but one example of such difficulties.

Shortly afterwards Olszewski's Government lost the confidence of the Sejm as a result of the 'lustration affair', when the Interior Minister provided Parliament with a dubious list of political leaders said to be former communist agents or informers.[24] The issue further divided the right, as three new parties emerged to promote lustration (cleansing), with accusations of communist conspiracy and presidential involvement in an alleged communist resurgence. This group alienated the KPN (the Confederation for Independent Poland), which accused Olszewski of falsely listing its leader as a collaborator. The Christian Nationalists and small peasant parties favoured lustration, but they joined the new Suchocka coalition and lacked the antipathy to Wałęsa, who came to be regarded as an object of almost pathological hatred by Olszewski's closest allies. The notion that Wałęsa had been a Soviet agent (his name was on the lustration list), that he was the collaborator identified by the code name 'Bolek', or that he would sacrifice Polish interests to Russia appeared utterly ludicrous; but many right-wing nationalists were firmly committed to this view.

Elements of the nationalist right continued to argue that Polish governments remained far too passive in accepting NATO's reluctance to expand its membership; they saw this as a fundamental strategic objective designed to free Poland definitively from the Russian sphere of influence. Olszewski's and Parys' supporters took this line,[25] which formed a crucial aspect of the jurisdictional dispute between Parys and Wałęsa. It provided an ingredient of the lustration issue, which strengthened links between Olszewski, Parys, and certain elements of the Centrum. Lustration was deemed essential to national security on the grounds that Poland could not be secure so long as former communists, Soviet and/or Russian agents, and Polish collaborators were still able to occupy positions of importance within the state apparatus, particularly the military. Their opponents argued that a literal interpretation of their demands would be a suicidal blow against the armed forces, which had already been 'cleansed' by the departure of over 18,000 officers but which could lose some 12,000–15,000 more to lustration.[26]

The Suchocka coalition of July 1992, again dominated by liberal parties, re-established the continuity of foreign and defence policy, but did not succeed in resolving the basic defence dilemma, which continued to plague Eastern Europe: namely, what to do about NATO in the face of the latter's distinct lack of enthusiasm for admitting new members. The answer was three-fold: first, keep banging loudly and insistently on NATO's door, while cultivating supporters of Polish membership, especially Germany; second, stress the links with other European bodies such as the European Union, the North Atlantic Cooperation Council, and the Western European Union; and third, work to maintain the good bilateral relations established with all Poland's neighbours and to strengthen the Visegrad Quartet. In autumn 1993 Boris Yeltsin's announcement (later retracted) that Russia would not object to Poland's membership of NATO was greeted with an audible sigh of relief from all major political parties, as Yeltsin (temporarily) appeared to have removed one of NATO's own major anxieties, namely fear of alienating and isolating the Russian Federation. None of these policy strands, however, resolved the longer-term strategic questions surrounding East European security. These were posed even more starkly for the new Pawlak Government by the significant performance of nationalist elements in the Russian elections of December 1993 and Yeltsin's shift to a less obviously pro-Western/pro-United States foreign policy, though it reacted calmly to these developments.

Whether membership of NATO could genuinely resolve the problems of European security was a question generally absent from political debate. It was even in some sense irrelevant, given NATO's symbolic importance in cementing the 'return to Europe'. However, clear divisions remained between the right-wing nationalist parties (almost all excluded from the Polish Parliament after the September 1993 election) and most others. The right stressed entry to NATO primarily as a means of securing Western military protection against Russia. NATO's reluctance was seen as part of a broader West European attempt to maintain a Central European buffer between West and East; it even revived notions of Western short-sightedness and betrayal, with Maastricht cast as the successor to Versailles and Yalta.[27] Other parties, including the governing coalition after October 1993, recognized the need to include Russia in the new security architecture of Europe and accepted that American concerns with Russian fears of isolation were not groundless. The SDRP–PSL coalition responded positively to President Clinton's 'partnership for peace' initiative, though the Foreign Minister pressed unsuccessfully for a specific timetable for the gradual extension of NATO's membership and the enunciation of specific criteria to be met by new members;[28] and President Wałęsa himself did not hide his disappointment at the second-rate status implied by the 'partnership'. In effect, it meant accepting proposals which themselves lacked any strategic underpinning but merely provided NATO with an interim recipe of 'more of the same'[29] until agreement could be reached among existing members as to the organization's new role in the post-Cold War period. The Polish Government accepted the 'partnership for peace' as an advance, albeit a slim one, on previous offers, and the first multinational manoeuvres involving Eastern Europe took place in Poland in September 1994. However, in late 1994 internal conflicts over defence policy and personnel resurfaced between government and President, within the government, and within the Ministry of Defence itself, resulting in the dismissal of the Minister of Defence and continuing uncertainty regarding the Ministry's internal organization. Though much posturing could be linked to the 1995 presidential election campaign, these disputes called into question Poland's ability to function as a genuine partner and raised wider issues of democratic control of the military.

THE EUROPEAN COMMUNITY

Following the collapse of communism the EC aimed to support the transition to capitalism and democracy by specifying conditions designed to make the processes of change irreversible. However, neither the individual states nor the European institutions sacrificed their short-term interests to their avowed long-term goal of fostering a stable, democratic and prosperous Eastern Europe. Indeed, often the structures of both the EC and the IMF appeared incapable of generating a new regional developmental framework for the East European states: the EC's institutions were structured to protect trade, while the IMF's role in the policing of debt was ill suited to a developmental role.[30]

Certainly the EC was very active, from the inception in July 1989 of the PHARE programme (Polish and Hungarian Assistance for the Reconstruction of Europe) and the rapid conclusion of trade agreements with Poland, Hungary and Czechoslovakia. It orchestrated, supported, and largely financed a considerable range of instruments and programmes, largely of an economic nature,[31] of which Poland was a privileged beneficiary. However, it was difficult to detect a coherent EC strategy for Eastern Europe in the first five post-communist years, not least because its member states had different views and priorities regarding Eastern Europe and because of internal preoccupation with Maastricht.

A major focus was the question of accession to the European Community. Here Poland was part of much wider issues of who should accede, when and how. By late 1994 the new European Union was still a long way from deciding where 'Europe' was to end, with all the attendant implications of a larger Community for its own internal functioning. However, Poland was in the first group of countries to achieve an association agreement with the EC (the so-called Europe Agreements, linking full implementation to the achievement of political, legal, and economic reforms).

Negotiations for the agreement proved arduous and often bad-tempered, with the Poles threatening to terminate the talks on several occasions. The final agreement was signed in December 1991, to facilitate economic co-operation and trade with the EC and provide assurances that the Community would aid Poland (and Hungary and Czechoslovakia, which signed identical agreements) to achieve the conditions necessary for full Community membership (previously, such agreements had not been linked to membership). However, the EC proved highly reluctant to commit itself to greater access to Polish goods, especially the 'sensitive products' of steel, textiles and agricultural products, because of its own existing surpluses. Although the Suchocka Government achieved an easy majority for ratification of the association agreement, numerous anxieties and tensions remained.

There was good cause for anxiety. The economic strategy urged on Poland's governments by Western advisers (often financed by the EC) led initially to reductions in output and to levels of inflation not anticipated by their architects. Wage restrictions and the removal of subsidies resulted in a dramatic reduction in purchasing power. The bulk of state-owned industry had been expected to restructure itself automatically in the face of loss of subsidy and competition from the West; instead the large state enterprises accumulated a massive burden of debt and responded very slowly to the demands of restructuring. Social confidence in shock therapy plummeted. By summer 1992 widespread strikes signalled a growth of serious opposition to privatization, with overtones of suspicion of the role of foreign capital. Trade union demands for an immediate cessation of privatization were echoed by a number of opposition parties – not only the Confederation for Independent Poland (KPN), which registered its own new trade union; and the Social Democratic Party (SDRP), still allied to the OPZZ union movement; but also the new nationalist groupings of Parys and Olszewski. Attacks on privatization described it as theft of national assets and a denial to workers of their basic rights. In September 1992 Minister Janusz Lewandowski narrowly survived a vote of no confidence in his stewardship of privatization. 'Europe' was often equated with issues of economic reform strategy, not least because of public anticipation that Europe would help develop the Polish economy, but also because of widespread expectations that Poland would rapidly achieve Western European levels of affluence. If the latter were unreasonable, the former surely was not. Indeed, the head of the European Bank for Reconstruction and Development urged the EC to renegotiate the agreements and in so doing to abandon its own protectionist tendencies.[32]

Such attitudes created some tension within the Suchocka Government, with its uneasy alliance of Christian Nationalists (ZChN), Liberals (the Democratic Union and the KLD), and small peasant parties. The latter in particular displayed their ambivalence about 'Europe', given the vocal demands of their constituency for continuing subsidies and protection against imports[33] and the challenge of a new, overtly anti-European peasant movement, Self-Defence [*Samo-Obrona*], which favoured disruptive methods of direct action. All the peasant parties represented in the 1991–3 Parliament were protectionist in relation to agriculture, and this reflected a generalized opposition of the peasants (and their leaders) to the 'unfair competition' of agricultural imports from Western Europe. However, the Suchocka coalition held firm and won an easy victory in the Sejm for the EC association agreement. In part this success represented an acknowledgement, sometimes grudging and reluctant, that EC aid brought economic benefits, including greater credibility with international debtors, and also gains in security from linkage with Western Europe. In part it reflected the rather nebulous nature of the association agreement itself; certainly it was not seen as an obstacle either to more interventionism in industrial policy or higher tariffs to protect the economy. The most uniformly pro-European parties were the Democratic Union and the Liberals, who were most receptive to West European prescriptions for the Polish economy. However, the social democratic SDRP, despite its determination that Poland should not fall victim to the predatory inclinations of giant European firms, was no less enthusiastic from a political point of view. Even the Christian National Union, anxious about pernicious Western commercial influences and moral pollution, saw proselytic opportunities for Poland to set an example serving the 're-Christianization' of Europe.

1994 brought no dramatic changes in the new Pawlak Government's policy regarding the European Union, though lack of co-operation from the Czech Government undermined co-ordination of policy with the Visegrad Quartet. However, tensions between and within the coalition partners were already beginning to appear; and the Foreign Minister, one of 'the President's men', was also caught up in conflicts between government and President. Successful pressure from the PSL for greater assistance to the peasantry also raised the spectre of further battles over the extent of agricultural protection and the most appropriate mechanisms of transition to European integration. Reports that the EU was 'dumping' foodstuffs in Eastern Europe[34] gave credence to peasant criticisms of EU practices.

EUROREGIONS

Euroregions constitute a third area illustrating the different approaches to Europe. Poland responded very positively to the Council of Europe's support for 'Euroregions' in Eastern Europe. This was an extension of the West European experience, intended to stimulate local co-operation in border areas.[35] Euroregions were to stimulate voluntary cross-border initiatives as a means of facilitating rapprochements between governments and local communities to reduce ethnic tensions, improve cultural understanding and promote commerce. In 1991 communities in southwestern Poland, northwestern parts of the Czech Republic, and the eastern tip of Germany inaugurated the Neiße Euroregion, the first to involve Poland. In January 1993 Poland signed a Council of Europe convention encouraging the creation of Euroregions. In February local representatives reached agreement on a 'Carpathian Euroregion' involving border provinces of Poland, Slovakia, Hungary and the Ukraine; its immediate focus was on communications: new telephone exchanges, new roads, and new border crossings. Communities in northwestern Poland also expressed interest in a Pomeranian region with several German *Länder*, Denmark and Sweden. A German–Polish Euroregion called 'Pro Europa Viadrina' was announced in December 1993, while a Trans-Bug Euroregion was also mooted in co-operation with the Ukraine.

The Social Democratic deputies welcomed Foreign Minister Skubiszewski's presentation of the proposals for the Carpathian Euroregion, promoted by the Liberals and the Democratic Union. However, there was an explosion of acrimony from the nationalist parties, especially from the ranks of the Centrum, the KPN and the ZChN (despite the latter's participation in the Suchocka coalition); some PSL deputies also joined them.[36] Jan Łopuszański of the ZChN accused Skubiszewski of preparing the way for a new partition of Poland and accused the Foreign Minister of collaboration with the 'dark forces planning to dismantle our frontiers'.[37] The ZChN viewed Euroregions as means of weakening Polish national identity through foreign influence, undermining Poland's territorial integrity and overriding its administrative divisions with alternative ones. The KPN's Janina Kraus saw them as aiding the urge to domination of the larger states. The Centrum for its part viewed Euroregions as a ploy to strengthen the hand of European federalists by eroding nation-state boundaries; Poland should join Europe through 'the entry of the Polish state as a whole into European structures, especially the EEC [sic] and NATO'; Poland should stoutly defend its national interests and prepare thoroughly for co-operation, not merely 'succumb to pressures of fashion from Brussels on the one hand and over-excited provincial governors on the other'.[38] Such conclusions were labelled 'laughable' by Skubiszewski and a 'tragicomedy of misunderstanding' by the spokesman of the Democratic Union,[39] but they gained credibility from Romanian President Iliescu's refusal to co-operate on the grounds that the Carpathian Euroregion was an instrument of Hungarian revisionism. The statute itself provided that decisions of the local communities must conform to the laws of their respective states;[40] but the debate revealed a great deal of conceptual confusion about Europe, whether the postulated Europe was to be a Europe of nations, of fatherlands, of regions or a supranational entity; it also reflected growing anxieties that such agreements would increase the possibility of mass immigration from the East. There were also underlying fears and insecurities about the strength of national identities in certain border areas, especially those previously part of Germany.

Of the parties hostile to the promotion of Euroregions, only the KPN retained parliamentary representation after the 1993 election. Its presence was small and its potential influence negligible. The electorate had not responded to attempts, notably by the ZChN, to elevate the issue of visas for eastern visitors to one of central importance. Local communities involved in Euroregion projects appeared to welcome and support them. How far they would achieve their optimistic goals was of course another matter. However, as a national political issue the Euroregions were dying a natural death by late 1994, though one which could be resurrected by an unexpected deterioration in Poland's relations with the Ukraine or Germany or even the reintegration of Belorussia with the Russian Federation.

CONCLUSION

Successive Polish governments since 1989 have recognized that their 'return to Europe' could not be achieved quickly or easily, though they were disappointed at the failure of the EC and NATO to extend their embrace more warmly. Polish élites shared a strong historical and cultural sense of belonging to Europe, a willingness to endorse Western-inspired economic strategies, and a commitment to the establishment of democratic institutions and processes which put Poland on the side of the integrationist angels during the first years of the post-communist transformation. Despite undoubted anxiety and insecurity amongst wide sections of the population as a result of upheavals in the economic system, despite a succession of minority governments and loss of public confidence in Solidarity and its heirs, and despite the ample presence of right-wing populist-nationalist demagogues, fears of political crisis proved unfounded during this period. By 1994 economic revival gave further hope of continuing political stability, though the forthcoming presidential elections generated a tense atmosphere as Wałęsa sought to distance himself from the left-wing government.

The stance of the West Europeans was more ambivalent in practice. The sudden, dramatic collapse of the common enemy which had done so much to unify Western Europe unleashed a new wave of state particularism and differently perceived national interests. Preoccupied with domestic political issues and European recession, shocked by the unravelling of policy which accompanied the ratification of Maastricht, frightened at the apparent resurgence of right radicalism and disagreeing over wider issues of membership, the countries of the EC, along with the wider Atlantic Alliance, proved incapable of agreeing a coherent strategy for the former countries of the Soviet bloc and the Soviet successor states. The East European position, including that of Poland, was largely reactive and dependent, forcing the aspiring democracies into the difficult military and foreign policy limbo of a commitment to a Europe itself uncertain of its aims and its boundaries.

FURTHER READING

K. Dawisha, *Eastern Europe, Gorbachev, and Reform*, 2nd edn, Cambridge: Cambridge University Press, 1990.

P. M. Lützeler (ed.), *Europe after Maastricht*, Oxford: Berghahn Books, 1994.

F. Millard, *The Anatomy of the New Poland: Post-Communist Politics in Its First Phase*, Aldershot: Edward Elgar, 1994.

G. Pridham (ed.), *Transitions to Democracy*, Aldershot: Dartmouth, 1995.

NOTES

1 P. G. Lewis, 'History, Europe and the Politics of the East', in: S. White, J. Batt and P. G. Lewis (eds), *Developments in East European Politics*, London: Macmillan, 1993, p. 271.

2 G. Ekiert, 'Peculiarities of Post-communist Politics: The Case of Poland', *Studies in Comparative Communism*, 1992, vol. 25 (December), pp. 341–61.

3 Walicki stresses this point; see: A. Walicki, *Trzy patrjotyzmy* [Three Patriot-isms], Warsaw: Res Publica, 1991; for a historical overview of the development of Polish national consciousness, see: P. Brock, 'Polish Nationalism', in P. Sugar (ed.), *Nationalism in Eastern Europe*, London: University of Washington Press, 1969, pp. 310–73.

4 See, for example: T. Gallagher, 'Vatra-Romaneasca and Resurgent National-ism in Romania', *Ethnic and Racial Studies*, vol. 15 (1992), no. 4, pp. 570–98; K. Verdery, 'Nationalism and National Sentiment in Post-socialist Romania', *Slavic Review*, vol. 52 (1993), no. 2, pp. 179–203; N. Cigar, 'The Serbo-Croatian War, 1991: Political and Military Dimensions', *The Journal of Strategic Studies*, vol. 16 (1993), no. 3, pp. 297–338; C. Job, 'Yugoslavia's Ethnic Furies', *Foreign Policy*, vol. 92 (1993), pp. 52–74.

5 J. Widacki, *Czego nie powiedział Generał Kiszczak* [What Gen. Kiszczak Did Not Say], Warsaw: BGW, 1992, pp. 45 and 47; the document is cited at length, pp. 37–58.

6 J. Rostowski, 'The Decay of Socialism and the Growth of Private Enterprise in Poland', *Soviet Studies*, vol. XLI (1989), no. 2, p. 194.

7 See, for example: L. Siemon (ed.), *Propozycje przekształceń polskiej gospodarki* [Proposals for the Transformation of the Polish Economy], Warsaw: Państwowe Wydawnictwo Ekonomiczne, 1989.

8 On the role of the Church in the communist period, see: B. Szajkowski, *Next to God . . . Poland*, London: Frances Pinter, 1983.

9 See G. Schöpflin and N. Wood (eds), *In Search of Central Europe*, Cambridge: Polity Press, 1989.

10 K. Skubiszewski, lecture to the Royal Institute of International Affairs, January 1991, published as: 'New Problems of Security in Central and Eastern Europe', *East European Reporter*, vol. 4 (1991), no. 4, pp. 61–4.

11 R. Linden, 'The New International Political Economy of East Europe', *Studies in Comparative Communism*, vol. XXV (1992), no. 1, p. 14.

12 President Havel's speech to the Polish Parliament, 21 January 1990 in *East European Reporter*, vol. 4 (1990), no. 2, p. 56.

13 'Dodawanie ułamków' [Adding Fractions], interview with Krzysztof Skubiszewski, *Polityka*, no. 42, 17 October 1992.

14 M. Piłka, 'Dwubiegunowa integracja' [Two-track Integration], *Rzeczpospolita*, no. 17, 21 January 1994.

15 'Gorzki smak wolności' [The Bitter Taste of Freedom], *Polityka*, no. 47, 20 November 1993.

16 *Zycie Warszawy*, no. 222, 22 September 1993.

17 *Gazeta Wyborcza*, no. 238, 11 October 1993.

18 See: F. Millard, 'The Polish Parliamentary Election of September 1993', *Communist and Post-Communist Studies*, vol. 27 (1994), no. 3, pp. 295–314.

19 Interview with Andrzej Olechowski, *Rzeczpospolita*, no. 268, 17 November 1993.

20 See: 'Na zwolnionym biegu' [In a Lower Gear], *Gazeta Wyborcza*, no. 220, 21 September 1994.

21 The poster is reproduced in *East European Reporter*, vol. 4 (1990), no. 2, p. 62; but its caption is incorrect (the correct caption is attached to a Slovene cartoon on p. 58).

22 See: J. DeWeydenthal, 'Political Problems Affect Security Work in Poland', *RFE/RL Research Report*, vol. 1 (1992), no. 16 (17 April), pp. 39–42.

23 *Rzeczpospolita*, no. 104, 4 May 1992.

24 J. Snopkiewicz *et al.*, *Teczki czyli widma bezpieki* [Files, or the Spectre of the Secret Police], Warsaw: BGW, 1992, pp. 20–3. For the full list, see: *Gazeta Polska*, no. 4, June 1993.

25 See, for example: J. Kwieciński, 'O bezpieczeństwo – dziś i w roku 2010' [On Security – Today and in 2010], *Rzeczpospolita*, no. 211, 8 September 1992.

26 Interview with Zbigniew Skoczylas, *Polityka*, no. 42, 17 October 1992.

27 See, for example, R. Sikorski, 'Porzucona Europa Srodkowa' [Central Europe Abandoned], *Rzeczpospolita*, no. 273, 23 November 1993.

28 See Olechowski's proposals in: *Rzeczpospolita*, no. 293, 16 December 1993.

29 Brzezinski has argued that the West has been particularly myopic in failing to build on opportunities created by Polish–Ukrainian co-operation; see: Ian Brzezinski, 'Polish–Ukrainian Relations: Europe's Neglected Strategic Axis', *Survival*, vol. 35 (1993), no. 3, pp. 26–37.

30 P. Gowan, 'Old Medicine, New Bottles: Western Policy toward East Central Europe', *World Policy Journal*, 1991–2 (Winter), pp. 1–33.

31 H. Kramer, 'The European Community's Response to the "New Eastern Europe"', *Journal of Common Market Studies*, vol. 31 (1993), no. 2, pp. 213–44.

32 *Financial Times*, 8 September 1992.

33 See: M. Cichowicz, 'Rolnicy o gospodarce rynkowej' [Peasants on the Market Economy], *Wieś i Rolnictwo*, 1993, no. 3, pp. 121–7.

34 *Independent*, 10 October 1994.

35 For a general discussion, see: J. deWeydenthal, 'Controversy in Poland over "Euroregions"', *RFE/RL Research Report*, vol. 2 (1993), no. 16 (16 April), pp. 6–9.

36 Z. Bosacki, *Pierwszy lepszy Sejm* [The First-Come Sejm], Poznan: SAWW, 1993, p. 228.

37 Quoted in: *Rzeczpospolita*, no. 44, 22 February 1993.

38 S. Siwek, 'Euroregiony–UD–PC–Polska' [Euroregions – the UD – the PC – Poland], *Rzeczpospolita*, no. 52, 3 March 1993. This view was echoed in somewhat different form by the geographer Piotr Eberhardt, who argued that the

Carpathian Euroregion made no sense, either geographically, historically or economically; P. Eberhardt, 'Euroregiony na wschodzie Polski' [Euroregions in the East of Poland], *Rzeczpospolita*, no. 81, 6 April 1993.

39 W. Klewiec, 'Kłótnia o euroregiony' [Rows over the Euroregions], *Rzeczpospolita*, no. 52, 3 March 1993; A. Potocki, 'Potrzeba dobrej woli' [The Need for Goodwill], *Rzeczpospolita*, no. 52, 3 March 1993.

40 deWeydenthal, 'Controversy in Poland' (n. 35 above), p. 6.

12 Bringing the East back in[1]

Robert Bideleux

In 1989 most of Eastern Europe embarked on an arduous 'triple transition': from communist dictatorship to pluralistic democracy; from centrally
administered to market economies; and from Soviet imperial hegemony to
fully independent national statehood. This was the third time that Eastern
Europe had embarked on a transition of such magnitude. After the First
World War much of the region underwent an analogous triple transition:
from semi-absolutist monarchies to ostensibly democratic republican
régimes; from a supranational imperial order to an order based on fully
independent nation-states; and from a social order dominated by imperial
bureaucracies and armies and large landed estates to societies with a
preponderance of peasant farmers, dominated by national bureaucracies,
national armies and ascendant national bourgeoisies. After the Second
World War, Eastern Europe attempted another triple transition: from
fascist imperial domination to independent national statehood; from fascist
dictatorship to pluralistic democracy; and from fascist (autarkic) administered economies to more open, semi-planned market economies.

The post-1918 transition came to grief on the rocks of illiberal 'ethnic' or
'integral' nationalism, irredentism, ruthless protectionism and increasing
'asymmetrical' commercial dependence on a resurgent German Reich and,
to a lesser extent, fascist Italy. The post-1945 transition succumbed to an
extension of Soviet imperial hegemony over Eastern Europe and the
imposition of neo-Stalinist régimes and programmes of coercive, centrally
planned industrialization and collectivization, whose limited positive
appeal rested partly on their alleged capacity to transcend the ethnic,
irredentist and economic problems that had plagued interwar Eastern
Europe.

Since 1918 Eastern Europe has been continually struggling to replace
the dynastic authority and legitimacy, the economic union, the (relative)
military and legal security and political stability and autonomy formerly
provided by the multinational Austro-Hungarian Empire. The military
defeat and collapse of that empire in 1918 left a major ideological and
power vacuum in the heart of Europe, a vacuum more readily filled by
illiberal 'integral' or 'ethnic' and economic nationalism, by native and

Italo-German fascism, and later by Soviet communism than by liberal democracy. Indeed, most of the new East European states were controlled by 'national' leaderships which upheld increasingly narrow and exclusive 'integral' or 'ethnic' conceptions of the nation, in contrast to the more inclusive 'civic' definitions of the nation that prevailed in Western Europe, excluding Germany. This in itself did not bode well for the 1990s. When, in addition, the (re-)establishment of democratic rule is not buttressed by the emergence of a multiplicity of autonomous social groups committed to the maintenance of individual and minority rights, while at the same time supporting and accepting the need for a viable framework of executive, legislative and judicial authority, fledgling democracies all too easily succumb to new forms of authoritarianism, especially when 'democratization' has been widely accompanied by economic collapse, mass impoverishment and unbridled criminality.[2] While the first priority after the collapse of communist rule was quite rightly the (re-)creation of formal democratic institutions, rights and procedures, these formal provisions would still have to be reinforced by a vigorous development of civil societies with liberal and multi-cultural 'civic' conceptions of the national state, if Eastern Europeans really wanted to become fully democratic, peaceful, prosperous and eligible for membership of the EU. Such a reorientation was bound to take time, however, as it would involve fundamental changes in political and cultural values and attitudes, in the social and economic structures of ownership and power, and in the way that East European states have been accustomed to seeing and defining themselves. The 'pre-accession strategies' championed by Sir Leon Brittain, Hans van den Broek and Henning Christophersen in 1994–5 recognized the tactical advantages of producing an EU White Paper setting out a series of concrete steps that East European states should take in order to make themselves 'eligible' for EU membership. This more positive, prescriptive approach, seeking to emulate the public relations success of the 1985 White Paper on the creation of a Single European Market, represented a major advance on previous EC passivity towards Eastern Europe. Yet this approach placed undue emphasis on formal economic and commercial preparations, to the relative neglect of the much more difficult and fundamental changes required in the political and cultural spheres. In May 1994 Pavel Sisa, then Minister-Counsellor at the Slovak Embassy in London, gave eloquent expression to the crucial political and cultural requirements:

> Our vision of Europe and of Slovakia's place in it is a vision of a multi-national and multi-ethnic community. In such a community, individuals must have equal rights and opportunities for self-realisation and for the expression of their own identity, based on the same rules everywhere and regardless of nationality, religion or ethnic background. The road to a unified Europe is not through a complete suppression of the role

of the national state within the European Union, but through a unification based on respect for individuals and the creation of a climate of trust in international relations. Then the borders will no longer stand in the way of human understanding.[3]

Nevertheless, as if to underline the difficulties, the 'civic-minded' Slovak government that Pavel Sisa represented was defeated in the October 1994 elections by an unholy alliance of ex-communists and extreme nationalists. The (re-)creation of strong and healthy civil societies, as prerequisites for civil economies as well as secure democracies, was likely to be equally difficult and protracted.[4] By definition, civil societies could not be created or re-created from above. Creatures of the state would tend to remain dependent upon and subservient to the state. But the insolvency, retrenchment and atrophy of the post-communist states vacated many social spaces that would have to be filled or taken over by autonomous civil associations and individuals, if they were not to fall under the control of the former communist *nomenklatura* and/or criminal elements. Above and beyond any private motives and ambitions, East European professionals, legitimate entrepreneurs, writers, journalists, broadcasters, trade unions and farmers' organizations had a historic opportunity and a civic responsibility to maximize their autonomy and self-reliance and to minimize their dependence on the state, in order to secure the conditions in which the post-1989 transitions to pluralist democracies and market economies could be consummated. Their degrees of success in this regard would be even more important in determining their countries' fortunes than either the crumbs of assistance received from the West or the more technical tasks of managing transitions to competitive capitalism. If they were to pass up this historic opportunity and responsibility, they would be among the first to suffer and they would have no one else to blame, for the re-creation of vibrant, autonomous and pluralistic civil societies was not something that could be done for them by the state or politicians or foreign assistance. Indeed, the post-communist states lacked the capacity to direct a vast range of social and economic activities, and any lingering insistence that they should attempt to do so in an endeavour to provide universal economic and social security would only lead back to forms of authoritarian paternalism and corporatism that had already been tried and found wanting. Unfortunately, outside the relatively developed and highly educated Czech Republic, Slovenia and, to a lesser extent, Hungary and Poland, conditions were not conducive to a healthy resurgence of civil society. For instance, the formal institutions of post-communist Bulgaria became democratic and 'civic', but the former communist *nomenklatura* and mafia-type gangsters exercised informal control over much of the economy and hence public life, while incompletely 'reconstructed' ex-communists continued to run Romania, Croatia and Slovakia in the mid-1990s. Such problems were not entirely absent from either Poland or Hungary, while large parts of Serbia and Bosnia were controlled by mafia-type gangsters, black-marketeers, paramilitary thugs and local 'war lords'.

Unfortunately, the initial 'national' euphoria that greeted the ending of communist dictatorship in Eastern Europe also unleashed potentially intolerant, exclusive and xenophobic nationalist and religious revivals and aroused hopes of welfare gains that the embattled, inexperienced and cash-strapped new régimes were unable to fulfil. The high hopes aroused in late 1989 and early 1990 were soon dashed by the grim realities of mounting insolvency, soaring inflation, escalating unemployment, infrastructural decay, environmental crisis and simmering inter-ethnic tensions (particularly in the Balkans and Slovakia). The generous and optimistic sentiments that were widely expressed during the initial 'national' jubilation would largely (and understandably) evaporate when varying degrees of political and economic 'liberalization' not only failed to deliver the commonly anticipated improvements in living standards, but also plunged most people into extremes of economic and social hardship for which they were almost totally unprepared and for which there were few 'social safety nets'. Indeed, a major report released by UNICEF in early 1994 claimed that the collapse of the Eastern European command economies and communist régimes had unleashed a great surge in poverty, death rates, morbidity rates, malnutrition, truancy, family breakdowns and violent crime and that by 1993 conditions in Eastern Europe were even worse than those in Latin America during the 'lost decade' of the 1980s or in Western Europe during the 1930s Depression.[5] There was a restoration of free elections, to be sure, but secure democracy involves much more than the holding of free elections, just as the restoration of market economies entails far more than the mere 'freeing' of prices. Universal suffrage could usher in 'the counter-revolution', as Proudhon had always feared it would. Free elections and price liberalization unleashed irrational and unruly forces which, paradoxically, made it all the more difficult successfully to consummate perilous transitions to pluralistic parliamentary democracy and thriving private-enterprise economies. As Patricia Clough remarked in 1992: 'The new political systems are still in their early infancy. . . . Politicians and parties are unsure of their roles. The accumulated experience of the West is of little use, for politics still centres on personalities rather than programmes or parties' and those who led the revolutions of 1989 were 'not necessarily the right leaders for their countries now'.[6] Indeed, by early 1995 variously 'reconstructed' ex-communists were back in power in almost all the East European states, with the notable exception of the Czech Republic, where President Václav Havel and Premier Václav Klaus managed to rise above the popular hardships, disillusionments and resentments which had by then unseated most of the revolutionary leaders of 1989. Most of the new political leaders who emerged in Eastern Europe between 1992 and 1995 were substantially less

'European-minded' than those of 1989-91 and had adopted rather more jaundiced views of the EU. Disillusionment and 'reform fatigue' were to be found even at the highest levels. As Hungary's Foreign Minister, Géza Jeszenszky, explained in October 1993:

> Three times in recent history Western powers have promised liberation to the peoples of Eastern Europe, but the East European nations finally won freedom for themselves. Today, however, a crisis of confidence is emerging on both sides: the West is questioning Eastern Europe's ability to make good use of freedom, while East Europeans are voicing doubts about the seriousness of Western helpfulness. In my region people feel disoriented and increasingly unhappy. They find themselves in a polluted environment wasted away by redundant industries. The attractions of consumer society beckon but prove unobtainable, except to the old political bosses, who profit in commercial business. The spirit of compassion and tolerance was not cultivated under communism. This social environment creates space for the demagoguery of onetime Communists now donning national colours, as well as for the resurgence of extremist (neo-Stalinist and/or neo-Nazi) tendencies. . . . People have been fed promises for generations and have been compelled to wait far too long.[7]

In some ways the post-1989 transitions to the market and multi-party democracy were even more fraught with difficulties than the post-1918 and post-1945 attempts. Up to half the industrial capacity inherited from the communist régimes was either technologically obsolete or environmentally hazardous or produced goods for which there was no longer a market. If stringent commercial and health and safety criteria had been ruthlessly applied, nearly half Eastern Europe's industrial capacity (including most of its power stations) would have had to be closed down, with massive loss of employment. This view is consistent with the slump in total output and employment which took place in the former GDR, the most highly developed of the former command economies, during the early 1990s. Between 1989 and 1993, the total number of jobs in the former GDR fell from 9.3 m to 6.2 m, employment in manufacturing dropped from 3.2 m to 1.3 m and the number of people working on the land fell from over 920,000 to 210,000, while the total available workforce shrank from 10.8 m to 8.2 m, mainly as a result of emigration to the West. By March 1994, 1.3 m people (16.8 per cent of the workforce) were registered as unemployed, but the true magnitude of the collapse was hidden in various ways. Indeed, 37 per cent of the reduced workforce were without employment in March 1994 and, if the total available workforce had not shrunk by 2.6 m, this percentage would have been even higher.[8] Moreover, between 1989 and 1991 East German GDP fell by 45 per cent, while the total number of hours worked plummeted from 8.9 bn to 4.0 bn.[9]

In other ways, however, the post-1989 transitions to independent national economies and multi-party democracy appeared much easier and more hopeful than the post-1918 and post-1945 attempts. This time around, Eastern Europe was not having to recover from the devastating effects of a world war. In addition, it was widely assumed that, because of the redrawing of East European state boundaries and the destruction and/ or expulsion of most of the former Jewish and German inhabitants of Eastern Europe during the 1940s, the scope for renewed inter-ethnic conflict in Eastern Europe had been greatly reduced. Moreover, Eastern Europe no longer appeared to be menaced by dangerous or potentially dangerous neighbours and the West appeared to be much more willing and able to assist the economic recovery and reconstruction of Eastern Europe in the early 1990s than it had been after 1918 or after 1945. Finally, the existence of a peaceful, prosperous and highly integrated EC appeared to hold out the prospect of much more propitious political and economic frameworks and mechanisms through which Eastern Europe could gradually be integrated into the mainstream of European develop-ment than was the case in the past. Certainly, the new post-communist East European governments entertained high hopes of a rapid 'return to Europe', starting with the bilateral trade and co-operation agreements between the EC and East European states signed in 1988–90, continuing with the bilateral 'Europe' (Association) Agreements that the EC con-cluded with Hungary, Poland and Czechoslovakia in December 1991 and with Romania and Bulgaria in late 1992 (providing for a phased reciprocal reduction and removal of trade barriers over a ten-year period) and pos-sibly culminating in the first East European accessions to full membership of the EU around the year 2000.

Unfortunately, the apparent advantages of the post-1989 transitions were in reality weaker than they appeared at first sight. Firstly, although Eastern Europe was not recovering from a world war this time, it was struggling to recover from a state of economic collapse, high levels of inflation, severe infrastructural neglect and decay, acute social strains, the draining effects of the Cold War, the lopsided economic priorities of com-munist rule, life-threatening environmental crises and long-suppressed inter-ethnic tensions, which soon boiled over into catastrophic fratricidal conflicts in the case of the former Yugoslav Federation. On the economic front, the tasks that Eastern Europe faced turned out not to be so very different from those involved in the reconversion of a ravaged and run-down war economy to civilian production.

Furthermore, even though the ethnic map of Eastern Europe had been subjected to drastic surgery since 1918, a considerable potential for violent inter-ethnic conflict still survived, sadly vindicating the view that no (acceptable) amount of resettlement and/or redrawing of East European state boundaries could either have satisfied all the conflicting territorial claims or have allowed all nations to occupy discrete territories (or even cantons, in cases such as Bosnia-Hercegovina and Macedonia), because they were often inextricably intermingled. Indeed, the ingenious territorial expedients and stratagems that Tito had adopted in his attempts to 'cut Serbia down to size' and thereby allay non-Serb fears of potential Serb dominance of Yugoslavia backfired disastrously in the early 1990s, when the Serbs brutally reversed some of the territorial losses inflicted on them by the 1946 and 1974 constitutions. Moreover, in the mid-1990s there were still aggrieved and/or vulnerable ethnic minorities in Serbia, Croatia, Macedonia, Bulgaria, Romania, Albania, Greece, Slovakia and the shattered remains of Bosnia-Hercegovina. Poland had potential territorial disputes with Lithuania and the Czech Republic, as did Italy with Slovenia and Germany with Poland, and the Greeks renewed their territorial disputes with Albania and the Macedonian Slavs, while Hungary was increasingly alarmed and incensed at the predicament of the three million Hungarians in neighbouring Romania, Slovakia and Serbia. Perhaps in part because the East European states did not feel themselves to be under any immediate external military threat from Russia or Germany or Italy, they now faced greater dangers of destructive internal and intraregional armed conflict than at any time since the end of the Second World War. External threats and patronage and policing had their uses, even though they were deeply resented. After all, fear of the external threats posed by Italy, Hungary and Germany was the main factor that had brought Southern Slavs and Czechs and Slovaks together to form the multinational states of Yugoslavia and Czechoslovakia respectively in 1918/19.

In addition, although Western politicians, economists and political commentators said and wrote a great deal about the need for a new 'Marshall Plan' to assist the transitions to the market and parliamentary democracy in Eastern Europe, and although it was widely recognized that it was in the self-interest of the West (especially Western Europe) to provide such assistance, the material and financial commitments that were actually made were exceedingly modest. The most blinkered and parsimonious Western politicians (e.g. Margaret Thatcher) tried to insist that the post-communist states should undertake major economic reforms first, as a precondition for the granting of large-scale Western assistance, on the grounds that Western assistance to unreformed post-communist states would simply be pocketed and/or wasted by the former communist *nomenklatura*. This mentality failed to grasp that the implementation of radical marketizing reforms and 'structural adjustment', including the promotion of small businesses and the restructuring of state enterprises to make them fit for privatization, would in practice require considerable inputs of capital, much of which could only come either from the West or from local black-marketeers and other criminal elements. It was therefore in the West's interests that much of the 'pump-priming' or 'seed' capital should come from the West, otherwise the West would in future have to 'do business' with seasoned gangsters and criminals. As Professor Jeffrey Sachs, the most prominent Western adviser to Poland and Russia, emphasized, Western aid would:

> help sustain political support for the reforms long enough for them to take hold. The Marshall Plan did not provide Europe with the funds for economic recovery. It provided governments with enough financial backing to achieve economic and political stability, give hope to the population and thus make economic recovery possible.[10]

Aid could buy time, which might not otherwise be available. 'In the absence of a generous and visionary approach by the West . . . it will prove impossible to achieve success in the reforms – no matter how resolute Eastern Europe is with its actions.'[11]

Nevertheless, while the US had transferred 1.3 per cent of its GNP to Western Europe between 1948 and 1952,[12] Western annual aid commitments to Eastern Europe (excluding East Germany and the former USSR) amounted to only $20–25 bn in 1991 and 1992,[13] or under 0.3 per cent of the EC's annual GDP. Compared to Eastern Europe's external financing needs or the $70–90 bn annual transfer payments from Western to Eastern Germany or the $500 bn that the Group of Seven (G-7) leading industrial countries spent on defence in 1990,[14] Western aid commitments to Eastern Europe were niggardly.

Moreover, whereas 80 per cent of Marshall Aid had been in the form of non-repayable grants, most of the Western 'aid' to Eastern Europe in the early 1990s took the form either of loans (which would eventually increase the recipients' already massive indebtedness and heavy burdens of debt service, just when they were supposed to open up their economies fully to EU exports) or of trade credits and guarantees to Western firms in order to promote Western exports to the region (thereby helping to retard economic recovery and the development of private enterprise by driving many East European producers of similar products out of

Table 12.1 Western aid commitments, January 1990 to June 1992 (bn ECU)[15]

From:	To: Eastern Europe	To: Former Soviet Union
Germany	7.5	39.2
Other EC states	5.5	9.7
EC institutions	8.1	3.5
EFTA	3.7	1.2
USA	4.4	6.8
Japan	2.5	2.0
Other bilateral	2.4	8.0
Multilateral	13.0	1.3
Total	47.0	71.7

business). Official aid flows to Eastern Europe (including the former USSR) added up to only $10.5 bn from 1989 to 1993 (inclusive).[16] In September 1991 William Pfaff remarked that 'more money is being paid annually to the West from the East in loan interest and loan repayments, than the East European countries have yet received from the West'.[17]

Finally, despite appearances to the contrary, the EC did very little to integrate Eastern Europe into the mainstream of European development. The 'Europe' Agreements concluded in late 1991 and late 1992 with Poland, Hungary, Czechoslovakia, Romania and Bulgaria seemed to have been designed to 'restrict their access to key western markets rather than to integrate them'.[18] They did so mainly by maintaining various 'safeguard' and 'anti-dumping' provisions (so-called 'contingent protection', which could and would be invoked against any 'disruptive' exports from Eastern Europe) and stringent EC import restrictions on their exports of agricultural products, processed foods, drinks, steel, chemicals, textiles, footwear, clothing and other so-called 'sensitive goods', which happened to be their main exports to the EC, for at least the next ten years (after which further restrictions could be written into prolonged 'transitional arrangements' for any states that might be granted so-called 'full' membership). A restrictive and defensive attitude was adopted by the EC even though these East European exports posed little threat to EC producers, as they amounted to less than one per cent of EC output and less than four per cent of EC imports of each of the products in question and were being more than offset by increased EC exports to Eastern Europe.[19] However, the development of common regional, social, industrial and agricultural policies and the veto powers of individual member states had left the EC hostage to producer interests which were much stronger, more effectively organized and better placed to apply pressure on national governments and EC institutions than were the West European consumers who would have been net beneficiaries of unrestricted access to East European products. The EC also steadfastly refused to offer a timetable for East European applications or negotiations for full membership of the EC, although the 'Europe' Agreements did make cosmetic provisions for regular 'political dialogue' with the states concerned. The EC's overriding aim seemed to be to keep the East European states at arm's length, mainly for fear of upsetting the EC 'apple-cart',[20] and East European governments felt increasingly insulted by the EC's defensive and patronizing language and attitudes. What they wanted was, in the words of Douglas Hurd, 'our partnership, not our patronage'.[21] As recognized by a *Financial Times* editorial on 22 September 1992, they needed 'a reappraisal of the European idea which would allow them to participate in framing an enlarged Community'.

Admittedly, premature admission of East European states to the EC could have been as damaging as it had been in the case of East Germany (via German reunification) in 1990. But the EC initially failed either to spell out the steps that the East European states would have to take in order to become eligible for EC membership in due course or to give them potent inducements to pursue an economic union of their own in the interim or to provide a clearer and more generous timetable for the removal of EC barriers against East European exports. Various EC 'carrots' and concessions were indeed necessary: first, to encourage the East Europeans to 'stay the course' of very painful and politically costly economic liberalization; second, to encourage Western firms to invest in Eastern Europe, secure in the knowledge that their products would be assured of unimpeded access to the EC market before long; and, third, because a generous attitude by the EC in opening up its markets to East European exports was absolutely essential if East European export-led recoveries were to be sustainable beyond the first year or two. Moreover, economic recoveries in the East European states could only be export-led, first, because their domestic markets were in most cases small and levels of domestic purchasing power were uniformly low as a result of the catastrophic declines in their meagre real incomes during the late 1980s and early 1990s (caused by the collapse of their former economic systems and 'captive' Comecon markets for their main exports), and partly because they would have to earn enough hard currency to service their extremely burdensome foreign debts and also pay for their reviving fuel requirements, most of which would have to be imported as Eastern Europe was becoming increasingly deficient in domestic fuel resources. By retarding the growth of East European exports to Western Europe, EC import restrictions would not only retard East European economic recovery and long-term economic growth, but would also (by the same token) substantially delay their potential eventual accession to the EU on the grounds that their economies were still too weak to withstand EU membership! Moreover, the accession of Austria, Sweden and Finland to the EU in January 1995 also diminished Eastern Europe's previous duty-free access to these markets, which now became subject to EU rules on 'sensitive goods' and EU 'safeguard' and 'anti-dumping' provisions.

Why was so little Western support forthcoming? In the first place, there was no longer a 'communist bogey', a fear of 'the Soviet threat', to encourage the West to give generously. This had undoubtedly been a major factor, possibly the main factor, explaining the scale of American Marshall Aid to Western Europe after the Second World War. During the early 1990s, the West's new bogies were predominantly Islamic, whether in the shape of Saddam Hussein, Iranian ayatollahs, Islamic revivalism in Algeria, Tunisia, Egypt and Turkey, or tidal waves of North African and Turkish migrants fleeing civil strife, mass unemployment and actual or perceived political and religious persecution. Far from encouraging Western generosity toward Eastern Europe, these new bogies prompted French and Spanish calls for a major redirection of Western resources away from Eastern Europe (including Russia) towards a strengthening of Europe's 'southern flanks'. Lurking beneath these xenophobic anxieties there were also French and Spanish fears that the accession of Austria, Sweden and Finland to the EU in January 1995 and concurrent moves to strengthen EU links with East European states during the later 1990s would shift the EU's centre of gravity towards *Mitteleuropa*, thereby helping Germany's increasing economic hegemony over the EU to eclipse the disproportionate political influence of the 'Romance axis' (France, Belgium, Italy, Spain and Portugal).

Furthermore, Western states were understandably preoccupied with their own internal problems: the United States with the effects of prolonged economic recession and vast budget deficits; Germany with the huge costs of reunification; France with mass unemployment and the paralysing prospect of imminent parliamentary and presidential elections in 1993 and 1995 respectively; Britain with a prolonged economic recession and a fraught, ambivalent relationship with the EC; and Italy with a deep economic, social and political crisis. In these circumstances, the potential electoral pay-offs or rewards from more substantial Western economic assistance to the former Soviet bloc would have been low or even negative. It was extremely unfortunate that the mammoth tasks of building liberal, pluralistic parliamentary democracies and market economies in Eastern Europe coincided with the onset of severe and prolonged economic recessions in the West and with politically problematic and divisive moves towards deeper integration within the EC, including the distractions and disorientations resulting from the fractious process of ratifying the increasingly unpopular and emasculated Maastricht Treaty. But there was also a grave failure of political leadership. As Edward Mortimer remarked in November 1992:

> No European leader has set out clearly for his electorate the nature of the opportunities and dangers which events in the east have produced for western Europe. As a result, it seems that none now has the authority to demand the sacrifices required from domestic vested interests, notably the farming and other producer lobbies which oppose the opening of the west European market to the most competitive east European products.[22]

Economically, as well as politically, the West was not in a strong position to assist the post-communist states at that time. During the Reagan and Bush presidencies the United States ran up vast trade and budget deficits and the world's largest foreign debt. The enormous cost of the Cold War and the attendant arms race, which had steadily sapped the strength of the Soviet bloc and paved the way for its disintegration between 1989 and 1991, also drained the economic strength of the United States, Britain and France by inducing them to concentrate too many resources and too much of their research and development expenditure on military and partly military projects, thereby accelerating the slippage of world leadership in many civilian industrial technologies from North America and

Western Europe to Japan and East Asia and weakening the balance of payments position of the major Western economies. In 1992 the combined current account trade deficit of the USA and Canada was a colossal $89 bn and that of the five largest EC economies was $77 bn, whereas Japan had a trade surplus of $118 bn. Even Germany had moved from large trade surpluses in the late 1980s to rapidly growing deficits by 1992, and its current account balance deteriorated by over $100 bn between 1989 and 1994.[23] This all added to the reluctance of the richer EC states to foot the bills for large financial transfers to Eastern Europe and the former Soviet republics, in addition to the steadily growing net financial transfers from the richer to the poorer members of the EC, even though it remained in their long-term self-interest to do everything possible to stabilize and develop the new economic hinterlands in Southern and Eastern Europe by transforming them into more prosperous partners and more lucrative markets.

Of all the advanced capitalist economies, Japan was in the strongest position to provide large-scale investment and economic assistance. But it showed little interest in either Eastern Europe or Russia (in contrast to mineral-rich and semi-Asiatic Kazakhstan, which attracted considerable Japanese investment and economic aid).[24] Unlike many Americans and West Europeans, the Japanese did not feel that they had any real 'stake' or 'responsibility' in either Russia or Eastern Europe, as they naturally did not see themselves as part of a wider European civilization, nor was Japan home to countless millions of East European immigrants. Moreover, the Japanese did not perceive Eastern Europe (as distinct from Russia and Kazakhstan) to be a potential major source of energy and raw materials and/or outlet for Japanese exports and investment. Instead, Japan has concentrated its overseas investment and export promotion within Asia, the Americas and the nascent Single European Market, that is, the world's largest and most promising markets. Indeed, Eastern European states also failed to attract much Japanese investment partly because there was no guarantee that their exports would gain (or, in the case of some industrial products, such as cars, retain) unimpeded access to the lucrative EC market (despite the so-called 'Europe' Agreements) and because they still entailed considerable political and economic uncertainties concerning property rights, enforceability of contracts, repatriation of profits, corporate taxation, reliability of supplies, infrastructure, future political stability and risk of military and/or inter-ethnic conflict.

The stark reality was that, during the early 1990s, there were no Western leaders with sufficient clout, motivation and 'vision' to lead a massive aid and reconstruction effort in Eastern Europe. There was a need for a George Marshall figure to mastermind, mobilize and co-ordinate Western assistance to the post-communist East. But the pusillanimity and deep-seated economic problems of the US in the early 1990s strongly contrasted with its commanding strength and sense of purpose in the late 1940s when it was riding on the crest of an enormous economic boom, and massive economic assistance in the reconstruction of an outward-looking, market-oriented and actively integrationist Europe was seen as a means of both prolonging the boom and containing the westward spread of communism. The commanding 'hegemonic' military, political and economic position of the United States in the aftermath of the Second World War helped to ensure that it would reap the lion's share of the trade and investment opportunities generated by West European economic reconstruction, recovery and integration. There was, therefore, no 'free rider' problem: there were no other large prosperous states which stood to gain large benefits from a massive US-funded European Recovery Programme and a US-sponsored Organization of European Economic Co-operation (OEEC) without incurring a proportionate share of the costs of these crucial ventures. (Canada shared some of the benefits, but it also bore part of the cost.) But in the early 1990s, paradoxically, there were too many potential Western aid donors and beneficiaries, giving rise to acute 'free rider' problems. Therefore, while paying lip-service to the importance of co-ordinated multilateral assistance to the post-communist East, in practice most Western 'aid' donors preferred to provide bilateral 'tied aid' on a more or less blatantly commercial basis, seeking to maximize the potential 'reciprocal' benefits and opportunities for their own companies, exporters and investors. Moreover, the actual Western preference for bilateral 'aid relationships', which encouraged economic disintegration rather than integration among the 'aid' recipients, was the opposite of what was needed and of the valuable integrative processes that Marshall Aid helped to initiate in Western Europe during the late 1940s and early 1950s. This limitation or reservation applied just as strongly to Germany, the biggest and most 'generous' donor, as it did to the more parsimonious and short-sighted donors. By 1993 Germany already accounted for 56 per cent of EC trade with Poland, Hungary, Czechoslovakia, Romania and Bulgaria[25] and, thanks to its great 'generosity', strategic location, technological virtuosity and business acumen, it could expect to consolidate its dominance of these fast-growing markets in the future, to the increasing detriment of its more mean-spirited and myopic EU partners.

If the EU were to enhance further its ties with the East European states during the late 1990s, Germany would still dominate those relationships as a result of its geographical proximity, its technological superiority and its inheritance of East Germany's long-standing economic relations, acquaintance and connections with its former Comecon partners. On the other hand, if the EU as a whole were to fail to develop much closer ties with Eastern Europe, then these same German advantages would ensure an even greater German dominance of their external economic relations and of foreign participation in their domestic economies. Either way, Germany would gain the main advantages. But the late Willy Brandt believed that 'reconciliation of Poles and Germans will someday have the same historical importance as the friendship between Germany and France'.[26] If so, it was in Western Europe's interests to promote the fastest possible deepening of multilateral relations between Eastern Europe and the EU or even the incorporation of Eastern Europe into the EU, in order to discourage the Germans and East Europeans from 'going it alone' or developing ever closer bilateral relations, to the exclusion of the West, as Germany did with Hungary, Romania, Bulgaria and Yugoslavia in the 1930s. But the more myopic West European politicians were held back by the perception that, either way, Germany stood to gain most of the benefits unless France, the Benelux countries and Britain were prepared to at least match Germany's financial, commercial and technological offer-ings to the region instead of complaining that Germany's generosity was 'showing up' Western European parsimony. However, fears that Germany could lose patience with its meaner and more blinkered EU partners and stake everything on a new relationship with the East were greatly exagger-ated or misplaced. Germany needed to maintain 'ever closer' ties with its Western European partners even more than it needed to promote new economic and political bonds with the East European states, as the value of German exports to Western Europe was several times the value of its exports to its new East European partners and would remain so for some time to come.

On the joint initiative of Jacques Delors and US President George Bush, the lead role in mobilization and co-ordination of Western assistance to Eastern Europe came to be entrusted to the Commission of the EC. The seeds of this initiative were sown in May 1989 at a lunch in the White House at which Delors was the guest of honour. Bush and Delors became 'deeply engrossed in a discussion of the Polish situation', during which Bush was 'struck by Delors' . . . expertise both on the Polish issue and on Eastern European affairs in general'.[27] One of the main agenda items for the approaching G-7 summit of major Western leaders in Paris on 14 July 1989 was Western aid for Poland and Hungary as they embarked on vital processes of political and economic liberalization. President Mitterrand wanted to use the occasion to launch a European Bank for Reconstruction and Development (EBRD). The Americans were never very keen on this idea, which (in their eyes) would involve an expensive and unnecessary European duplication of and rivalry with functions that were already being performed to US satisfaction by the World Bank, alias the Inter-national Bank for Reconstruction and Development (IBRD). Instead of the EBRD concept, the US was proposing a potentially more ambitious Western aid 'consortium' to assist Poland and Hungary in their gradual 'negotiated' retreat from communist dictatorship and central planning. It seemed likely that the US would 'upstage' or even fall out with their French hosts at the July 1989 G-7 summit. At the eve-of-summit banquet, with France and the US set on a collision course, Delors took 'the oppor-tunity to tell President Bush that he welcomed the US idea of an aid

Coordinatio
of assistance

...ush responded by suggesting that its running should be ...hands'. Moreover, it was arranged that these 'twin ...e presented to the official summit meeting by Chancellor ...drawing the teeth of any French opposition'.[28] As a ...cialist with a trade-union background and as President ...sion (1985–95), Delors was seen as the ideal person to ...s with the new Catholic/Solidarity Government in ...w Catholic/nationalist Democratic Forum Government ...over, the hard-pressed President of an over-burdened ...eager to relinquish the main responsibility for mobiliz-...ng Western efforts in the post-communist East to the EC. The principal outcomes of the July 1989 G-7 summit were the setting up of a Group of 24 aid donors (G-24) comprising all the large and medium-sized Western states, including Japan, and an initial EC-sponsored programme of aid for Poland and Hungary which was given the acronym PHARE ('*Pologne, Hongrie: activité pour la restructuration économique*'; appropriately, 'phare' is also the French for a 'lighthouse' or a beacon of light). The name became something of a misnomer, however, when PHARE was extended to include Czechoslovakia, Romania, Bulgaria and Yugoslavia in May 1990, Albania and the three Baltic states in December 1991 (when the shattered Yugoslav Federation was dropped) and Slovenia in 1992. The designated priority areas for the PHARE programme(s) were agriculture, industry, investment, energy, training, environmental protec-tion, trade and services, with an over-arching emphasis on promotion of private enterprise. The main focus was on microeconomic and technical assistance for agriculture, food processing and distribution, restructuring of industrial enterprises and banking, urgent projects to raise energy effi-ciency and safety, retraining, promotion of small businesses, provision of very rudimentary social 'safety nets', guidance/encouragement on demo-cratic procedures, legal reform and the promotion of human/minority rights and civil society.[29] PHARE also claims to have acted as a catalyst, 'unlocking funds for important projects from other donors through studies, capital grants, guarantee schemes and credit lines',[30] although this mainly involved a cosmetic re-packaging or re-designation of existing bilateral programmes and export guarantees. PHARE tried not to involve itself in programmes of macroeconomic stabilization, which were seen as tasks for the International Monetary Fund (IMF), nor in large-scale pro-grammes of structural adjustment, which were to be left to the World Bank and the International Finance Corporation. PHARE was originally intended to have expired at the end of 1992, but in November 1992 the EC Council decided to prolong it at least until 1997.

In addition to launching PHARE, and despite US misgivings, the EC summit held in Strasbourg in December 1989 approved Mitterrand's pro-posal for the establishment of EBRD (with an initial capital of 10 bn ECU to be subscribed by the G-24) to promote private enterprise and related infrastructure in Eastern Europe. The man chosen to head the new bank was Mitterrand's former political adviser, Jacques Attali. EBRD opened for business in April 1991: early in 1992 it was decided to extend membership to the Commonwealth of Independent States (CIS), to commence operations in these former Soviet republics from April 1992 and to earmark 60 per cent of its funds for Eastern Europe and the three Baltic states and the other 40 per cent to the CIS.[31] In Attali's own words:

> The vision was and is to build the first pan-European institution, in order to make totally irreversible the end of the split of the European continent in two. . . . We could have thought about a confederation, about political institutions. But today the main problem is finance.[32]

He hoped that, in helping to transform the post-communist states into democracies and market economies, the EBRD would metamorphose into a truly 'pan-European institution', much as the ECSC 'merged into the Common Market'. By early 1993, however, the EBRD had gained notoriety for lavishing more money on itself than on its intended clients. Attali was obliged to resign amid a barrage of Western political and press criticism in June 1993. Yet the low disbursements were not entirely the fault of either Attali or the EBRD. The bank was 'boxed in by the EBRD's founding charter and the powerful directors shareholding countries put in place to rein Mr. Attali's ambitions'.[33] The charter debarred it from disbursing more than 40 per cent of its loans to public sector projects or enterprises, in economies that were still dominated by publicly owned enterprises in desperate need of finance for new investment and restructuring (including, in some cases, preparation for privatization). Moreover, it was required both to refrain from trying to act as a substitute for potential private investors and to confine its support to commercially viable enterprises and projects, in collapsing economies whose existing enterprises were mostly making massive losses and struggling to stave off bankruptcy. Consequently, most of the profitable projects and enterprises had to be left to foreign private lenders and investors (including foreign multinationals), while those in greatest need of external funding were to be denied it. This US-inspired 'Catch 22' could not have been better calculated to stymie the initial operations of the EBRD. When Attali tried to secure a relaxation of these unduly restrictive terms of reference, he was slapped down by the US shareholders and the US Treasury Secretary Nicholas Brady, partly as a result of the American knee-jerk aversion to public enterprise and US misgivings about setting up the EBRD in the first place. Attali himself had protested that, as a result of these constraints, 'The bank has more money than it has projects.'[34] By 1994, fortunately, the rapid expansion of private enterprise in Eastern Europe had created a plethora of would-be borrowers who fell within the EBRD's narrow terms of reference, causing most of the problems that had bedevilled the Attali presidency to 'go away'. But the EBRD had permanently lost a bold leader who had dared to 'rock the boat' and challenge Western vested interests.

In May 1990 the EC also launched the Trans-European Mobility Scheme for University Studies (TEMPUS). This was designed to promote links, co-operation and student and staff exchanges between East European and EC institutions of higher education, mainly to help East European universities to change the structure and content of their higher education and research and to upgrade their books and equipment. Training programmes such as TEMPUS, the European Training Foundation (ETF) and Technical Assistance to the CIS (TACIS) were very valuable as far as they went.

Nevertheless, total EC-coordinated Western assistance to Eastern Europe amounted to a few drops in some very large buckets. Furthermore, this assistance was rendered within an essentially unchanged structure of East–West relations; it made little attempt to change or challenge long-established frameworks. When Attali tried to do so, he was both 'slapped down' and 'boxed in'. Indeed, partly as a result of the over-hasty, informal and almost Olympian manner in which a deal was struck between the US President and the President of the EC Commission, with the apparent acquiescence of other G-7 leaders, there was hardly any serious inter-governmental, inter-parliamentary or even national exploration and discussion of the various 'architectural', institutional and policy options for Europe as a whole after the Cold War, let alone Europe's dealings and relationships with newly 'liberated' Eastern Europe. Europe was simply presented with a *fait accompli* that had been 'stitched up' in private, even over the banqueting table, 'President to President'. The timorous West European governments were only too happy to abdicate responsibility for fleshing out the details to the EC Commission which, in the words of Heinz Kramer, 'resorted mainly to well-established means and procedures in EC foreign relations'. These comprised two main planks, 'one concentrating on aid measures in various forms and the other emphasising the establishment of a long-term trade régime to which are added measures of economic and political co-operation'. The *leitmotif* of the former was 'help for the promotion of self-help', whereas the latter essentially relied on 'integration by organised free trade'.[35]

It was extremely significant that relations with Eastern Europe were to be treated as part of the 'foreign relations' of the EC, on much the same basis as EC relations with former European colonies in Africa and the Caribbean, rather than as part of the internal relations of an increasingly unified Europe. Thus there was to be no fundamental search for the most suitable new 'European architecture', but simply a civil servants' strategy for preserving as much as possible of the *status quo*. Aid and trade were gradually to be grafted on to the existing EC structure, causing minimum disturbance to current members, institutions and procedures and avoiding any fundamental re-think. This incremental approach would help to perpetuate and institutionalize the pre-existing East–West division of Europe and dampen the quest for new structures more capable of bridging the divide and bringing Russia and Ukraine 'in from the cold'. Thus the more interesting proposals for a (pan-)European Confederation put forward by President Mitterrand of France and President Havel of Czechoslovakia in 1990 and 1991 were almost immediately kicked into touch. Yet such a European Confederation, dealing primarily with matters of European security and high politics, could have avoided some of the dilemmas that the EU and NATO later confronted over how to deal with Russia and Ukraine and could have provided a more appropriate and effective forum for handling border disputes and threats to minority rights, of the sort that re-ignited long dormant inter-ethnic conflicts in the Caucasus region and former Yugoslavia. One of the chief merits of these European Confederation proposals was that they could have embraced the former Soviet republics as well as Eastern Europe and the 'Little Europe' of the EC. Such a Confederation would also have made it easier to offer viable security guarantees to East European states and the smaller ex-Soviet Republics within an over-arching framework that need not have excluded or antagonized Russia. (Indeed, to offer so-called 'security guarantees' in forms that are bound to exclude or alienate Russia is rather self-defeating, even in terms of the objective self-interest of those who short-sightedly clamour for this illusory 'security'. Such 'guarantees' would be about as effective as those that Britain and France gave to Poland and Greece in 1939). Admittedly, Mitterrand favoured a European Confederation primarily in order 'to preserve the EC in its present shape, which, for Paris, is the best means of containing Germany'.[36] Nevertheless, as emphasized by Václav Havel in Aachen in May 1991, 'no future European order is conceivable without the European peoples of the Soviet Union, who are an indivisible component of Europe'.[37] In his speech to the US Congress in July 1991, on the eve of the abortive *Putsch* by Soviet hardliners, Havel declared that it was essentially:

> in the interests of my country, of Europe and of the whole world to make the Soviet Union a more free, more democratic and more stable place. . . . You can help us most of all if you help the Soviet Union on its irreversible but immensely complicated road to democracy.[38]

Edward Mortimer has similarly emphasized that 'a stable and peaceful order in Europe presupposes that Russia and the states associated with it must find their rightful place'.[39] Moreover, not until late 1994 and early 1995 was there any serious consideration of proposals for subsuming NATO and the expanding European Union into a wider 'Atlantic Community' with economic and security dimensions, and designed to address the changing nature of the economic and security challenges confronting Europe without completely marginalizing and antagonizing Russia and Ukraine, which cannot be accommodated in NATO and the

EU in their existing forms and yet cannot and should not be frozen out of 'our common European home'.

While it has to be duly acknowledged that Delors publicly contemplated an EC that would eventually embrace twenty to thirty members[40] and that he acted as one of the principal 'cheer leaders' for Western financial assistance to Eastern Europe, calling for aid commitments of up to £100 bn over a ten-year period,[41] the media and the political establishment have probably been over-generous in their judgements on his dynamism and achievements as President of the EC Commission. His vaunted 'federal vision' was a relatively limited one and, under his stewardship, EC aid and trade commitments to Eastern Europe were developed in ways that would do more to reinforce than to recast the existing bilateral structural relationships with East European states. Increased aid and trade were simply to be 'added on' to existing structures, keeping the East Europeans in the position of economically 'dependent' foreign states or supplicant 'orphans at the gate'. Eastern Europe would become the EU's 'backyard', just as the Central American 'banana republics' became 'Uncle Sam's backyard'. Such a relationship would demean and diminish both sides, morally as well as economically. Moreover, much as one might admire the skill and tenacity with which he 'fought his corner', Delors encouraged the EC to become increasingly preoccupied with its own internal affairs and structures at a time when another equally challenging and exciting Europe was finally emerging from its 42-year-old communist cocoon on the EC's eastern doorstep. He also piloted the EC into a Treaty and into a particular trajectory of monetary union that proved to be so seriously flawed and divisive that it threw away much of the momentum for deeper and wider integration achieved by the 1985 White Paper on a Single European Market and the 1986 Single European Act, during the more constructive first half of his presidency. History may judge that his clever footwork in 1989–90 did the wider cause of European union a long-term disservice by helping to lead the EC into an institutional and monetary minefield and by tending to re-jig rather than replace Europe's East–West divide. According to Kramer:

> the EC, in its response to the challenges posed by the Central and East European economic and political transformation processes, has not been very daring. Its activities do not go beyond the established instruments of Community foreign relations and the normal range of Western international activities in economic restructuring.[42]

Fundamentally, above and beyond the special culpability of particular individuals, the EC was ill-equipped to play the roles assigned to it, which may of course be a principal reason why the EC was given them. Composed of 12 (now 15) quarrelsome, cantankerous and mutually competitive national states, it was a somewhat introverted organization, increasingly preoccupied by its own internal problems, disputes and objectives. With nominal control over a mere 1.2 per cent of the European Community's GDP (roughly half of it in the rigid form of 'compulsory expenditure' on the Common Agricultural Policy (CAP)), the supra-national institutions of the EC were grossly under-resourced in comparison with the magnitude of the ever-proliferating tasks that were ceded to it by national governments that typically controlled 40 to 60 per cent of their respective national GDPs. The EC Commission did not possess the wherewithal or the political muscle or the strength of resolve to break the mould of the East–West division of Europe. Moreover, the EC lacked well-developed institutions, procedures and competences for dealing with external relations, as demonstrated by its divided and ineffectual handling of the 1990–1 Gulf crisis, the early 1990s Yugoslav conflicts and the 1986–93 Uruguay Round of the General Agreement on Tariffs and Trade (GATT) negotiations. The EC was hostage to too many vested interests which could all too easily block any radical overtures to Eastern Europe, whether in terms of economic assistance or trade liberalization or funda-mental changes in the architecture of Europe. In 1992 Professor Richard Baldwin argued that in the final analysis a combination of Southern Eur-opean and farming interests would probably veto East European member-ship of the EC for at least another twenty years.[43] However, this view was countered by arguments that the particular economic profile and techno-logical level of the Southern European economies meant that they would have the most to offer and to gain from future East European membership of the EC. A study conducted by National Economic Research Associates on behalf of the EC Commission in 1993 concluded that, if EC trade with Eastern Europe were to be liberalized, this would initially reduce total EC output by 0.2 per cent, but by 2010 the subsequent increase in East Euro-pean imports of EC products would (on balance) raise EC industrial output by 1.2 per cent and total EC output by 0.8 per cent, with the largest increases (2.2 per cent and 1.0 per cent, respectively) occurring in Spain, Portugal and Greece, because their industries and products are best suited to the import needs of Eastern Europe and Greece is so advantageously located.[44] Moreover, opinion polls conducted in May 1994 on behalf of eight West European newspapers found that popular opposition to East European membership of the EU was lowest in Southern Europe. Asked 'Do you favour EU enlargement to [include] the Czech Republic, Hungary, Poland and Slovakia?', the percentage of negative replies was 13 in Spain, 14 in Italy, 17 in Portugal, 24 in the Netherlands, 28 in Eastern Germany, 29 in Greece, 31 in Belgium and Ireland, 38 in the UK and Luxembourg, 40 in France, 43 in Western Germany and 46 in Denmark.[45] Unfortunately, the question of eastward enlargement will probably be decided by politicians over-influenced by sectional producer lobbies, while the public at large will have as little say in this as in previous EC enlargements.

The potential effects of a major 'eastward enlargement' on the CAP will pose political rather than economic problems, but they are not insurmountable and could diminish quite rapidly. Taking 1990 as a base year, it seems that the admission of all the East European states to the EU would nearly double the EU's cultivated area and more than double its agricultural population. Therefore, in doomsday scenarios, total claims on the CAP could roughly double and, when offered CAP prices and full access to West European markets, East European agriculture could greatly increase the EU's farm surpluses, wrecking the CAP. In fact, those surpluses largely disappeared in 1994–5 and the East European states need not all be admitted at the same time, but two by two, as into the Ark. The Czech Republic, Slovenia, Slovakia and Albania would pose no great problems for the CAP, in view of their small size and/or infertile terrain. Like Portugal and Greece, they could be net importers of temperate farm products, helping to relieve pressures on the CAP. The real problems concern the admission of Hungary and Bulgaria, because their farms are relatively productive and export-orientated, and Poland and Romania, because their relatively unproductive farmers are so numerous. But, if the 70 per cent reduction in East Germany's farm workforce between 1989 and 1993 is at all indicative, one should expect the East European farm population to decrease as and when opportunities for leaving the land (including emigration) open up, and this should lead to significant reductions in cultivated area, restraining potential increases in agricultural output. As in the West, few young East Europeans want to remain on the land. Prolonged transitional arrangements could blunt the challenge to the CAP long enough for domestic and Western investment in East European industrial regeneration to reduce Eastern Europe's agricultural sectors to more manageable proportions. The potential problems have been grossly exaggerated by alarmists, some of whom want either to scrap or to 're-nationalize' EU farm support, which they regard as nothing more than a very costly and corrupt system of 'outdoor relief' for ne'er-do-well farmers. The more blinkered critics fail to grasp that the CAP was an essential component of the political contract that created the EEC, not just to placate rural constituencies and apoplectic Frenchmen, but also in order to banish *national* agricultural protectionism, which, if it were to return in the guise of 're-nationalization' of farm support, could precipitate tit-for-tat *national* protectionism in other sectors and quickly unravel the great achievements of the Common Market and the Single European Market. Thus the CAP is not merely a system of farm support, but a fee that we pay for the avoidance of any repetition of the beggar-my-neighbour trade wars that bedevilled interwar Europe, politically as well as economically. At a cost of less than 0.6 per cent of the EU's GDP, it is worth every penny.

Unfortunately, the total fixation of the first post-communist East European governments on eventual accession to the EU discouraged any consideration of interim alternatives to EU membership, even though rapid accession was out of the question. An interim scheme to foster political and economic integration and supranational institutions within Eastern Europe, going far beyond the minimalist commitments to an East-Central European free-trade area and inter-governmental co-operation agreed at Visegrad in February 1991, would help to prepare East European states for eventual membership of a wider EU and to develop and demonstrate their capacities for constructive participation in joint institutions, resolving bitter intraregional disputes and promoting national reconciliation between former foes. That in turn could help to convince West European opponents that an eastward enlargement would not simply import into the EU all the conflicts that have for so long soured relations between East European nations and states. Conversely, those opponents would be handed an almost unassailable objection to any eastward enlargement of the EU (beyond perhaps Slovenia and the Czech Republic) if East Europeans prove incapable of integrating *among themselves* as a first step towards integration between Eastern and Western Europe.

Since the First World War, or longer in the case of Poland, East Europeans have laboured under persistent illusions concerning the scale of economic, military or political assistance that West European states might be willing to provide, whether in support of national self-determination or democracy or 'free-market' economies or against a common foe (usually Germany or Russia). East Europeans repeatedly deluded themselves that, when the West avowedly shared their concerns or aspirations, significant practical support would be forthcoming. But Poles looked in vain for West European assistance against the 'Partitioning Powers' in 1791–5, in 1831 and 1863, as did Hungarian nationalists during their 1848–9 revolution against the Habsburgs. The Western Allies did re-establish or 'call into existence' independent East European states in the wake of the First World War. During the 1920s and 1930s, however, these East European states looked in vain for substantial Western financial, commercial, technical or even moral support for their faltering crisis-torn democracies and fragile trade-dependent economies. The 'appeasers' who governed Britain and France did little to discourage Hitler's dismemberment of Czechoslovakia in 1938–9 or Mussolini's occupation of Albania in 1939. Many East Europeans also felt betrayed by the agreements reached by Churchill and Stalin in Moscow in October 1944 and by the Allied leaders at Yalta and Potsdam in 1945, which in effect surrendered Eastern Europe to the post-war Soviet sphere of influence. Many Poles and Czechs felt that their heroic anti-fascist resistance during the Second World War should have been rewarded by a more spirited Western resistance to Soviet encroachments on their post-war sovereignty. However, as Professor Doreen Warriner remarked in 1950, 'Western Europe, so far as it was interested in eastern Europe at all, was interested in keeping it backward, as a source of cheap food and cheap labour'; and, if the Western Powers had been able to have their way in post-1944 Eastern Europe,

> they would have put back into power the same kind of governments which had existed before, and whose failure led to Fascism. . . . During the war the Western Powers had evolved no new policy for eastern Europe: they supported the emigre governments in London, at best, liberal politicians of the old style, at worst, near-Fascists.

It therefore fell to the communists to break the mould of post-1918 East European politics. While the West had 'learnt nothing' from the failure of the 1919–20 peace settlements in interwar Eastern Europe,

> the Soviet Union and the Communist parties of eastern Europe had learnt a great deal. Their conception of the future was clear, and so also was their grasp of the strategy of gaining power. In conformity with that conception, they have carried through a revolution . . . which is transforming the political and economic life of the region.[46]

Warriner astutely observed that the significance of the East European Revolutions of 1945–50 lay not only in the political change, 'the destruction of the old ruling groups', but also in 'the economic dynamic' that accompanied it. 'What eastern Europe primarily needed was the industrial revolution and, without the shift in the European balance of power resulting from Soviet victory, it would never have come.'[47] Nevertheless, despite Western reluctance to come to the assistance of the Hungarian Revolution of October 1956, the Prague Spring of 1968 or Poland's Solidarity movement in 1981, East Europeans still expected Western Europe and the United States to underwrite their post-1989 transitions to multi-party democracy and a market economy.

These delusions were partly a consequence of centuries of subjugation by powerful Russian, Austrian, German and Turkish neighbours and the resultant belief that Eastern Europe could only be liberated and economically developed with external assistance. This fostered a damaging psychological dependence on an ill-founded faith in the West. It was commonly assumed that external powers would decide Eastern Europe's destiny and deal with its problems to suit themselves. It was a self-fulfilling expectation, inducing a 'satellite mentality'. Western Europe, for its part, had regularly raised and disappointed East European hopes and that cycle was to be repeated yet again during the 1990s, when the East Europeans ceased to be 'satellites' of the former Soviet Union only to become 'satellites' of the EU and Germany. It is important not to be naive about international relations. Strong states normally dominate weaker neighbours and highly developed economies are usually in a position to reap greater gains from international trade and investment than are less developed ones. These asymmetrical power relations and unequal exchanges lie at the root of many colonial, neo-colonial and hegemonic relationships. Just as the EU's relationships with less developed countries have been open to serious accusations of neo-colonialism, unequal exchange and 'dumping' of EU agricultural surpluses, so one must not automatically assume that EU relations with Eastern Europe are necessarily benevolent. For the EC itself, the emergence of Eastern Europe from its communist cocoon in 1989 was highly inconvenient, for the EC had partly relied on the Cold War partition of Europe for much of its cohesion, sense of purpose and stability. The new Europe would be much less stable and cohesive and would take time to gain a new sense of direction.

Ever since the collapse of the Austro-Hungarian Empire in 1918, Eastern Europe has been an economic and power vacuum waiting to be filled, usually by Germany and/or Russia, but since 1989 by Germany and/or the EU. This is almost a law of physics. Nature abhors a vacuum. The most likely outcome is German domination under an EU mantle. As Otto von Bismarck, the creator of modern Germany, once remarked: 'I have always found the word "Europe" in the mouths of politicians who wanted from other powers something they did not dare to demand in their own name.'[48] Moreover, there will continue to be real dangers that Eastern Europe could become an informal colony or a 'captive' market for the EU states and/or a provider of very cheap labour to EU subcontractors, subsidiaries and 'screwdriver' industries, helping EU economies to survive increasing low-waged competition from Asia. West European investors could be primarily interested in: saving the 'plums' among East European enterprises, while leaving the rest to founder; buying up potential competitors before they can find their feet; pocketing any available subsidies or investment grants; acquiring and spiriting away key East European personnel and their technological know-how; or simply making 'a quick killing', before turning their attention elsewhere, like the Northern carpet-baggers who descended like vultures on the defeated American South after the Civil War. West European entrepreneurs may be less interested in sustainable long-term development for the benefit of East Europeans than in cornering markets for their own benefit. In practice, the main role of the EU could be simply to open up fertile hunting grounds for West European 'sharks', 'consultants' and speculative 'developers', while helping to subjugate Eastern Europe to West European capitalism by facilitating its penetration and domination of East European markets, financial institutions and state structures. The main consolation is to be found in Professor Joan Robinson's legendary remark that 'If there is anything worse than being exploited by foreigners, it is not being exploited by foreigners.' This may be too cynical a picture, but it is a necessary antidote to the widespread naive assumptions that capitalist Western Europe is engaged in a great philanthropic venture in Eastern Europe and that it is there to help. One must not be deluded by the hypocritical language of 'aid'. In May 1991 Premier Felipe Gonzalez described how he had told a stream of official visitors from Eastern Europe, seeking 'lessons' from Spain's transition from 'totalitarianism' to democracy:

> Spain went through a deep economic crisis between 1975 and 1985. We got a great deal of moral support, but we never had a single peseta in assistance. . . . Western Europe is not going to foot the bill for 40 years of communism. Just like it didn't pay for 40 years of Franquismo. No one feels obliged to pay this bill.[49]

The great danger in this is that the traumas of transition and painful disappointment at the parsimony, protectionism and pusillanimity of the West might translate into further disillusionment with liberal democracy and the market system. After all, 'serfdom' is always said to have arrived later, but to have persisted longer, in the East than in the West.

FURTHER READING

R. Baldwin, *Towards an Integrated Europe*, London: CEPR, 1994.
C. Bryant and E. Mokrzycki (eds), *The New Great Transformation: Change and Continuity in Eastern Europe*, London: Routledge, 1994.
J. Bugajski, *Nations in Turmoil: Conflict and Cooperation in Eastern Europe*, Boulder, CO: Westview Press, 1993.
G. Kolankiewicz, 'Consensus and Competition in the Eastern Enlargement of the EU', *International Affairs*, vol. 70 (1994), no. 3, pp. 477–95.
H. Kramer, 'The European Community's Response to the "New Eastern Europe"', *Journal of Common Market Studies*, vol. 31 (1993), no. 2, pp. 213–44.
H. Miall (ed.), *Redefining Europe*, London: Pinter, 1994.
S. Nello, *The New Europe: Changing Relations between East and West*, London: Harvester Wheatsheaf, 1991.
J. Pinder, *The European Community and Eastern Europe*, London: Pinter, 1991.

NOTES

1 By 'Eastern Europe' I mean the former communist states lying in between Germany and Italy, to the west, and the former Russian Empire and Soviet Republics, to the east. German writers used to call this area *Zwischeneuropa*. Unfortunately, this very apt word has no exact English equivalent, although the title of a book by R. R. Palmer shrewdly rendered it into English as 'the lands between'. We are not helped by the fact that, in this neck of the woods, the usages and political/cultural connotations of regional designations have changed repeatedly in the course of the twentieth century. I am well aware that many of the region's inhabitants prefer the designation 'Central and Eastern Europe', but this just adds to the confusion, since for many people the concept of 'Central Europe' (or *Mitteleuropa*) primarily includes Germany and Austria, more than Hungary, Poland, Slovakia or the Czech Republic. The 'lands between' are most usefully subdivided into 'East-Central Europe', comprising Poland, Hungary, Slovakia, the Czech Republic and, at least until the Second World War, Austria; and 'the Balkans', comprising Romania, Bulgaria, Albania, the former Yugoslav republics and, for most purposes, Greece. I wish to thank Eleanor Breuning for her helpful comments on this chapter.

2 When I diffidently expressed a fear that I might have exaggerated the threats to democracy posed by the persistence or revival of 'ethnic' nationalism and the continuing weakness of civil society and of civic conceptions of the state in the Balkans at a conference on the Balkan states held in Bucharest in July 1994, Gramoz Pashko (a former Deputy Premier of post-communist Albania) urged me to regard the vaunted constitutional guarantees of individual and minority rights in the 1990s Balkan states as 'pieces of paper which anybody can write'. What matters is the capacity and willingness of civil society to defend those rights and uphold an impartial 'civic' conception of the state and the nation. But on this score he was decidedly pessimistic, as were the Bulgarian delegates.

3 P. Sisa, 'Towards a United Europe: A View from the East', Cardiff: Welsh Centre for International Affairs Occasional Paper no. 7 (Summer 1994), p. 2.

4 The concept of a 'civil economy' is expounded in: R. Rose, 'Toward a Civil Economy', *Journal of Democracy*, vol. 3 (1992), no. 2, pp. 13–26.

5 Summarized by A. Bridge, *Independent*, 28 January 1994.

6 *Independent*, 24 April 1992.

7 *International Herald Tribune* (hereafter *IHT*), 22 October 1993.

8 J. Dempsey and Q. Peel, *Financial Times Survey: Restructuring of East Germany*, 4 May 1994, pp. ii and iv.

9 M. Wolf, *Financial Times* (hereafter *FT*), 17 July 1992, and D. Goodhart and A. Fisher, *FT*, 13 September 1991.

10 J. Sachs, 'Lay Out Reform Dollars. . . .', *IHT*, 16 May 1991.

11 J. Sachs, *Poland's Jump to the Market*, Cambridge, MA: MIT Press, 1994, p. 6.

12 J. Pinder, *The European Community and Eastern Europe*, London: Pinter, 1991, p. 98.

13 S. Fidler, *FT*, 17 April 1991.

14 *FT* editorial, 9 July 1992.

15 Data from the EC Commission, quoted in *The Economist*, 17 April 1992, p. 4.

16 F. Williams, *FT*, 8 April 1994.

17 W. Pfaff, *IHT*, 14 September 1991.

18 *FT*, 29 October 1992.

19 E. Balls, *FT*, 19 October 1992; D. Marsh and L. Barber, *FT*, 7 June 1993; J. Rollo, *FT*, 18 June 1993.

20 For example, in Berlin on 19 September 1991 President Mitterrand called on the EC twelve 'to build on the Community they had created and the policies at its heart – the common market, customs union and common agricultural policy – and not allow them to be diluted by enlargement' (Q. Peel, *FT*, 29 September 1991). In the House of Commons on 21 May 1992 Edward Heath declared that East European states were being 'misled' by false prospects of EC membership. 'We can't just say we'd like to have lots of friends, so we welcome them in. . . . How many years is it going to take before they catch up with the Community? . . . It worries me that they are being misled by the things which are being said' (S. Goodwin, *Independent*, 22 May 1992).

21 *The Observer*, 1 March 1992.

22 *FT*, 18 November 1992.

23 W. Rees-Mogg, *The Times*, 27 January 1995.

24 The long-standing Russo-Japanese territorial dispute over the Kurile Islands and profound mutual mistrust between Russian and Japanese nationalists deterred large-scale Japanese investment in Russia, causing the Japanese to miss a golden opportunity to develop and acquire control of the vast under-exploited energy, timber and mineral resources of the Russian Far East. However, Japan's loss could be South Korea's gain, as President Yeltsin assiduously courted South Korea's public and private investors in 1992. Potentially, there

was a lot of mileage in this new relationship, since Russia and South Korea shared bad memories of Japanese imperialism and brutality during the first half of the twentieth century and South Korea needed reassurance that Russia would not resume its former military supplies and/or assistance to North Korea. Moreover, South Korea's increasingly industrialized, energy-deficient and capital-rich economy was even better placed than Japan's to benefit from preferential access to eastern Russia's natural resources. Moreover, it could do so without being seen as a potential threat and without raising the fears and hackles of Russian nationalists since, unlike 1930s Japan, it had never seriously contemplated a conquest of the Russian Far East.

25 *FT*, 7 June 1993.
26 W. Brandt, 'A Peace Policy for Europe' (1968), in: K. Harprecht (ed.), *Willy Brandt: Portrait and Self-Portrait*, London: Abelard-Schuman, 1972, p. 272.
27 G. Merritt, *Eastern Europe and the USSR: The Challenge of Freedom*, London: Kogan Page and Office for Official Publications of the European Community, 1991, p. 21.
28 Merritt, p. 22. Significantly, Merritt's book was 'written with the encouragement and support of the European Commission' and with 'privileged access to key officials' (p. 11).
29 In February 1993 PHARE initiated a five-million-ECU sponsorship of so-called 'democracy projects' to 'help fledgling parliaments nurture emerging legal systems, promote objective journalism and encourage trade unions and other democratic organizations', for example, by 'training parliamentary staff to draft legislation' and 'translating human rights texts into local languages'; *The European*, 4 February 1993.
30 PHARE 'Operational Programmes 1994, Update No. 4', Brussels: PHARE Information Office, European Commission, November 1994, p. 7.
31 J. Dempsey, *FT*, 28 February 1992.
32 *FT*, 15 April 1991.
33 N. Denton, *FT*, 15 April 1992.
34 N. Denton and J. Dempsey, *FT*, 13 April 1992.
35 H. Kramer, 'The European Community's Response to the "New Eastern Europe"', *Journal of Common Market Studies*, vol. 31 (1993), no. 2, p. 222.
36 Ibid.
37 *FT*, 19 May 1991.
38 *IHT*, 15 July 1991. Havel was deliberately echoing the words of his previous speech to the US Congress in February 1990.
39 *FT*, 9 September 1992.
40 In October 1991 Delors called for a further EC conference (after Maastricht) 'to prepare a structure for 24 to 30 countries' (T. Redburn, *IHT*, 14 October 1991).
41 J. Palmer, *Guardian*, 18 and 20 January 1990.
42 Kramer (n. 35 above), p. 234.
43 *FT*, 9 November 1992.
44 E. Balls, *FT*, 13 September 1993.
45 *FT*, 1 June 1994, p. 4.
46 D. Warriner, *Revolution in Eastern Europe*, London: Turnstile Press, 1950, p. xiv.
47 Ibid., p. xiii.
48 J. Kirkpatrick, *IHT*, 19 July 1994.
49 *FT*, 9 May 1991.

13 The double-headed eagle: Russia – East or West?

Richard Taylor

As post-communist Russia emerges from the ruins of the Soviet Union it has sought to rediscover its national identity as a sovereign state distinct from the multinational entity that previously encompassed it. This has been a peculiarly difficult task for Russia and the Russians, in part because they saw themselves, and were indeed seen by other national groupings, as synonymous with the old Soviet state. The Russian Federation was by far the largest republic in the USSR in terms of population, land area and industrial muscle, but until 1990 it had none of the trappings of Soviet republican statehood: no separate Communist Party organization, no separate Academy of Sciences, no separate police or secret police organizations, no separate trade union or Party youth organizations, and no radio or television stations aimed purely at Russians.[1] As late as the March 1991 referendum on the future of the USSR 71 per cent of those voting in the Russian Federation cast their votes in favour of the preservation of the Union, and this confusion of identity hindered the emergence of a Russian national front to parallel those in other republics.[2]

The awakening national identity of the minority nationalities of the old USSR was associated in the minds of their populations with a reaction against the multinational ideology of the system that furnished that state's foundations and against the perceived domination of that state by Russians, since the Russian Federation constituted 51.4 per cent of the population and 76.2 per cent of the territory of the Union.[3] For the Russians national self-consciousness came as a product of the process of democratization that was unleashed by Gorbachev's policies of perestroika and glasnost, and it came upon them very suddenly in the stormy days of the August 1991 *Putsch*, when the Russian/Soviet choice was put so starkly before them. Furthermore, more than seven decades of rule in the name of an ideology that claimed class rather than nation as the basis for its political analysis and its policies meant that Russians also carried with them a burden of guilt about the expression of their own national identity, because they had been inculcated with the notion that patriotism was all too easily confused with, or all too easily slid into, 'bourgeois nationalism' and 'great-power chauvinism'. Nevertheless, when it came to the crunch, it was Russia, led by its first directly elected President, Boris Yeltsin, which led the final and decisive battle that brought about the disintegration of the Union, even if the motivation was an internecine power struggle, rather than more elevated ideals of liberty and democracy.

Russian *state* consciousness thus preceded Russian *national* consciousness: in the new post-Soviet Russian state ethnic Russians comprise 81.6 per cent of the total population (far outstripping the Tatars, who come second at 3.75 per cent), so that Russia is now an ethnically more homogeneous state than at any other time in its modern history.[4] The clear separation of Russia from the old Union and from the other successor states has required not merely the building of a state, but the building of a *Russian* state, and has consequently also involved the process of nation building for Russia that most European nation-states underwent in the late nineteenth or early twentieth centuries.[5] This process of nation-building has depended on a perception that Russia's greatness lay in the dim and distant past, before the so-called Great October Socialist Revolution (nowadays more frequently dismissed as the 'October coup' and thus conveniently bracketed with the August 1991 *Putsch* as the beginning and end of Soviet communism), so that, in order to approach the future with some sense of their own national identity, Russians have looked exclusively to their past, to a past that is all too frequently seen through rose-tinted spectacles. Last, but not least, there has been a linguistic ambiguity in Russian over the words for 'Russia' and 'Russian'. The historic Russian heartland that emerged in the Middle Ages around Kiev and later Moscow is known as *Rus'*, a largely archaic term still used in poetry, and ethnic Russians are referred to as *russkie*, their language as *russkii*. The more modern state that emerged during and after the reign of Peter the Great is known as *Rossiia*, its inhabitants as *rossiiane*, the institutions and characteristics of this state as *rossiiskie*, 'of the Russias'.[6] The distinction between these two sets of terms, between the ethnic and political concepts of 'Russianness', is a distinction that has emerged as post-Soviet Russian national consciousness has itself begun to re-appear.

The arguments since 1991 over Russia's national identity have been variously categorized as a contrast between 'empire-saving' and 'nation-building' ideas,[7] between 'big-state' and 'small-state' concepts,[8] or between 'Westernizing' and 'Eurasian' tendencies, yet the essence of the more recent debates is all too often obscured, rather than clarified by these oppositions. We can however trace a shift in Russian perceptions of Russia's national identity and it is a shift that in turn reflects a shift in Russian attitudes towards the West and its possible, or impossible, role in the regeneration of this vast country. Two things unite almost all commentators: first, agreement on the current catastrophic state of Russia in political, economic and *spiritual* terms; second, similar agreement that the cause lies with seven decades of Soviet communism.

Boris Orlov has argued in the Writers' Union newspaper, *Literaturnaia gazeta*, that the Bolsheviks:

> were the cause of many misfortunes. They destroyed the best part of our nation. For three generations they cut people off with an 'iron curtain' from the rest of the world. They turned one sixth of the earth into an ecological disaster zone. But they had their most insidious effect on the minds of men, filling them with the idea that they must act in accordance with the orders of the Party, without regard to considerations of morality, because the Party was the mind, the honour and the conscience of our epoch.[9]

A similar point has been made by the Abkhazian novelist, Fazil Iskander:

> People who have been in prison for too long suddenly begin to be afraid of freedom. Often they ask to be let back into prison. With all its terrible restrictions, prison liberates man from the labour of choice, from the pressure of choice, from the responsibilities of choice. In prison everything is decided in advance by the authorities. . . .
>
>   Suddenly, after a long stay . . . the people find themselves in conditions of disorganised freedom, in which they have to decide everything for themselves, they have to move around, take action, use their imagination and take risks.[10]

Iskander also argues that the corruption of the Soviet régime, especially in the 'period of stagnation' under Brezhnev, explains the huge rise in crime in post-Soviet Russia:

> The whole of Soviet society was riddled with crime, but the criminal inclinations of the 'lower orders' were kept in check by fear of an even more criminal government. Up there were the criminal bosses. So, when these bosses were suddenly removed, even those who had not even suspected that they had criminal inclinations rushed to grasp their opportunity.[11]

Agreement on the scale and causes of the catastrophe does not of course mean agreement on the means by which that catastrophe might be overcome. The debates on those means, and their implications for Russia's role East and West, form the focus of the rest of this chapter. For many years, while an iron curtain cut the Russian people off from the outside world, many of them dreamed, largely in ignorance and almost entirely without personal experience, of life in the West as some kind of ideal model to which Russia might one day aspire. The mass of the Russian population has formed its image of the West, not through direct experience of the Western way of life, but through the sudden influx of Western films, pop music and television programmes in recent decades. While soap operas and pop music are not necessarily the best guide to reality, they do effectively stimulate demand for Western goods and lifestyles. The promise of material prosperity offered by the Western media is something that those who live in the West have to some extent become used, if not immune, to. The shock to a closed society, unused to any form of advertising other than centrally directed political propaganda, has been enormous.[12] The Soviet Union had, of course, already been opening to the West as a result of Gorbachev's 'new thinking' and desire to construct a 'common European home'. But the speed of the change is illustrated by the fact that the USSR had only opened economic discussions with the EC in November 1988, three years before its own demise. Avid Westernism was nevertheless the background popular attitude when the first economic reforms were being contemplated in post-Soviet Russia, and this undoubtedly made the prospect of 'shock therapy' more acceptable to the population at large than it otherwise might have been: after all, if the people wanted a Western way of life, why not adopt Western economic ways at all possible speed?

This first period of post-Soviet economic reform, described by one commentator as the 'romantic' or 'heroic' period,[13] was associated with Yegor Gaidar, the academic economist who was originally appointed Deputy Prime Minister in charge of economic reform in November 1991, then First Deputy PM in March 1992, and finally Acting PM from June until December 1992, when he was replaced by the former Soviet Minister for Energy Resources, Viktor Chernomyrdin, but reappointed as Deputy PM until resigning in January 1994, after his Russia's Choice party performed badly in the December 1993 elections. The 'heroic' period of reform was characterized not only by faith in the accelerated application of a Western-inspired model through 'shock therapy' but also by a parallel belief that the West would somehow step in to 'save Russia'.[14] The West was more cautious, preferring to channel much of its potential assistance (apart from short-term humanitarian aid) through the International Monetary Fund, which laid down stringent conditions for Russia, as it is obliged to do and indeed as it has done elsewhere (including Britain under the last Labour Government). 'Shock therapy' however took little account of Russia's cultural distinctiveness, and in particular of the 'insidious effect on the minds of men' of seven decades of communism.[15] It had proved impossible to develop the infrastructure necessary to boot the Russian economy into the 1990s in Shatalin's '500 days' despite, or perhaps because of, 'savage surgery on the body economic'.[16] Inspired by the ideas of another academic economist, Harvard's Professor Jeffrey Sachs (who had played an influential part in the economic reforms in Poland and Bolivia), Gaidar tried to push through the radical economic reforms that President Yeltsin had omitted to gain a democratic mandate for when he failed to capitalize on his immediate post-*Putsch* success and call elections in the autumn of 1991.[17] Given the historical peculiarities of Russia, especially the importance of both religion and nationalism in its culture, and given the lack of democratic experience, this omission proved politically fatal to the policy of 'shock therapy' and highly damaging to the actual process of reform.[18] While the population certainly wanted a Western standard of living for themselves and what they regarded as a 'normal life' for their country, they were ill-prepared for the devastating effects of the transition to a market economy: inflation destroyed their savings and price liberalization reduced their living standards, so that the overwhelming majority of the Russian population was deemed to be living at or below the poverty level.[19] Privatization led all too often to the emergence of a subclass of *mafiosi*, and Russia seemed to have acquired – rather too rapidly for comfort – the disadvantages of the Western way of life, such as a rapidly rising crime rate, without the advantages, while simultaneously losing the advantages of 'prison life' in the former Soviet Union.

Whatever the fate of Russia's reforms, Sachs manfully struggled to persuade Western governments that the cost of those reforms could not be met from Russia's own current resources and therefore necessitated a significant infusion of funds from outside.[20] Speaking in November 1992, Sachs called the West's reluctance to meet the challenge 'tragic' and Bush's foreign policy 'vacuous', warning of 'Weimarization', the creation of conditions similar to those that brought Hitler to power in Germany six decades earlier:

> The stakes are huge. History shows that hyperinflation usually leads to violence in one form or another. The Weimar Republic is just one example.
>
> In Chile hyperinflation led to a military take-over. In Argentina it resulted in a civil war. In Russia it is particularly worrying. We are talking about a country with thousands of nuclear warheads, chemical weapons, simmering ethnic problems and a lack of social consensus. . . . Russia is at an extremely dangerous juncture. . . . The West has left the reformers dangling out there by themselves.[21]

It has to be said that, under both the Bush and Clinton administrations, American policy towards Russia has been somewhat lacking in what Bush so characteristically called 'the vision thing', and there can be little doubt, given the nature and scale of the problems, that, even in purely economic terms, Sachs was absolutely right. But economic reform on this scale has also to be a political process, and the immediate, short- and medium-term dislocation caused by economic reform would have been more palatable to the Russian electorate had there been, or seemed to be, some light at the end of the tunnel. This is not merely a matter of the scale and nature of the aid granted but, more importantly in political terms, a matter also of coalition-building and presentation. Had Western aid been packaged along the lines of US aid to Europe under the Marshall Plan, it might well have been that the darkness in the tunnel of economic and social dislocation would have been more tolerable, its rationale more widely understood.[22] Growing disillusionment with the West, and with the Western model, has led increasingly to an examination of alternatives.

Just before Gaidar's replacement by Chernomyrdin, Arkadi Volsky, the leader of Chernomyrdin's Civic Union grouping (a coalition of former Soviet industrial managers), was dismissive of Western advisers:

> Most of them are Americans. Just one model for imitation has been chosen – call it the Anglo-Saxon model. But the reason why the Russian eagle is two-headed is that only one of its heads looks to the West. The other looks to the East.[23]

Volsky went on to dream of importing the Chinese model, combining economic reform with continued espousal of socialism, but such dreams have so far found little resonance among the public, and even less among the experts. If Russia were to look East, the post-1945 Japanese model might be more pertinent, but it has been largely ignored.

In the period since Gaidar's resignation as Acting PM in December 1992 there has been little improvement in the economic situation. In 1994 Russian industrial output fell by 21 per cent and by the end of the year stood at 45 per cent of its 1991 level. Gross domestic product was estimated to have fallen by 15 per cent and overall capital investment by 27 per cent, while inflation was running at an annual level of 320 per cent. The gap between the rich and poor was growing dramatically wider: Russian Economics Ministry statistics suggested that the top 10 per cent of the population were earning fourteen times the income of the poorest 10 per cent, compared to a ratio of 5:4 in 1991. It is small wonder that the Economics Minister, Yevgeni Yasin, remarked in December 1994 that Russia could soon face a stark choice between war or reform.[24]

The growing belief that Russia is heading for some kind of civil unrest and violent confrontation may well, of course, become a self-fulfilling prophecy. It is not, however, a new prophecy and, given the enormity of the problems Russia faces, it is perhaps surprising that the prophecy has not so far (with the exception of Chechnya) been fulfilled. In February 1994 the commentator Andrei Bystritsky argued that 'Russia is quite unable to decide what exactly it is doing: is it leaving the past behind it, or moving towards the future?'[25] Bystritsky claimed that:

> nobody is governing Russia. We are experiencing an elemental process of the self-organisation of society, even in criminal forms. In this process we also see reflected the fundamental conflict between the forces of civilisation and anti-civilisation, between those who see Russia as belonging to the European and Christian nations and those whose inclination is to cling parasitically to the idea of Russian exclusivity. . . . Russia's key problem remains infantilism, and this involves not just the population at large but also the élites in our society. As before, the intelligentsia and the democrats feel themselves to be aliens in this society and, as before, they are afraid of their own people.[26]

Bystritsky has here put his finger on two parallel but related themes: is Russia a Western or European (in the Western sense) country or does she have a unique mission? What is, or should be the role of that peculiarly Russian social stratum, the intelligentsia, in the transformation of the country? These are themes that have haunted Russian political thought since its effective beginnings after the failure of the Decembrist Uprising of a small group of noblemen in 1825. They find their roots in the ambiguous works of the writer Peter Chaadayev.

In the first of a series of *Lettres philosophiques*, written in French (then still the language of much Russian intellectual discourse) in 1829 and first published in 1836, Chaadayev argued that Russia's allegiance to 'miserable Byzantium' had cut her off from mainstream cultural and historical developments in Europe and left her with an inorganic culture based entirely on the wholesale appropriation of the superficial products of other cultures. Russians were:

> like illegitimate children, without a heritage, without a link with those who have lived on earth before us, we have in our hearts none of those lessons learned before we came into being . . . we are, in a certain sense, strangers to ourselves. . . . This is a natural consequence of a culture based entirely on importation and imitation. . . . Since we take only ready-made ideas, the indelible trace that is left in men's minds by the progressive development of ideas and that gives those ideas their strength does not impinge upon our intelligence. We grow, but we do not mature; we advance, but obliquely, i.e. in a way that leads nowhere. We are like children who have not learned to think for themselves; when they become men, they have nothing of their own.[27]

Chaadayev was detained as a lunatic (another precedent) and recanted somewhat in his *Apologie d'un fou* [*The Apology of a Madman*], written and published in 1837. While drawing the same conclusions about Russia's past, Chaadayev was now more optimistic about the country's future. He saw strength in the fact that Peter the Great had found Russia to be a 'blank sheet of paper': Russia's past isolation from the West meant that she had no historical baggage to restrain her. Russia was therefore 'called upon to resolve the greater part of the social problems, to perfect the greater part of the ideas that have emerged in older societies, to pronounce judgement on the most serious questions that preoccupy mankind'.[28] Here Chaadayev was drawing on a long tradition of Russian Messianism, stretching back to the notion of Moscow as the 'Third Rome' following the fall of Byzantium to the Turks in 1453. This was the special role destined for Russia by providence: it was her *mission civilisatrice*. Untainted by the West, Russia could become the bearer of some new historical truth that would propel mankind towards the next stage in its progress.

If we can see in the *Lettre philosophique* the origins of the Westernizing tendency in subsequent Russian political thought, we can see in the

Apologie the origins of the Slavophile tendency, which opposed and contradicted it, and in both we can see the basic framework that has shaped all subsequent debates about Russia's historical destiny and her future role in the world. Ever since, these debates have been carried on by the Russian intelligentsia, which has played a unique and distinctive role in Russian history.

The nineteenth-century lexicographer, Vladimir Dal, defined the intelligentsia as 'the rational, educated, intellectually developed part of the population',[29] and that is how it emerged in the 1860s. In a country where poverty, ignorance, illiteracy and the other symptoms of cultural backwardness were widespread, it rapidly became a self-conscious and self-identifying cultural and *political* force. Mikhail Berg has recently argued that:

> for a *true intelligent* it is not action but contemplation and advocacy that are canonic distinguishing features. . . . The *intelligent* above all else has taught, educated, enlightened himself, as if he were preparing himself for his future and extremely important activity.

He also remarked, 'How much copy has been expended . . . to prove that the intelligentsia exists only in Russia, and that *over there in the West* they have only intellectuals and professionals, while here we have our "speaking conscience".' The Russian intelligentsia has played a particularly significant part in the political history of the country because it:

> has been an intermediary . . . between the people, whom it has perceived in a fairly mythologized way, and the government, which, however strange it might seem, has always approached its own people (and indeed itself) in a more sober fashion than has the Russian [*rossiiskaia*] intelligentsia.[30]

Although it was theoretically possible for someone from the people [*narod*] to become an *intelligent*, through the process of self-conscious self-enlightenment that Berg describes, the people and the intelligentsia *as social entities* were, and still are, seen as discrete.

The writer Anatoli Utkin has taken this argument further. Citing Disraeli's notion of 'two nations', Utkin maintained:

> But the British Prime Minister was talking of the rich and poor in England. In Russia, however, the two nations were the vehicle of Western civilisation, on the one hand, and the followers of Byzantium, of Asia, the masses who had lost touch with their Kievan inheritance, on the other.
>
> The pride of Russia – its intelligentsia – never recognised itself for what it in fact was: a pro-Western intellectual élite, selfless and almost regarding its alienation from the people as a natural state of affairs. . . .

. . . the Romanov dynasty created only a thin stratum of Westernised aristocracy, mainly a military élite, whose recognition by the people depended on immediate practical results. When these results proved lamentable there arose . . . the question of two peoples within one, two cultures within the confines of a single nation. The small pro-Western élite itself realised how small its internal base was, how far removed were the masses of the people, living their own lives, from the glittering 'citizens of the world' of the two capital cities.[31]

Other writers have extended this divide to a broader one between the centre and the provinces in general. The historian Mikhail Korablev described Russia as:

a country which, if you leave the capital and a few large cities aside, has made no progress whatsoever in its democratic development. The former Party *nomenklatura*, together with young careerists who more often than not do not even pretend to be democrats, hold the provinces firmly in their hands. . . . The local administration . . . is composed of 99.9 per cent members of the former Party and economic *nomenklatura* who, as before, take bribes, build themselves houses, make fun of honest and principled people and at the same time call themselves the democratic power.[32]

Bystritsky however took a more optimistic view. Describing the Russians as 'inclined to the contemplative', he argued that, in this division between the intelligentsia and the people, it was the intelligentsia that in post-Soviet Russia had let the people down. In June 1994, he argued that 'The élite has proved itself to be incapable of making a significant effort and is now isolated from the people. But it is the people who are quietly, bit by bit, building a new country.'[33] He went on:

The tragedy is that in Russia there is no democratic state capable of standing up for democracy, and our society is only in the process of for-mation. . . . Russia is short of leaders of the calibre of the founding fathers of the United States. These leaders need to combine willpower, reason, strong convictions, faith and political talent. Russia is ready for a decisive leap into the future.[34]

In the rest of this chapter I shall discuss the ideas of three people with aspirations to influence that 'decisive leap'. First, I propose to examine the ideas of one of the first people who could be said to have revived the notion of Russia's uniqueness: the writer, Alexander Solzhenitsyn, who in January 1974 had dismissed the Soviet intelligentsia as 'The Smatterers'.[35] Twenty years later he was equally dismissive:

Gorbachev proclaimed glasnost in order to use the intelligentsia of the capital against his own enemies in the *nomenklatura*. . . . Instead of more actively employing glasnost to purge the country of communism, the intelligentsia of the capital condemn one another, while the *nomenklatura* rub their hands and occupy the important positions.[36]

Exiled from the Soviet Union later in 1974, he returned to Russia in the summer of 1994 in a triumphal progress along the Trans-Siberian Railway from Vladivostok to Moscow, where he was hailed ecstatically as a possible 'future President of Russia'.[37] Although Solzhenitsyn's entire *oeuvre* may be seen as a political critique of the Soviet system, his first overtly political tract was *Letter to Soviet Leaders*, written in 1973 and published in the West shortly before his exile. This was followed in 1990 from that eventually American exile by his *Rebuilding Russia*, which laid out a programme for the renewal of Russia and its institutions.[38]

Envisaging a Russian Union [*Rossiiskii soiuz*], consisting of the three Slav republics – Great Russia, White Russia [Belarus] and Little Russia [the Ukraine] – and part or all of Kazakhstan[39] – Solzhenitsyn argued that the other republics should be allowed to secede because 'sharing a communal apartment can at times make life itself seem intolerable'.[40] 'But even then such an entity would contain a hundred different nationalities and ethnic groups'; however, the absence of the bitterness caused by the enforced sharing of the 'communal apartment' (which is, of course, also Iskander's 'prison'), would facilitate the consolidation of 'a fruitful commonwealth of nations, affirming the integrity of each culture and the preservation of each language',[41] a re-creation of what Solzhenitsyn saw as 'the peaceful coexistence of nationalities, that almost drowsy nonperception of distinctions that had virtually been achieved . . . in the final decades of pre-revolutionary Russia'.[42] He argued for the spiritual benefits of a reduced Russian state:

> The time has come for an uncompromising *choice* between an empire of which we ourselves are the primary victims, and the spiritual and physical salvation of our own people. . . . By separating off twelve [republics] . . . Russia will in fact free itself for a precious *inner* development.[43]

It is this inner development that lies at the heart of Solzhenitsyn's vision of Russia's future:

> The strength or weakness of a society depends more on the level of its spiritual life than on its level of industrialization . . . a tree with a rotten core cannot stand . . . because of all the possible freedoms the one that will inevitably come to the fore will be the freedom to be unscrupulous: that is the freedom that can be neither prevented nor anticipated by any law. . . . And that is why the destruction of our souls over three quarters of a century is the most terrifying thing of all.[44]

One might have expected Solzhenitsyn to allot a central role to the Orthodox Church in the moral and spiritual regeneration of his country, but he has been almost as scathing about the corruption of the Church as about the failings of the intelligentsia. In this respect he has echoed the Slavophiles' attacks on the servility of Church to state in tsarist Russia. Solzhenitsyn argued that the Church must 'free itself completely from the yoke of the state and . . . restore a living bond with the people'.[45] The widespread 'destruction of souls' during the Soviet era could only begin to be purged through a public repentance on the part of the Communist Party.[46] This theme has been taken up by subsequent writers, who have contrasted the de-Nazification programme in post-war Germany favourably with the failure to call those prominent in the Soviet régime to account, and indeed with the continuing privileged position of the former Soviet *nomenklatura* in post-Soviet Russia. Particular criticism has been levelled at the failure of the Supreme Court of the Russian Federation to try those involved in the August 1991 *Putsch*.[47] Paradoxically, perhaps, some writers have also warned of a continuing slide into anarchy that would provide a fertile breeding ground for the 'Weimar scenario': democracy would be undermined and fascism triumphant.[48]

Solzhenitsyn, however, has not bothered himself with these comparisons. Rather than human rights as the basis on which Russian society should be organized, he has instead proposed the idea that:

> A stable society is achieved not by balancing opposing forces, but by conscious self-limitation . . . for the freedom to seize things and gorge oneself is something even animals possess. Human freedom, in contrast, includes voluntary self-limitation for the sake of others.[49]

He therefore proposed that the future Russian state form should be highly decentralized, growing organically from the people [*narod*] up to those at the centre. He opposed the party system as manipulative and unrepresentative of public opinion: 'Party rivalry distorts the national will. The principle of party-mindedness necessarily involves the suppression of individuality, and every party reduces and coarsens the personal element. An individual will have views, while a party offers an ideology.'[50] Modern elections, dominated by the media, 'invariably entail the degradation of political thought'.[51] For Solzhenitsyn, as for many major Russian writers before him, democracy in the Western sense – including universal and equal suffrage, direct elections and the secret ballot – represents the tyranny of the minority over the majority in the name of the majority.[52] In the light of the Soviet experience of party government that view is perhaps understandable.

What then to put in its place? Arguing that, 'For a given people, with its specific geography, history, traditions and psychological make-up, the task is to set in place a structure that will lead to a flourishing of this people rather than its decline and degeneration',[53] Solzhenitsyn proposed the notion of 'the democracy of small areas'.[54] The dominance of the capital(s) over the provinces had to be broken: 'Our country will not be able to lead a full and independent life unless there emerge perhaps forty centres of vitality and illumination throughout the breadth of the land.'[55] 'Democracy must be built from the bottom up. . . . Democracy becomes genuinely effective where citizens' assemblies can appropriately take the place of assemblies of representatives.'[56] He suggested a development of the pre-Revolutionary *zemstvo* upwards from the local to the national level.[57] This would ensure the necessary degree of organicity that has been so central to proponents of Russia's uniqueness. To a non-Russian such proposals might seem at best eccentric and at worst extreme, but they do fall within a Russian tradition that stretches back to the early mediaeval *veche*, or popular assembly, which ruled Novgorod and other Russian cities, and which Solzhenitsyn cited as a useful precedent and proof that Russia has its own organic democratic traditions. He defined democracy as 'a system under which the people [*narod*] determine their own fate. Democracy requires enormous efforts. It is not the easiest way of governing. It requires willpower and obedience to the law.'[58]

In his speech to the State Duma on 28 October 1994, televised live throughout Russia, Solzhenitsyn reiterated many of the points made in *Rebuilding Russia* and elsewhere. But he also attacked the pace and scale of the privatization programme, especially that of land: 'Selling land at auction to precocious *nouveaux-riches* means selling Russia itself. The rest will become hired labourers [*batraki*]. But a country of farm labourers will never become a democracy.'[59] He also reminded his audience, which of course included representatives of the government, the former Communist Party, and Zhirinovsky's Liberal Democratic Party of Russia: 'Power is not a reward, it is not food for personal ambition. Power is a heavy burden. It is a responsibility, a duty and hard, hard work. And until those in power recognise this, Russia will not find wellbeing.'[60]

The really eccentric, if not actually extreme, aspect of Solzhenitsyn's proposals lies in the fact that he devoted *no attention whatsoever* to Russia's foreign or security policy.[61] It is almost as if Russia were to return to the Middle Ages before the onslaught of the Tatar hordes, when Russia was the world and the world was Russia. The kind of decentralized Russia that Solzhenitsyn envisaged would either implode or explode from within or provide rich pickings for a variety of predatory neighbours. One does not have to be a Zhirinovsky to see this: power does, after all, abhor a vacuum.

The perceptive veteran dissident and Orientalist Grigori Pomerants has remarked:

I am worried that Solzhenitsyn loves the Russia that he perceives, his project for Russia, more than the individual Russian people who would like to stay in their apartments in Tashkent and Baku and do not aspire to become migrants, eking their existence from minuscule grants in the corridors of the local Russian authorities who have been sold out through and through. . . . But he can and must have a role as one of the leaders of our national dialogue.[62]

If there is to be a national dialogue in Russia, then there will have to be at least two sides to that dialogue. One parallel figure on the 'Westernizing' side is the distinguished and widely respected cultural historian from St Petersburg, Academician Dmitri Likhachev, who, like Solzhenitsyn and Pomerants, spent some years in the Gulag.[63] For Likhachev the role of the intelligentsia as a culture-bearing force has been crucial to Russia's historical development, even though he has shared the doubts expressed by others about its present and future potential.[64] While accepting Solzhenitsyn's idea that 'an *intelligent* is not just an educated person',[65] he argued that the intelligentsia was defined by its 'intellectual honesty':

> All *intelligenty* are to some extent 'creative' but, on the other hand, somebody who writes, teaches or creates works of art, but who does it to order, on the instructions and in the spirit of a party, a state or a client with an 'ideological proclivity', is not in my view in any way an *intelligent*, but a mercenary. . . . The basic principle of the intelligentsia is intellectual freedom, freedom as a moral category.[66]

That is why the intelligentsia was the prime target for the Bolshevik terror from the very first days of Soviet power.[67] But intellectual freedom is a product of what he called 'European education',[68] and this raises the central question of Russia's national identity:

> Is the intelligentsia a Western phenomenon or an Eastern one? The answer to this question depends upon whether we consider Russia to be the West or the East. One of the central pillars of the intelligentsia is the character of its education. For the Russian intelligentsia education has always been of a purely Western type.
> If Russia is the East – or even Eurasia[69] – then the Western European character of its education makes it easy to isolate the intelligentsia from the people, to justify to some extent the negative attitude towards it of Russia's ruling caste of semi-intelligentsia, of the half-educated and the trained. Is it not because of this, because of a desire to isolate the one from the other, that Eurasianism has in recent years taken on a dark and obscurantist character?
> In actual fact Russia is by no means Eurasia. If you look at Russia from the West, of course it lies between the West and the East. But this is a purely geographical – I might even say, 'cartographic' – point of view. The West is divided from the East by a difference in culture, not by a conditional frontier drawn upon a map. There is no doubt that Russia is European in both religion and culture. Moreover, in its culture you will find no great differences between St Petersburg in the West and Vladivostok in the East.

Russia is no more distinct in cultural terms from the countries of the West than they are from one another: England from France, or Holland from Switzerland. There are many cultures in Europe. The principal medium linking Russia to the West is, of course, the intelligentsia, although it is not alone.[70]

Elsewhere Likhachev has specifically rejected the notion of Russia's special mission. Bemoaning the tendency of the common people [*prostoliudin*] towards gullibility, Likhachev argued:

Why does a country with such a large population and such a great culture find itself in such a tragic position? Tens of millions of people shot and tortured, dying of hunger and perishing in a 'victorious' war. A country of heroes, martyrs and . . . prison warders. Why?

Once again some people are searching for a special 'mission' for Russia. This time the most widely held belief is that old but 're-worked' idea: Russia is fulfilling its own mission to protect the world from the disaster of artificial state and social formations, and demonstrate the impracticality, and even the catastrophic nature, of socialism – on which rested the hopes of 'forward-looking' people, especially in the nineteenth century. I refuse to believe in even a hundredth or a thousandth part of the beneficence of this 'mission'.

Russia had and has no special mission![71]

Likhachev has, as we have seen, also rejected the notion of Eurasianism as a solution to the problem of Russia's post-Soviet national identity, deriding it as the product of Russian *émigré* thinkers:

seduced by the simple solution of the complex and tragic problems of Russian history, proclaiming Russia to be a special organism, a special territory, orientated principally towards the East, towards Asia, rather than to the West. From this they drew the conclusion that European laws were not written for Russia and Western norms and values had no relevance to her whatsoever.[72]

Likhachev's attitude towards Asia is that of the traditional Westernizer: Russia has received its culture largely from Europe and in turn used that predominantly Western culture to civilize parts of Asia. 'There is extremely little of the real East in Russian culture', and what there is has entered Russia's 'cultural sphere' [*kul'turosfera*] from Western European culture 'which preserves within it all the cultures of the past and present. . . . European culture is a culture that is common to all mankind. And we, belonging to the *culture of Russia*, should belong to the *culture of all mankind* through the fact that we belong to *European culture*.' Russians, therefore, 'should be *Russian Europeans*, if we want to understand the spiritual and cultural values of both Asia and the ancient world'.[73]

Like Solzhenitsyn, Likhachev has expressed regret at the passing of Russia's organic democratic institutions under the influence of Westernization and denied that tsarist Russia was a 'prison-house of the peoples'.[74] He has also sympathized with the idea that Russia must return to its roots in the small towns and the countryside, arguing that large cities are 'jungles of anticulture':

> We must not develop our culture by orientating it towards two or three gigantic cities, which have weak links with the rest of our 'backward' country. We must put a stop to the excessive expansion of cities like Moscow and St Petersburg for the further reason that in their concrete jungles anticulture is growing faster than culture itself.
>
> I must say that I place great hopes on the small Russian towns. In small towns people live more closely to one another, they are less spoiled, there our traditions are better preserved. And – and this is very important – there it is much more obvious 'who is who'.[75]

But Likhachev has gone further than Solzhenitsyn in advocating the actual construction 'of a chain of small towns between Moscow and Petersburg, linked to one another by a high-speed motorway', even though this might appear to contradict his advocacy of the small-scale urban and rural ways of life.[76] Unlike Solzhenitsyn, and more consistently with that vision, Likhachev has openly proclaimed that 'religion must be at the summit of culture'.[77] He sees religion not, as some have argued, as *Orthodoxy* – one of the factors dividing Russia from the West, but as *Christianity* – one of the factors making Russia indisputably European.[78]

The most original part of Likhachev's world view has been his attempt to question the prevailing East–West view of Russia's destiny. Instead he has tried to argue that Russia's history has been shaped by North–South factors:

> For Russia the main problem has always been that of the North and the South, rather than the West and the East, even in her wars in the Balkans, the Caucasus and Kazakhstan. For Russia the defence of Christianity was always the defence of European cultural principles: individual, personified, intellectual freedom.[79]

Russia, he has argued, is not 'Eurasia' but rather 'Scandoslavia':

> Russian culture is usually characterised as an intermediary between Europe and Asia, between the West and the East, but this frontier situation is apparent only if you look at Russia from the West. In actual fact the influence of nomadic Asian peoples in settled Rus was minute. Byzantine culture gave Rus its Christian spiritual character, while Scandinavia gave it its basic military arrangements.[80]

It is the strength of a country's culture and the depth to which that culture penetrates among the mass of the population that protect the country from the dangers of totalitarianism:

Culture is a complex concept with many levels. Culture penetrates all aspects of the life of a country: the way we behave on the street, how we preserve and study our cultural treasures, our attitude towards science (especially our basic knowledge), the level of our television programmes and, of course, literature and art. The various elements of culture develop in different ways. Whereas in matters of 'high' culture we are on the level of the world's best achievements, in terms of every-day ordinary culture we are behind many civilised countries. We must not idolise the common people: despite all their outstanding qualities, they frequently display a tendency towards all sorts of extremes, towards anarchistic principles, hooliganism, scandal – doesn't this to some extent explain Zhirinovsky's success? In part this is today's reaction to seven decades of boring, regimented life.[81]

Earlier in 1994 Likhachev had called upon the Russian people to recognize the strengths that underlay their 'thousand-year culture':

The Russians are prepared to risk what they value most, they are reck-less in realising their intentions and ideas. They are prepared to starve, to suffer, even to go as far as self-immolation (as did hundreds of Old Believers) because of their faith, their convictions, because of an idea. And this did not just happen in the past – it is happening now. (Surely the voters did not really believe in the unrealistic promises of Zhirinovsky, who now sits in the State Duma?)

We Russians must at last find the right and the strength to take upon ourselves the responsibility for the present, to decide our policy our-selves – in culture, in economics, in state law – relying on real facts, real traditions, and not on the various kinds of prejudice associated with Russian history, on myths about the universal historical 'mission' of the Russian people and on its supposed destiny because of mythic suppositions about some kind of particularly difficult heritage of slavery, which never was, or of serfdom, which many did endure, on a supposed absence of 'democratic traditions', which we did in fact have, on the supposed absence of entrepreneurial qualities, of which we had more than enough (the opening up of Siberia alone is proof of that), etc., etc. Our history is no worse, and no better, than that of other nations.

We must ourselves take responsibility for our own current situation, we are responsible before Time and must not dump everything on to our forefathers, who deserve every respect and honour, but, in so doing, we must, of course, take account of the serious consequences of the communist dictatorship.

We are free – and for that very reason we have responsibilities.[82]

While both Solzhenitsyn and Likhachev, with their differing visions of Russia, its identity, and its relationship with the West, might lay claim to the intelligentsia role of 'conscience of the nation', there is another man in Russia who also has a vision. He is a populist, a demagogue who has set himself up as a tribune of the people, and with some considerable success: Vladimir Zhirinovsky.

Zhirinovsky has been all too easily dismissed as a comic clown, but a politician who, in the desperate circumstances of post-Soviet Russia, climbs from gaining 7.8 per cent of the votes cast in the presidential elections of June 1991 to 24 per cent in the elections to the State Duma in December 1993 could well turn out to be a tragic clown instead. Zhirinovsky has also been described as a 'fascist' but that term has been so abused that in this case it is less than helpful. Although the party that he leads is rather curiously called the Liberal Democratic Party of Russia (LDPR), Zhirinovsky himself claims to be a 'National Socialist', which signifies that he represents the 'philosophy of the man in the street', a philosophy 'that Hitler has discredited'. Zhirinovsky's *Weltanschauung* is laid out in his book *The Last Thrust to the South*, published by the LDPR in 1993, and augmented by press reports of his various outbursts in Russia and around the world.[83] As one Russian observer has remarked:

> A politician of Zhirinovsky's type does not have to worry about making precise predictions: if he doesn't win, nobody will ask any questions, because he is not in power; if he does win, the same situation will arise, because nobody will be able to ask questions any more.[84]

The key to Zhirinovsky's outlook lies in his account of his own life, which is spattered with inconsistencies and contradictions and infused with self-pity and self-delusion; the major part of his book transposes these attributes on to a view of the situation of Russia itself. Born and brought up in what was then Alma Ata, the capital of the Kazakh Soviet Socialist Republic, he claims to have felt isolated: 'Alma Ata was a Eurasian city. There was almost nothing Asiatic about it but geographically you have to think of it as Asia. 4,000 kilometres from Moscow to the southeast. China and India were closer to us than Moscow.'[85] He grew up surrounded by Kazakhs who were allegedly given privileged access to better housing, better jobs, better education. This increased his isolation: 'From the moment of my birth I went everywhere on my own, alone, stopping at nothing, pushing ahead. And I always felt angry, bitter, dissatisfied, because I never experienced happiness, any happiness at all.'[86] He saw in his own experience a microcosm of the experience of the Russian [*russkii*] people as a whole:

> A whole life of humiliation and suffering. This, evidently, was the state of the whole nation. . . . First of all the Tsar and the Russian Empire, then Revolution and Civil War, then the Great Patriotic War,[87] always travelling from one place to another, always formalities, passports, permits, always being told you can or you can't. Transported across

the country from Europe to Asia, people died before their time. Whole lives were spent travelling. Changing cities, changing flats. . . . We put the entire nation on wheels. The whole Russian people on carts, jingling along dirt-tracks and over potholes. The entire twentieth century. We went into space and we beat the Germans. But we destroyed all our families, all our roots, we lost all our archives, all our family links. How many people were uprooted, how many lost? But how good everything was at the beginning of the century. The Russian Empire.[88]

Although Zhirinovsky has made no attempt to pass himself off as an *intelligent*, he has presented himself as a man with an education in the humanities (as opposed to the technocrats who ran the Soviet Union), who has thought carefully about the major issues in world politics:

> there has always been a foreign element in my life; since childhood I have been surrounded by the representatives of various nations. For that reason I am well aware of other cultures, other civilisations, other psychologies. I cannot be some kind of blinkered chauvinist, limited by national horizons. I am in favour of the broadest possible development – the main thing is that there should be no enmity, no domination by one nation, no discrimination. . . . My planetary *Weltanschauung* is that we are all citizens of a single planet.[89]

This led on eventually to an expression of faith in pluralism,[90] yet in the previous breath he had complained about having to share a room in a student hostel 'with a Frenchman, while for a whole year I had to share with a Mongol'.[91] This contradiction is typical: Zhirinovsky has borrowed ideas, consciously or unconsciously, from a variety of diverse sources and thrown them together into a hotchpotch that does not bear close examination. From Solzhenitsyn comes this notion: 'Politics, which involves the lives of millions of people, is the most responsible work: it is impossible to imagine anything more responsible.'[92] Having 'reached an understanding of the causes of the deep processes of political life and of the turning points in the state', having 'acquired a vast sum of knowledge',[93] Zhirinovsky claimed that, by the time that Gorbachev came to power:

> I had already begun to work out my own geopolitical conception. I do not want to give it my name, for example 'the Zhirinovsky formula', but the last 'thrust' to the South, Russia's outlet on to the shores of the Indian Ocean and the Mediterranean, is really a matter of the salvation of the Russian nation. When other parties speak about cutting off Kazakhstan, Kyrgyzia, Central Asia, they do not realise that we are driving Russia into the tundra, where there is nothing but mineral resources, where nothing can live or grow. The development of civilisation has always begun in the South.[94]

Conversely, Zhirinovsky argued elsewhere that 'All Russia's misfortunes are in the South.'[95] Likhachev would not agree with either of these statements, even though he has argued the case for the North–South divide, while in the 1970s Solzhenitsyn argued the opposite, seeing the mineral resources and empty spaces of what he termed Russia's 'North-East' as 'Russia's hope for winning time and winning salvation', a future 'centre of national activity and settlement and a focus for the aspirations of young people'.[96]

Like both Solzhenitsyn and Likhachev, however, Zhirinovsky has regretted the historical rupture in Russia's organic development:

> the too rapid Europeanisation of Russia had both positive and negative consequences. The destruction of the traditions of the patriarchal Russian family also had negative consequences. Drunkenness and binge-ing probably date from Peter the Great's time. And smoking and other attributes of European life. That is why, as well as civilisation, Europe also brought elements of corruption to Russia. After all, under Stalin we were a closed country. For instance, we were almost completely free of venereal disease.[97]

The new Russia, in Zhirinovsky's view, will be like the old Russian patriarchal family. There will be no divisive internal frontiers, there will be cultural, linguistic, political and religious pluralism, there will be security and stability because this will be the last division of the world, the end of history:

> We stand in the South, but it is volatile, inflammable, rebellious. . . . Mankind will not permit constant war to the South of Russia. . . . For this reason the last 'thrust' to the South will also exclude the possibility of a third world war. This will mean not merely the resolution of Russia's internal problems and the pacification of the peoples of this region from Kabul to Istanbul. It will mean the resolution of a global task of planetary significance. . . .
>
> The last 'thrust' to the South. I can see Russian soldiers washing their boots in the warm waters of the Indian Ocean and forever wearing summer uniform. Lightweight shoes, lightweight trousers, short-sleeved shirts, with an open collar and no tie, lightweight forage caps. And the compact modern Russian sub-machine-gun . . . so that a platoon of Russian soldiers can enforce order anywhere.[98]

In this paradise on earth, there would be a single economic, judicial and political space in which all could live freely: 'where there was a compact Muslim population they could keep their own customs and possibly even retain polygamy, with women wearing the veil and houses divided into male and female quarters.'[99] Zhirinovsky too is an advocate of the joys of small-town living: 'We do not need vast metropolises. Let there be small towns convenient to live in. . . . This is the cure that we need.'[100]

City-states would be spread across the land. It would be a 'multilingual world' but nevertheless, 'It would be easier for everybody to speak Russian than to learn five languages. And in this new space, right up to the shores of the Indian Ocean, everyone would speak Russian.'[101]

> This would be a purification for us all. And the sound of the bells of the Russian Orthodox Church on the shores of the Indian Ocean and the Mediterranean would proclaim peace to the peoples of this region, brotherhood . . . prosperity, tranquillity, the end of any military conflicts and interethnic clashes. . . . Russia will only be doing what she is destined for, she will be fulfilling her historic mission – to free the world from wars, which always begin in the South. And this plan – the last 'thrust' to the South – is . . . determined by Russia's destiny. Otherwise Russia itself will not be able to develop but will perish; we shall be crammed with nuclear power stations and nuclear weapons, which will eventually explode and destroy the entire planet. . . . If we do not pacify this region, unrest, corruption, disease and war will increase and engulf the whole of Russia.[102]

Russia's interests in a last 'thrust' to the South are, in Zhirinovsky's view, part of a global arrangement:

> The idea of a world government is fallacious. Regional collaboration is better. On the North–South principle. If our paths cross again, we shall start to interfere with one another once again. We must come to an agreement and we must hope that this will be a worldwide agreement that we should divide the entire planet into spheres of economic influence and action along North–South lines. The Japanese and the Chinese will cover Southeast Asia, the Philippines, Malaysia, Indonesia, Australia. Russia will deal with its South: Afghanistan, Iran, Turkey. Western Europe will turn to its South, the continent of Africa. And, last of all, Canada and the USA will have the whole of Latin America to their South. This will all be done on an equal footing. Nobody will be privileged. The direction will be one and the same – to the South.[103]

In Zhirinovsky's view, this division of the world will enable Germany to 'restore East Prussia at the expense of Poland, or parts of it. And possibly take parts of Moravia from the Czechs.'[104] Germany's labour shortage could be solved by the return of Russia's 2–3 million Germans.[105] France would also benefit: 'We could help it to free itself from US and Zionist influence. Otherwise the French capital will be an Arab city. Because on the quiet the Algerians are taking over Paris and moving on. Europe needs our help.'[106] Elsewhere – and this is even more revealing of Zhirinovsky's amateurishness in foreign affairs – 'South Africa will receive a guarantee that there will be a White Republic in Southern Africa.'[107] Russia will have a special place in this scheme of things: 'We could resolve all these problems for our Western and Eastern, and our Southeastern, neighbours, but only on one condition – that Russia gets what it needs'[108] because 'The world should be grateful to Russia for its role as saviour.'[109] Zhirinovsky is by no means unique in arguing that the world owes Russia an unpaid debt for saving European civilization from, first, the Mongol Horde; second, the Turks (for whom he reserves particular bile: 'Nothing would happen to the world if the entire Turkish nation were wiped out. Proportionately the Turks have brought as much evil to the world as the Germans. But the Germans, their Party and their ideology were brought to trial. . . . Nobody has punished the Turks');[110] and third, the Nazis. 'Russia is fated to a great historical mission. Perhaps it will be the last.'[111] This time, this final time, Russia will be rewarded for its sacrifices: 'Russia will in part become once more a single-storeyed country: cottages, saunas, garages, country houses, gardens. These provide better living conditions than those stone jungles, those concrete blocks.'[112] 'It is not necessary to promise "pineapples in champagne", but we can promise a quiet life, a life of satisfaction. . . . I think the pensioner will support us, his mind will be at ease.'[113]

> You would know that wherever you walked, whether you were visiting friends or at work, nobody would be breaking into your apartment, nobody would be raping your daughter, she would grow up in peace and marry, and you would know that your son would not be killed or maimed, either by local hooligans in the street, or in the army, or on a business trip, or while he was away on holiday, especially in the South – all these would be the attributes of the state in which you would be living.[114]

'The warm breath of the ocean would calm everyone who lived in this new geopolitical space, within these new frontiers of Russia.'[115]

The attractions of law and order as a political platform are not, of course, confined to Russia, and Zhirinovsky offers an idyll that has proved seductive to an electorate experiencing deprivations and tribulations on a scale previously unknown in Europe in peacetime. He appeals to a Messianic tradition, to the notion of Russia's special mission and historic destiny, to a sense of self-pity and self-justification, to a longing for peace, prosperity and what so many Russians call 'a normal life', even thought they have never experienced it. Zhirinovsky has a dream, which, like most dreams, is based partly on reality, partly on perceptions of reality, and partly on fantasy and wish-fulfilment. He has been able to manipulate the media to great effect, running what was generally regarded as the slickest television campaign in the December 1993 elections.[116] His appeal has been to the downtrodden and oppressed and to the infinitely greater number of Russians who feel themselves to be downtrodden and oppressed. To them it does not matter that the 'Zhirinovsky phenomenon', as the Russian press called it, offered a programme that was at best inconsistent and at worst incoherent, a programme that could only be realized through a third world war that would obliterate everything that they hold dear.

The war in Chechnya has offered the West a further reason (or excuse) for procrastination in its efforts to support and strengthen the reform process in Russia. As at April 1995 nobody knows what the long-term consequences for Russia's domestic politics of that originally profoundly unpopular campaign will be. Zhirinovsky was the only major party leader to support Yeltsin in what may well turn out to be his own last 'thrust' to the South. Zhirinovsky's reasons were clear: Chechnya represented in microcosm all the problems emanating for Russia from the South and stood geographically on one path to the Indian Ocean. Chechnya may well do for Yeltsin and his faltering reform programme what Afghanistan did for the Soviet system. But Chechnya may not benefit Zhirinovsky. If the effect of the war is to persuade Russian mothers that their sons should never again die in a 'foreign' land – and there is considerable evidence that this may be the case – Chechnya may finally bury Russia's 'imperial' ambitions.[117] But equally, it may not persuade the Russians to turn back to the 'Western model', to 'democracy', privatization and the market economy.[118] The long-delayed release in March 1995 of IMF funds may have come too late, and the legacy of the 'Zhirinovsky phenomenon' may persuade the electorate to reject what it might regard as economic colonization by the West. It may turn Russia, for once, to the 'real' East, to the 'Asiatic' model of development, combining rapid modernization and computerization with authoritarian social and political structures. One obvious model, at least to Western analysts, is Japan, but Japan is unlikely to offer the necessary economic support until the problem of the Kurile Islands (to the Japanese, the Northern Territories) is solved, which currently seems highly improbable. South Korea provides another possible model, and certainly has the necessary surplus resources, but those could well be diverted in the very near future to the development of a reunited North Korea. There are, however, powerful cultural and historical reasons why the Russians will never look to the 'real' East for their paradigms: they have always regarded themselves as bulwarks of European civilization against Asia, as bearers of Western cultural values to the East. As Likhachev has argued, the notion of East and West depends very much on where you are standing. In the Russian East–West debate, East does not mean what we in Western Europe would call the Far East: after all, Russia itself, in the far reaches of Siberia, stretches further to the East than either China or Japan. East means Russia itself, whether defined geopolitically as Eurasia, or spiritually as the centre of Orthodox Christianity.

It has sometimes been stated anecdotally that, wherever you find four Russians, you will find at least five opinions. Likhachev remarked that:

The drama of Russian gullibility is deepened by the fact that the Russian mentality is not in the least bothered by everyday concerns, but strives to make sense of history and life, of everything that is happening in the world, in the most profound sense. The Russian peasant, sitting in front of his wooden house, will be discussing with his friends the fate of the Russian, the destiny of Russia. This is a normal occurrence, not an exception![119]

Whether Russia turns East or West, North or South is of crucial import-ance to Europe, but it may be a policy choice that Europe is no longer in a position to influence, perhaps even less to comprehend.[120] As Winston Churchill remarked in 1939: 'I cannot forecast to you the action of Russia. It is a riddle wrapped in a mystery inside an enigma.'[121]

FURTHER READING

J. Barber, 'Russia: A Crisis of Post-imperial Viability', *Political Studies*, vol. 42, Special Issue 1994: Contemporary Crisis of the Nation State?, pp. 34–51.

I. Bremmer and R. Taras (eds), *Nations and Politics in the Soviet Successor States*, Cambridge: Cambridge University Press, 1993.

G. Frazer and G. Lancelle, *Zhirinovsky: The Little Black Book*, Harmondsworth: Penguin, 1994.

E. Gellner, 'The Struggle to Catch up. Russia, Europe and the Enlightenment', *Times Literary Supplement*, 9 December 1994, pp. 14–15.

D. Likhachev, *Reflections on Russia*, Boulder, CO: Westview Press, 1991.

J. Löwenhardt, *The Reincarnation of Russia: Struggling with the Legacy of Communism*, Harlow: Longman, 1995.

R. Sakwa, *Russian Politics and Society*, London and New York: Routledge, 1993.

V. Solovyov and E. Klepikova, *Zhirinovsky: Russian Fascism and the Making of a Dictator*, Reading, MA: Addison-Wesley, 1995.

A. Solzhenitsyn, *Rebuilding Russia. Reflections and Tentative Proposals*, London: Harvill Press, 1991.

A. Solzhenitsyn, *The Russian Question at the End of the Twentieth Century*, London: Harvill Press, 1995.

NOTES

1 R. Sakwa, *Russian Politics and Society*, London and New York: Routledge, 1993, p. 39.

2 J. Dunlop, 'Russia: Confronting a Loss of Empire', in: I. Bremmer and R. Taras (eds), *Nations and Politics in the Soviet Successor States*, Cambridge: Cambridge University Press, 1993, p. 45.

3 Russia also had 90 per cent of the oil, 80 per cent of the natural gas, 70 per cent of the gold production and 62 per cent of the electricity production of the former USSR. Population figures from the 1989 census; all figures cited in Sakwa, pp. 38–41.

4 Figures from the 1989 census, cited in Sakwa (n. 1 above), p. 113.

5 See: A. Bystritsky, 'Rossiia: vyzov istorii' [Russia: The Summons of History], *Literaturnaia gazeta* (hereafter *LG*), 15 June 1994. However, the fact that a Russian *state* concept has preceded the development of a strongly defined *national* concept may make it easier to maintain an inclusive 'civic' notion of Russia as a nation state on the Western European pattern, rather than the exclusive 'ethnic' conception that has prevailed elsewhere in Eastern Europe.

6 This point is made by John Barber in: 'Russia: A Crisis of Post-imperial Viability', *Political Studies*, vol. 42, Special Issue 1994: *Contemporary Crisis of the Nation State?*, pp. 34–51, on p. 35.

7 This distinction dates from the late Soviet era in the excellent analysis by Roman Szporluk, 'Dilemmas of Russian Nationalism', *Problems of Communism*, July–August 1989, pp. 15–35. See also: J. Morrison, *Boris Yeltsin*, Harmondsworth: Penguin, 1991, pp. 131–4.

8 See, for instance: N. Moiseyev, 'Sumerki Rossii (Rassvet ili zakat? Rossiia na pereput'e)' [Russia's Twilight (Dawn or Sunset? Russia at the Crossroads)], *Polis. Politicheskie issledovaniia* [Polis. Political Research], 1993, no. 1, pp. 12–13.

9 B. Orlov, 'Kogda demokratiia prevrashchaetsia v fars' [When Democracy Turns into Farce], *LG*, 26 January 1994.

10 Iskander, interviewed in: 'Ne nado slishkom mnogogo zhdat' ot politiki' [We Shouldn't Expect Too Much from Politics], *LG*, 19 January 1994.

11 Ibid.

12 This point is made by Maria Rozanova in a round-table discussion: 'Pochemu my okazalis' porozn'?' [Why Have We Found Ourselves Apart?], *LG*, 2 March 1994.

13 Alexander Borin in conversation with Gaidar; 'Strashnyi soblazn tsentrizma' [The Terrible Temptation of Centralism], *LG*, 16 March 1994.

14 This reliance on the West also dates back to the late Soviet period; see, for example: Q. Peel, *Financial Times* (hereafter *FT*), 29 May 1990. For the post-*Putsch* continuation of the argument, see: A. Pankin, *FT*, 21 November 1991; J. Lloyd, *FT*, 23 November 1991; Ye. Gaidar, *FT*, 22 January, 5 February and 4 March 1992.

15 For a useful survey of the literature on shock therapy in Eastern Europe as a whole, see: A. Smith, 'Shock Therapy or Gradualism? Economic Controversies with Political Undercurrents', *Slavonic and East European Review*, vol. 72 (1994), no. 4, pp. 692–701. See also: M. Ellman, 'Shock Therapy in Russia: Failure or Partial Success?', *RFE/RL Research Report*, vol. 1, no. 34 (28 August 1992), pp. 48–61.

16 Q. Peel, 'Savage Surgery on the Body Economic', *FT*, 24 September 1990. The Shatalin plan was the most drastic of the economic reform proposals touted in the early 1990s and the inspiration for many of the policies adopted by Gaidar. See also this volume, Chapter 12.

17 Gaidar's policies were outlined in: 'Memorandum ob ekonomicheskoi politike Rossiiskoi Federatsii' [Memorandum on the Economic Policy of the Russian Federation], *Ekonomika i zhizn'* [Economics and Life], 1992, no. 10 (March).

18 See: J. Gray, *Post-Communist Society in Transition*, London: Social Market Foundation, 1994. Gray argues that the prevailing Western attitude has been 'not only intellectually indefensible; it is politically frivolous and dangerous in the highest degree'. Compare: J. K. Galbraith, 'Revolt in Our Time: The Triumph of Simplistic Ideology', in: G. Prins (ed.), *Spring in Winter: The 1989 Revolutions*, Manchester: Manchester University Press, 1990, pp. 1–12; S. Brittan, *FT*, 24 February 1994.

19 Alexander Solzhenitsyn, citing the newspaper *Argumenty i fakty*, in: 'Khochu vo vsem razobrat'sia sam' [I Want to Find Out Everything for Myself], *LG*, 13 July 1994. See also this volume, Tables 10.1–10.4 (pp. 194, 196, 201).

20 Once again the arguments go back to the late Soviet period; see: G. Allison and R. Blackwill, *Guardian*, 7 June 1991; H. Kopper, *FT*, 10 July 1991; R. Blackwill and W. Hogan, *International Herald Tribune* (hereafter *IHT*),

12 September 1991; A. Pankin, *FT*, 21 November 1991; L. Boulton, *FT*, 12 November 1992.

21 M. Campbell, *Sunday Times*, 15 November 1992.

22 See also: J. Sachs, 'The West Can Help the Soviets Democratize', *IHT*, 15 May 1991, and 'Lay out Reform Dollars for Soviet People', *IHT*, 16 May 1991; G. Tett, 'Harvard Economist Backs "Shock Therapy" for Russia', *FT*, 13 December 1991; J. Sachs and D. Lipton, 'Russia on the Brink', *FT*, 16 October 1992; J. Sachs, letter to *FT*, 22 November 1993; 'Reform's Setback in Russia Indicts an Arrogant IMF', *IHT*, 24 January 1994; and 'Russia: IMF Gives Too Little, Too Late', *FT*, 31 January 1994.

23 Volsky, cited in: Campbell (n. 21 above).

24 Data cited in: J. Thornhill, *The Times*, 1 January 1995. The continuing decline occurs after interpretations of the resurgence of reformed communists and the success of nationalist extremists in the December 1993 State Duma elections, such as that given by A. Kaletsky, *The Times*, 16 December 1993, who argued that 'From the strictly economic standpoint, the abyss does seem to have a bottom. The collapse in Russia's industrial and agricultural production is probably nearly over.'

25 A. Bystritsky, 'Kto upravliaet Rossiei?' [Who Governs Russia?], *LG*, 16 February 1994.

26 Ibid.

27 P. Chaadayev, '*Lettre première*', in: *Polnoe sobranie sochinenii i izbrannye pis'ma* [Complete Collected Works and Selected Letters], 2 vols, Moscow: Nauka, 1991, vol. 1, pp. 92–3.

28 Chaadayev, '*Apologie d'un fou*' in: *Polnoe sobranie*, p. 300.

29 V. Dal, *Tolkovyi slovar' zhivago velikorusskago iazyka* [Explanatory Dictionary of the Living Great-Russian Language], 2nd edn, St Petersburg: M. O. Vol'f, 1880–2 (reprinted, Moscow: Russkii iazyk, 1978–80), vol. 2, p. 46.

30 M. Berg, 'Provody mavra?' [Exit the Moor?], *LG*, 3 August 1994. I have used the Russian word *intelligent* to denote member of the *intelligentsia*, rather than the English word 'intellectual', because Berg and others make this distinction themselves.

31 A. Utkin, 'Dva naroda. Rossiia i Zapad' [Two Nations. Russia and the West], *Nezavisimaia gazeta*, 22 October 1993.

32 M. Korablev, 'I stanem kormit' krest'ianskikh detei . . .' [And We'll Start Eating Peasant Children . . .], *LG*, 23 February 1994.

33 Bystritsky (n. 5 above).

34 Ibid. See also Bystritsky, 'Kto . . .' (n. 25 above). Oleg Morozov developed a different critique, arguing that the Gaidar Government had been the first intelligentsia government in Russian history but that 'the Russian intelligentsia scarcely noticed this and did not value it'; O. Morozov, 'Tipazhi vlasti' [Stereotypes of Power], *LG*, 22 June 1994.

35 This is the title of one of the articles in: A. Solzhenitsyn *et al.* (eds), *From Under the Rubble*, New York: Little, Brown, 1975; paperback edn, Chicago, IL: Regnery Gateway, 1980. In this last edition the article appears on pp. 229–78. The book was first published in Russian in Paris: YMCA Press, 1974.

36 Solzhenitsyn, 'Khochu . . .' (n. 19 above).

37 V. Baskov, 'Vo chto oboidetsia Bi-bi-si etot voiazh?' [What Is this Trip Costing the BBC?] and O. Batalina, 'Demokratii sverkhu my ne dozhdemsia' [We Are Not Waiting for Democracy from Above], *LG*, 15 June 1994.

38 A. Solzhenitsyn, *Letter to Soviet Leaders*, London: Collins Harvill, 1974; *Rebuilding Russia. Reflections and Tentative Proposals*, London: Harvill, and

New York: Farrar, Straus & Giroux, 1991. Originally published as 'Kak nam obustroit' Rossiiu?' [How Can We Rebuild Russia?] in both *Komsomol'skaia pravda* (then the organ of the Communist Youth League) and *LG* in September 1990.

39 Solzhenitsyn notes that Kazakhstan has, since its establishment as a Union Republic in 1936, 'been transformed and built up by Russians, by inmates of forced-labour camps, and by exiled peoples. Today the Kazakhs constitute noticeably less than half the population of the entire inflated territory of Kazakhstan': *Rebuilding Russia*, p. 13. At the same time Solzhenitsyn is withering in his contempt for those who argue that the *Slav* republics of the Ukraine and Belarus should be separate: ibid., pp. 17–21. It is consistent with this position that he has said in 'Khochu . . .' (n. 19 above): 'Chechnya has every ground for separation: 80 per cent of the population there really are Chechens.'

40 Solzhenitsyn, *Rebuilding Russia* (n. 38 above), p. 12.

41 Ibid., p. 13.

42 Ibid., p. 11.

43 Ibid., p. 15.

44 Ibid., pp. 44–5.

45 Ibid., pp. 46–7.

46 Ibid., p. 29.

47 See, for instance: Orlov (n. 9 above), and: Iskander (n. 10 above). Another writer, Anatoli Krasikov, has cited the transition to democracy in Spain as a model for Russia: 'Ot Kremlia do Monkloa i obratno' [From the Kremlin to Moncloa and Back], *LG*, 27 April 1994.

48 See, for instance, A. Arbatov, 'Fashizm ne proshel, no demokratiia poterpela porazhenie' [Fascism Did Not Pass, But Democracy Suffered a Defeat], *Nezavisimaia gazeta*, 22 October 1993.

49 Solzhenitsyn, *Rebuilding Russia* (n. 38 above), p. 48. See idem, 'Repentance and Self-Limitation in the Life of Nations', *From Under the Rubble* (n. 35 above), pp. 105–43.

50 Solzhenitsyn, *Rebuilding Russia*, p. 70.

51 Ibid., p. 63.

52 Ibid., pp. 85–71.

53 Ibid., p. 54.

54 Ibid., p. 71–4.

55 Ibid., p. 37.

56 Ibid., pp. 71–2.

57 See also the discussion in *LG*, 23 February 1994, in which Yelena Panina, Chairperson of the Russian Zemstvo Movement, put the case for the *zemstvo* ('Rossiiu spasat' ne nuzhno' [Russia Does Not Need to Be Saved]), while the historian Mikhail Korablev accused her of 'caricaturing the past' and warned, 'While we are moved by the wisdom of the people, the mass goes and votes for Zhirinovsky' ('I stanem kormit' krest'ianskikh detei . . .' [And We'll Start Eating Peasant Children . . .] (n. 32 above)).

58 Solzhenitsyn, 'Khochu . . .' (n. 19 above).

59 'Odin den' Aleksandra Isaevicha' [One Day in the Life of Alexander Isayevich], *LG*, 2 November 1994. On the land question see also: *Rebuilding Russia* (n. 38 above), pp. 29–32.

60 'Odin den' . . .', ibid.

61 He did, however, mention Russia's international position almost in passing in: '"Russkii vopros" k kontsu XX veka' [The 'Russian Question' at the End

of the Twentieth Century], *Novyi mir*, 1994, no. 7, pp. 135–76. An English translation has been published by Harvill Press, London, 1995.

62 G. Pomerants, 'S nadezhdoi na dialog printsipov' [In Hope towards a Principled Dialogue], *LG*, 27 July 1994. See also his: 'Dialog natsii na granitse vekov' [Dialogue of the Nations at the Turn of the Century], *LG*, 9 October 1994.

63 Likhachev, who was born in 1906, can be seen reminiscing about his seven years in the far-northern ex-monastery of Solovki in Marina Goldovskaia's documentary film *Solovki Power* [Vlast' Solovetskaia], 1988. A collection of his earlier writings is available in English in: D. S. Likhachev, *Reflections on Russia*, ed. N. N. Petro, Boulder, CO: Westview Press, 1991. These were first published in part as 'Zametki o russkom' [Reflections on Russian], *Novyi mir*, 1980, no. 3, pp. 10–38.

64 D. S. Likhachev, 'O russkoi intelligentsii' [On the Russian Intelligentsia], *Novyi mir*, 1993, no. 2, p. 9, where he asked, 'Are we perhaps beginning, as we did before "in the Bolshevik style", to overestimate the intelligentsia and its role in the life of our peoples?'

65 Ibid., p. 3.

66 Ibid.

67 Ibid., pp. 5 and 7. Likhachev argued that the eminence of the pre-Revolutionary intelligentsia was such that in 1922 the Bolsheviks had to hire two steamships to carry into exile those members of the intelligentsia whose international reputations protected them against the Red terror.

68 Ibid., p. 4.

69 For the history of the 'Eurasian' interpretation of Russia's specific geopolitical imperative, see: M. Hauner, *What Is Asia to Us? Russia's Asian Heartland Yesterday and Today*, paperback edn, London and New York: Routledge, 1992.

70 Likhachev, 'O russkoi intelligentsii' (n. 64 above), p. 8.

71 Likhachev, 'Nel'zia uiti ot samykh sebia . . . Istoricheskoe samosoznanie i kul'tura Rossii' [We Cannot Escape from Ourselves . . . Historical Self-Awareness and the Culture of Russia], *Novyi mir*, 1994, no. 6, pp. 118–19.

72 Likhachev, 'Kul'tura kak tselostnaia sreda' [Culture as an Integral Milieu], *Novyi mir*, 1994, no. 8, p. 7.

73 Ibid., p. 8.

74 Likhachev, 'Nel'zia . . .' (n. 71 above), pp. 115 and 117.

75 Ibid.

76 Ibid.

77 D. Likhachev, 'Velikaia kul'tura primiritel'na po svoei puti . . .' [Great Culture Is Conciliatory in its Ways], *LG*, 13 April 1994.

78 Likhachev, 'O russkoi intelligentsii' (n. 64 above), p. 5.

79 Ibid., p. 6.

80 Likhachev, 'Nel'zia . . .' (n. 71 above), p. 113.

81 Likhachev, 'Velikaia kul'tura . . .' (n. 77 above).

82 Likhachev, 'Nel'zia . . .' (n. 71 above), p. 120.

83 V. Zhirinovsky, *Poslednii brosok na iug* [The Last Thrust to the South], Moscow: LDP, 1993. Extracts from this and various newspaper interviews are included in: G. Frazer and G. Lancelle, *Zhirinovsky: The Little Black Book*, Harmondsworth: Penguin, 1994. See also: A. Higgins, 'Rise and Rise of the Wild Man who Would Be Tsar', *Independent*, 15 December 1993; 'Sad Vlad, a Hitler with a Degree', *Independent*, 18 December 1993; M. Sutherland, 'The Right Image for Russia', *Independent*, 22 December 1993; P. Hobday, 'Eyeball to Eyeball with Mad Vlad in Moscow', *Observer Magazine*, 9 January

1994; A. Higgins, 'Vlad the Mad, and Dangerous', *Independent on Sunday Magazine*, 1 May 1994; A. Higgins, 'Zhirinovsky Plays to Gallery in Pyongyang', *Independent*, 4 October 1994. The notorious Zhirinovsky map of Europe was published as 'Le continent vu par Vladimir Jirinovski', *Le Monde*, 29 January 1994, while a text originally published in *Izvestiya* on 28 August 1993 was published in *Le Monde* on 23 December 1993.

84 Otto Lacis, adviser to President Yeltsin, *Izvestiya*, 28 August 1993 and *Le Monde*, 23 December 1993.

85 Zhirinovsky, *Poslednii brosok* (n. 83 above), p. 20.

86 Ibid., pp. 18–19.

87 The name by which the Soviet contribution to the Second World War effort was known in the former USSR.

88 Zhirinovsky (n. 83 above), pp. 19–20.

89 Ibid., p. 55. See also pp. 60–1.

90 Ibid., p. 81.

91 Ibid., p. 54.

92 Ibid., p. 58.

93 Both quotes from ibid., p. 62.

94 Ibid., pp. 63–4. There is, however, nothing new in the idea that Russia needed a warm-water port in the Indian Ocean; see: F. Kazemzadeh, *Russia and Britain in Persia, 1864–1914*, New Haven, CT: Yale University Press, 1968; and Hauner (n. 69 above), especially ch. 5.

95 Zhirinovskii (n. 83 above), p. 45.

96 Solzhenitsyn, *Letter to Soviet Leaders* (n. 38 above), pp. 27 and 32.

97 Zhirinovsky, *Poslednii brosok* (n. 83 above), p. 90. Stalin himself argued that Peter the Great had erred in allowing too many Western influences into Russia, while praising Ivan the Terrible for effectively cutting the country off; see: R. Taylor (ed.), *S. M. Eisenstein, Selected Works. Vol. 3: Writings, 1934–47*, London: British Film Institute, 1996.

98 Zhirinovsky, *Poslednii brosok* (n. 83 above), p. 66.

99 Ibid., pp. 66–7.

100 Ibid.

101 Ibid., pp. 76–7.

102 Ibid., pp. 75–7.

103 Ibid., pp. 71–2.

104 Ibid., p. 137.

105 Ibid., p. 138.

106 Ibid.

107 Ibid.

108 Ibid., p. 139.

109 Ibid., p. 124.

110 Ibid., pp. 130–1.

111 Ibid.

112 Ibid.

113 Ibid., p. 102.

114 Ibid., p. 114.

115 Ibid., p. 124.

116 M. Sutherland, 'The Right Image for Russia' (n. 83 above).

117 O. Moroz, 'O pol'ze Chechni' [On the Use of Chechnya], *LG*, 18 January 1995.

118 There are, after all, several groups on Russia's extreme right which make even Zhirinovsky look like a Western liberal. These include Russian National Unity, whose leader Barshakov has declared that 'Genocide is . . .

a phenomenon of the national racial struggle.' See: V. Iliushenko, '"Evange-
lie" ot Barshakova' [The Gospel According to Barshakov], *LG*, 30 November
1994. See also: A. Arbatov, 'Fashizm ne proshel', ibid.; and: 'Russkii fashizm
– mif ili real'nost'?' [Russian Fascism – Myth or Reality?], *LG*, 11 May 1994.
See also the works of L. N. Gumilev: *Etnogenez i biosfera zemli* [Ethnogenesis
and the Biosphere of the Earth] and *Tysiacheletie vokrug Kaspiia* [A Thousand
Years Around the Caspian], both Moscow: Mishel, 1993.
119 Likhachev, 'Nel'zia . . .' (n. 71 above), p. 120.
120 See, for instance, A. Marshall, 'EU Ponders the Russian Riddle', *Independent*,
18 March 1995.
121 Winston Churchill in a radio broadcast, 1 October 1939.

14 In lieu of a conclusion: East meets West?

Robert Bideleux

Relations with Eastern Europe and the former Soviet republics have posed some of the greatest challenges that the EC/EU has ever had to face. If these challenges are adequately met, European peace, prosperity and integration will be enormously enhanced. If they are not met, the damaging consequences will not be confined to the East. Unfortunately, the Western democracies made 'a terrible mess' of the first five years of transition, because 'we never really understood what we ought to be doing. We never saw, you might say, what history expected of us.'[1] By December 1994 President Václav Havel was lamenting that:

> the birth of a new and genuinely stable European order is taking place more slowly and with greater difficulty and pain than most of us had expected five years ago. Many countries that shook off their totalitarian régimes still feel insufficiently anchored in the community of democratic states. They are often disappointed by the reluctance with which that community has opened its arms to them. The demons we thought had been driven for ever from the minds of people and nations are dangerously rousing themselves again, and are surreptitiously but systematically undoing the principles upon which we had begun to build the peaceful future of Europe . . . Europeans continue to suffer and die in the former Yugoslavia, and with them is dying the hope that Europe will be able to bring these horrors to an end.[2]

If the EU does not help to prevent further escalations of the conflicts and crises that have afflicted many former communist countries since 1989, individual West European states could find themselves being increasingly drawn into those maelstroms, backing different sides and/or courses of action, and obliged to absorb additional millions of migrants and refugees. Such a scenario would fuel the further growth of nationalist and neo-fascist extremism across Europe. 'Eastern Europe cannot be separated arbitrarily from the rest of the Continent, for the problems of the part are indissolubly connected with those of the whole.'[3] The degree of stability achieved in the East will have a crucial bearing on the further integration and development of Europe as a whole and on its peace and prosperity.

The security of Europe is indivisible. The Hungarian historian and premier Jozsef Antall commented shortly before his untimely death, 'It is not by chance that both world wars broke out in this region, from Sarajevo to Danzig. The danger zone is precisely this area which is always neglected.'[4]

During the Cold War the EC was rarely called upon to play an independent political role. Indeed, to a considerable extent, the outcome of the Second World War had marked 'the collapse of Europe as an autonomous actor and the transfer of control over its destiny to the non-European superpowers'.[5] But the sudden disintegration of the Soviet bloc, followed by that of the USSR itself, and the incipient disengagement of the US from Europe, now that the main justification for a massive US military presence in Europe had gone, gave rise to a new political and military vacuum that offered the EU an unprecedented opportunity to reassert Europe's sovereign control over its own affairs and yet thrust upon the EC momentous tasks for which it was ill prepared. The timing of this challenge was less than convenient. Nonetheless, if the vacuum is not soon filled by a European Confederation or an expanded EU and NATO, it will probably be filled in due course either by a new German economic imperialism, or by a resurgent Russian imperialism or by a Rapallo-style partnership between the two, on the potent pretext that their presence in the region is again becoming necessary in order to reduce or forestall chaos and conflict. This is not a determinist judgement on the innate proclivities of either Germany or Russia, but simply a statement that, if a vacuum is allowed to persist, one or both of the major powers in that vicinity will eventually fill it.

During the first half of the 1990s the EU enjoyed a breathing space because Germany was preoccupied with the problems of unification, while Russia was temporarily incapacitated by the disintegration of the Soviet imperium, the ensuing power struggles, lawlessness and economic collapse, and the need to reconstitute the Russian state on a new basis. However, once Germany has achieved economic recovery and the full reconstruction and integration of its new eastern *Länder*, it will emerge even stronger than it was before 1990 and even better placed to fill any continuing economic or political vacuum in Eastern Europe. Similarly, the power struggle and political deadlock between Russia's extreme nationalists, ex-communists and free-marketeering democrats will most probably be resolved one way or the other by the 1996 presidential election, heralding a potential revival of Russia's capacity to act decisively by the year 2000. Future German dominance of Eastern Europe is likely to be economic rather than political, as economic dominance offers most of the potential fruits without the formal responsibilities, and Germany will probably remain, in Willy Brandt's famous phrase, 'a political pygmy but an economic giant'. The reverse could be true of Russia. However, if it took Hitler only four years to rescue Germany from political and economic collapse in the 1930s, then a similar feat could conceivably be achieved by Russia in the late 1990s.

The 'founding fathers' of the EC never intended it to remain an exclusively West European club.[6] On 9 December 1989 the European Council issued a proclamation on Central and Eastern Europe stating that 'The Community and its member states are fully conscious of the common responsibility that devolves upon them in this decisive phase in the history of Europe.'[7] However, if they wish to reap in full the potential political, economic and security dividends of pan-European integration, EU members will have to act far more decisively and generously than hitherto and in ways that will call for significant innovations in the EU's structures. Indeed, inasmuch as Western Europe helped to bring about the end of communist rule in Eastern Europe, through its anti-communism, championship of human rights, support for East European dissidents and willingness to escalate the arms race until it finally overburdened the Soviet bloc economies, Western Europe incurred *some* responsibility for ensuring that the new political and economic systems are more successful than those it helped to undermine. The communist régimes did not collapse entirely under their own weight. Having spent several decades working and calling for political and economic liberalization in the former Soviet bloc, Western Europe was in no position to complain when the desired outcome actually materialized, even if the scale and timing of the collapse were daunting and inconvenient. Ignoring the problems unleashed by the lifting of the 'iron curtain' will not make them go away, but will simply make them fester and become more intractable.

On the other hand, the predicament of the post-communist East poses difficult questions as to how far the West can or should try to impose or 'transplant' democracy, the rule of law, civil liberties and capitalism. Both in the 1920s and again in the 1990s, East Europeans have been expected to telescope into a few years developments that occurred organically over several centuries in Western Europe. The institutions and practices that evolved in one area cannot easily be replicated in other areas that have had very different historical experiences and political traditions. Moreover, one must beware the great dangers of attempting to impose rigid economic blueprints on the arrogant assumption that Western free-marketeers have all the answers to questions that they imperfectly understand. The East is recovering from one disastrous experiment in social engineering and 'revolution from above'. It should not now be subjected to other such experiments in the opposite direction.

It has been widely assumed that the East–West division was essentially a product of the Cold War and communist ascendancy over Eastern Europe and that, with the end of the Cold War and communist rule in Europe, the two halves of Europe can simply be 'united' in the way that Germany was in 1990. Thus, in Aachen in May 1991, President Havel declared that Europe was closer than ever before to realizing 'the age-old hope of becoming an area of friendship and co-operation for all its inhabitants' and that East Europeans were seeking to return to a civilization that they had helped to develop. 'This is not a question of . . . being fascinated by another world. It is just the opposite. After decades of unnaturally following the wrong track, we are yearning to rejoin the road which was once ours too.'[8] Indeed, East-Central Europe has been home to some of Europe's greatest writers and intellectuals and some of its oldest universities, and 'nowhere in the world is there so widespread a belief in the reality, and the importance, of a European cultural community'.[9] This belief in the 'oneness' of Europe is very important to the East-Central European intelligentsia in its drive for wider European integration. It will help East-Central Europe to surmount many difficulties. Nevertheless, it rests on a very partial reading of European history.

The Cold War certainly gave more definite institutional expression to the East–West division of Europe, but there were deep-seated cultural, political, social and economic differences between Eastern and Western Europe long before the epoch of communism and Cold War. The traumatic experience of communist dictatorship was but a brief episode in the history of Eastern Europe, which has been much more enduringly marked by various political, cultural and economic influences that lasted far longer than the communist experiment, even if that is still the freshest memory. It was these older, profounder, temporarily suppressed influences that resurfaced most powerfully after 1989, and the more Eastern Europe is denied adequate access to West European markets, capital and technology and thrown back on its own resources, the longer the East–West divide will persist. This divide can partly be traced back to the East–West partitions of the Roman Empire in 285 and 395 AD and to the growing divergence and eventual schism between Western Catholic and Eastern Orthodox Christianity. The fifth-century disintegration of the Western Roman Empire paved the way for the gradual evolution of Western Europe through fragmented and decentralized feudal polities to the precocious development of capitalism within the interstices of feudal society. In Eastern Europe, by contrast, outwardly splendid but ultimately stultifying imperial polities remained dominant until 1918. The Eastern Roman Empire (Byzantium) survived until the fifteenth century, only to be succeeded by the Ottoman Empire, while East-Central Europe gradually fell under absolutist imperial control from the sixteenth to the early twentieth centuries, partly in response to Ottoman onslaughts. Admittedly, there was a period when it seemed as if East-Central Europe was being fully assimilated into the emerging 'modernity' of Western Christendom. During the fourteenth and fifteenth centuries, monarchical power and authority were circumscribed and eroded in Hungary, Poland and Bohemia, which experienced significant expansions of commerce, crafts, mining, towns and decentralized, autonomous activity. The region's educated élites vigorously participated in the humanist intellectual currents that gave rise to the Reformation, the Renaissance and the early stages of the Scientific Revolution. Unfortunately, these promising developments were nipped in the bud by the religious wars of the sixteenth and seventeenth centuries, the expansion of intolerant Eastern empires and the attendant reinforcement of seigneurial privileges and serfdom and persecution and/or emigration of dissenters and free-thinkers, including large numbers of merchants and skilled craftsmen. These increasingly took refuge in Protestant Northeastern Europe, whose economic and intellectual gains were to be East-Central Europe's loss. The consequent cultural, political and social straitjackets cramped East European development and this, together with the rise of West European maritime colonial commerce and the displacement of major trade routes toward Europe's Atlantic seaboard, caused East-Central Europe and the Balkans to fall far behind maritime Western Europe, which developed increasingly secular 'civic' societies and freedom of thought and commerce. The subsequent West European Industrial Revolution, coupled with East European specialization in unsophisticated and less remunerative primary products, widened the East–West disparity in per capita GNP from about 2:1 to about 3:1 in the space of fifty years.[10] This crucial economic disparity has widened still further in the twentieth century[11] and will persist for several decades, even if the East European economies were to grow at an impressive 5 or 6 per cent per annum. It will be an even longer haul if the East European states continue to be dogged by recurrent crises like those they have experienced this century.

An even more important consequence of these East–West divergences is that East European politics is seriously 'out of phase' with West European politics, and this constitutes another crucial hindrance to pan-European integration. Fundamentally, the East European states are still in a 'state-building' and 'nation-building' phase, whereas most West European states have long since completed (or exhausted) their state-building and nation-building projects and have moved into an essentially post-nationalist era. This is not to deny that Turkish and non-European immigrants have been subjected to prejudice, discrimination and violence in Western Europe in recent years, but these problems have arisen from racism and xenophobia rather than nationalism in the territorial state-building mode; such phenomena are ugly, deplorable and pose serious threats to West European democracy but, as with European antisemitism, no European borders or territories are in dispute. Nor is it to deny that nationalism is still a seductive force in areas such as Flanders, Catalonia, the Basque Country or Europe's 'Celtic fringes'. But these 'minority nationalisms' have survived mainly on the peripheries of West European politics and, except for a few violent extremists, operate within the laws and political 'rules of the game' of the larger post-nationalist polities within which they are embedded. The non-violent champions of minority nationalisms in Western Europe have not, on the whole, been attacked as 'traitors' or 'fifth columnists' as they have been in the Balkan states (including Greece), Latvia, Estonia and Slovakia in recent years. For most West Europeans, politics has become mainly concerned with mercifully prosaic 'bread and butter' issues such as employment, education, health and taxation, rather than territorial claims, the 'ethnic' complexion of the state or the plight of co-nationals in neighbouring states. Likewise, the EC has been more concerned with mundane issues of 'low politics', such as trade, farm prices and health and safety regulations, than with more highly charged issues of 'high politics', although EMU could alter that. Indeed, the EC was created essentially in order to defuse and/or lay to rest the issues of 'high politics' that had repeatedly convulsed Western Europe from 1870 to 1945. The existence of the EC facilitated the consolidation of relatively tolerant and inclusive 'civic' West European nations, each secure in the knowledge that their neighbours were engaged in similar processes and no longer posed territorial threats, thereby helping nationalism to lose much of its former emotive force and appeal and largely reducing it to relatively harmless forms of nostalgia, clinging to comforting illusions and ritual commemoration of wartime heroics. The obsolescence of large conscript armies and the widespread abandonment of obligatory 'national' service has deprived West European nationalism of its former 'functional' roles in inducing and requiring the 'nationals' of each state to be ready to kill and to die for their country.

In Eastern Europe, unfortunately, politics is still locked into the primordial state-building and nation-building projects that have largely run their course in Western Europe. These nationalist projects and preoccupations, rather than the more high-minded projects of democratization and economic reform, are the ones that most effectively engage and mobilize political energies and passions in the East, where men are still being conscripted to kill and/or die for their country. The seemingly settled, solid and secular (albeit repressive) polities created by communism have unravelled. Indeed, the successor states of the former Soviet, Yugoslav and Czechoslovak Federations have virtually begun the projects of state-building and nation-building all over again. Worse still, the nationalism that pervades East European politics is mainly intolerant and exclusive 'ethnic' nationalism rather than the more tolerant and inclusive 'civic' nationalism that prevails in Western Europe.[12] 'Ethnic' nationalism and 'ethnic' conceptions of the state make it much harder to implant and/or uphold impartial and uniform administration of the law and economic, educational and political rules and opportunities. Indeed, 'ethnic' conceptions of the nation postulate collectivities whose claims and interests override and diminish not only the rights of minorities, but also those of the individual members of ethnic majorities. Hence nations defined in this way more easily lend themselves to fascist and/or racist conceptions of the nation and the state than do 'civic' nations.

It is widely assumed that the fundamental reason why 'ethnic' national-ism and inter-ethnic tensions have been so much more persistent and pervasive in Eastern than in Western Europe is that the East presents a much more variegated and intermingled ethnic patchwork, with the result that it has been impossible either to draw boundaries that would create ethnically homogeneous national states or to include everybody in the states to which they 'belong' by ethnic affiliation. In reality, however, the West European national states comprise almost as many different ethnic and linguistic strains as do their East European counterparts. Most Euro-peans are mongrels, if their ancestry is traced back far enough, and every European nation is actually a *mélange*, the product of centuries of migra-tion, acculturation and intermarriage. The crucial difference between the two halves of Europe lies not so much in their differing degrees of ethnic diversity and intermingling as in the marked contrast between the extensive coalescence and fusion of diverse and intermixed ethnic 'strains' into discrete territorial nations and national polities in Western Europe and the equally striking perpetuation of a multiplicity of separate ethnic identi-ties within most states in the East. In Eastern Europe, thanks to the pre-dominance of various multi-cultural imperial polities from Roman times to 1918, the emergence of smaller proto-national kingdoms capable of fusing or welding ethnically diverse subjects into 'civic' nations never managed to progress very far, with the result that successive inward migra-tions and conquests established layer upon layer of ethnic groupings, many of which have maintained their separate identities into the twentieth century. Whereas the feudal kingdoms of Western Europe gradually assimilated their diverse subjects and successive waves of inward migrants and conquerors into 'civic' proto-nations, whose national identities, allegiances and ideologies were fostered in order to mobilize and enhance popular loyalty towards and identification with these embryonic nation-states, in Eastern Europe national identities, allegiances and ideologies developed somewhat later and in reaction *against* the existing imperial states. Thus the East European nations were conceived as pre-existing ethnic and cultural entities that eventually overthrew their imperial over-lords and established narrowly 'ethnic' nation-states. Furthermore, while most of Western Europe's nation-states were forged and defined *before* the popularization of pernicious doctrines extolling (spurious) ethnic and racial 'purity', East European conceptions of the nation and the nation-state have developed under the direct influence of such doctrines.[13] This has been partly a result of the prominent ('hegemonic') role of 'national' intelligentsias in nurturing and defining national identities and ideologies in Eastern Europe during the nineteenth and twentieth centuries. Out of 'myths of the past and dreams of the future' East European nationalists postulated 'an ideal fatherland' that was not yet a political reality, enabling them 'to adorn it with traits for the realization of which they had no immediate responsibility, but which influenced the nascent nation's image of itself and of its mission'.[14] Thus 'eastern European nationalism became *messianic*', emphasizing the 'historic' and 'God-given' rights of the nation rather than those of the individual, who was simply required to render unquestioning obedience to the nation.[15] It was but a short step from East European 'ethnic' nationalism to fascism.[16]

Since 1918, moreover, the ascendancy of exclusive 'ethnic' nationalism in Eastern Europe has been greatly enhanced by the principle of national self-determination, which presupposes that nations are essentially defined in ethnic terms and that an ethnic majority has an exclusive sovereign right to control the state. Thus Eastern Europe's 'nationality problems' have been greatly exacerbated by implicit assumptions that a nation-state should ideally be ethnically homogeneous and that people who are not members of the majority ethnic group do not strictly 'belong' in that state, even though they and their forebears may have lived and worked there for centuries. This pernicious conception of ethnic homogeneity as the ideal basis for national statehood was espoused by the Western states-men gathered at the 1919 Paris Peace Conference and accepted by the governments of most of the East European 'successor states', in the mis-taken belief that they were merely transposing the Western European system of nation-states to Eastern Europe. In fact they were doing nothing of the sort, since ethnically homogeneous nation-states have never existed in the West any more than in the East. This tragic misreading of modern West European history helped to create the disruptive and potentially explosive 'ethnic minority' problems that have bedevilled twentieth-century Eastern Europe. Indeed, if genuinely West European conceptions of the nation, nationality and the nation-state had been transposed to the new or reconstituted states of Eastern Europe, all the people whose families had been living and working there for centuries would have been defined and treated as full citizens and 'nationals' of those states, irrespective of their ethnic affiliations. But what has actually happened is that the majority ethnic group in each state has constituted itself as 'the nation', while the other ethnic groups within that state have been classified as implicitly 'alien' and barely tolerated ethnic minorities, even though the latter have often richly contributed to the culture and economic development of that society. Thus the narrow and exclusive manner in which East European nations have been defined has served to entrench political and social exclu-sion and to foster antagonistic relationships between ethnic majorities and minorities, preventing the latter from playing the fullest possible roles in the further development of the successor states, even in areas that used to enjoy harmonious inter-ethnic relations. The tragic mistake was repeated when the EC misguidedly tried to apply national self-determination to Bosnia-Hercegovina in the early 1990s. National self-determination is an extreme form of the 'winner-takes-all' syndrome, for whoever has a major-ity at the outset is likely to retain it indefinitely, while ethnic minorities tend to become permanent underdogs or at best second-class citizens. The attainment of full national independence has given the ethnic majority of each of the successor states the opportunity to claim sole possession of the state apparatus and all state-funded institutions. Each has promoted its own language and culture as the official language and culture of the state, while doing as little as possible (or worse) for the languages and cultures of ethnic minorities, many of whom enjoyed greater cultural autonomy under Habsburg or Ottoman rule. Ethnic majorities have rejoiced in their new-found national 'freedom', even when this took the form of political dictatorship and was far removed from Western concepts of liberty.

Paradoxically, the Western sponsors of the post-1918 order in Eastern Europe saw only too clearly that their handiwork would still leave large and vulnerable ethnic minorities within most of the successor states and that this could pose major problems in the future. However, instead of going back to the drawing board to reconsider the inherently flawed basis of the new order, they decided to treat the symptoms rather than the causes of the problems by forcing the new or expanded successor states grudgingly to sign 'minority protection treaties' pledging them to respect the fundamental rights of ethnic minorities and granting aggrieved minorities a right to appeal to the League of Nations, whose approval was supposedly a prerequisite for any change in the laws governing those fundamental rights. However, while ethnic minorities did occasionally appeal to the League of Nations under the terms of these treaties, their grievances were not redressed and no means was found of enforcing the intended safeguards. The treaty provisions were resented as encroachments on the exclusive territorial jurisdictions of the ethnic majorities, while conflicting with their frequent resentment or mistrust of ethnic minorities and prompting accusations of hypocrisy (as such arrangements would never have been accepted for the UK, for example). This virtually invited German, Italian and other external interference in the internal affairs of the successor states, without providing effective protection for the rights of ethnic minorities. The interwar experience thus suggests that Western attempts to impose minority protection treaties on multi-ethnic East European states in the 1990s could both antagonize ethnic majorities and yet be similarly ineffectual in safeguarding the rights of ethnic minorities, especially when so few states are prepared to get involved in the provision of adequate long-term means of multilateral enforcement of the treaty provisions. The concept is fundamentally flawed, since it aims at costly, hazardous and impractical long-term containment or suppression of inter-ethnic tensions, instead of constructing states that are neither built around ethnicity nor defined in inherently exclusive and antagonistic ethnic terms. One of the most effective steps that the EU and NATO can take is to insist that, in future, membership of these organizations will be confined to 'civic' states that have dismantled and outlawed all forms of ethnic discrimination and exclusion; otherwise, Eastward enlargements could simply import into the EU and NATO the nationalist feuds and inter-ethnic conflicts that have poisoned internal and inter-state relations in Eastern Europe in recent decades, and could damage or even paralyse both organizations, undoing the achievements that have made them so attractive. However, inasmuch as the Western powers unwittingly compounded Eastern Europe's ethnic minority problems by enunciating and instituting the principle of national self-determination as the linchpin of the post-1918 East European states system, they should not try to wash their hands of responsibility for the baleful outcome.

'Ethnic' conceptions of the nation, nationality and the state are clearly at odds with the 'civic' ideals of the EU and most of its member states. This is the fundamental qualitative difference between Eastern and Western Europe, just as the above-mentioned economic disparities are the basic quantitative difference, and both constitute serious impediments to the full integration of East European states into the EU. Nevertheless, such barriers do not loom equally large for all the East European states. The crucial advantages that have placed Poland, Hungary, Slovenia and the Czech Republic ahead of the more Easterly states in the post-1989 transitions to democracy and market economies and at the front of the queue for eventual EU membership are not just their significantly higher levels of education, technology and economic development, but, even more importantly, the fact that they have more quickly become law-governed societies in which the legal underpinnings of democracy and the market system are upheld and enforced in a relatively impartial manner.[17] This was also what has made them the preferred locations for Western companies and investment in Eastern Europe. The rule of law has acquired special significance in relation to eventual membership of the EU. The EU rests upon a supranational rule of law, requiring the uniform acceptance and application of common policies, procedures, laws and legally binding treaty provisions, and only states which can fully comply with such requirements ought to be accorded membership, even if this raises awkward questions concerning one or two of its current members.

It is sometimes asserted that moves towards EMU in Western Europe could make it harder for East European states to join the EU. This is certainly true for the financially undisciplined CIS and Balkan states (apart from Slovenia). However, the successes of the East-Central European and Baltic states and Slovenia in reducing budget deficits and bringing rampant inflation under control (see Table 10.4, p. 201), while average wages are still only 10–15 per cent of the German level, have prompted suggestions that these countries may soon be more able to participate in EMU (while remaining internationally competitive) than some current members of the EU. Certainly, various West European companies have been persuaded to relocate some of their productive activities in East-Central Europe by such considerations. In principle, moreover, membership of the EU need not be a prerequisite for participation in EMU, which could still take place outside the framework of EU law and institutions, even if most EU members decide not to go ahead with it and/or fail to meet the so-called 'convergence criteria' laid down by the Maastricht Treaty. Thus EMU probably poses greater problems for current EU members and for EU unity than it does for the leading East European candidates for EU membership. Meeting the convergence criteria will involve degrees of monetary and fiscal stringency and a renunciation of exchange rate flexibility for which the Greek, Italian, Spanish, Swedish and Finnish economies, in particular, are not yet ready. (Portugal could perhaps meet the convergence criteria if its economy were not so closely tied to that of Spain, whose repeated devaluations of the peseta in 1992–5 pulled down the escudo). In order to bring their budget deficits, public debts, interest rates and currency fluctuations within the permitted limits by the late 1990s, these countries would have to make enormous economic and fiscal adjustments, exacerbating already acute social strains and economic recessions, and the economic and social costs would be politically suicidal for those administering such draconian programmes within such a tight timetable. However, assuming that they will not become eligible to participate in EMU at its inception, they will still be subject to growing pressure to match the fiscal and monetary discipline of the most eligible countries in order to remain competitive and attractive to foreign investors within the Single European Market, to become eligible to join a single currency in due course and to avoid political and economic marginalization. Such marginalization would be even harder to swallow in view of the painful adjustments they have already made as part of the price of EU membership and would negate one of their main reasons for joining the EU in the first place. However, the potential economic and political advantages of EMU are neither so certain nor so overwhelming that it absolutely has to commence in 1997 or 1999. The costs of postponing the start date by a few years would be minimal, while the political and economic advantages of being able to include most of the laggards as well as the frontrunners in EMU from the outset would be considerable. EMU would then become a means of strengthening EU unity and cohesion, instead of precipitating a potentially enduring cleavage between a strong 'core' and a weak 'outer circle'. The larger the number of countries eligible to participate in EMU at its inception, the greater will be the pressure on the recalcitrants to join in. But any attempt to force the pace of EMU could inflict lasting damage on the EU, compounding the mistakes made at Maastricht and threatening to recreate the former split between the EC and EFTA in a new guise.

Austria's accession to the EU in January 1995 can only intensify the internal pressure to grant full EU membership to the Czech Republic, Hungary, Slovenia, Poland and possibly Slovakia before 2000, since Austria has maintained its historic links with these lands and sees itself as a natural conduit for and beneficiary of ever-closer economic relations between them and the EU, just as the concurrent accession of Finland and Sweden to the EU will increase the internal lobbying for the Baltic states to be granted associate membership of the EU by 1996 and full membership shortly after 2000. Carl Bildt, who as Swedish Premier from 1991 to September 1994 was the chief architect of Sweden's internal economic liberalization and external realignment with the EC (which he presented as two sides of the same coin), has provided incisive Nordic perspectives on the implications of EU enlargement. He sees EU membership partly as a means of rectifying the marginalization, over-regulation, over-taxation and under-performance of the Swedish economy, which worryingly contracted by 5 per cent between 1990 and 1993, much as the integrationist lobby in Finland expects EU membership to open up new economic relationships to offset the loss of Finland's economic 'special relationship' with the former USSR, whose collapse was the chief cause of an alarming 15 per cent contraction of the Finnish economy between 1991 and 1993. But he also emphasizes the geopolitical implications of EU enlargement:

> Russian power in Europe now directly meets the West . . . in the areas of the Baltic and Barents Sea. . . . The region around St Petersburg . . . is set to recover its old role as the window to the West. . . . These border lands between Russia and the West may become the most impressive growth region in Europe. . . . In their own interests, as well as those of the wider Europe, the Nordic countries will want early progress towards bringing the Baltic states firmly into the structures of European co-operation. With EU agreements on Baltic trade and economic co-operation now in place, the Nordic members will be pressing for the Baltic countries to take part in the EU's future enlargement towards eastern and central Europe.[18]

The over-representation of small states in the EU Commission, Council of Ministers and Parliament will give Austria and Scandinavia disproportionate influence on the EU's future direction, as their combined weight will be greater than that of any one of the four largest members and they can count on support for expeditious Eastward enlargements of the EU from Germany and, on some days, Italy and the UK. Moreover, the declining strength of Austrian, Finnish and even Swedish neutrality after the collapse of the Soviet bloc and the end of the Cold War, which played a major role in persuading them to join the EU for fear of being left 'out in the cold', will also help to erode former barriers to pan-European integration.

The problems of transition to democracy and market systems have been even greater in most of the former Soviet republics than in the Balkans and East-Central Europe. Some of them have never existed as independent states before, or have only briefly done so. Even Russia has never previously assumed its present form. Their current territories and boundaries are the arbitrary consequences of tsarist and Soviet imperialism, just as those of most African states were arbitrarily created by Western imperialism. They have all faced enormous problems of state-building and nation-building. Before far-reaching political and economic reforms could be implemented, they all had to establish institutions with sufficient power, competence and authority to enact them. The supposed advantages of being able to write on 'blank sheets of paper' were soon discovered to be not so much a freedom from irksome constraints as a lack of much-needed institutional capabilities and infrastructure, without which very little could be done. Hence reform programmes tended to get off to slow starts. In attempting transitions to democracy and market systems, they also had to contend with the smallness of their entrepreneurial middle classes, their surfeits of white-collar state employees and the often unchecked abuses and criminality of the former *nomenklatura*, black-marketeers and gangsters (the 'mafia'). Thanks to the extreme interregional specialization and interdependence of the former Soviet economy, the disintegration of the USSR caused quite drastic economic dislocations and declines in output. Moreover, the rulers of the newly independent republics initially seemed to have about as much idea how to create a market system as the Bolsheviks did on how to create a centrally planned economy. A market economy is essentially a network of contractual relationships underpinned by the sanctity of private property and contracts, yet these republics have encountered great difficulties in their half-hearted efforts to (re-)establish private property, the rule of law, the enforceability of contracts and 'horizontal' contractual relations, in place of the 'vertical' power relations of the former 'command economy'. Unable to make much headway with reform, and even less able to reap any electoral credit for the few (often painful) reforms that they have enacted, CIS governments increasingly played the nationalist card, the last refuge of scoundrels. But this nationalism is merely camouflaging a lack of effective institutions and coherent programmes.

All in all, the former Soviet republics have found it extremely difficult to make clean breaks with their Soviet past. Neither the rulers nor the ruled have shown much understanding of the prerequisites for successful transitions to democracy and market economies, if indeed that was what they really wanted. Political parties have remained poorly developed. There were few attempts either to mobilize support or to obtain proper democratic mandates for radical political and economic reform early on, while the prestige of the democrats was still riding high and before the old economic system completely seized up. Having missed that initial window of opportunity, popular support for the democrats and for economic reform was rapidly eroded by economic collapse, mass impoverishment and the enrichment of the few, making it increasingly difficult to press on with the restructuring and/or privatization of state industries and collective and state farms. This has resulted in growing disillusionment, demoralization, lawlessness and falling political and electoral participation, although the desperate need for Western investment and economic assistance will probably ensure that the outward trappings of democracy and desultory economic liberalization, privatization and restructuring will survive just sufficiently to avert total political and economic collapse. This will make it very difficult for the EU to go much beyond arm's-length trade treaties and economic assistance in its relations with the CIS. The EU should therefore concentrate its limited power and resources on helping to ensure the successful consummation of pluralistic democracy and competitive market economies in East-Central Europe and Slovenia, the countries with the strongest prospects of success, followed by the Baltic states, Bulgaria, Romania and Albania. It would be far more constructive and rewarding to help these countries to 'rejoin Europe' economically and politically, as true partners in the shaping of a new European architecture, than to reduce them to dependence on Western handouts. The 'failure' of several of these countries would palpably diminish the chances of success in the more Easterly post-communist states; conversely, any successes on the Balkan, Baltic or East-Central European fronts would at least provide the latter with positive role models and beacons of hope.

The almost universal demise of highly centralized communist rule and command economies has cleared the way for a simpler North–South division of the world into 'haves' and 'have nots', as the more successful East European and East Asian states are gradually joining the ranks of the rich North, while the poorer or less successful post-communist states are becoming part of the impoverished South. This momentous realignment has stiffened the resolve of the more successful post-communist states to gain acceptance into the ranks of the rich North, including the EU, in order to avert the ignominy and discomfort of sinking into the ranks of the impoverished South. The Eastern frontier of the EU is becoming the main demarcation line between Europe's 'haves' and 'have nots'. That also helps to explain why Turkey, Cyprus and Malta are so anxious to get feet in the door.

NOTES

1 B. Beedham, *International Herald Tribune*, 9 May 1994.
2 V. Havel, 'A New European Order?', *The New York Review of Books*, 2 March 1995, p. 43.
3 H. Seton-Watson, *Eastern Europe between the Wars*, Cambridge: Cambridge University Press, 1945, p. xv.
4 Interview in *Financial Times* (hereafter *FT*), 1 January 1993.
5 J. Rothschild, *Return to Diversity*, New York: Oxford University Press, 1989, p. 25.
6 H. von Brentano, *Germany and Europe*, London: André Deutsch, 1964, p. 200.
7 Office for Official Publications of the EC, *The European Community and its Eastern Neighbours*, Luxembourg, 8/1990, p. 6.
8 *FT*, 10 May 1992.
9 H. Seton-Watson, quoted in *The Times*, 20 March 1992.

10 I. Berend, 'The Historical Evolution of Eastern Europe as a Region', *International Organization*, vol. 40 (1986), no. 2, p. 339.

11 See: EBRD *Transition Report*, London: EBRD, October 1990, p. 7.

12 In adhering to 'ethnic' rather than 'civic' definitions of the nation, Germany and Greece are more like Eastern than Western Europe and this exacerbates their immigrant and ethnic minority problems.

13 Especially from Germany, where similarly exclusive and illiberal 'ethnic' conceptions of the nation were ascendant.

14 H. Kohn, *The Idea of Nationalism*, New York: Macmillan, 1944, p. 330.

15 P. Sugar, 'External and Domestic Roots of Eastern European Nationalism', in: P. Sugar and I. Lederer (eds), *Nationalism in Eastern Europe*, Seattle: University of Washington Press, 1971, p. 11.

16 J. Linz, 'Some Notes Towards a Comparative Study of Fascism in Sociological Historical Perspective', in: W. Laqueur (ed.), *Fascism: A Reader's Guide*, Harmondsworth, Penguin Books, 1979, pp. 18, 28, 50–1.

17 It is significant that, before 1918, their territories were ruled by the relatively law-governed and efficiently administered Habsburg and Prussian monarchies rather than the more arbitrary and corrupt Ottoman or tsarist empires. It may be objected that most of pre-1915 Poland was under tsarist rule, but in fact those territories were largely lost to Belorussia, Ukraine and Lithuania in 1945, ostensibly because most of their inhabitants were not Polish.

18 C. Bildt, 'Importance of Nordic Influence in EU', *FT*, 22 November 1994.

Index